❖ Searching the Scriptures

Volume One:
A Feminist Introduction

In Celebration of Anna Julia Cooper's
Feminist Thought and Work

Now, I think, if I could crystallize the sentiments of my constituency and deliver it as a message to this congress of women, it would be something like this: Let women's claim be as broad in the concrete as in the abstract. We take our stand on the solidarity of humanity, the oneness of life, and the unnaturalness and injustice of all special favoritisms, whether of sex, race, country, or condition. . . . The colored woman feels that women's cause is one and universal; and not till the image of God whether in parian or ebony, is sacred and inviolable; not till race, color, sex, and condition are seen as the accidents and not as the substance of life, not until the universal title of humanity to life, liberty, and the pursuit of happiness is conceded to be inalienable to all; not till then is woman's lesson taught and woman's cause won— not the white woman's nor the black woman's, nor the red woman's. . . . The acquirements of her rights will mean the final triumph of all right over might, the supremacy of the moral forces of reason, and justice, and love in the government of the nations of the earth.

From Anna Julia Cooper's speech
at the 1893 Congress of Representative Women

Searching the Scriptures

VOLUME ONE:
A Feminist Introduction

Edited by
ELISABETH SCHÜSSLER FIORENZA
with the assistance of Shelly Matthews

CROSSROAD ◆ NEW YORK

1993

The Crossroad Publishing Company
370 Lexington Avenue, New York, NY 10017

Copyright © 1993 by The Crossroad Publishing Company

Printed in the United States of America

Library of Congress Cataloging-in-Publication Data

Searching the Scriptures / Elizabeth Schüssler Fiorenza
    p.   cm.
  Includes bibliographical references.
  Contents: V. 1. A feminist introduction.
  ISBN 0-8245-1381-9
  1. Bible. N.T.—Feminist criticism. 2. Bible. N.T.—Criticism, interpretation, etc. 3. Women in Christianity—History—Early church, ca. 30–600. I. Schüssler Fiorenza, Elizabeth, 1938–.
BS2379.S43 1993
220.6′082—dc20   93-31336
                                                  CIP

Contents

v

Part II: Changing Patriarchal Blueprints:
  Creating Feminist Frames of Meaning

Part III: Scrutinizing the Master's Tools:
  Rethinking Critical Methods

Rethinking *The Woman's Bible*

IN THE PAST FIVE YEARS the Women in the Biblical World section of the Society of Biblical Literature has sponsored discussions on rethinking *The Woman's Bible* in preparation for the 1995 centennial celebration of the publication of *The Woman's Bible*. The present feminist commentary project has grown out of these discussions, which set out to explore the ambiguous feminist heritage of Elizabeth Cady Stanton's work.

Like the work of Cady Stanton and her collaborators, this commentary underlines the political character of biblical interpretation and the impact of biblical religion on women's self-understanding. Yet, unlike Cady Stanton's work, which on the whole engaged mostly Protestant white women from the United States and was not able to attract women schooled in "higher criticism," this feminist commentary project brings together some of the finest scholarship in contemporary biblical and historical studies, not only from the United States but from around the world.

A Feminist Introduction, the first volume of *Searching the Scriptures,* is dedicated to the memory of Anna Julia Cooper, whose "unparalleled articulation of black feminist thought," in the words of Helen Washington, appeared in 1892, in her major work, *A Voice from the South* (1892; reprint, The Schomburg Library of Nineteenth-Century Black Women Writers; New York: Oxford University Press [editor's introduction]). The second volume, *A Feminist Commentary,* is dedicated to the memory of Elizabeth Cady Stanton. Through these dedications I want to mark the whole work as a forum and space where different voices and discourses can be heard. By invoking Anna Julia Cooper as the "other foremother" who has inspired this commentary project, I intend to position its discourses within the tensions, contradictions, and as yet unrealized possibilities of the diverse locations and divergent traditions of feminist biblical interpretation.

The title of the entire work, *Searching the Scriptures,* seeks to indicate the ambivalent relationship that women as marginalized people have to the scriptures. A critical hermeneutics is not only conscious that the process of canonization has selected those texts that were acceptable to the hegemonic communities and leadership in biblical religions; it also must consider that canonical authority has been established in and through the silencing and exclusion of writings by women and other marginalized people. Any feminist introduction and commentary, therefore, must signal its problematic relations with hegemonic canons and scriptures by transgressing their boundaries and authority claims. At the same time it must claim the power of "the Word" as the heritage of the dispossessed in their struggles for liberation and transformation.

Searching the Scriptures is the offspring or brainchild of many different "godmothers." Several years ago Esther Fuchs and I proposed to the co-chairs of the Women in the Biblical World section that we initiate discussions on *The Woman's Bible* in view of the upcoming centennial of its first publication. These discussions explored theoretical and practical issues at stake in undertaking a commentary project that is rooted in feminist biblical studies and committed to the women's liberation movements in different sociopolitical and religious-cultural situations. Hence I am much indebted to professors Esther Fuchs, Katherine Kroeger, Gale Yee, and Mary Rose D'Angelo for their initiative and assistance in organizing these panel discussions. The contributions of many scholars who as panelists or audience participants shared their intellectual insights, critical questions, and practical experience have greatly advanced the articulation of this project.

This first volume of *Searching the Scriptures* raises issues of perspective, sociohistorical location, method, and communication. It explores the multifaceted voices shaping a feminist approach, elaborates modes of inquiry and theological approaches, samples the history of interpretation by women, and elucidates various ways in which the scriptures are read and feminist biblical studies are taught. Women scholars from different religious, cultural, and global locations were invited to articulate their feminist theoretical frameworks, methodological approaches, and hermeneutical goals. While they were encouraged to bring to this task their particular experiences and scientific methods of interpretation, they were also urged to abandon a value-detached, objectivist stance and to engage a "feminist" hermeneutical perspective that does not focus simply on gender but also on class, race, ethnicity, and other structures of oppression. Needless to say, the sociopolitical location of this project in the history of American women's biblical interpretation engenders at one and the same time its limit and strength.

This introduction is quite different from the standard forms of introduction in biblical studies. It does not focus on historical-theological information about biblical writings or limit itself to a discussion of critical exegetical method. Rather, this volume attempts to chart a comprehensive approach to feminist interpretation and to prepare the way for a second volume that engages in critical feminist interpretation of individual texts. The goal of the whole project is to empower readers for the tasks of engaging in critical analysis and for developing a different sociohistorical and theo-ethical imagination.

Audre Lorde's much quoted assertion "the masters tools will not destroy the masters house" serves as an organizing framework for this volume's plurivoiced explorations. Lorde's assertion, however, functions not as an infallible dictum but as a heuristic instrument and hermeneutical map for sorting the intellectual building materials and critical working tools that are necessary both for deconstructing the master's house and for reconstructing a "Room of Our Own." Hence, the four main parts of this book should not be read as dividing and organizing multifaceted chapters into unified arguments. Rather, they should be seen as overlapping structures that seek to make connections and to map the terrain of biblical studies as a feminist site of intellectual labor and spiritual transformation.

Such a feminist interpretive work of deconstruction and re-vision begins in the first part with a reflection on different sociopolitical locations as strategic starting points of feminist interpretation. The essays of the second part point out forms of distorted patriarchal lenses that prevent us from en-visioning a "different house of meaning." They also make suggestions for creating new frames of meaning on feminist grounds. The contributions in the third part of the book scrutinize the intellectual toolbox of critical methods and suggest how these methods can serve feminist ends. Finally, the last part of this introduction explores critical and constructive practices of feminist communication that seek to integrate feminist theoretical and practical work for transforming patriarchal societies and religions.

Many different persons were involved in the construction and completion of this project. Rev. Shelly Matthews, who assisted in editing the essays and in preparing the publication of *Searching the Scriptures,* deserves special acknowledgment. Her critical reading of several drafts of some contributions and her competent and patient prodding of individual contributors even during the time of her comprehensive exams have been invaluable. The project has greatly benefited from her painstaking editorial work, critical feedback, and patient enthusiasm.

At the stage of its conception, Professors Bernadette Brooten, Katie Cannon, Elizabeth Castelli, Esther Fuchs, Karen King, Ross Kraemer, Kwok

Pui-lan, Clarice Martin, Rita Nakashima Brock, Mercy Amba Oduyoye, Jane Schaberg, Luise Schottroff, Elsa Tamez, and Mary Ann Tolbert served as special advisors to the project and have recommended possible authors for it. I am especially grateful for their prompt response and creative suggestions for "naming the child." Since I could use only one title I was forced to choose a "single name" from their rich and variegated proposals. In this process of "naming," I have learned to appreciate the quandary of a feminist postmodernism that insists on the indeterminacy and multiplicity of meanings.

This feminist commentary project was fortunate to have not only "godmothers" but also "godfathers." Without the enthusiastic encouragement and the financial commitment of its "godfathers" Werner Linz and Frank Oveis of the Crossroad Publishing Company, *Searching the Scriptures* would never have seen the day of publication. By relinquishing both editorial control and "the power of naming," Crossroad has taken considerable promotional and financial risks.

Above all, editor Frank Oveis has my warmest appreciation and gratitude for his consistent and constructive support of this feminist project. He has worked untiringly and creatively for its successful completion. Thanks are also due to Maurya Horgan and Paul Kobelski of The HK Scriptorium for their careful editing and typesetting of this volume.

As always, my work has greatly benefited from the tireless backing and efficient assistance of my secretary, Dr. Margaret Studier. Her deft handling of accumulating correspondence has expedited its completion. To her as well as to my research assistant Solveig Nilsen-Goodin I am especially grateful for careful proofreading and attentive correction of the manuscript. I also want to thank Harvard Divinity School, and especially Dean Ronald Thiemann, for the continuing support of my work.

Finally, my profound appreciation and thanks go to all those unnamed women and men who have supported this work over the years and have encouraged me to undertake this project. I am especially indebted to the scholars who have contributed their insights and research to this volume of *Searching the Scriptures*. Needless to say, I alone am responsible for the faults and deficiencies that limit its scope and execution. Such limitations are not just personal but are also due to sociohistorical academic conditions that define and restrict feminist work. Whereas a representative number of European and American "white women" have entered advanced theological education during the past quarter of a century, it is only in the past ten years or so that significant numbers of "women of color" from all over the world have gained access to the academy and completed doctoral studies. As a result of such patriarchal academic conditions, the women scholars "of color" who shape and define feminist biblical scholarship and studies in religion are few in number and overburdened by work. I am very grateful to those scholars who were able to contribute to this volume as well as to those who had expressed interest but for various reasons could not participate in it. I do hope that this volume will not only assist individual readers in their reading of the scriptures but will also influence and shape the discourses of malestream biblical scholarship.

Elizabeth Schüssler Fiorenza

❖ Transforming the Legacy
of *The Woman's Bible*

Elisabeth Schüssler Fiorenza ◆

In her book *Women of Ideas (And What Men Have Done to Them): From Aphra Behn to Adrienne Rich,* the Australian feminist Dale Spender has pointed out that historical forgetfulness is fundamental to the perpetuation of patriarchal power.[1] In every generation feminists have to reinvent the wheel, so to speak, and rediscover feminist knowledge. Throughout the centuries, women thinkers who have claimed that the world looks different from the perspective of women have disappeared again and again from historical consciousness and remained unknown not only to men but also to women. Because of this patriarchally induced "forgetfulness," women have had again and again to discover anew feminist theories and perspectives.

Most recently, the historian Gerda Lerner has made a similar point, stressing that women have not built on the previous intellectual work of women.[2] This insight, however, does not protect her from falling prey to the same historical inattentiveness. She neither mentions Dale Spender's pioneering insights nor seems aware of Elisabeth Gössmann's work on medieval women's biblical interpretation. As Gössmann has done before her, so Lerner argues now that in the past thousand years or so women have expounded the Bible in reaction to male interpretations rather than in conversation with explications by women. As a case in point, Lerner refers to *The Woman's Bible,* a work written by committee, which does not make any reference to the preceding work of Sarah Grimké or to any other prior work of biblical interpretation by women. Lerner also points out that Sarah Grimké, in the introduction to her book, had in turn expressed her belief that she was "venturing on nearly untrodden ground."[3] However, Lerner does not note that *The Woman's Bible* is equally oblivious to the biblical interpretation of Maria Stewart, which, as Paula Giddings remarks, precedes that of Sarah Grimké and Elizabeth Cady Stanton by several years.[4]

CONTEXTUALIZING *THE WOMAN'S BIBLE*

Since scant attention has been paid to the intellectual history of biblical interpretation by women until very recently, the present feminist commentary project deliberately positions itself within such a history. The dedication of its volumes to two nineteenth-century women invokes the centennial anniversary of two American feminist publications: Anna Julia Cooper's *A Voice from the South* (1892) and Elizabeth Cady Stanton's *The Woman's Bible* (1895 and 1898). Positioning this work in the history of American women's interpretation of the Bible allows one to scrutinize its legacy and difference.

In general, introductions to biblical books and scriptural interpretation still recount only the history of interpretation by elite white men but not the work of women. Furthermore, William Myers has detailed how Eurocentric biblical scholarship and theological education focus on the interpretive history and questions of white European-American men while they neglect the traditions and questions of the African-American hermeneutical tradition.[5] Even feminist biblical scholars and writers of women's religious history have not paid sufficient attention, for instance, to the different ways black and white women have read the Bible in the nineteenth century.[6] We therefore lack sustained research into the history of biblical interpretation not only by African, Asian, or Hispanic Americans but also by women of all cultures.

A rich multicultural heritage waits not only to be "unearthed" by feminist intellectual, social, historical, and critical interpretive work but also to be discovered and owned by feminist movements in society and religion. Such a critical reconstruction of the history of women's biblical interpretation would not only reclaim women's intellectual work, but, as Dale Spender has pointed out, it would also

> make clear that for centuries women have been saying many of the things that we are saying today and which we have often thought as new. . . . There are industries built upon the discussion of men's ideas, and for women it would be a productive change to build upon, elaborate and modify the ideas of our foremothers.[7]

But such a feminist reconstruction of the history of women's biblical interpretation must be consistently self-critical. In her poem "Heroines," Adrienne Rich celebrates our feminist foresisters and foremothers, who draw "their long skirts deviant across the nineteenth century," speak in the "shattered language of a partial vision," and "register injustice" without being able to abolish it. She characterizes these feminist heroines as having "fair skin," "white power," and "class privilege," as well as being different from the Indians who were believed to "live in filth." The poem concludes with a series of rhetorical questions asking, How can one fail to love their clarity and fury, to give them all their due, to honor their "exact legacy as it is/recognizing as well that it is not enough"?[8]

A critical history of biblical interpretation by women not only would have to give insight into the ways women have read and used the Bible throughout the centuries, but also would have to show how women's readings were limited by their socioreligious location and cultural situation. It would not only need to make us conscious of our rich feminist history, now almost completely lost to us, but would also need to explore why we have lost it. Such a critical recovery of women's intellectual history of biblical reading could document that women's biblical interpretation is not a recent phenomenon. Rather, it is as old as the scriptures themselves and has spanned all centuries and cultures that have been touched by biblical cultures. But such a history of women's biblical interpretation must not be taken as identical with the history of feminist biblical interpretation.[9] Rather, it must be subjected to a critical analysis of its implicit and explicit feminist achievements and possibilities.

Contextualizing Elizabeth Cady Stanton's work within such a critical history of biblical interpretation by women prevents us from uncritically idolizing her as the foremost heroic foremother of women biblical interpreters. In response to those who used the Bible against women's emancipation, Elizabeth Cady Stanton and her co-workers conceptualized *The Woman's Bible* in order to investigate and to elaborate accurately what the Bible says about the subjection of women. Cady Stanton's project starts with the realization that throughout the centuries the Bible has been invoked both as a weapon against and as a defense for subjugated wo/men in their struggles for access to citizenship, public speaking, theological education, or ordained ministry.

In these often bitter debates, the warring parties have cited — and still do — biblical normativity and revelatory authority not only for and against women's full ecclesial participation and religious leadership but also for and against the full citizenship of freeborn women, for and against the emancipation of slave women and men, for and against the rights of lesbians and gay men, as well as for and against economic equity for poor women and their children. Opposing sides in this debate have appealed — and continue to appeal — to the Bible as the word of God in order to legitimate their arguments for and against the civil and religious emancipation of women and other nonpersons.

Against the advice and opposition of her suffragist friends, Cady Stanton asserted the political importance of women's biblical interpretation and therefore together with her collaborators initiated and completed the project of *The Woman's Bible.* Hence, she deserves our respect and honor, although we must not forget that she could not overcome the limitations set by her privileges of race and class. For as Toni Morrison so forcefully elucidates, racial ideology has "horrific results" not only "on its objects" but also on the mind, imagination, and behavior of the masters who perpetuate it.[10]

In short, *The Woman's Bible* and its interpretive traditions remain positioned within the space defined by patriarchal argument and women's apologetic response to it, although the intention of the Revising Committee was to produce a "scientific" commentary on the biblical passages speaking about women. Nevertheless, the project of *The Woman's Bible* proved to be very unpopular because of its radical political implications. In response to those who contended that a suffragist critique of the Bible was a waste of time or a political mistake, Cady Stanton argued that one cannot reform one area of society without also reforming all the others at the same time. Since "all reforms are interdependent," one cannot attempt to change the law, education, and other cultural institutions without also seeking to change biblical religion.

However, *The Woman's Bible* was unpopular not only because of its political implications, but even more so because of its radical interpretive perspective. Its hermeneutics sought to expand and replace the apologetic argument of other suffragists who insisted that the Bible, correctly understood, does not preach women's subordination. Rather, they argued, the true message of the Bible was obstructed by the faulty translations and biased interpretations of clergy men. Although Cady Stanton agreed with them that the translations and interpretations of the Bible reflect male bias, she nevertheless also insisted that the Bible has not just been misinterpreted but that scripture itself is androcentric and biased in the interest of men.

Over against those who held to the notion of "plenary inspiration" and understood the Bible as the direct "word of God," Cady Stanton stressed that it is written by men and reflects the male interests of its authors. She categorically states: "No man ever saw or talked with God." By treating the Bible as manmade and not as a fetish, and by denying divine inspiration to its degrading ideas about women, her committee, she claims, has shown more reverence for God than have the clergy or the church. Hence, *The Woman's Bible* comes to the ordinary reader "like a real benediction." It tells her that "the good Lord did not write the book."[11] Consequently, every biblical statement about woman must be carefully analyzed and assessed with respect to its male bias. Such a radical critical demythologizing of the Bible, however, solidifies several assumptions: it reifies the text in a positivist way, distinguishes between "good" and "bad" texts, and also works with the Western universalizing gender construct of woma[e]n[12] understood as over and against man. In so doing, it centers its discourses on the significance of biblical authority and normativity for woma[e]n, rather than on an exploration of how women's religious agency and intellectual power has used the Bible in emancipatory struggles.

In this century women's biblical studies have continued Cady Stanton's hermeneutical focus insofar as, like *The Woman's Bible,* they have centered on the question of biblical authority and woma[e]n. Therefore, questions of scriptural authority have taken center stage in the discussion of feminist theological hermeneutics. Since the last century, feminist biblical hermeneutics has agonized and argued about what kind of authority the Bible can claim in the lives of women. Today, feminist biblical discourses still appear to be caught up in this apologetic debate which seeks to show that the Bible, or at least parts of it, is *either* liberating and therefore has authority for women and other nonpersons, to use an expression of Gustavo Gutierrez, *or* that it is totally patriarchal and must be rejected.

The Bible not only functions in Christian discourse as a resource for critical insight and hope in the liberation struggle. It also serves as an authoritative means of reinforcing a Christian identity formation based on the patriarchal exclusion and subordination or vilification of "the others," be they women, heretics, or other subjugated peoples. Hence, it not only becomes important to scrutinize the contemporary patriarchal arguments which cite the Bible against movements of emancipation. It is also necessary to deconstruct the patriarchal "politics of otherness" that not only is inscribed in the pages of the Bible but also permeates modern discussions of biblical normativity and authority.

In the footsteps of Cady Stanton, women's biblical studies have developed a dualistic hermeneutical strategy that is able to acknowledge two seemingly contradictory facts. On the one hand, the Bible is written in androcentric language, has its origin in the patriarchal cultures of antiquity, and has functioned throughout its history to inculcate androcentric and patriarchal values. On the other hand, the Bible has also served to inspire and authorize women and other nonpersons in their struggles against patriarchal oppression. Women's biblical studies today in one way or another still presuppose and seek to address this dual problematic. Thus, what Adrienne Rich has said about the research of Marie Curie can equally be said of women's biblical heritage: it is at one and the same time a source for women's religious power and for women's suffering.[13]

In contrast to that of elite white women, the point of departure for African-American women today and in the nineteenth century has not primarily been the white women's struggle for emancipation and self-development. Rather, African-American women have heard and read the Bible in the context of their experience of slavery and liberation. The womanist ethicist Katie Cannon has underlined that in the last century racial slavery was the sociopolitical context not only of African-American but also of white hegemonic biblical interpretation. She identifies three ideological constructs that made it possible for white Christians to justify the enslavement of Africans as chattel.

As *property,* slaves were seen as not fully human; as *Africans* they were classified as heathen savages to be saved through enslavement; and as *Christians,* white and black, they were expected to believe that slavery was divinely willed in the Bible.[14] Within this context, Africans used the Bible as a "matrix" for the transformation of cultural meaning. Such an Afro-centric reading of the Bible incorporates texts that affirm the dignity of the African person in the face of dehumanization, rejecting those texts that can be used to legitimize slavery. Read in the rhetorical space of the struggle for liberation from slavery, the Bible offered enslaved Africans dignity, equity, and citizenship. "Redemption and salvation incorporated economic and political empowerment and a restoration to civil status."[15]

Since slaves were prohibited from learning how to read and write, their biblical interpretation did not so much focus on the exegetical explanation of texts. Instead, it freely engaged the stories and images of the Bible to illuminate their own sociopolitical experiences. As Vincent Wimbush has suggested,

> Interpretation was therefore controlled by the freeing of the collective consciousness and imagination of the African slaves as they heard the biblical stories and retold them to reflect their actual situation as well as their visions for something different.[16]

Moreover, African-American women such as Sojourner Truth, Amanda Berry Smith, Jarena Lee, Julia Foote, Maria Stewart, or the Quaker Elizabeth (of whom we know only her baptismal name) derived their authority for biblical interpretation and preaching first of all from a mystical experience in which they encountered God or Jesus directly. It was this confidence in the privileged nature of their relationship with the divine that compelled African-American women to transcend the limits imposed on them by the patriarchal gender-race system.

Like white suffragists and black men, African-American women evangelists sought valorization and authentication from the Bible. But unlike white women and black men, African-American women spoke from a doubly disadvantaged location. As *blacks* they had to address white audiences who doubted the human capacity of African-Americans for learning and religious salvation. As *women* they had to address audiences, black and white, who questioned both their ability to exercise authority and the legitimacy of their speaking in public. This critical interplay between "spiritual" experience and the authorizing interpretation of scripture leads to an implicit privileging of sociopolitical experience.

In her famous speech at the Akron Convention on Women's Rights, Sojourner Truth argued for women's theological authority and civil rights with reference to her own experience of slavery.[17] The much-quoted statement of Howard Thurman's grandmother, a freedwoman who could not read or write, similarly articulates experience as a criterion for assessing scripture:

> During the days of slavery, she said, "the master's minister would occasionally hold services for the slaves. Always the white minister used as his text something from Paul. 'Slaves be obedient to them that are your masters . . . , as unto Christ.' Then he would go on to show how, if we were good and happy slaves, God would bless us. I promised my Maker that if I ever learned to read and if freedom ever came, I would not read that part of the Bible."[18]

The African-American scholar Mae Gwendolyn Henderson has pointed out that black women have been free from both the elite male "anxiety of influence" and white women's "anxiety of authority and authorship." Therefore, they had no need to define themselves in relation to elite white men, to write about them or to become like them. However, insofar as the history of biblical interpretation by African-American women has scarcely been written and recognized in biblical studies, its hermeneutical approach could not develop its corrective power in the feminist discussion of biblical authority and theological authorization.

Hence, the hermeneutical discussions engendered by *The Woman's Bible* continue to evoke the elite white female anxiety about biblical authority. These discussions have centered on the question of how the Bible as a grammatically androcentric (male-centered) book that often advocates patriarchal (the rule of the father) or kyriarchal (elite male domination; *Herrschaft*) values is or can be authoritative for feminists in biblical religions and authorize their emancipatory struggles in Western culture. Even in the discourses of feminist liberation theology, the Bible as the authoritative and authorizing "word of God" has occupied center stage.

Such a hermeneutical approach that focuses on canonical authority runs the risk of prematurely foreclosing a critical rhetorical analysis of biblical texts by either passing over so-called "negative" texts in silence or by reading so-called "positive" texts in an anti-Jewish fashion. It thereby tends to neglect the Bible and biblical interpretation as the site of competing discursive practices. At the same time, it does not sufficiently appreciate that the Bible is a cacophony of interested historical voices and a field of rhetorical struggles in which questions of truth and meaning are being negotiated.

SEARCHING THE SCRIPTURES

Alicia Ostriker therefore has called for a "hermeneutics of indeterminacy" that rejects the notion of scripture as a consistent, unitary, true text and instead insists on its multilayered, contradictory indeterminacy of meaning. Hence, scripture does not have meaning only in relation to those who rule. It also is claimed by those who struggle to undermine and change kyriarchal oppressions. "If the Bible is a flaming sword forbidding our entrance to the garden, it is also a burning bush urging us toward freedom. It is what we wrestle with all night and from which we may, if we demand it, wrest a blessing."[19] The title of this work, *Searching the Scriptures,* seeks to underscore this ambiguous character of canonical texts and feminist interpretations.

In the introduction to the second volume of *The Woman's Bible,* Cady Stanton reflects on the criticisms of the chosen title, to which both "friend and foe" objected:

> The critics say that our title should have been "Commentaries on the Bible." That would have been misleading as the book simply contains short comments on the passages referring to woman. Some say that it should have been "The Women of the Bible"; but several books with that title have already been published.[20]

I expect that both "friend and foe" will have similar critical reactions to the title chosen for this "daughter" of *The Woman's Bible,* which decidedly seeks to avoid its predecessor's hermeneutical and methodological pitfalls.

In order to transform the ambiguous hermeneutical and methodological legacy of *The Woman's Bible,* the present feminist project has deliberately not identified itself as a *biblical* project nor claimed to be a *Bible* commentary. Rather, the title *Searching the Scriptures* was adopted in order to signify a more interactive approach between reader, text, and context. The second volume of commentary will not discuss the Hebrew Bible, nor will it restrict its inquiry to canonical Christian texts. Thereby it seeks to avoid Western Christian women's anxiety about "canonical authority." Instead it engages in an act of *historical imagination* by exploring writings which women in the first centuries might have rejected or claimed as their own "scriptures."

Although Cady Stanton sought to shift the apologetic argument in defense of biblical authority, the discourses engendered by *The Woman's Bible* did not break through their canonical limitations and theological frameworks. Insofar as they restricted their attention to the women's passages of the Bible, they reinforced the discursive boundaries set by the canon. By contesting the authority claims of the women's passages, they reinscribed canonical authority. Hence, a critical feminist approach to scripture cannot remain within the boundaries of the canon. Rather, it must transgress the canonical paradigm because the selection of some writings as "canonical" and the exclusion of others as "apocryphal" has also coopted, silenced, or marginalized those voices and visions that were not acceptable to the emerging exclusive paradigm of biblical religions. By claiming to be the only "orthodox" word of God, the canon scripturalized traditions of subordination and domination which in a kyriarchal society and church could develop greater historical power than the canonical traditions of equality and liberation.

Because women's biblical studies have focused for too long on the canonical authority of the Bible, a feminist political interpretation for transformation must become canonically transgressive. Hence, a multivocal feminist interpretation cannot conceptualize its project as a canonical *biblical* project if it does not wish to accept the exclusive religious boundaries that are set by the process of canonization. Because the ethos of a feminist critical interpretation is inclusive, ecumenical, and multicultural, it may not limit its scope to canonical writings, accept the authority claims of the canon, or focus exclusively on the teachings of the Bible.

Just as the canon must be transgressed, so also must the term "Bible/biblical" be problematized. The expression Bible/biblical generally connotes the Protestant notion of a revealed text or a canon of books that serve as the primary locus of authoritative teaching. In order to avoid such a Western authoritarian understanding of the Bible, a comparative religions perspective has attempted to develop the notion of scripture as a relational/contextual category. Such a comparative conceptualization of scriptures that is derived not from Western understandings of the Bible but from the function of sacred texts in various world religions refers to the kinds of religious experiences and the dynamics of relationships that people have had with specially sanctioned texts.

Miriam Levering circumscribes "scriptures" as "a special class of true and powerful words, a class formed by the ways in which these particular words are received by persons and communities in their common life."[21] Such a generic understanding of scriptures problematizes the Western notion of scripture as a singular form that offers a sacred story or moral instruction and instead pays attention to the relations between people and their sacred texts. It challenges the assumption that scriptures have fixed canonical boundaries. It underlines the porousness and unsettledness of scriptural boundaries and brings to consciousness that new scriptural forms are created over and over again. Emphasizing the relations between scriptures and people rather than the authority and normativity of canon also underlines that scriptures are to be seen as contingent historical manifestations which must be reinterpreted in ever new situations. Such an approach can pay attention to the various modes of reception and the different ways of scripturalizing that determine the power of communities in relation to their specially sanctioned texts.

Moreover, by replacing the notion of *Bible* with that of *scriptures,* the title of this project seeks to express the ambivalent relationship that marginalized people, such as women, have had with the Bible. It is not only conscious that the process of canonization has selected those texts that were acceptable to dominant communities and their leadership in biblical religions. It also must consider that canonical authority has been established in and through the silencing and exclusion of writings by women and other marginalized people. A feminist commentary therefore must signal its problematic relations with hegemonic canons and sacred scriptures by transgressing their boundaries and authority claims. At the same time, however, it must claim the power of "the word" as the heritage of the dispossessed in the struggles for liberation and transformation.

In an influential article Claudia Camp has explored feminist biblical hermeneutics in terms of three biblical women: Hulda, who authorizes the biblical word; personified Wisdom, who embodies the authority of the text; and Esther, who personifies the tradition of her people, binding authority and life together in shared celebration.[22] In order to shift the paradigm of feminist biblical interpretation, I would like to introduce here Sheba, the black queen, who travels far from home to test the wisdom and knowledge of Solomon (1 Kgs 10:1–13; 2 Chr 9:1–12). Like Sheba, the authors of *Searching the Scriptures* put "hard questions" not only to the reigning epistemology of biblical studies but also to the scriptures themselves. Like the Queen of the South (Luke 11:31 [Q]), they search the "rich dark depth" of submerged religious wisdom and knowledge that can inspire sacred visions for a *different* future.

The verb *searching* evokes two different images for characterizing the "doubled vision" of a feminist hermeneutics and for construing its relationship to the tradition of *The Woman's Bible* differently. A *hermeneutics of suspicion* invites readers to investigate biblical texts and traditions as one would "search" the place and location where a crime has been committed. It approaches the canonical text as a "cover-up" for patriarchal murder and oppression. It seeks to identify the crime by carefully tracing its clues and imprints in the texts in order to prevent further hurt and violations.

A *hermeneutics of re-vision* in turn "searches" texts for values and visions that can nurture those who live in subjection and authorize their struggles for liberation and transformation. Scriptures have power and meaning not only for those who rule but also for those who seek to undermine and change kyriarchal oppressions. Like the woman of the [G]ospels searching diligently for the lost coin so a hermeneutics of re-vision investigates biblical texts for submerged meanings, lost voices, and authorizing visions.

Such a doubly "doubled" feminist strategy of suspicion and re-vision, of critical evaluation and different reconstruction[23] seeks to dislodge texts from their patriarchal frame by reading them against their kyriocentric (master-centered) grain. Its attempts to articulate a *different* reading would be misunderstood, however, if they were construed as one more sophisticated apologetic variation that seeks to recuperate the authority of the androcentric canonical text and thus to coopt women's religious energies for kyriarchal biblical religions.[24] *Searching the Scriptures* invites readers to move away from the prevalent feminist posture of either accepting or rejecting biblical texts on the whole to a careful critical assessment of and feminist engagement with ancient texts that can challenge sociocultural stereotypes and produce a different cultural and religious imagination. In order to do so, readers also have to reflect on their own religious perspectives and the conceptual frameworks with which they approach these texts.

TOWARD A FEMINIST READING:
THE DARKENED EYE RESTORED

The intellectual legacy of the nineteenth-century suffragist movement is not only methodologically problematic and hermeneutically ambivalent. Its feminist inheritance is also conceptually ambiguous.[25] Insofar as interpreters in the tradition of *The Woman's Bible* have focused on biblical texts *about* women or on symbolic constructions of woman and the feminine, they also have imported the cultural meanings of *woman* and of *the feminine.* Therefore, singling out *The Woman's Bible* as *the* milestone in the history of women's biblical interpretation not only risks overlooking the contributions of women of color to biblical hermeneutics. It also continues a white feminist gender discourse inscribed in *The Woman's Bible* that does not recognize the constitutive kyriarchal *differences* among and within women. In so doing, it is not only in danger of perpetuating a feminist historical discourse that celebrates the work of those nineteenth-century feminists with "fair skin" and forgets or represses feminist achievements of women from the "Dark Continent" but also in danger of perpetuating the cultural myth of "true womanhood."

This danger was recognized by Anna Julia Cooper, whose black feminist work, *A Voice from the South,* also appeared one hundred years ago. In it she argues that the strongest vindication of woman's speaking is "that the world needs to hear her voice." She likens the world to a man with one eye who has to limp and wobble along without being able to see the truth from women's standpoint. "Suddenly the bandage is removed from the other eye and the whole body is filled with light." The "darkened eye restored," the world "sees a circle where before it saw a segment."[26] As long as feminist interpretation focuses on the universalizing white gender discourse, its vision remains one-sided and partial. As Cooper puts it: "The colored woman of today occupies, one may say, a unique position in this country. . . . She is confronted by both a woman question and a race problem and is as yet an unknown or an unacknowledged factor in both."[27] In short, Cooper argues, the struggle of the women's movement and its power to challenge patriarchal power must be located at the juncture of racial and sexual politics.

However, Mary Helen Washington has pointed out that Cooper herself was never quite successful in connecting race, class, and gender issues. She could not make them pivotal in women's resistance to all forms of subjection because she too was not able to escape the ideological entanglements of the cult of "true womanhood" and its dictates. Writing as a middle-class black woman, she was not able to imagine ordinary black working women, sharecroppers, or domestic maids either as her audience or as the vanguard of her politics. Rather, because of her class privilege, Cooper, like other educated middle-class black women, had an even greater stake than her white compatriots

> in the gentility guaranteed by the politics of true womanhood. . . . Burdened by the race's morality, black women could not be as free as white women or black men to think outside of these boundaries of "uplift"; every choice they made had tremendous repercussions for an entire race of women already under the stigma of inferiority and immorality.[28]

Although some writers of women's history have suggested that the nineteenth-century tenets of "true womanhood" represent an incipient form of radical feminism, such a positive assessment of the middle-class cult of femininity overlooks its cultural-ideological entanglements. Since the ideal of "the white lady" has determined the dualistic formation of gender feminism, such feminism has supported racist, classist, and colonialist domination. Only when the "darkened eye" is restored can we begin to "see a circle rather than just a segment" of feminist biblical interpretation.

The recognition that Cady Stanton's work was "racist and classist" cautions white feminists in religion not to adopt the conceptual approach of *The Woman's Bible* that limits its theoretical focus to gender. The pitfalls of Anna Julia Cooper's work in turn also warn feminists not to adopt an essentialist notion of woman, femininity, and womanhood that does not understand women as diverse historical agents but rather as a universal class or caste with a special nature and essence. Because of its focus on woma[e]n and the feminine, gender feminism was not able to develop a complex analysis of women's subordination, marginalization, and exploitation. Thus, it was not able to explicate that gendered theological-cultural discourses on woman are produced by the patriarchal "politics of submission," which has its philosophical-political roots both in the tradition of the Middle East and in the classical philosophical traditions of Greece. Theologians such as Augustine, Thomas Aquinas, or Luther, and philosophers such as Kant, Nietzsche, or Freud (to name a few!) have espoused a negative theology or philosophy "of woman."

In the face of the gradual changes in society and religion that were brought about by the emancipatory movements of modernity, the theology of free women's and slave wo/men's inferior nature and subordinate status changed to a "separate but equal" position. Feminist cultural theories or essentialist theologies that glorify "true womanhood" and "the feminine," whether their godfathers be Goethe, Schleiermacher, Jung, Tillich, Lacan, Derrida, Teilhard de Chardin, or Pope John Paul II, have valorized abstract universal Woman as body, sexuality, maternity, or nature, or as feminine archetype, essence, or divinity. Yet in their attempt to construct a positive discourse on Woman, these theories or theologies of the feminine have kept in sustained circulation the discourses of classical Western philosophy and theology on gender asymmetry, gender polarity, and gender complementarity—discourses that understand Man as the subject of history, culture, and religion while seeing Woman as the Other.

This essentialist European-American elite male discourse on Woman as the Other of Man—the politics of Otherness—has also been perpetuated by women's and gender studies. A theoretical approach that professes to read the Bible *as a woman* remains within the dualistic gender/sex framework of Western culture and often assumes an essentialist understanding of woman. Further, one cannot assume that texts are liberating just because they are articulated by women. Anyone who is familiar with the religious right knows that women are among its most ardent supporters. If one has seen the women of Operation Rescue on the nightly news or read drafts of articles arguing that feminist interpretation must respect conservative women's attempts to construct meaning when reading patriarchal biblical texts, or heard women doctoral students assert that women and blacks receive "privileged" treatment in academic employment procedures, one can readily see that speaking, writing, or reading *as a woman* does not produce a critical or liberating interpretation of the world.

To the contrary, women's writing and speaking often function to mediate and reinforce kyriarchal behavior. While the "politics of submission" of the Pastoral Epistles, for instance, forbids women to teach and have authority over men (1 Tim 2:11), it also instructs women elders to be "good teachers" in encouraging younger women to practice their patriarchal household duties, "so that the word of God may not be discredited" (Titus 2:3–5). Another historical example of women reinforcing the patriarchal politics of submission is Proba, whose Virgilian poem, *Cento,* "elaborates upon the biblical materials in ways that render woman's status worse than it actually is in the Bible."²⁹ Unlike the so-called church fathers, Proba does not extol asceticism but rather recommends to women as Christian values the traditional patriarchal Roman values "of respect for parents and kin, sanctity of home, and marital chastity."³⁰

Reading the Bible "self-consciously as women" or reading it "as a woman in the company of women,"³¹ therefore, does not necessarily produce a feminist biblical interpretation, but it may in fact reinscribe the cultural myth of femininity and womanhood. If one cannot assume that the reading of the Bible from a woman's point of view or its reading in the community of women will necessarily amount to a *feminist* reading, then the focus of *The Woman's Bible* on texts about women or that of *The Women's Bible Commentary* on "reading as a woman"³² underscores the hermeneutical problem engendered by *The Woma[e]n's Bible* but does not transform it.

Instead of assuming that a feminine style of thinking or writing from a woman's perspective promotes the interests and the well-being of women, one needs to explore critically how much such a reading perpetuates patriarchal mind-sets and whether and to what degree the women characters of the kyriocentric text communicate kyriarchal values and visions. One must also consider that women, even more than men, have internalized cultural-religious feminine values and that they consequently tend to reproduce uncritically the patriarchal "politics of submission and otherness" in their speaking and writing.

Therefore, the category of *woman* must be problematized. More and more the diverse resistant discourses of emerging feminist political movements around the world interrupt those discourses of gender studies that conceptualize feminist interpretation as the practice of reading *as a woman*. These political discourses challenge Western universalist claims that all women have a special, essential nature in common and that all women are defined in the same way in their otherness to men. If feminist theology should displace the kyriarchal "politics of submission and otherness," it can no longer construct women's identity as unitary and universal and establish it in terms of either the exclusion and domination of the Others or the self-negation and subordination of the Others. The emerging feminist movements around the world insist on the specific historical-cultural contexts and on the historically defined subjectivity as well as on the plurality of women. By so doing they unravel the unitary universalizing tendency of Western philosophical-political and religious discourses to define *woman* as the natural Other of *man,* an Otherness which in reality is only that of elite Woman to elite Man.

By deconstructing the ideological constructs of Woman and the Feminine, such global feminist discourses bring to the fore how the identity of women who belong to subordinated races, classes, cultures, or religions is constructed as the "Other" of the "Others," as a negative foil for the feminine identity of the white Lady and the masculine identity of the men of their own people. For instance, in her analysis of lynching, Ida B. Wells has elucidated the kyriarchal manipulation of race and gender in the interest of perpetuating political terrorism, economic oppression, and sexual exploitation in America.[33] She argued that the miscegenation laws did not protect females from rape, only white women. In the name of protecting the honor of womanhood, they granted to white men the power to terrorize black men, who were seen as a threat to white womanhood. The charge of having raped a white woman became the excuse for the murder of any black man.

The insights articulated by emerging feminist discourses around the globe into the collusion of race, gender, class, and culture in the production and continuation of kyriarchal oppression compel middle-class feminists in the so-called First World not to duplicate the whitemale universalistic discourse of gender dualism.[34] At the same time they caution middle-class feminists of the "Two Thirds World"[35] not to reproduce the neocolonialist discourse on Woman and femininity, in order to prove their cultural stature. As a result, a feminist commentary project concerned with the multiplicative forms of women's oppression may no longer conceive of itself as either a "Woman's Bible" or a "Women's Bible" commentary that reads *as a woman* in the company of women. Rather, it must understand itself as reading in *a feminist* way[36] by destabilizing the category of *woman* and by continually problematizing the feminist paradigm of interpretation that is conceived of in terms of the Western dualistic sex/ gender system.

THE MANY VOICES
OF FEMINIST INTERPRETATION

Just like the category "woma[e]n," the term "feminist" has become problematic, since it is often understood in essentialist rather than historical, cross-cultural terms. If feminism is understood as a universalized women's movement and a gender theory that concerns itself with the universal and unilateral oppression of all women by all men, it reproduces the cultural patriarchal discourse on Woman and the Feminine. Hence, for many women of the Two Thirds World the term "feminist" designates the movement of white European and American women. To designate this volume of *Searching the Scriptures* as *feminist* might thus easily provoke the misunderstanding that it is conceptualized within such a totalizing gender perspective.

Therefore, some advisors to the project have suggested that the qualifier "feminist" should be displaced and replaced with a proliferation of names and self-designations. An identification of this project as "womanist," "*mujerista*," or as written from an Asian/African/Latin-American, lesbian, differently-abled, Protestant, or Jewish women's perspective, they argue, would interrupt the gender perspective of *The Woman's Bible* and positively mark the particular social-religious locations and hermeneutical perspectives of the contributions to this project. However, such a suggestion indicates at the same time its infeasibility and impracticality, since the book's title could not possibly name all the perspectives and standpoints of its authors. Moreover, while some of the proposed neologisms and self-designations explicitly claim to be feminist (see Alice Walker's definition of womanist), others reject the term as too radical for many women.

Other feminists of color have argued to the contrary for retaining the qualifier "feminist" in the title. Abandoning the term "feminism," they point out, would be a "mixed blessing" for women in the Two Thirds World. Not only would such a practice credit the historical achievements of feminism as a worldwide *political* movement to white European and

American women, but it would also relinquish the claim of feminists around the world that they continue to define and practice feminism in a different key.[37] Instead of rejecting feminism as white middle-class, these feminists maintain that women of color have always engaged with feminism or "feminist movement"—to use bell hooks's expression. As Cheryl Johnson-Odim suggests, it is more important for feminists of color to be concerned with participating in shaping

> and defining feminism than with changing the terminology. . . . Since "modern day" feminism is still in the process of incarnation, especially at the international level, I question whether the coining of a new term simply retreats from the debate, running the risk of losing sight of the fair amount of universality in women's oppression.[38]

Rather than retreat from the debate, feminists of the Two Thirds World thus continue to challenge white European and American feminist movements and articulations to abandon their cultural imperialism, white supremacy, and exclusivist definition of feminism in terms of middle-class white women's experiences. Although as an educated white European woman teaching at Harvard I write from an "infinitely privileged position"— to borrow Gyatri Chakravorty Spivak's words—I also believe it would be politically fatal for the women's movement in biblical religions if we were to restrict the label "feminism" to white European and American women and then go on to define it as *different* from Asian, Latin American, African women's, womanist, or *mujerista* biblical interpretation. Rather than reify "feminist/feminism" as a white supremacist definition by theorizing it in terms of the Western sex/gender system, I argue, one needs to destabilize and problematize its meanings.

While it is important that diverse feminist communities proliferate their own positive self-designations, such a proliferation is also in danger of engendering the "balkanization" of feminism in academy and church. Such a nationalist, territorial fragmentation turns differently articulated feminist movements into "special interest groups" and unwittingly serves the interest of established powers. If feminists continue to define our particular voices along the oppressive structures and dividing lines engendered by kyriarchal domination, we are in danger of jeopardizing and undermining the effectiveness of feminism as a theoretical and practical political movement for changing relationships of domination.

In order to avoid such a debilitating impact on feminist movements around the globe, different feminist formations must be conceptualized as open political discourses that are repeatedly problematized, destabilized, and defined differently. Only if the term "feminist/feminism" is not reified as a fixed, essentialist classification can it function as an "open-ended" category which must be questioned, destabilized, and redefined in ever-shifting historical-political situations of domination. It is my hope that readers engage the diverse contributions to this volume in such a critical feminist way.

Hence, this commentary project explicitly claims the adjective "feminist" rather than positioning itself within the essentialist cultural tradition of *The Woman's Bible*. Its authors have been invited to articulate their diverse feminist perspectives and to spell out the theoretical assumptions and methods of analysis with which they have approached their task. They have also been asked to reflect on how their own particular social locations and political engagements impinge on their feminist perspectives and shape their biblical interpretations. In this way, I hope this commentary project provides a discursive forum in which different and even contradictory voices can define the outline and shape of a *feminist* biblical interpretation.

A "feminist" reading, I argue, must time and again rearticulate its categories and focus its lenses of interpretation in particular historical situations and social contexts. It may not subscribe to a single method of analysis nor adopt a single hermeneutical perspective or mode of approach. It also may not restrict itself to one single reading community or audience. Rather, it must *search* for appropriate theoretical frameworks and practical ways of interpretation that can make visible oppressive as well as liberative traces inscribed in ancient Jewish and Christian scriptures. A collection of feminist perspectives from different subject locations that does not construe these particular approaches as exclusive totalizing strategies can articulate them as different *feminist* practices of collaboration for changing particular relations of domination and alienation.

At stake here is a theoretical shift from the paradigm of domination to one of radical equality.[39] Emancipatory movements have to create discursive communities based on shared assumptions and values that define boundaries and validate claims to authority. In the past decade political or liberationist rather than gender feminism has offered one of the most dynamic examples of such a counterdiscourse in society in general and in biblical religions in particular. It has constituted an oppositional public arena for generating critical analyses of patriarchal oppression and for articulating feminist interests and visions. Still, insofar as such feminist movements have projected themselves as a single oppositional front, defined their ethos in terms of the sex/gender system, and generated a universalizing critique of sociopolitical structures from the standpoint of [European-American elite] *Woman,* they have tended to constitute a feminist counterpublic as a hegemonic sphere of privileged, white European-American women.

Recent feminist work that does not position itself within the Western "politics of otherness," but rather within the ethical-political space of the democratic paradigm, seeks to theorize differently such a public feminist space from which to speak. In order to move away from essentialist notions of "women's perspective," Chandra Talpade Mohanty has suggested that the "imagined community" for oppositional struggles of the Two Thirds World should be

> political rather than biological or cultural bases for alliance. Thus it is not color or sex which constructs the ground for these struggles. Rather it is the way we think about race, class and gender—the political links we choose to make among and between struggles. Thus, potentially, women of all colors (including white women) can align themselves and participate in these imagined communities.[40]

Following her suggestion, I have argued that within the logic of radical equality one can theorize *biblical interpretation* as a site of feminist struggles for transforming societal and religious institutions. Such a theoretical frame can displace that of the gender alterity construct *woman* as the theoretical space from which to struggle and to speak.

Situating feminist theorizing and theologizing within the logic of radical equality rather than within that of female/ethnic identity allows one to contextualize so-called natural binary sexual arrangements together with those of race, ethnicity, or class as sociopolitical ideological constructions. Women live in structures that are not simply pluralist. Rather, "they are stratified, differentiated into social groups with unequal status, power, and access to resources, traversed by pervasive axes of inequality along lines of class, gender, race, ethnicity, and age."[41] Consequently, feminist theories must take care not to reinscribe such patriarchal structures and status *divisions* of women as positive pluralistic *differences*. Rather, a critical feminist political discursive practice of liberation must "denaturalize" patriarchal racial, gender, cultural, and other status inscriptions and show how they are historically and socially constructed.

As the intersection of a multiplicity of public feminist discourses and as a site of contested sociopolitical contradictions, feminist alternatives, and unrealized possibilities, *feminist interpretation* requires a rhetorical rather than a scientific positivist conceptualization. Such a rhetorical conceptualization of feminist discourses on scripture must develop a *methodological* approach that is different from that of Cady Stanton's project. In the tradition of *The Woman's Bible*, women's biblical studies have concentrated on *topical* analyses that do not sufficiently take into account the rhetorical character of androcentric and kyriocentric texts. They have focused on male injunctions for woman or on the great women of the Bible. Since *The Woman's Bible* and its tradition of interpretation focused on what men have said about women, subsequent discussions have adopted a similar *methodological approach.*

Historical studies of biblical women have taken biblical texts about women as comprehensive and descriptive sources rather than as prescriptive rhetorical texts. Women's Bible commentaries focus on the women characters in the Bible as well as on what biblical authors have written about women. Such a methodological focus on woma[e]n is in danger of identifying women's reality with women's representation and of succumbing to the totalizing power of the grammatically masculine so-called generic text.

Because of their methodological focus on texts about woma[e]n, women's biblical studies have neglected to develop biblical interpretation and historical reconstruction as a critical praxis of emancipatory struggles for liberation. Such interpretive practices must not only be able to break the hold of the sacred androcentric text by resisting its ideological patriarchal directives and hierarchically arranged binary oppositions. They must also be adept at unmasking the patriarchal politics of biblical texts about women, must reject textual determinism that understands the texts about woma[e]n as the only texts speaking about females, must engage in a historical reconstruction that imagines the social and ecclesial reality of wo/men in antiquity differently, and must trace the dynamic interaction between text, reader, and sociopolitical context. Feminist critical interpretations must engage with and move back and forth between different rhetorical strategies of interpretation, rather than construct them as fixed positions that exclude each other.

By elucidating not only the gender politics but also the patriarchal — or better kyriarchal — politics of biblical texts, such a critical rhetorical model of interpretation can enable readers to resist the prescriptive rhetorics and identity formation of canonical biblical texts. In such a way, it can make available polyglot discourses through which individual women can shape their own stories in conversation with the stories of other contemporary, historical, or biblical women.

Such discourses must render those women who have remained invisible even in feminist discourses visible again. By insisting in its own discourses on the theoretical visibility and difference, for instance, of black, poor, colonial, lesbian, or working women, feminist theory and theology make it clear that "women" do not have a unitary essence but represent a historical multiplicity, not only as a group but also as individuals. In addition, feminist discourses must also take care not to portray one group of women — for example, lesbians — as a monolithic, essentialist, and undifferentiated group with no competing interests, values, and conflicts.[42]

In order to minimize the possibility of its cooptation in the interests of Western patriarchy, I argue, feminist biblical interpretation must place at the center of its attention everywoman's struggles to transform patriarchal structures, both in biblical and in our own times, rather than focusing its gaze solely on the androcentric biblical text and its authority. Since throughout the centuries patriarchal theologies and churches have silenced women and excluded us from religious institutions of authority, feminist theology and theory seek to empower women to become theological subjects, to participate in the critical construction of biblical-theological meanings, and to claim women's authority to do so. In reclaiming the authority of women from all walks of life to shape and determine biblical religions, feminist theology attempts to reconceptualize the act of scriptural interpretation as a moment in the global praxis for liberation. I hope that this volume of *Searching the Scriptures* will help readers to claim their authority of interpretation and their spiritual power of vision for the struggle to change kyriarchal relationships of exploitation, marginality, and injustice.

NOTES

1. Dale Spender, *Women of Ideas (And What Men Have Done to Them): From Aphra Behn to Adrienne Rich* (Boston: Routledge & Kegan Paul, 1982), 8.

2. Gerda Lerner, *The Creation of Feminist Consciousness* (New York: Oxford University Press, 1993), 165.

3. Sarah Moore Grimké, *Letters on the Equality of the Sexes and the Condition of Woman* (Boston: Isaac Knapp, 1838), 3.

4. See *Productions of Mrs. Maria W. Stewart*, "published by friends of freedom and virtue" (Boston, 1835; reprinted in *Spiritual Narratives* [The Schomburg Library of Nineteenth-Century Black Women Writers; New York: Oxford University Press, 1988]); see also Paula Giddings, *When and Where I Enter: The Impact of Black Women on Race and Sex in America* (New York: William Morrow, 1984), 49–54.

5. William H. Myers, "The Hermeneutical Dilemma of the African American Biblical Student," in *Stony the Road We Trod: African American Biblical Interpretation*, ed. C. H. Felder (Minneapolis: Fortress, 1991), 40–56.

6. See the critique of white feminist scholarship by Jaqueline Grant, *White Women's Christ and Black Women's Jesus: Feminist Christology and Womanist Response* (Atlanta: Scholars Press, 1989); and Barbara Hilkert Andolsen, *Daughters of Jefferson, Daughters of Bootblacks: Racism and American Feminism* (Macon, GA: Mercer University Press, 1986).

7. Spender, *Women of Ideas*, 19f.

8. Adrienne Rich, *A Wild Patience Has Taken Me This Far: Poems 1978–1981* (New York: Norton, 1981), 33–36.

9. Sharon Sievers argues in a similar fashion that one must distinguish between women's history and feminist history ("Six [or More] Feminists in Search of a Historian," in *Expanding the Boundaries of Women's History: Essays on Women in the Third World,* ed. Cheryl Johnson-Odim and Margaret Strobel [Bloomington: Indiana University Press, 1992], 319–30).

10. Toni Morrison, *Playing in the Dark: Whiteness and the Literary Imagination* (Cambridge: Harvard University Press, 1992), 12.

11. Elizabeth Cady Stanton et al., *The Woman's Bible,* 2 vols. (1895, 1898; reprint, New York: Arno Press, 1974) 2:8.

12. This spelling is intentionally jarring in order to bring to consciousness that "woma[e]n" is a culturally constructed signifier that must be destabilized.

13. Adrienne Rich, *The Dream of a Common Language: Poems 1974–1977* (New York: Norton, 1978), 33–36.

14. K. G. Cannon, "Slave Ideology and Biblical Interpretation," *Semeia* 47 (1989): 9–24.

15. C. Townsend Gilkes, "Mother to the Motherless," *Semeia* 47 (1989): 65.

16. Vincent L. Wimbush, "The Bible and African Americans: An Outline of an Interpretative History," in *Stony the Road We Trod,* ed. Felder, 88.

17. See the introduction by Margaret Washington, ed., *Narrative of Sojourner Truth* (New York: Random House, Vintage Books, 1993; reprint of 1850 edition).

18. Howard Thurman, *Jesus and the Disinherited* (Nashville: Abingdon, 1949), 31–32.

19. Alicia Suskin Ostriker, *Feminist Revision and the Bible* (Cambridge: Blackwell Publishers, 1993), 86.

20. Cady Stanton, ed., *The Woman's Bible,* 2:7.

21. Miriam Levering, "Introduction," in *Rethinking Scripture: Essays from a Comparative Perspective,* ed. M. Levering (Stony Brook: State University of New York Press, 1989), 2.

22. Claudia V. Camp, "Female Voice, Written Word: Women and Authority in Hebrew Scripture," in *Embodied Love: Sensuality and Relationship as Feminist Values,* ed. P. M. Cooey, S. Farmer, and M. E. Ross (San Francisco: Harper & Row, 1987), 97–114.

23. For such a four-dimensional feminist model of interpretation, see my *Bread Not Stone: The Challenge of Feminist Biblical Interpretation* (Boston: Beacon Press, 1984).

24. For instance, Lone Fatum criticizes the project of a feminist reconstruction in terms of such a positivist understanding of androcentric language ("Women, Symbolic Universe and Structures of Silence: Challenges and Possibilities in Androcentric Texts," *Studia Theologica* 43 [1989]: 61–80).

25. See Karen Offen, "Defining Feminism: A Comparative Historical Approach," *Signs* 14/1 (1988): 119–57, for a historical account of the ambiguity in the definition of feminism in Europe and America. However, she does not elaborate a cross-cultural history of the term "feminism" as it was used, for example, in Egypt, India, China, or Japan. My own distinction between gender and liberation feminism is different from her distinction between relational and individualist feminism.

26. Anna Julia Cooper, *A Voice From the South* (Xenia, OH: The Aldine Printing House, 1892; reprint, The Schomburg Library of Nineteenth-Century Black Women Writers; New York: Oxford University Press, 1988), 120–23.

27. Ibid., 134.

28. Mary Helen Washington, "Introduction," in *A Voice from the South,* xlvii.

29. Elizabeth A. Clark, *Ascetic Piety and Women's Faith: Essays on Late Ancient Christianity,* Studies in Women and Religion 20 (Lewiston: Edwin Mellen Press, 1986), 135.

30. Ibid., 143.

31. This is the hermeneutical perspective stated by the editors of the *Women's Bible Commentary*, ed. Carol A. Newsome and Sharon H. Ringe (Louisville: Westminster/John Knox Press, 1992), xv.

32. See Jonathan Culler, *On Deconstruction* (Ithaca, NY: Cornell University Press, 1982), 43–64.

33. See Hazel V. Carby, "'On the Threshold of Woman's Era': Lynching, Empire and Sexuality," in *Race, Writing and Difference*, ed. H. L. Gates (Chicago: University of Chicago Press, 1986), 301–28; Emily M. Townes, *Womanist Justice, Womanist Hope* (Atlanta: Scholars Press, 1993) for a critical discussion and exploration of Ida B. Wells's work.

34. Since "Third World" often carries the negative connotation of "undeveloped," feminists of color have coined the term "Two Thirds World" in order to stress the fact that they represent not a minority of the world's population but rather the majority.

35. For the expression "whitemale," see Houston A. Baker, Jr., "Caliban's Triple Play," in *Race, Writing, and Difference*, ed. Gates, 382.

36. See Adrienne Munich, "Notorious Signs, Feminist Criticism and Literary Tradition," in *Making a Difference: Feminist Literary Criticism*, ed. Gayle Green and Kopelia Kahn (New York: Methuen, 1985), 238–60.

37. See, e.g., Barbara Smith, ed., *Home Girls: A Black Feminist Anthology* (New York: Kitchen Table: Women of Color Press, 1983); bell hooks, *Feminist Theory: From Margin to Center* (Boston: South End Press, 1984).

38. Cheryl Johnson-Odim, "Common Themes, Different Contexts: Third World Women and Feminism," in *Third World Women and the Politics of Feminism*, ed. C. T. Mohanty, A. Russo, and L. Torres (Bloomington: Indiana University Press, 1991), 316.

39. For further elaboration, see my books *But She Said: Feminist Practices of Biblical Interpretation* (Boston: Beacon Press, 1992) and *Discipleship of Equals: A Critical Feminist Ekklesia-logy of Liberation* (New York: Crossroad, 1993).

40. Chandra Talpade Mohanty, "Introduction: Cartographies of Struggle," in *Third World Women and the Politics of Feminism*, ed. Chandra Talpade Mohanty et al., 4.

41. Nancy Fraser, *Unruly Practices: Power, Discourse and Gender in Contemporary Social Theory* (Minneapolis: University of Minnesota Press, 1989), 165.

42. E. Frances White, "Africa on My Mind: Gender, Counter Discourse and African-American Nationalism," *Journal of Women's History* 2/1 (1990): 87.

RECOMMENDED READINGS

Cady Stanton, Elizabeth et al. *The Woman's Bible*, Parts I and II. 1895, 1898. Reprint, New York: Arno Press, 1974.

Chung Hyun Kyung, *Struggle to be the Sun Again: Introducing Asian Women's Theology*. Maryknoll, NY: Orbis Books, 1990.

Cooper, Anna Julia. *A Voice from the South*, ed. Mary Helen Washington. 1892. Reprint, The Schomburg Library of Nineteenth-Century Black Women Writers. New York: Oxford University Press, 1988.

hooks, bell. *Feminist Theory: From Margin to Center*. Boston: South End Press, 1984.

Johnson-Odim, Cheryl, and Margaret Strobel, eds. *Expanding the Boundaries of Women's History: Essays on Women in the Third World*. Bloomington: University of Indiana Press, 1992.

Lerner, Gerda. *The Creation of Feminist Consciousness: From the Middle Ages to Eighteen-Seventy.* New York: Oxford University Press, 1993.

Mohanty, Chandra T., Ann Russo, and Lourdes Torres, eds. *Third World Women and the Politics of Feminism.* Bloomington: University of Indiana Press, 1991.

Plaskow, Judith, and Elisabeth Schüssler Fiorenza, eds. *The Journal of Feminist Studies in Religion.* Atlanta: Scholars Press, 1985.

Russell, Letty, ed. *Feminist Interpretation of the Bible.* Philadelphia: Westminster, 1985.

Schüssler Fiorenza, Elisabeth. *But She Said: Feminist Practices of Biblical Interpretation.* Boston: Beacon Press, 1992.

Spender, Dale. *Women of Ideas (And What Men Have Done to Them): From Aphra Behn to Adrienne Rich.* Boston: Routledge & Kegan Paul, 1982.

Suskin Ostriker, Alicia. *Feminist Revision and the Bible.* Cambridge: Blackwell Publishers, 1993.

PART ONE

Charting Interpretation From Different Sociohistorical Locations

1

❖ History of Biblical Interpretation by European Women

ELISABETH GÖSSMANN ◆

How DID CHRISTIAN WOMEN read the Bible in the centuries that preceded modern feminist interpretation? Did they only internalize and reproduce the biblical interpretation of the fathers of the church, the male scholastic theologians, the male leaders of the Reformation and the Counter-Reformation, and so on? This is often assumed, not only by male but also by female scholars of our time. Although much research work on medieval women writers has been done by Kari Elisabeth Børresen, Peter Dronke, Caroline Walker Bynum, and others, women's biblical interpretation as a countertradition and a more or less concealed reaction against the official (male) tradition is very seldom the focus of our sex- and gender-bound studies of today. But this is my special feminist hermeneutical perspective, from which I try to understand female writers of the Middle Ages and the early centuries of the modern era. If one compares male and female theological writers' biblical interpretation, especially from the twelfth to the eighteenth century, the differences become evident.[1]

It seems to me that because women writers were more or less obliged to introduce themselves with an expression of modesty and an excuse for their writing in spite of being female, they adopted the negative portrayal of woman (poor, little, uneducated, miserable, wretched) used by scholastic male theologians. Alluding to 1 Cor 1:27, however, these women writers made use of the cultural understanding of "female weakness" by interpreting it as a sign of their election and exaltation by God. According to their self-understanding, they were tools of divine inspiration and wisdom and did not need any instruction from human teachers. Women writers understood themselves as prophetesses, experiencing visions and auditions in which they often received the "correct" biblical interpretation from Christ himself, an interpretation different from that of male teachers and preachers.

It is evident that medieval women writers, who had to be obedient to 1 Tim 2:9ff. and consequently had to avoid the appearance of teaching others, consciously or unconsciously developed their own hermeneutics in two different directions: on one hand, they wanted to pass the tests of ecclesiastical control by male authorities; on the other hand, they wanted to convey spiritual nurture to those who were hungry and thirsty and unsatisfied with the "usual" way of (male) teaching and preaching.

Consequently, the official interpretation of biblical texts used in the church appears at the beginning of "books" and "chapters" of women's works, but very often these texts are interpreted in some other way, or even undermined, in other passages of their works. Different from the conspicuous passages confirming orthodoxy, the countertraditional biblical interpretation of women cannot be recognized at first sight, neither by readers of their own time nor by those of today. It was often concealed, only to be discovered by those who looked more deeply for women writers' spirituality. This way of concealment through writing in a double-voiced discourse[2] not only functioned in their own time but still is effective today, since scholars still tend to regard medieval women writers as male-identified.[3]

The subject of women's countertraditional biblical interpretation was often the first three chapters of the book of Genesis; the women wrote in reaction to male writers who drew from these chapters when working out their hierarchical anthropology. Women writers' chief concerns included woman's *imago Dei* (Gen 1:26–27); woman's special creation and Eve's dignity before the Fall (Genesis 2); the role of woman in the Fall (Genesis 3); functions of women and female God-language in the Christian Old Testament; the competence and functions of women in the Gospels and Acts; confrontation with Paul's letters; and the great sign of the woman with the sun, the moon, and the stars (Revelation 12).

Women interpreted the Bible not only in an affirmative way through their writing, but also negatively by their silence. Concerning Genesis 2, male theologians sometimes wrote about the "perfect" and "not so perfect" mixture of elements in the creation of the bodies of Adam and Eve, a mixture that was believed to influence the "higher" and "lower" intelligence of the two sexes; yet women kept silent on this point. Concerning Genesis 3, male theologians generally wrote much about Eve's evil motives in committing original sin. Medieval women kept silent on this point, while Renaissance women contradicted it.

The scholastics degraded the female human being through their integration of Greek—mostly Aristotelian—philosophy and a patriarchal view of the Bible. Women preferred Plato and Neoplatonism for their own integration of philosophy and biblical interpretation.

For medieval writers of both sexes the meaning of the biblical text was *sensus historicus* ("the historical sense"), but women writers anticipated some of the results of modern critical methods by resisting the limitations of their life-style and activities which this sense seemed to impose.

HILDEGARD VON BINGEN

Hildegard von Bingen (twelfth century) can be called an ardent defender of God's image (*imago Dei*) in woman (Gen 1:26–27), which she not only mentions but also describes (*De operatione Dei* 2.5 [*PL* 197:952]). Male scholastics before and after her time attributed only one element of the *imago Dei* to women as well as men—that is, the three faculties of the soul: *memoria, intelligentia, voluntas* (memory, intelligence, will), which Augustine considered an image of the Trinity. They denied to women the second element, which is human resemblance to God as the creator and ruler of the world.[4] Like other women, Hildegard did not mention such a distinction. In contrast to male theologians, who regarded the *imago Dei* as a quality of the soul that has no sex (*ubi sexus nullus est;* Augustine, *De trinitate* 12.7.12), Hildegard included the body with the five senses by which the human being becomes wise, knowledgeable, and intelligent (*sapiens, sciens, intelligens; Explanatio Symboli Sancti Athanasii* [*PL* 197:1073]).

A striking example of Hildegard's anthropology can be found in her exegesis of Genesis 2, where she distinguishes between God's creation of man and of woman. Man was created from the loam (*de limo*) and had to be changed into flesh (*mutatus in carnem*). His privilege, derived from the earth as the material of his creation, is physical strength, enabling him to do his work in an agricultural society. But woman was created from human flesh and therefore did not need to be transformed. "Flesh from flesh," she remained what she was from the beginning and did not need to be changed (*Caro enim de carne, in aliud non mutanda permansit; De operatione Dei* 3.7 [*PL* 197:963]). "Taken from the flesh, she remained flesh, and therefore a skillful work of her hands is committed to her" (*De carne sumpta, caro permansit, et ideo datum est ei artificiosum opus manuum*).[5] This is her privilege. Her hands are skilled for textile work "to cover man," who would be naked without her labor, and her body is skilled "to cover" the child with the human flesh to be born from her.

Hildegard's theory of woman's better qualification for skilled work because of her creation from human flesh is also a kind of compensation and consolation for women living in a patriarchal culture, where they were under juridical obligation to be obedient to husbands and to work for them. But according to Hildegard, the obligation is mutual: man has to nurture woman, while she has to "cover" him. Both sexes, from the "privileges" of their special creation, are qualified for social cooperation. It seems that Hildegard intended to raise esteem for woman's work by her interpretation of Genesis 2.

In one of her variations of the patriarchal opinion concerning man's strength and woman's weakness, Hildegard writes: "God created the human being: the male of more strength, the female of a softer kind of power" (*Deus creavit hominem, masculum scilicet maioris fortitudinis, feminam vero mollioris roboris; De operatione Dei* 2.5 [PL 197:945]). Accordingly, man's strength needs "mildness" (*mansuetudo*). Man's "strength in the kind of mildness" (*fortitudo in specie mansuetudinis*)[6] and woman's "softer kind of power" (*mollius robur*) indicate Hildegard's concept of the human being. As her interpretation of God's creation of the human being shows, she is convinced of the equality of the two sexes, even if she is not able to abolish the patriarchal matrimonial law of her time. However, concerning monks and nuns living in virginity, she uses expressions of equality: they are "the same among the angelic orders" (*idem inter angelicos ordines; Solutiones quaestionum* 38 [PL 197:1039]).

It is necessary to mention here that Hildegard's macro-microcosmic concept of creation is different from the corresponding male interpretation, according to which the mixture of elements in the male and female body confirms the hierarchy of the two sexes. In male interpretations of Genesis 2, fire and air as the two higher elements prevail in the male body, and water and earth as the two lower elements prevail in the female body. But according to Hildegard, air and water as the two intermediate elements prevail in the female body. In this way she dissolves the cosmic fixation of the man–woman hierarchy.[7]

In her interpretation of woman's "subjection" to man (Gen 3:16), Hildegard uses biological terms in order to undermine its patriarchal, legal connotation: "A Woman is placed under her husband that he may sow his semen into her womb. . . . A woman as a receiver of her husband's semen remains under his potency."[8] The juridical term of subjection is reinterpreted by its biological use. The biological act of generating a human being with the cooperating woman as *subiecta* symbolizes the creature's subordination to God.

Hildegard distinguishes between the newly created Eve as the splendid feminine form (*feminea forma*) and model of virginity on one hand and the fallen Eve on the other. But according to the persuasive argument of Barbara Newman, Hildegard, in contrast to male theologians, magnifies the role of Satan. Disregarding the question of Eve's motivation, Hildegard's Eve was "more sinned against than sinning, not so much tempted as deceived."[9] Eve's frailty as a sinner calls up God's mercy and grace. Consequently, Hildegard is not far from interpreting Eve's guilt as *felix culpa* (a happy fault).

Since in scholastic theology woman's subordination makes her dissimilar to God,[10] Hildegard connects subordination with awe (*timor*) and wisdom (*sapientia*), two of the seven gifts of the Holy Spirit (Isa 11:1ff.). According to Hildegard's allegorical interpretation of the "house of wisdom" in Prov 9:1, woman is, so to speak, a house of wisdom (*quasi domus sapientiae*) in her awe (*timor*) toward God and her husband (*Liber vitae meritorum* 1.82.96 [ed. Pitra, 44]). Here, in a spirit of solidarity, Hildegard equates married women bearing children and nuns delivering works of charity. All of them are "the house of wisdom," the only difference being that the virgin is *timida* toward God directly, while the married woman is *timida* toward God indirectly, through her awe toward her husband. But, as we know already, the reverse of humiliation is exaltation.

"House of wisdom" in Prov 9:1 was interpreted by most of the male exegetes of that time as the body of Christ. For Hildegard, it means womanhood. She also discovers a parallel between woman and Christ or Eve and Christ. Christ (Luke 1:26–38) and Eve (Gen 2:21–22) have the same origin—"not from semen but from human flesh" (*non ex semine sed ex carne; De operatione Dei* 3.7 [PL 197:974]). Christ's and woman's work are similar too: humankind was born from woman's "weakness," not from man's "strength," and reborn from the "weakness" of Christ's human nature, not from the "strength" of his divine nature.[11]

Hildegard's female God-language is pervasive in her works. I will only mention here her stress on divine wisdom (*divina sapientia*), whose incarnation is Christ[12] and her paraphrase of Isa 42:14 (God as a woman in childbirth), in which she enjoys the use of the feminine gender of Latin grammar (*De operatione Dei* 2.5 [PL 197:928]). Interpreting Luke 15:8–10, Hildegard enthusiastically writes: "Holy divinity had ten drachmas" (*Sancta divinitas habuit drachmas decem; Scivias* 3.2 [PL 197:587]) CC CM 43A, 366). Different from the fathers, who identified the woman in the parable as God's wisdom, Hildegard understands the woman as divine substance (*divina substantia*).[13]

In her interpretation of the Prologue of the Fourth Gospel, Hildegard mentions both sexes as being given the "power" to become God's children: ". . . to all human beings of both sexes who received him" (*omnibus hominibus utriusque sexus qui eum receperunt; De operatione Dei* 1.4 [PL 197:896]). The addition of *utriusque sexus* ("both sexes") also in other women's texts shows that women realized that male writers often used the word *homo* (human being) only in the sense of "male."

The prophecy of Joel, quoted in Peter's sermon on Pentecost (Acts 2:17), which mentions the prophesying sons and daughters, was one of Hildegard's favorite texts of the Bible. It was important not only for her self-understanding as a prophet but for that of other women as well.

Hildegard quotes and completes Paul's text of 1 Cor 11:9: "Woman is created because of man, and man is made because of woman."[14] Against the dualistic concept of woman becoming man in eschatological perfection, Hildegard, in a context alluding to 1 Cor 15:52, stresses the eschatological integrity of the female human being: "All human beings will rise from the dead in body and soul . . . with integrity of their sex."[15]

GERTRUD THE GREAT
AND OTHER MEDIEVAL WOMEN WRITERS

Typical for medieval mysticism is the individualistic interpretation of the Song of Songs, succeeding the collective interpretation of earlier centuries, which had identified the figure of the bridegroom with God or Christ and that of the bride with God's people or the church. The medieval type of interpretation, connected with the name of Bernard of Clairvaux, identifies the figure of the groom with God or one of the persons of the Trinity, and that of the bride with the individual human soul. The female contribution to this type of interpretation of the Song is important. The beguine Mechthild of Magdeburg, who wrote *The Flowing Light of the Godhead* (in the vernacular), is probably the most significant author in this regard.[16]

It is not inconceivable that the individualistic interpretation of the Song of Songs might have been developed first by women mystics and have been adopted later on by men. But because some of the earliest mystical texts of this type are handed down anonymously, this is difficult to demonstrate. Nevertheless, bridal mysticism (*Brautmystik*) is a much more "natural" expression of female mystic experience and spirituality. As Caroline Walker Bynum has shown, only in an act of humiliation could a male mystic identify with the female role of the bride—but such an act of humiliation seems to be a second step.[17]

Mechthild of Magdeburg spent the last years of her life in a convent in Helfta in which the nuns lived under Cistercian rule. The two Mechthilds (M. von Magdeburg and M. von Hackeborn) and the two Gertruds (G. von Hackeborn and G. the Great) can be regarded as Bible scholars, well versed in the scholasticism and mysticism of the twelfth century and of their own time. Johanna Lanczkowski's German translation of the *Legatus divinae pietatis* (Herald of Divine Love), by Gertrud the Great and other nuns of Helfta, has a scripture index of seven pages.[18] The biblical interpretation of the *Legatus* alone, not to mention Mechthild of Hackeborn's *Liber specialis gratiae* (Book of special grace),[19] can provide material for a thesis on this woman's biblical interpretation. I confine myself here to some examples.

Like Hildegard, Gertrud defends the dignity of woman as God's image, without any restriction. In *Legatus* 2.6, she describes an experience of meditation in which she perceived the words of Christ: "As I am the image of God the Father in divinity (Heb 1:3), you will be the image of my essence toward humankind, since you received in your God-created soul the efficiency of my divinity, just like the air which receives the rays of sunshine." Christ in dialogue with Gertrud does not regard womanhood as an impediment for any religious functions.

In 2.20 the praying Gertrud mentions gratefully that she received from Christ the commission to hear confessions and to judge the seriousness of the sins confessed to her. In 4.32 a fellow sister reports that, in a vision, Christ breathed upon Gertrud and spoke to her the words of John 20:22–23: "Receive the Holy Spirit. Whose sins you remit shall be remitted," and that she, not daring to believe, mentioned the restriction of this power to the priests, but received the following answer from Christ: "Those whom you, discerning through my spirit, judge to be not guilty, will surely be accounted innocent before me, and those whose case you judge to be guilty, will appear such to me, for I will speak through your mouth."[20]

The same is affirmed in 1.14, Gertrud's biography, written by the Convent of Helfta after her death:

> After several days, remembering this promise of the Lord without forgetting her own unworthiness, she asked how it was possible . . . and the Lord replied: "Is not the faith of the universal Church that promise once made to Peter: 'Whatever you bind on earth will be bound in heaven' (Matt 16:19), and firmly she believes this to be carried out by all ecclesiastical ministers. Therefore why do you not equally believe because of this that I can and will perfect that which, moved by love, I promise to you by my divine mouth?" And touching her tongue he said: "Behold, I give my words into your mouth."[21]

According to this text, Christ regards Gertrud as a minister of the church by his special gift.

A word of Christ to Gertrud, reported in *Legatus* 3.60 by a fellow sister, shows that she, in spite of feeling personally unworthy, was conscious of being in possession of all the seven sacraments: "Why are you troubled, my love? For as often as you desire it of me I, the sovereign priest and true pontiff, will enter you and will renew in your soul all the seven sacraments in one operation more efficaciously than any other priest or pontiff can do by seven separate acts."[22] Similar to Gertrud, Mechthild von Hackeborn too was conscious of her ecclesiastical ministry. But how did these nuns use their ministry? We know from the texts only that they counseled many people and that they confessed their sins not only to a priest but also to their abbess (*Legatus* 4.2).

Whereas Hildegard had reinterpreted the parable in Luke 15:11–32 by exchanging the lost son for a lost daughter, Gertrud interprets the parable in a different way so that the son who stays home with the father appears as a daughter. After an experience of God's absence, she hears the words of Luke 15:31, spoken to herself: "My daughter, you are always with me . . ." (*Legatus* 3.30).

We learn from Gertrud also that God was addressed in Helfta as Father and Mother and that Christ reveals his love as a maternal one. God's word in Isa 66:13 that he will console his people like a mother who consoles her child is applied to Christ and Gertrud and is paraphrased by Christ in a vision (*Legatus* 3.30). Christ appears not only as a tender mother but also as a strict mother, a mother teaching her daughter, referring to his eternal wisdom. Christ as the incarnation of Eternal Wisdom is always present in the consciousness of the Helfta nuns.

Thus, it is evident that the texts of the New Testament applied to one's own self are the horizon of these women's lives, an attitude which nearly transcends the genre of biblical interpretation.

WOMEN WRITERS OF THE EARLY MODERN ERA

In northern Europe, the situation of women writers became more difficult at the end of the Middle Ages. In 1455, the *Devotio moderna* (Windesheim Congregation) threatened the sisters with prison for writing *revelationes*.[23] Women as potential heretics suffered special restrictions. But in southern Europe, women seemed to enjoy more freedom. In 1399, Christine de Pizan wrote her ardent *Epître au Dieu d'amour* with a theological defense of women against the misogynist male writers of her time and the time before. She used the women's tradition of Genesis interpretation for her arguments: Woman, like man, was created in God's image. She was created from a better material, human flesh. Woman, but not man, was created in paradise. Thus, woman's noble nature is guaranteed by God himself, and man has no reason to offend her. Christine also tried to excuse Eve and to demonstrate the responsibility of man for original sin.[24]

This is the main argument of women's countertradition in the Renaissance. Before so-called male feminists such as Henricus Cornelius Agrippa von Nettesheim and others adopted the concept of Eve as God's masterpiece of creation, many women had worked it out.[25] But one finds also a very important variation of this type of argument in the work of Isotta Nogarola, a writer of fifteenth-century Verona who lived in her parents' house with her books like a nun without a convent. In spite of exchanging letters with prominent humanists, she seems to have suffered from the isolation of a woman who entered the more or less male preserves of humanist studies. Her *topoi* of humility are very one-sided, since they are without the expression of divine election. She excuses herself for writing in spite of being a woman, but also complains of male arrogance and confesses to having been often deterred from a certain undertaking by men who called learning in a woman poison.

In her dialogue *De pari aut impari Evae atque Adae peccato* (Concerning the equal or unequal sin of Adam and Eve), Isotta accepts from her male partner in the dialogue all the reasons for female weakness and insignificance taken from medieval scholasticism, but only in order to demonstrate with reference to woman's weakness her lower degree of responsibility for original sin. Thus she beats men with their own weapons. Yet to do so she has to subscribe to the notion of woman's intellectual and moral frailty. Even if the dialogue lacks a clear conclusion, Isotta may have intended to demonstrate the paradox that a weak woman can be successful in a discussion with a man.[26]

However, for the mainstream of this countertradition, Eve as the splendor of creation was a better model for encouraging women. Marguerite de Navarre (sixteenth century), sister of King Francis I, for instance, wrote letters to defend her sex in which she combines a matriarchal theory with the interpretation of Eve as the last and most perfect creature of God in Genesis. Fighting against the Salic law, by which women were excluded from the French throne, Marguerite used the Bible to work out her image of the strong woman.[27]

In 1600, the self-conscious Venetian Lucretia Marinella, who did not use a *topos* either of modesty or of humility, did not hesitate to use apocryphal gospels as sources for her *Life of the Virgin Mary*. She is only one of three famous women writers in this town who composed special compendiums to defend their own sex against male attacks. It was the time of the famous debate about the status of women known as "Querelle des femmes." Lucretia Marinella clearly defended Eve's innocence. "If men say that Eve was the cause of Adam's sin and in consequence of all our misery, I answer: She did nothing but propose that he eat from the fruit of the tree because she believed it was good for them. Not she but Adam was forbidden by God to do so. If that is so—and it is so—how can you say that she sinned? The person who sinned is Adam. Therefore, according to the Old Testament, only males are punished by circumcision."[28]

Marie de Jars de Gournay, an ardent Catholic, defender and friend of the Jesuits, wrote in 1622, more than one and a half centuries before the French Revolution, her *Egalité des hommes et des femmes* (Equality of Men and Women), in which she ridicules the male sex for confounding their beard with the "image de Dieu" (image of God), and for thinking that only males can be like God. Incisively and with irony she criticized the concept of God as an old man with a beard. She also reduced to this syndrome of the beard the male monopoly of power and the subordination of women, to whom public and ecclesiastical functions were denied.[29]

But the Jesuits could be found not only on women's side; they were also on the opposite side in the Querelle des femmes. François Loryot, S.J., who in his *Secretz Moraux* (Paris, 1614) had explained men's courtesy toward women as due to the necessity of women for the propagation of the human race and for nothing else, had to take advice from Marguerite de Valois, who called God as a witness to the perfection of his last creature:

> God proceeds in his works by such a succession that he creates the lowest things first and the most excellent, most perfect, and most dignified last, what he has shown in the creation of the world when he created the human being last of all—the human being for whom he had made all the other creatures. Therefore it is necessary to admit that the supreme degree of dignity must be attributed to woman, who was created after man as God's last creature. The highest perfections can be found in her as well, emerged as she is from God's hands just like man, but from a material as much more elaborated in its degree of excellence as the rib of man is which surpasses the mud.[30]

Because in seventeenth-century France women philosophers were tolerated, especially writing on topics of moral philosophy, Suzanne de Nervèze could publish in her *Oeuvres spirituelles et morales* (1642) an "Apologie en faveur des femmes," in which she complains of male arrogance despising women's intellectual faculties. Her refutation of this antifeminist position is a demonstration of the strength and wisdom of the women in the Bible, daughters of Eve, the "chef d' oeuvre" of God's works of creation. According to Suzanne de Nervèze, it is meaningful that God called his work of creation "very good" (Gen 1:31) only after finishing the creation of Eve.

In addition to self-defense, women writers used their biblical interpretation with a didactic intention. In her *Nouvelles observations de la langue*

Françoise (1668), Marguerite Buffet wanted to teach women how to speak and how to write. But to encourage them, she first had to explain the Bible in a different way than women were generally taught. Using an argument from tradition, she maintained that the human soul is sexless and therefore equal in both sexes. But this had been acknowledged already by medieval scholastics with the addition that a soul could develop its faculties much better in a male than in a female body. Therefore Marguerite Buffet had to stress the bodily prevalence of women enabling them to develop all the faculties of their souls without any limitation:

> . . . since the body of man was formed from the loamy soil of the earth, which is a material not at all comparable to that from which the body of woman was formed; since we know that everything that is stronger in the body of man was used to form that of woman. In whom, however, can we trust with more submission than in the God of truth who assures us that the perfection of the universe depended on the creation of woman who was the last of his works as well as their coronation? (She was it) in such a way that without this excellent creature, the world would not have gained the complete extension of its beauty and loveliness.[31]

The continuity of European women's countertradition of biblical interpretation from the Middle Ages to modern times is evident. Phyllis Trible with her Eve-oriented Genesis interpretation and Virginia Mollenkott with her feminist reading of the Bible have many foresisters. Whether it be Genesis interpretation or emphasis on women's functions in the Gospels, especially on Easter morning, women have always criticized the patriarchal reading of the Bible and have always developed new concepts. But seldom was the exegesis of women integrated into the official doctrine of the churches. Those male writers who adopted the feminist interpretation of the Bible did not quote the women writers from whom they had learned, but only from their male forerunners, since women were not acknowledged as authorities. Nor did women belong to the powerful teachers of the churches. Hence, in every generation women were forced to begin the hermeneutical task anew.

NOTES

1. Most of the biblical interpretation by women can be found in these centuries, although Hrotsvith von Gandersheim (tenth century) is also very interesting in this regard. For Chris-

tian antiquity, see Anne Jensen, *Gottes selbstbewußte Töchter: Frauenemanzipation im frühen Christentum?* (Freiburg: Herder, 1992); Monika Leisch-Kiesl, "Eva in Kunst und Theologie des Frühchristentums und Mittelalters" (Dr. theol. Diss., Salzburg, 1990).

2. See Elaine Showalter, "Feminist Criticism in the Wilderness," *Critical Inquiry* 8 (1981): 179–205.

3. Peter Dinzelbacher regards medieval women writers as male-identified in his essay "Das politische Wirken der Mystikerinnen in Kirche und Staat: Hildegard, Birgitta, Katharina," in *Religiöse Frauenbewegung und mystische Frömmigkeit im Mittelalter,* ed. P. Dinzelbacher and D. R. Bauer (Cologne and Vienna: Böhlau, 1988), 265–302.

4. See Elisabeth Gössmann, "Glanz und Last der Tradition: Ein theologiegeschichtlicher Durchblick," in *Mann und Frau: Grundproblem theologischer Anthropologie,* ed. Theodor Schneider (Freiburg: Herder, 1989), 25–52.

5. *Causae et curae,* ed. P. Kaiser (1903; reprint, Basel, 1980), 59.

6. *Liber vitae meritorum* 4.23.36, ed. J. B. Pitra (Monte Cassino, 1882; republished, Farnborough: Gregg Press, 1966/67), 160.

7. See Prudence Allen, *The Concept of Woman: The Aristotelian Revolution* (Montreal and London: Eden Press, 1985); eadem, "Two Medieval Views on Woman's Identity: Hildegard of Bingen and Thomas Aquinas," *Studies in Religion: A Canadian Journal* 16 (1987): 21–36.

8. *Mulier viro subiecta est in qua ipse semen suum seminet. . . . Mulier autem susceptrix seminis est unde et mulier sub potestate viri manet* (*Scivias* 1.3 [PL 197:398], ed. A. Führkötter, CC CM 43,29; *Scivias* 1.2 [PL 197:392] CC CM 43,19).

9. Barbara J. Newman, "*O feminea forma:* God and Woman in the Works of St. Hildegard" (Ph.D. diss., Yale University, 1981), 167.

10. Elisabeth Gössmann, "The Image of the Human Being according to Scholastic Theology and the Reaction of Contemporary Women," *Ultimate Reality and Meaning* 11 (1988): 183–95.

11. *Liber vitae meritorum* 4.24.32, ed. Pitra, 157–58: *Ipse etiam Deus virum fortem et feminam debilem creaverat, cuius debilitas mundum generavit. Et Divinitas fortis est, caro autem Filii Dei infirma, per quam mundus in priorem statum recuperatur.*

12. See *De operatione Dei* 1.1 [PL 197:743), where *divina sapientia* speaks: *Integra namque vita sum, quae de lapidibus abscissa non est, et de ramis non fronduit, et de virili vi non radicavit, sed omme vitale de me radicatum est. Rationalitas enim radix est, sonans vero verbum in ipsa floret* ("For I am the integral life, which is not cut off from the trees, not greened from the twigs, not rooted in a man's potency. But all that is living is rooted in me. Rationality, indeed, is the root, and the sounding word is blossoming in her").

13. See *De operatione Dei* 1.1 (PL 197:743), where *divina sapientia* speaks: *Sed et ego ignea vita substantiae divinitatis . . .* ("But I am also the fiery life of the substance of divinity").

14. *Scivias* 1.2 (PL 197:393) CC CM 43,21: *Mulier propter virum creata est, et vir propter mulierem factus est.*

15. *Scivias* 3.12 (PL 197:727) CC CM 43A, 608: *Omnes homines in anima et corpore . . . in integritate . . . sexus sui . . . resurgunt.*

16. Lucy Menzies, trans. *The Revelations of Mechthild of Magdeburg (1210–1297) or The Flowing Light of the Godhead* (London: Longmans, Green & Co., 1953).

17. See Caroline Walker Bynum, ". . . And Woman His Humanity: Female Imagery in the Religious Writing of the Later Middle Ages," in *Gender and Religion,* ed. C. W. Bynum, S. Harrell, and P. Richman (Boston: Beacon Press, 1986), 257–88.

18. Gertrud die Grosse von Helfta, *Gesandter der göttlichen Liebe* (*Legatus divinae pietatis*), trans. Johanna Lanczkowski (Heidelberg: Verlag Lambert Schneider, 1989). See also Sabine B. Spitzlei, *Erfahrungsraum Herz: Zur Mystik des Zisterzienserinnenklosters Helfta im 13. Jahrhundert,* Mystik in Geschichte und Gegenwart, Abteilung I, Christliche Mystik 9, ed. Margot Schmidt and Helmut Riedlinger (Stuttgart-Bad Cannstatt: Frommann-Holzboog, 1991).

19. See Gertrud Jaron Lewis, *Bibliographie zur deutschen Frauenmystik des Mittelalters,* Bibliographien zur deutschen Literatur des Mittelalters 10 (Berlin: Erich Schmidt-Verlag, 1989), 184–95.

20. Trans. Caroline Walker Bynum in *Jesus as Mother: Studies in the Spirituality of the High Middle Ages* (Berkeley: University of California Press, 1982), 205.

21. Ibid., 206.

22. Ibid., 202.

23. See Leen Breure, "Männliche und weibliche Ausdrucksformen in der Spiritualität der Devotio Moderna," in *Frauenmystik im Mittelalter,* ed. P. Dinzelbacher and D. R. Bauer (Ostfildern bei Stuttgart: Schwabenverlag, 1985), 247.

24. See Elisabeth Gössmann, ed., "Introduction" in *Archiv für philosophie- und theologiegeschichtliche Frauenforschung,* vol. 1 (Munich: Iudicium, 1984), 12. See also Christine de Pizan, *The Book of the City of Ladies* trans. Earl Jeffrey Richards (New York: Persea Books, 1982) I.9.2 and 3, pp. 23–24.

25. See E. Gössmann, ed., "Introduction" in *Archiv,* vol. 4 (Munich: Iudicium, 1988), 12–15.

26. See Katharina Fietze, *Spiegel der Vernunft: Theorien zum Menschsein der Frau in der Anthropologie des 15. Jahrhunderts* (Paderborn: Schöningh, 1991).

27. See Gössmann, "Introduction" in *Archiv,* vol. 1, 13.

28. See E. Gössmann, ed., *Archiv,* vol. 2 (Munich: Iudicium, 1985), 40–41.

29. See Gössmann, *Archiv,* vol. 1, chap. 1.

30. "Discours docte et subtil fait par la feue Reyne Marguerite et envoyé à l'autheur des secrets Moraux," in *Réponse des Femmes à l' Autheur de l' "Alphabet"* (Paris, 1618), 11.

31. (Paris, 1668), 201.

[Editor's Note. In her most recent book, *The Creation of Feminist Consciousness* (New York: Oxford University Press, 1993), Gerda Lerner covers similar material and comes to the same conclusions as Elisabeth Gössmann, although she does not refer to Gössmann's work.]

RECOMMENDED READINGS

Bynum, Caroline Walker. *Jesus as Mother: Studies in the Spirituality of the High Middle Ages.* Berkeley: University of California Press, 1982.

Demers, Patricia. *Women as Interpreters of the Bible.* New York: Paulist Press, 1992.

Lerner, Gerda. *The Creation of Feminist Consciousness: From the Middle Ages to Eighteen-Seventy.* New York: Oxford University Press, 1993.

Newman, Barbara. *Sister of Wisdom: St. Hildegard's Theology of the Feminine.* Berkeley: University of California Press, 1987.

Petroff, Elizabeth A., ed. *Medieval Women's Visionary Literature.* New York: Oxford University Press, 1986.

Pomeroy, Sarah B., ed. *Women's History and Ancient History.* Chapel Hill: University of North Carolina Press, 1991.

Schmitt Pantel, Pauline, ed. *A History of Women: Vol. 1, From Ancient Goddesses to Christian Saints.* Cambridge: Harvard University Press, 1992.

Shahar, Shulamith. *The Fourth Estate: A History of Women in the Middle Ages.* New York: Methuen, 1983.

——, Stevan Harrell, and Paula Richman, eds. *Gender and Religion: On the Complexity of Symbols.* Boston: Beacon Press, 1986.

Wilson, Katharina M., ed. *Medieval Women Writers.* Athens: University of Georgia Press, 1984.

❖ Anna Julia Cooper and Sojourner Truth: Two Nineteenth-Century Black Feminist Interpreters of Scripture

KAREN BAKER-FLETCHER ◆

BLACK WOMEN'S INTERPRETATION of the Bible in the nineteenth century deserves more exploration and more space than is possible to pursue in a short essay. This essay considers the biblical hermeneutics of Anna Julia Cooper and some suggestions for comparing Cooper's interpretation of scripture with that of Sojourner Truth. Anna Cooper and Sojourner Truth were different in age, class, literacy, and region of origin. Cooper, born in 1858 in Raleigh, North Carolina, attended St. Augustine's Normal and Collegiate Institute during the Reconstruction period. She was an Oberlin-trained (1884) black woman educator who received a doctorate from the Sorbonne in 1925 and had few but painful memories of slavery. Sojourner Truth, eighty years Cooper's senior, was born in 1779 in Dutch-speaking New York, lived as a slave for thirty years, and never learned to read or write. Both women were highly intelligent, self-possessed, and irrepressible black feminists and social reformers. Truth died in 1883 at the age of 104 shortly before Cooper's career took off. Cooper died in 1964 at the age of 105.

ANNA JULIA COOPER'S INTERPRETATION OF SCRIPTURE

Along with women such as Harriet Tubman, Fannie Barrier Williams, Ida B. Wells, Frances E. W. Harper, and Josephine St. Pierre Ruffin, Anna Julia Cooper was part of a vanguard of spokeswomen who were counted on to speak as advocates of the feminist and suffrage movements.[1] She entered the public arena as a speaker for women's rights in 1886, when she delivered her essay "Womanhood a Vital Element in the Rengeneration of a Race" before colored clergy in Washington, D.C. She delivered it many times before both black and white audiences.[2] In 1893, Cooper, along with Fannie Barrier Williams and Fannie Jackson Coppin, was invited to address a special meeting of the Women's Congress in Chicago. Cooper believed that black women were created equal in intelligence to women and men of all races. She employed her religious belief and education to interpret the social message of the gospel.

Biblical principles were foundational to Anna Julia Cooper's views on womanhood. In "Womanhood a Vital Element . . . ," Cooper called the church to act according to gospel principles in its treatment of women.[3] She challenged the church to provide equal educational and economic opportunity for black women. Cooper argued that the church is the source of the vitalizing principle of women's amelioriation "so far as the church is *coincident with Christianity.*" She asserted "that the idea of the radical amelioriation of womankind . . . was to come from that . . . bounteous fountain from which flow all our liberal and universal ideas—the Gospel of Jesus Christ."[4]

Cooper described the church as struggling to understand Christ's teachings and as being in tension in its attempt to comprehend the "spirit" and the "letter" of Christ's precepts. She averred that for the church to be congruous with the gospel, it must espouse principles of freedom and equality for women. Historically, Cooper lamented, the church often has trampled "under foot both the spirit and the letter of his [Jesus'] precepts." But Jesus' precepts were indestructible and eternal, continuing "to the end of the world."[5]

THE HISTORICAL JESUS AS A GIVER OF IDEALS

Cooper saw the principles of the gospel as giving the church and culture an eternally unfolding source of truth and vitality:

> Christ gave ideals not formulae. The Gospel is a germ requiring millennia for its growth and ripening. It needs and at the same time helps to form around itself a soil enriched in civilization, and perfected in culture and insight without which the embryo can neither be unfolded or comprehended.[6]

Christ, Cooper asserted, gave certain *ideals* which required the development of society to be comprehended. She describes Christ as a sower, planting certain principles in the soil of civilization. Without the enriching soil of civilization, culture, and insight, Cooper wrote, the gospel could not be comprehended. In Cooper's thought, the gospel is nurtured in and helps form the rich soil of civilization. As civilization progresses, helped by the gospel, the gospel unfolds before it and reveals itself, generating a more perfected comprehension which enriches and perfects society over millennia. For Cooper, the ideals Christ has given require a continuous process of interpretation. Misunderstanding is part of the interpretive process. No interpretation of the gospel is ever complete.

Among the ideals Christ gave was "a rule and guide for the estimation of woman, as an equal, as a helper, as a friend, and as a sacred charge to be sheltered and cared for."[7] Cooper emphasized the equality of women. Because black women who worked as laborers and domestics were often sexually and physically abused by white male employers, she employed the rhetoric of the day to refer to women as sacred charges to be cared for. Cooper argued for the development and education of black women of the South so that they would be more economically independent. Equal education and economic opportunities for black women were modes of shelter and care.

For Cooper, every progressive social force was foreshadowed mutely or directly enjoined in the tale of Jesus Christ:

> With all the strides our civilization has made from the first to the nineteenth century, we can boast not an idea, not a principle of action, not a progressive social force but was already *mutely* foreshadowed, or directly enjoined in that simple tale of a meek and lowly life.[8]

Much of the language Cooper employed to represent Jesus is the kind of language she used to describe the black woman of the South, whose voice Cooper described as voiceless and as a "muted" note. Similarly, Jesus' face "foreshadows" progressive social forces *mutely*. Both have a liberating message that has been suppressed and that must be heard. For Cooper, "the Nazarene is ever . . . leading onward . . . the tottering childish feet of civilization." Likewise, "only the BLACK WOMAN can say 'when and where I enter, in the quiet, undisputed dignity of my womanhood . . . the whole *Negroe race enters with me.*"[9] Both melioriate culture through the gospel.

Select Scripture Texts

Cooper copied five pages of scripture passages, which she apparently found essential to the Christian message. The first page of the text is missing. The second page instructs the reader to humble oneself as a little child and not to "offend one of these little ones which believe in me . . ." (Matt 18:6).[10] Throughout her writings, Cooper was concerned with the domination of the "weak" by the "strong." Children were among the weak, and they required equal opportunities for nurture, education, and economic development across race and gender lines.

The second scripture text is what Jesus cited as the greatest commandment, according to Matt 22:37–39: "Thou shalt love the Lord thy God with all thy heart and with all thy strength and with all thy mind . . . the second is . . . Thou shalt love thy neighbor as thyself."[11] For Cooper, the most important question was, Who is my neighbor? She therefore went on to record the parable of the Good Samaritan (Luke 10:29–37).

The Lukan version records Jesus asking the lawyer what the law says one must do in order to inherit eternal life. The lawyer responds with the commandments to love God and neighbor, which Jesus affirms as the correct answer. The Gospel of Matthew does not record the parable of the Good Samaritan, although Matthew 22 records Jesus speaking the commandments to love God and neighbor in response to a lawyer's question. Cooper preferred the Lukan account, which depicts the lawyer asking, "Who is my neighbor?" and Jesus presenting a parable.

The parable of The Good Samaritan was central to Cooper's understanding of the Christian message. Cooper's question to American churches was, Who is my neighbor? She criticized American churches for assisting the white poor and excluding the black poor. Cooper published a short story entitled "Christ's Church," in which she revised the Good Samaritan parable to address the race problem in America.

In Cooper's revision of the parable, a poor black man beset by thieves was refused entry into a white church. While the poor black man was made to understand that he really was not welcome, the preacher announced that he would be preaching on the text "I was a stranger and ye took me not in." "But you see, the stranger at the door was—Black!," Cooper wrote. "And, of course, that settles it."[12]

Cooper also recorded verses from Matthew 25 regarding feeding the hungry, giving drink to the thirsty, and visiting the sick and the imprisoned as ways of honoring Jesus. She understood altruism as service to the needy and as compassion toward one's neighbors of whatever race. Such compassion and altruism were normative in Cooper's interpretation of scripture.

To supplement her reading of the Synoptic Gospels, Cooper transcribed from James 2:3–10 the injunction that those in the faith of the Lord Jesus Christ should not be respecters of persons; that the poor must be treated no differently than the wealthy. This text emphasizes the importance of being impartial with regard to class and status. From there she went on to transcribe into her notes Acts 10:34, which records Peter as saying that "God is no respecter of persons." This scripture supports Cooper's arguments that God requires unconditional, impartial love of persons regardless of class, gender, and color.

THE SOCIAL GOSPEL

Cooper read sermons and articles on the social teachings of Jesus with great interest. In an undated letter "to the editor of *The Outlook*," Cooper wrote that the sermons in *The Outlook*, more than in any other series of sermons she had seen or heard in a long time brought "this man-loving, practical, social teacher & reformer in touch with our own daily life."[13] She requested a sermon focusing on the problem of racism in America.

She particularly addressed the work of "Dr. Abbott" in the body of the letter. This was probably Lyman Abbott (b. 1835), who was a prominent Social Gospel leader. In 1881, he became editor in chief of the *Christian Union*, a nondenominational religious weekly. Abbott was the successor to Henry Ward Beecher's pulpit in Plymouth Congregational Church in 1888. Like Beecher, he promulgated ideals of social reform which included historical-critical analysis of the Bible and a liberal evolutionary theory.[14] In 1893 the *Christian Union* became *The Outlook*. Originally liberal and reformist in his views on the race problem, by the 1890s Abbott had retreated to an accommodationist position.[15]

Cooper criticized *The Outlook's* accommodationist philosophy. She requested sermons directly addressing the race problem. She argued that Christ was concerned for the poor and oppressed regardless of race or nationality. Thus the problem of racism ought to be addressed by American pulpits:

> I have read with deep interest the weekly talks in the Outlook on *Xt's Teachings on Social Topics* & there has come to me, as always from Dr. Abbott's unfolding of a truth a quickening sense of the reality of Xt's hold on the everyday problems that vex and harass us. I have often tried to imagine Xt (not a theological abstraction but the man Xt Jesus) living in our world of today. What would he say, what would he scourge, with whom would he "associate" . . . whom would he choose to minister to him in tender sympathy & grateful affection, what pew would be assigned him in the Churches? The man whom Mary & Martha cheered & refreshed, whom Peter admired & John loved, who offended the upper crust of society by . . . receiving publicans & sinners . . . the man who made it the climax of his peroration

that "the poor have the Gospel preached to them,"—what would be his sermon to the Churches of America today.[16]

Cooper appreciated *The Outlook*'s portrait of Christ as an exemplar and teacher of social ethics. Cooper and black Social Gospel leaders like her friend Francis Grimké emphasized a concrete, historical interpretation of Jesus rather than an abstract concept, as did their white Social Gospel peers. But Cooper interpreted scripture as speaking to the oppressive social situation of black women and men as well as whites. She re-envisioned Social Gospel ideals. Renita Weems has observed that substantial portions of the Bible describe a norm of liberation which stands "at the center of the biblical message" for "oppressed readers."[17] Cooper appealed to such a norm from a black feminist perspective to re-envision Social Gospel ideals.

Cooper emphasized Jesus' socially ameliorative acts. For Cooper he embodied eternal principles of freedom, equality, compassion, and altruism. She interpreted the New Testament as presenting a norm of altruism for the poor, the weak, and the dominated. She challenged white Social Gospel leaders to address the race problem to be truly consistent with Christ's social teachings. Cooper criticized white clergy for sympathizing with poor European immigrant laborers to the exclusion of poor black laborers. She accused white churches of neglecting the "weightier matters of the law," comparing them to Pharisees who oppressed the poor, and of being "timid about antagonizing local prejudices" where "the black man is the laborer, poor, . . . oppressed." She asked rhetorically, "Has Xt no special message on this subject?"[18]

SOJOURNER TRUTH

Sojourner Truth is well known for her participation as a speaker at the 1851 Convention on Women's Rights in Akron, Ohio. Of Sojourner Truth in relation to Cooper, Louise Daniel Hutchinson writes:

> Sojourner Truth is most often depicted as an itinerant preacher, while Harriet Tubman is pictured as the unlettered conductor of the Underground Railroad. . . . But each uniquely advanced the women's rights movement in America. . . . Later, Anna Cooper would become an effective protagonist for equal opportunities for women, at a time when black women had begun to view pragmatically the feminist and suffrage movement as a tactically viable tool for gaining full civil rights for blacks.[19]

Both Sojourner Truth and Anna Cooper were effective protagonists for equal opportunities for women, and both worked to advance the women's rights movement in America. Anna Cooper participated in a women's meeting with Tubman at least once.[20] Cooper entered the women's rights movement after slavery, but Sojourner Truth and Harriet Tubman were the mothers of black feminism. Whereas Cooper was literate not only in English but also in Greek, Latin, and French, Sojourner Truth learned scripture by hearing it and having it read to her, as most black women did until the Reconstruction period. As Renita Weems has noted, only in the last one hundred years have black women been taught to read. It was illegal for slaves to read. "The slaves' earliest exposure to the Bible was aural."[21]

Sojourner Truth memorized scripture, which she quoted at length in her sermons and speeches. Margaret Washington observes that Truth's memorization of most of the Bible, "reflected her African heritage more than her American environment."[22] Western culture tends to devalue oral/aural knowledge. It uplifts the kind of scholarship Cooper had the opportunity to engage in to the effective exclusion of oral/aural forms of knowledge. It tends to value book-learning over and against oral/aural learning traditions. A comparison of Cooper and Truth, however, challenges Western assumptions about power and knowledge. Both Truth and Cooper were brilliant masters of their subject matter despite differences in modes of learning.

Sojourner Truth did not place a high valuation on book literacy. It was not a necessary means of knowing for her. Truth said several times: "You read books, I talk to God."[23] She relied on personal communion with God for knowledge about God and in interpreting the Bible. Washington ascribes Sojourner Truth's "intuitive religious insights" to her African orality. Sojourner Truth learned mystical customs like going "out at night to commune with the stars, moon, and a god" from her mother, Elizabeth (or Mau-Mau) Bett. These were not taught by the Dutch Reformed Church but were vestiges of African ontology.[24] Moreover, Mau-Mau Bett narrated stories about her children who had been sold, saying that the stars shone on these children too. Though separated, they were part of one universe. Mau-Mau Bett taught Truth that when she was in trouble she should pray to God and he would hear her. When her own son was illegally sold, Truth relied on such faith in her efforts to recover her son. Truth inherited gifts of memory, orality, and African ontology from her mother. Washington describes these African practices for preserving history and communicating knowledge as an alternative discourse, closely tied to *visionary literacy.*[25] Sojourner Truth was literate in this sense.

Truth meditated on, contemplated, and studied the Bible with sharply honed oral/aural skills. She was highly reflective. She did not simply memorize and quote scripture; she critically interpreted the Bible. She was irritated by adults who commented on scripture for her and preferred

to have a child read the Bible to her so that she could interpret it
herself:

> when she was examining the scriptures, she wished to hear them without
> comment; but if she employed adult persons to read them to her, and she
> asked them to read a passage over again, they . . . commenced to explain,
> by giving her their version of it; and in this way, they tried her feelings
> exceedingly. In consequence of this, she ceased to ask adult persons to read
> the Bible to her, and substituted children in their stead.[26]

Children would re-read the same sentence to Sojourner Truth as often
as she wished without commentary. This allowed her to *examine* scripture, to "see what her own mind could make out of the record, and that,
she said, was what she wanted, and not what others thought it to mean."
Moreover, Truth wanted to "compare the teachings of the Bible with the
witness within her." She came to the critical conclusion "that the spirit
of truth" spoke in scripture "but that the recorders of those truths had intermingled with them ideas and suppositions of their own."[27] Sojourner Truth
was an independent, reflective thinker who placed her reasoning authority
in the witness within her.

Margaret Washington refers to Sojourner Truth's "intuitive religious
insight." In the modern era, intuition has been juxtaposed with reason as
an inferior form of knowing. Anna Julia Cooper in "The Gain From a
Belief" argues for feeling and belief as ultimate forms of knowing.[28]
Similarly, Truth trusted in the witness within her to interpret scripture in
relation to her personal and social-historical context. For Cooper and Truth,
feeling and the witness of the spirit were forms of knowing. From an
Afrocentric womanist perspective the separation between feeling/intuition
and reason is artificial. Truth and Cooper employed both forms of reason
to interpret scripture.

Sojourner Truth questioned literal interpretations of the Bible by contrasting scripture with her personal, theophanous experiences of God and
her everyday work experience. For example, at first she took the book of
Genesis literally. But to conceive of God as working by day, getting tired,
and resting conflicted with her logic. It contradicted her knowledge of God's
inconceivable greatness, which she had perceived in mystical experience.
Truth did not cite Mark 2:27, which presents Jesus saying that "the sabbath was made for man [*sic*], and not man for the sabbath" to support
her argument. Rather, she reasoned out an innovative argument based on
her experience of God:

> Why, if God works by the day, and one day's work tires him, and he is obliged
> to rest, either from weariness or on account of darkness, or if he waited for

the "cool of the day to walk in the garden," because he was inconvenienced by the heat of the sun, why then it seems that God cannot do as much as *I* can; for *I* can bear the sun at noon, and work several days and nights in succession without being much tired. . . . No, God does not stop to rest, for he is a spirit, and cannot tire; he cannot want for light, for he hath all light in himself. . . .[29]

Sojourner Truth's theophanies had revealed a God who needs no Sabbaths, although "Man might need them." Her personal experience of the brightness of God's light—unbearable until Jesus came to stand between her and God—was a witness to her that God who is all light has no need for light and needs no rest by night.[30]

Sojourner Truth broke with conventional interpretations of scripture that relegated women to inferior roles in relation to men. In her famous "Ar'n't I a Woman?" speech she contended that:

I can't read, but I can hear. I have heard the bible and have learned that Eve caused man to sin. Well, if woman upset the world, do give her a chance to set it right side up again. . . . And how came Jesus into the world? Through God who created him and a woman who bore him. Man, where is your part? But the women are coming up blessed be God and a few of the men are coming up with them.[31]

For Sojourner Truth, knowledge and literacy were not the same thing. Hearing and reflecting critically on what she heard in light of the witness within her was a valid form of learning and knowledge. She interpreted Christ's nativity through Mary as indicating women's ability to be public leaders. Women could govern the world. If a woman had borne the child of God, women were leaders who could "set the world right side up again."

Anna Julia Cooper has been described as a black woman intellectual and Sojourner Truth as an illiterate, itinerant preacher. Such distinctions fail to value African concepts of literacy. Truth was a visionary, oral, and aural literate.[32] She corrected book-literate persons in their interpretations. Cooper employed book-learning and Western historical-critical methods with moral feeling; Truth employed an inherited oral/aural, mystical hermeneutical tradition. Both women were innovative interpreters of scripture who forged a distinctively black feminist hermeneutic to argue for black women's equality. They publicly challenged whites who questioned their humanity because they were black, and whites and blacks who questioned their authority to speak because they were women.

Weems observes that the "significant portions" of the Bible that "speak to the deepest aspirations of oppressed people for freedom, dignity, justice, and vindication," have captured the imaginations of African American women.[33] Cooper and Truth examined scripture to consider its message for an oppressive social context. They interpreted scripture from black and feminist social-critical perspectives, perspectives from the underside, unearthing a message of freedom and equality for all.

NOTES

1. Louise Daniel Hutchinson, *Anna J. Cooper: A Voice from the South* (Washington, DC: The Smithsonian Institution, 1981), 85–86. See also Karen Baker-Fletcher, *A Singing Something: The Literature of Anna Julia Cooper as a Resource for a Theological Anthropology of Voice* (Ann Arbor, MI: University Microfilms, 1991).

2. Hutchinson, *Anna J. Cooper,* 87.

3. Anna Julia Cooper, "Womanhood a Vital Element in the Regeneration and Progress of a Race," in *A Voice from the South,* ed. Mary Helen Washington (New York: Oxford University Press, 1988), 9.

4. Ibid., 14.

5. Ibid., 16–17.

6. Ibid., 17.

7. Ibid., 18.

8. Ibid., 17. The term "mute" is a musical metaphor that refers to a muted note that sounds suppressed and distant.

9. Ibid., 31.

10. "Bible Quotations," Anna Julia Cooper Papers, Box 23-4, Folder 30, Courtesy of the Moorland-Spingarn Research Center.

11. Ibid.

12. Cooper, "Christ's Church," Anna Julia Cooper Papers, Box 23-4, Folder 31, Courtesy of the Moorland-Spingarn Research Center.

13. Richard Hofstadter, *Social Darwinism in American Thought* (Boston: Beacon Press, 1955), 13–50, 29, 106–8. Charles Hopkins, *The Rise of the Social Gospel* (New Haven: Yale University Press, 1940), 130.

14. Ronald White, *Liberty and Justice for All* (New York: Harper & Row, 1990), 24–26.

15. Cooper, "Christ's Church," Anna Julia Cooper Papers, Box 23-4, Folder 31, Courtesy of the Moorland-Spingarn Research Center.

16. Cooper, "Letter to the Editor of the Outlook," Anna Julia Cooper Papers, Box 1, Folder 5, Courtesy of the Moorland-Spingarn Research Center.

17. Renita Weems, "African American Women and the Bible," in *Stony the Road We Trod: African American Biblical Interpretation,* ed. C. H. Felder (Minneapolis: Fortress Press, 1991), 70–71.

18. Cooper, "Letter to the Editor of the Outlook." Cooper was conventional in interpreting "the Pharisees" as oppressive and was unaware of the anti-Jewish overtones.

19. Hutchinson, *Anna J. Cooper,* 85–86.

20. Ibid., 96–98.

21. Weems, "African American Women," 60. Weems notes that women like Howard Thurman' s grandmother, a former slave, practiced a selective, liberating hermeneutic.

22. Margaret Washington, ed., *Narrative of Sojourner Truth* (New York: Random House, 1993), xxvii. Olive Gilbert is the writer who wrote Sojourner Truth's narrative.

23. Ibid., xxvii–xxviii.

24. Ibid.

25. Ibid.

26. Ibid., 87–88.

27. Ibid.

28. Cooper, "The Gain from a Belief," in *A Voice from the South*, 294–95.

29. Washington, *Narrative of Sojourner Truth*, 86.

30. Ibid., 86, 50–51. See also Jacquelyn Grant, *White Women's Christ and Black Women's Jesus: Feminist Christology and Womanist Response* (Atlanta: Scholars Press, 1989), 211–14 for a discussion of Truth's and Jarena Lee's contextual and experiential interpretation of scripture.

31. Washington, ed., *Narrative of Sojourner Truth*, 118.

32. One definition of "literate" is "having or showing extensive knowledge, experience, or culture." Although a primary definition of "read" is to interpret something written, it also means "to understand the nature or significance of; to interpret, as dreams, signs." *Webster's New Twentieth Century Dictionary, Unabridged, Second Edition* (New York: World Publishing Company, 1961). Truth read God, the world, visions, and all that she heard.

33. Weems, "African American Women," 70.

RECOMMENDED READINGS

Baker-Fletcher, Karen. *A Singing Something: The Literature of Anna Julia Cooper as a Resource for a Theological Anthropology of Voice*. Ann Arbor, MI: University Microfilms, 1991.

Cooper, Anna Julia. *A Voice from the South*, edited by Mary Helen Washington. The Schomburg Library of Nineteenth-Century Black Women Writers. New York: Oxford University Press, 1988.

Grant, Jacquelyn. *White Women's Christ and Black Women's Jesus: Feminist Christology and Womanist Response*. Atlanta: Scholars Press, 1989.

Hutchinson, Louise Daniel. *Anna J. Cooper: A Voice from the South*. Washington, DC: Smithsonian Institution, 1981.

Schüssler Fiorenza, Elisabeth. *But She Said: Feminist Practices of Biblical Interpretation*. Boston: Beacon Press, 1992.

Washington, Margaret, ed. *Narrative of Sojourner Truth*. New York: Random House, 1993.

Weems, Renita. "African American Women and the Bible." In *Stony the Road We Trod: African American Biblical Interpretation*, edited by Cain Hope Felder. Minneapolis: Fortress Press, 1991.

❖ Politicizing the Sacred Texts:
Elizabeth Cady Stanton
and *The Woman's Bible*

CAROLYN DE SWARTE GIFFORD ♦

NEARLY A CENTURY AGO, in 1895, Part I of *The Woman's Bible* was published in book form, after appearing serialized in *The Woman's Tribune,* earlier in the year. Primarily the work of Elizabeth Cady Stanton, the venerable pioneer of women's rights, *The Woman's Bible* aimed, as Stanton stated in her preface, "to revise only those texts and chapters directly referring to women, and those also in which women are made prominent by exclusion."[1] The revising took the form of commentaries, written mainly by Stanton herself, on selected biblical texts, with a small number authored by other women. Part I covered the Pentateuch; the biblical texts were printed in small type, and the commentaries appeared below the biblical texts in a larger size. Part II was published in 1898, again after having been serialized. It dealt with the remaining portion of the Old Testament and the New Testament, following the same format as Part I.[2]

The Woman's Bible was a controversial and politicizing document from its inception. It was conceived by Stanton as a tool in the struggle for women's equality with men, one that would challenge what Stanton insisted was the most formidable adversary in that struggle—the authority and power of the Jewish-Christian traditions and their sacred texts, not simply in the religious realm specifically but far more broadly in Western civilization generally. Not only was *The Woman's Bible* itself politicizing; it exploded onto a highly politicized environment, that of the women's rights movement of the last decade of the nineteenth century, creating a crisis in which already contending factions wrestled over control of the movement and the direction it would take in the twentieth century. This essay will focus on *The Woman's Bible* in its political context, examining its development during the late 1880s and early 1890s; its entry onto the political scene in the mid-1890s and the resulting crisis; and, finally, its relationship to the political environment of feminist biblical criticism in the 1990s.

At the time *The Woman's Bible* was published, Elizabeth Cady Stanton had been engaged for a half century in the battle for women's equality. Thus *The Woman's Bible* must be understood, first of all, as one event in an unfolding history of Stanton's personal struggle for women's rights, one strategy in a lifetime spent devising many different strategies to further the reform to which she had committed herself.[3] At the same time, it could be called her final or culminating strategy, the capstone of the edifice of argumentation she had labored to build from the time of the first women's rights convention she and Lucretia Mott had called at Seneca Falls, New York, in 1848. It was the strategy that she believed crucial to weakening and finally breaking the hold that institutional Christianity maintained over women.

A decade before the publication of *The Woman's Bible*, Stanton wrote an article in which she analyzed the roots of the power that Christianity had over women and the ways in which it wielded that power for the subjection, even the degradation, of women. In late 1884 the three-part article "The Christian Church and Women" ran in the *Index;* it contained the core of ideas Stanton would continue to refine over the next decade and ultimately include in her commentaries on *The Woman's Bible.*[4] She began the article by attacking the claim very often made by many leaders in the women's rights movement as well as by those opposed to women's rights that "woman owes all the advantages of the position she occupies today to Christianity." Not so, Stanton insisted.

> The facts of history show that the Christian Church has done nothing specifically for woman's elevation. In the general march of civilization, she has necessarily reaped the advantage of man's higher development; but we must not claim for Christianity all that has been achieved by science, discovery and invention.[5]

Indeed, according to Stanton, it was the institutional church—its theology and practices—with its power to influence the content of civil law and social custom, to permeate the whole of Western civilization with its ideas and ideals that had "plung[ed] woman into absolute slavery." For eighteen hundred years, she charged, Christianity in all its variety of forms had created and maintained a humiliating definition of womanhood and of woman's relation to man and God which perpetuated the notion of women's inferiority and consequent subjection.[6]

Stanton was quick to distinguish between the teachings of Jesus, which promised a radical equality of women and men, and the teachings of the institutional church, which had continued to ignore or subvert Jesus' message for eighteen hundred years. "[Jesus' teaching] represents the ideal the race is destined to attain; [that of the church] the popular sentiment of its time."[7] Church teachings on woman contained for Stanton no trace of the egalitarian vision of Jesus. She set them out simply and starkly:

> According to Church teaching, woman was an after-thought in the creation, the author of sin, being at once in collusion with Satan. Her sex was made a crime; marriage a condition of slavery, owing obedience; maternity a curse; and the true position of all womankind one of inferiority and subjection to all men.[8]

Perhaps most shocking and frustrating to Stanton was her discovery, over decades of traveling around the country stumping for women's rights, that the vast majority of women uncritically accepted the church's definition of womanhood with a gullible acquiescence which she quite ruthlessly derided. It was incomprehensible to her that women of the nineteenth century—the beneficiaries of the age of rationalism, the rise of science, the questioning attitude fostered by disciplines such as higher biblical criticism and comparative study of religions—could not see the church's teachings on women for what they were: a fabrication over centuries by men in power, who cleverly authorized that power by claiming to speak the truth on behalf of God. Their definition of woman and delimitation of her sphere, though apparently invested with divine sanction, were actually instruments of domination; "the priesthood, claiming apostolic descent, so interpret Christianity as to make it the basis of all religious and political disqualifications for women, sustaining the rights of *man* alone."[9] Males in power, not only in positions of religious authority but throughout the civil realm as well, manipulated women's guilt over their purported evil nature and sinfulness, their fears of damnation for themselves and their children, and their self-abasement, in order to constrain women in a subordinate position inhabiting a restricted sphere.[10] And, Stanton concluded, women were unwitting accomplices in their own subjection.

What could be done to break the power of this insidious system of domination and subordination? Stanton had been searching for the answer to this dilemma since her mid-twenties. A good part of her women's rights career had been devoted to appealing to men—the power holders—by various means including influence, petitioning, and speeches, to relinquish some of their power through enacting married women's property rights laws, giving women the vote, and the like. As Stanton approached seventy, she had long since concluded that men—with very few exceptions—would not willingly relinquish power. Thus, she argued, it was time—in fact, long past time—to persuade women to extricate themselves from their own dilemma and not rely on men to do it. Women must become self-conscious agents of their own liberation. To do so required that they confront their own complicity in their subjection, unmasking it and analyzing it, in order eventually to rise up from it.

Stanton believed it was, above all, woman's self-sacrifice and obedience, carefully inculcated in her by centuries of Christian civilization, which both allowed and obliged her to remain in a subordinate position. Although self-sacrifice and obedience were touted as Christian virtues in imitation of Jesus and were ostensibly meant for men and women alike, the burden of expressing them had always fallen unequally on women, anxious to overcome through their practice the shame and guilt of what they understood as their original sinfulness. Women must be brought to realize that their willing acceptance of the role of self-sacrificer crippled them, ensuring their domination by men and guaranteeing the continued humiliation of inferiority.

In her 1884 article Stanton noted that earlier, in 1878, at a women's rights convention celebrating thirty years of struggle since Seneca Falls, she had introduced three resolutions that endorsed the notion of self-development as women's primary duty. For a number of years before, she had tried unsuccessfully to get such resolutions considered, a failure which served to underscore her realization that women could not bring themselves to go against their socialization to deference and self-sacrifice. That they might seek self-development was apparently nearly unthinkable even to women's rights leaders. Nevertheless, a series of three related resolutions was finally passed in 1878; taken together, these resolutions could be seen as one of Stanton's earliest manifestos on women's self-liberation. The first resolution in the series announced self-development as "the first duty of every individual," male or female, and charged that women's self-sacrifice and obedience were detrimental not only to women but to the entire human race since they allowed men to assume an attitude of superiority. The third resolution described the excessive hold the clergy had over women by playing on their religious superstitions and fears about their future life, which led women to concentrate on life after death while ignoring their earthly situation of subordination.

The first resolution was a charter for woman's self-liberation; the third analyzed the cause of her enslavement; and the second proclaimed the means by which her self-liberation could be achieved. It read:

Resolved, that the great Principle of the Protestant Reformation, the right of individual conscience and judgement, heretofore exercised by man alone, should now be claimed by woman; that in the interpretation of Scripture, she should be guided by her own reason, and not the authority of the Church.[11]

Let women seek for themselves the meaning of the sacred texts and not accept what men told women was in them. Never mind that men claimed priestly authority, wielded sacred and secular power, or dazzled women with their erudition; men had never been and could not, at present, be reliable interpreters of the texts because their authority, power, and knowledge were flawed, having been based on a false premise — male superiority and female inferiority. Stanton was convinced that this hierarchical definition of human being could not possibly be the design of the great Creator of the Universe. Now was the time for women to exercise the right of individual scriptural interpretation decisively won for them through the Protestant Reformation, and peruse the Bible in order to determine what God really did have in mind about the nature of woman and man and the relationship between them.

In her 1884 article she suggested that the first step toward women's reinterpretation of scripture — and consequently toward women's self-liberation — be taken by calling a council of women who would work together on a revision of the Bible.[12] By that time a group of prominent male biblical scholars had produced a Revised Version of the New Testament (1881) and were preparing to publish a Revised Version of the Old Testament (1885). Stanton's call for a women's revising committee was prompted by this revision, which was heralded as the great achievement of a century of biblical scholarship and the last word in modern scriptural interpretation. For Stanton, it simply could not be the last word because it would not (and did not) address the nature of woman as a hermeneutical issue.[13]

Throughout the second half of the 1880s Stanton pushed on a number of fronts for the analysis of women's position in the churches and for a women's revision of the Bible. In March 1886 she sent a resolution to the American Woman Suffrage Association (AWSA), the more conservative rival of her organization, the National Woman Suffrage Association (NWSA), asking that they place the securing of women's rights in the church on their agenda since the church was the greatest barrier to women's full emancipation.[14] By August of that year she had announced the organization of an international committee to revise the scriptures, with a rationale for its task and a general plan of work for the process.[15] In October she published a detailed description of the committee's planned mode of operation and indicated a growing interest by women in the progress of the work, as well as the reception of some letters critical of the undertaking for a variety of reasons, one of which was that it was not good political strategy for women's rights leaders to risk antagonizing the many clergy and other religious leaders who supported woman suffrage. This criticism presaged the controversy that would erupt in the wake of the publication of *The Woman's Bible* a decade later. In 1886 Stanton's reply to her critics' warning was that limiting the critique of the causes of women's subordinate position because of political expediency was compromising and cowardly. Moreover, it was ultimately self-defeating since it did not strike at the root of women's oppression.[16]

In the late 1880s Stanton decided that she herself would take the responsibility for gathering a committee of women to produce *The Woman's Bible.* She sought women with knowledge of Greek and Hebrew from both the United States and England to join her in the project. In the meantime she, her daughter Harriot Stanton Blatch, and an English suffragist friend Frances Lord identified the biblical passages that dealt with women. By winter 1887 Stanton and her daughter had written commentaries on the Pentateuch. However, the response to Stanton's invitations to join the project was disappointing; Lord and Blatch lost interest in the work; and Stanton put it aside for several years.[17]

In 1890 Stanton once again floated the idea of *The Woman's Bible,* asking Clara Bewick Colby, the editor of the *Woman's Tribune* if she would like to publish it in her newspaper.[18] But she was still unable to find women to help her, and in 1892 she wrote Colby:

> As to the Bible, I thought the moral effect of *a committee of women* to revise the scriptures . . . would be very great. But I could not get a committee of leading English and American women. For me to do it as an individual would not have the same effect or dignity. And now I prefer to use my eyes for more pleasant occupations.[19]

Yet the idea remained important to Stanton, and in February 1895 she arranged with Colby to publish *The Woman's Bible* week by week and began negotiations with a publisher to bring it out in book form.[20]

Her renewed enthusiasm for the undertaking and her belief that a revised version of the Bible by women would be a powerful strategy in the struggle to break the domination of women by the clergy are evident in a letter to Colby:

> I think The Woman's Bible will create a great interest. . . . I have felt for years that this work should be done. When these . . . men from their pulpits presume to tell us the scriptural position of woman we can tell them we have revised the scriptures & know all about it. A committee of women revising the Old & New Testament! to find out their true position in the scale of

being, will make Priests and Bishops open their eyes & say "What will these women do next?"[21]

Once again she sought a committee to work with her, hoping to interest leading evangelical women as well as her more liberal colleagues in order to present a spectrum of views on biblical authority and scriptural interpretation, thereby creating a kind of dialogue among commentators about these issues. But she was unable to persuade any evangelical women to take part. They could not accept her contention that the Bible was not in any way the inspired Word of God but rather the words of men. Nor were they willing to agree, as Stanton insisted, that one "cannot twist out of the Old Testament or the New Testament a message of justice, liberty, or equality from God to the women of the nineteenth century."[22] This had not been their understanding or experience of the Bible's message, and they did not want be associated with a project clearly based on suppositions with which they differed so radically. Stanton finally wrote most of the commentaries herself and enlisted a few other women with equally heterodox opinions on the scriptures to add their comments.[23]

Evangelical woman suffragists also feared—as did many nonevangelical leaders of the woman suffrage movement, particularly Stanton's close friend Susan B. Anthony—that attacking the Bible would needlessly alienate supporters of the cause. While Stanton saw the publication of *The Woman's Bible* as the key strategy in her lifelong struggle for women's independence and equality, many others felt it was a disastrous move sure to bring about a political setback from which the movement might not recover. Shortly after the publication of Part I, the National American Woman Suffrage Association (NAWSA, formed in 1890 through an uneasy merger of NWSA and AWSA) went on record disclaiming any official connection with *The Woman's Bible*.[24] Not only did many NAWSA leaders personally disagree with the views expressed in it; their organizers were reporting from the field that the controversial book was damaging efforts to build support for woman suffrage in the South and West, from evangelicals and from others who found the radical religious and social views of *The Woman's Bible* commentators threatening. A majority of the organization's leadership believed that disassociating itself from the book was a necessary step of political prudence even though it meant repudiating the latest work of Stanton, their honorary president and, for over fifty years, the leading women's rights reformer.

For her part, Stanton felt that NAWSA's repudiation of *The Woman's Bible* (and indirectly of her and those who, like her, held radical views) was a dangerous step backward for the organization and the entire women's rights movement, which until then had maintained a tradition of free discussion of all issues. "If women may not comment on what the Bible says of women . . . ," she wondered, "then I would like to know what freedom we acquired under Christianity."[25] She worried that the move by the NAWSA would alienate political and religious liberals who were alarmed at the growing power of more conservative women within the suffrage movement, seeking the vote in order to enact an agenda of restrictions in government such as religious tests for candidates for office, strict sabbath laws, required teaching of the Bible in schools, nontaxation of church property, and so on.[26] Furthermore, she was convinced that by focusing its efforts only on the narrow goal of suffrage while avoiding potentially divisive but crucial women's rights issues such as those raised on the pages of *The Woman's Bible,* the NAWSA pursued a course ultimately detrimental to the broad aims of women's liberation for which she and the founders of the women's rights movement stood. Women might win the right to vote, but that was merely one step toward their full emancipation, which would be won only when women's equality became manifest in all of the institutions of society.

Until the end of her life Stanton continued to call for women to demand the same equality within the church that they demanded of the state. Just months before her death in 1902 she published "The Duty of the Church to Woman at This Hour," in which she outlined a plan of work that would put increasing pressure on the governing bodies of denominations for a fundamental and thoroughgoing change in the institutional church's attitude toward women. She argued:

> It matters little that here and there some clergyman advocates our cause, on our platform, so long as no sectarian organization has yet recognized our demand as a principle of justice, and the debate is rarely opened in their councils, being generally treated as a speculative, sentimental question, unworthy of serious consideration. Neither would it suffice if they gave their adhesion to the demand for political equality, so long as by scriptural teachings they perpetuate our social and religious subordination.[27]

Thus she insisted once again that a crucial element of the process of change must be a revision of sacred scripture. This time she suggested an expurgated edition of the Bible with all passages detrimental to women removed, to be published after a convocation of delegates from temperance and suffrage associations, the National Council of Women, and the Consumer's League (an alliance of middle- and working-class women for women's economic rights) met to produce such an edition. "In view of the intelligence, morality and liberal education of this period," she wrote, all those texts of scripture and parables referring to woman as "author of sin", as "an inferior", "a subject", "a weaker vessel", should no longer be read in our churches, as they humiliate and destroy the respect that is her due from the rising generation. . . . All these old ideas should be relegated to the ancient mythologies as mere allegories, having no application whatever to the womanhood of this generation. Everything points to a purer and more rational religion in the future, in which woman, as mother of the race, will be recognized as an equal in both Church and the State.[28]

Still holding fast to her dream of a dialogue among women of differing religious and political views and widening that dream to include women of different class backgrounds, Stanton envisioned a woman's Bible which would be a sacred scripture worthy of the purer, more rational religion she foresaw. It would then be a fitting expression of the inspiration of the "Great Spirit of All Truth."[29]

What relevance can *The Woman's Bible* have for the 1990s since it is a document written a century ago and definitely—self-consciously, even—the product of its politically and religiously liberal, upper-middle-class authors, all of whom were what we have come to call WASPs—white, Anglo-Saxon, Protestants—and none of whom were professionally trained in biblical criticism? When one of the most imperative goals of feminist biblical criticism is to widen the "lens of interpretation" to include the perspectives and views of women of color and of women from a great variety of Christian faiths as well as from non-Christian traditions, what can be the value of a volume whose lens is so narrow, whose editor neither included commentaries from the African-American, Roman Catholic, and Jewish women with whom she was acquainted nor seemed aware of elements of anti-Judaism within the commentaries in the volume she edited?[30] When feminist biblical critics grounded in the liberation theologies of the late twentieth century work to de-center Western European and North American religious thought and experience and to foreground the richness of non-Western traditions, of what use is a biblical commentary whose editor believed her editing committee was "international" because it included women from England and continental Europe as well as from the United States? When women biblical scholars have labored so long to win entry into and respect from their professional guild by becoming adept at the latest theories and methodologies, why should they pay attention to commentaries so obviously outmoded in their interpretation, so dependent on nineteenth-century ideas about biblical criticism, comparative religions study, and history? Can *The Woman's Bible* really be anything more than a quaint artifact, interesting mainly to historians of the nineteenth century, but worthy only of a footnote in a discussion of feminist biblical criticism?

Surely the answer to these questions about relevance lies in the intent of *The Woman's Bible* and the spirit in which it was created. As a controversial and politicizing document that generated discussion and action and as a sophisticated strategy for liberation that revealed the root causes of oppression and insisted on a restructuring of society at all levels to eradicate the injustice of sexism rather than a mere tinkering with the processes to ease or ameliorate a sexist system, it can be a model of radical reform for late twentieth century feminists. As an impassioned call for women's dignity and self-development whose author steadfastly refused to countenance the notion of women's inferiority in the face of powerful institutions and sacred texts which seemed to justify that power, it can be an empowering text for women of all times who struggle for a similar sense of dignity and worth. Finally, as a testament to the tremendous intelligence, morality, and courage of one who labored over half a century to realize her ideal of equality for women and men, *The Woman's Bible* and Elizabeth Cady Stanton, its editor and chief writer, merit our honor and remembrance.

NOTES

1. Elizabeth Cady Stanton et al., *The Woman's Bible,* Part I (New York: European Publishing, 1895, reprint, Salem, NH: Ayer, 1986), 5.

2. Elizabeth Cady Stanton et al., *The Woman's Bible,* Part II (New York: European Publishing, 1898; reprint, Salem, NH: Ayer, 1986).

3. For the latest biography, see Elisabeth Griffith, *In Her Own Right: The Life of Elizabeth Cady Stanton* (New York: Oxford University Press, 1984). For interpretations of the meaning and significance of Stanton's life and thought, see Maureen Fitzgerald, "Religion and Feminism in Elizabeth Cady Stanton's Life and Thought" (M.A. thesis, University of Wisconsin-Madison, 1985); and Ann D. Gordon, "The Political is Personal: Two Autobiographies of Woman Suffragists," in *Fea(s)ts of Memory,* ed. Margo Culley (Madison: University of Wisconsin, forthcoming).

4. Elizabeth Cady Stanton, "The Christian Church and Women," *Index* (October 30, November 6, and December 4, 1884). All articles and correspondence by Stanton cited in this essay may be found in the microfilm edition of *The Papers of Elizabeth Cady Stanton and Susan B. Anthony,* ed. Patricia G. Holland and Ann D. Gordon (Wilmington, DE: Scholarly Resources, 1991). Since the microfilm edition was not used to prepare this essay, footnotes will not refer to reel or frame numbers when citing material from the edition.

5. Stanton, "Christian Church and Women," 1.

6. Ibid., 7.

7. Ibid., 1.

8. Ibid.

9. Ibid., 5 (emphasis in original).

10. Ibid., 2.

11. Ibid., 6.

12. Ibid., 4.

13. For a discussion of the history of the development of the nature of woman as a hermeneutical issue over the course of the nineteenth century, see Carolyn De Swarte Gifford, "American Women and the Bible: The Nature of Woman as a Hermeneutical Issue," in *Feminist Perspectives on Biblical Scholarship*, ed. Adela Yarbro Collins (Chico, CA: Scholars Press, 1985).

14. Elizabeth Cady Stanton, "Woman Suffrage and the Church," *Index* (March 25, 1886) n.p.

15. Elizabeth Cady Stanton, "The Woman's Bible," *Index* (August 9, 1886) n.p.

16. Elizabeth Cady Stanton, "The Woman's Bible," *Index* (October 21, 1886) n.p.

17. Elizabeth Cady Stanton, *Eighty Years and More: Reminiscences, 1815–1897* (1898; reprint, New York: Schocken Books, 1971), 389–93.

18. Elizabeth Cady Stanton to Clara Bewick Colby, April 10, 1890, Clara B. Colby Papers, Archives Division, State Historical Society of Wisconsin.

19. Stanton to Colby, December 8, 1892, Clara B. Colby Papers, Archives Division, State Historical Society of Wisconsin.

20. Stanton to Colby, February 16, 1895, Clara B. Colby Papers, Archives Division, State Historical Society of Wisconsin.

21. Stanton to Colby, February 21, 1895, Clara B. Colby Papers, Archives Division, State Historical Society of Wisconsin.

22. Elizabeth Cady Stanton, *The Woman's Bible*, Part II Appendix, 214.

23. For a description of the religious perspectives of the women who contributed commentaries in *The Woman's Bible*, see Barbara Welter's introduction to the Arno Press reprint of *The Woman's Bible* (Elizabeth Cady Stanton, *The Original Feminist Attack on the Bible* [New York: Arno, 1974]).

24. For a detailed discussion of the repudiation of *The Woman's Bible* by NAWSA, see Kathi Kern, "The Woman's Bible: Gender, Religion and Ideology in the Work of Elizabeth Cady Stanton, 1869–1902" (Ph.D. dissertation, University of Pennsylvania, 1989).

25. Stanton to Colby, February 5?, 1896, Clara B. Colby Papers, Archives Division, State Historical Society of Wisconsin.

26. Stanton to Colby, December 21, 1887, printed in the *Woman's Tribune* (January 21, 1888) n.p.

27. Elizabeth Cady Stanton, "The Duty of the Church Toward Woman at This Hour," *Boston Investigator* (October 5, 1901) n.p.

28. Elizabeth Cady Stanton, "An expurgated Edition of the Bible," *Free Thought Magazine* (December 1902 [no. 20]) 704.

29. Ibid.

30. For a discussion of anti-Judaism in *The Woman's Bible* and in contemporary Christian feminist theology, see Judith Plaskow, "Anti-Judaism in Feminist Christian Interpretation" (in this volume). For a discussion of Stanton and racism, see Barbara Hilkert Andolsen, *Daughters of Jefferson, Daughters of Bootblacks: Racism and American Feminism* (Macon, GA: Mercer University Press, 1986).

RECOMMENDED READINGS

Gifford, Carolyn De Swarte. "American Women and the Bible: The Nature of Woman as a Hermeneutical Issue." In *Feminist Perspectives on Biblical Scholarship,* edited by Adela Yarbro Collins. Biblical Scholarship in North America 10. Chico, CA: Scholars Press, 1985.

Gordon, Ann D. "The Political is Personal: Two Autobiographies of Woman Suffragists." In *Fea(s)ts of Memory,* edited by Margo Culley. Madison: University of Wisconsin, forthcoming.

Griffith, Elisabeth. *In Her Own Right: The Life of Elizabeth Cady Stanton.* New York: Oxford University Press, 1984.

Holland, Patricia G., and Ann D. Gordon, eds. *The Papers of Elizabeth Cady Stanton and Susan B. Anthony.* Microfilm edition. Wilmington, DE: Scholarly Resources, 1991.

Kern, Kathi. "*The Woman's Bible:* Gender, Religion and Ideology in the Work of Elizabeth Cady Stanton, 1869–1902." Ph.D. dissertation, University of Pennsylvania, 1989.

Stanton, Elizabeth Cady, and the Revising Committee. *The Woman's Bible,* Parts I and II. New York: European Publishing, 1895, 1898. Reprint editions: Seattle: Coalition Task Force on Women and Religion, 1974; Salem, NH: Ayer, 1986; and New York: Arno, 1974, under the title *The Original Feminist Attack on the Bible (The Women's Bible),* Introduction by Barbara Welter.

4

◆ Dusting the Bible on the Floor:
A Hermeneutics of Wisdom

RITA NAKASHIMA BROCK ◆

AMY TAN in *The Joy Luck Club* tells the story of a Chinese mother whose son drowns in the California surf. She believes she can make things happen, and her Baptist church had taught her to believe that faith could make up the difference when the sheer force of her will faltered. She is convinced her will and faith can bring back her son. They fail; so she places the church's gift Bible on the floor, under the leg of a kitchen table, to steady it, and says she no longer sees a purpose for such faith. Her daughter notices, however, that the Bible is always carefully dusted.

THE HERMENEUTICS OF WISDOM

The mother in Amy Tan's story makes a paradoxical choice to both reject and keep her Bible. Ambiguity emerges in her hedging of bets and in her refusal to discard something that might retain some power. Navigating through paradoxical, ambiguous territory is a major element in the works of Asian American women,[1] writings that describe our search for identity and meaning in a complex environment.

This maneuvering within ambiguity is guided by a hermeneutics of wisdom that determines how the history of one's people and one's experiences are interpreted. Ripening insights, which are learned through experience and observation of life, and collected knowledge and strategies, which are handed down through generations, inform this interpretation. The hermeneutics of wisdom has at least three aspects: (1) Asian culture and personal memories of that culture are understood to give meaning and life to the present at the same time that patriarchal traditions lose their authoritative status; and (2) innocence, especially as it reinforces victimization, is rejected because it has no survival value and is not empowering. These two themes — the importance of the past and innocence rejected — interlock around a third aspect, (3) the retention of multiple perspectives that create a fluid, multilayered self. That complex sense of self allows life to be maintained and passed on in communities of meaning and accountability.[2] Through examination of these themes in Asian-American women's writings, I will develop a multilayered approach to biblical hermeneutics. Examples of the development of the three elements of wisdom can be found in novels by Cynthia Kadohato, Wendy Law-Yone, and Amy Tan and in the memoirs of Maxine Hong Kingston.[3]

In Kadohato's story of a Japanese-American adolescent girl's travels with her migrant family, the past lingers through the ghost of her tormenting grandmother and through the stories the girl hears of Japan, which sounds both strange and familiar to her. She is too implicated in her grandmother's death and knows too much about her parents to pretend she is innocent. Instead she strives to remember everything and to refuse to forget any part of herself, no matter how troubling. That tenacity of remembering moves her toward greater insight and courage.

The young immigrant woman in Law-Yone's novel struggles to learn a new culture and to cling to her memories of Burma as she is abandoned by all those she has loved. She describes herself as knowing too much and never being innocent. She survives alone by her wits until she breaks. Through the searing crucible of an attempt at suicide, she comes to terms with her life of sorrow and grieves the losses of her life. In her gradually increasing remembrance of the many parts of her life, she finds the resources for a complex multifaceted identity.

In Tan's novel a critical memory of the past and the rejection of innocence emerge through the stories of four Chinese women who are rebellious survivors in China and who emigrate to the U.S. Their stories combine with the confusion of their American-born, assimilated daughters. This combination of mothers and daughters creates a complex picture of Chinese-American women's identities through the development of stronger relationships between them and the subsequent transmission of memory.

In Kingston's memoirs a similar tension is found between a strong Chinese mother, who is a tough survivor, and an American-born daughter who struggles to fit in with the dominant culture at the same time that she is fascinated by stories of China. Her confusion of identity, her love–hate relationship with being Chinese, and her ambiguous relationship with her mother are explored through Kingston's use of different voices. She scrutinizes her own multiple identities by experimenting with voices and trying out versions of stories. And she creates as her primary imaginary figure a woman warrior who lives in several worlds, crosses gender lines, and carries memory carved into her own flesh.

Perhaps because the cultural roots of many Asian Americans lie to some extent in Confucian values, which respect the wisdom and sophistication of age, rather than the innocence of children, innocence is placed in these Asian-American women's novels in proper perspective. Innocence is something one outgrows, or else one risks remaining superfluous and disempowered, which is the designated state of women and children. Innocence may be appropriate to babies, but innocence in men is foolish—and the women in these works see it as dangerous to themselves. Hence, innocence is not described as lost, but as rejected because it leads to victimization. Innocence is not a survival skill. It does not nurture and empower life or pass it on. Cunning, wits, tolerance for ambiguity, manipulation, imagination, moral reflection, and active agency are the survival skills that emerge with the rejection of innocence and the ripening of wisdom. Life is nurtured and survives through the works of those who are wise. Rather than seeking to be good or clinging to a naïve trust in the power of others, which is how one remains innocent, the stories of Asian-American women depict them as seeking to minimize the forces that threaten their lives and those they love. They reject innocence in order to enlarge and enhance their capacities to alleviate pain and sustain the loving bonds that keep people alive. They are neither innocent nor good; they learn to be strong, cunning, caring, and wise.

This negative attitude toward innocence is in sharp contrast to Western Christian attitudes that prize innocence, even in adults. Doctrines about the sinless purity of Jesus and the image of him as an innocent lamb taken to slaughter reinforce the idea that victims ought to be innocent and virtuous or else pain and suffering are deserved, even though the Gospels tend to depict a more ambiguous and politically savvy Jesus. It seems to me that as long as we romanticize victims and want innocence, we operate with the assumption that suffering is deserved by the guilty and the knowledgeable, that mechanisms of oppression are not inherently wrong, but serve the protection of goodness, and that punishing the wicked is a divine mandate, no matter what structures do this. This emphasis on the innocence of victims can lead both to the tendency to blame victims, if anything can be found wrong with them, and to the kind of dichotomies that paint oppressors as one-dimensionally evil and victims as helpless.[4]

The impact of ideologies about good and evil on women is described by Nel Noddings in her work on a phenomenology of evil.[5] Noddings uses the experiences of women to argue that the moralistic and dualistic dichotomizing of evil creates greater forms of it by favoring "masculine virtues" that encourage the need to dominate, control, and destroy others. In a dualistic framework, the only moral ground for women is innocence. Noddings argues that a woman's moral claim on life is understood to rest in her feminine nature, an unconscious essence that is associated with being archetypally chaste and good. This goodness is evidence of a superior force working through her, which is part of her biologically given destiny as wife and mother. A woman's goodness, to be real goodness, must be innocent— unconscious, passive, and dependent. A woman who claims her actions are both learned and chosen becomes like a man, which she cannot be. Hence, she becomes morally unreliable.

In constructing another way to understand moral behavior, Noddings suggests that we must give up the ideology of good, evil, and innocence. As resources for understanding ethics, she looks to the activity of women who struggle to alleviate pain, maintain relationships, and empower the actions of others—women who seek to be wise. She argues that life is ambiguous and that evil will never be destroyed or overcome but that it can be managed in such a way as to make life more humane by our abilities to minimize pain, lessen separation from relationships, and reduce helplessness.

In refusing the polarization of good and evil and seeing the agency of ethical human action as the minimizing of evil, we can view women not simply as victims to be pitied or helped, but as agents of their own lives— survivors who are neither innocent nor good, but who, within the limits of power given them, make conscious willed choices for good and ill. Neither are oppressors simply evil. They are both conscious agents and victims enmeshed in the same systems of violence and oppression that afflict everyone.

The questions that emerge from a refusal to cling to innocence and to split our identities into externally projected forms of evil and internally defensive forms of self-righteousness are not who is right and who is wrong, but what strategies can we develop for minimizing harm and what resources can we develop to give dignity and agency to people. How can we speak to each other with mutual respect, so that our speaking is neither accusatory nor acquiescent? How can we identify the problem in ways that allow us all to be agents of change, people who can take responsibility?

In all the above works by Asian-American women, the maintenance of multiple perspectives is crucial to understanding the identities of Asian American women. The ability to refuse polemics and hold onto multiple perspectives comes through the emergence of several voices that contain suspicion and retrieval—and more, for they seek healing and hope.

These voices focus on what I call a tribal consciousness, as in the old Latin meaning of *tri-bu—tri,* which means three, and *bu,* which means being—three forms of being. A tribe identifies itself with a common ancestry, but it has more than one being because it values kinship. A tribal consciousness has trinitarian resonances, and contains perhaps, a post-colonialist sensibility.[6] The Asian-American women writers named above speak in chords, with two cultural discourses fused in one language and a third discourse, which is neither of the others, that integrates the two, a process that creates a multifaceted identity.

Most Asian-American women know something of the ragged and worn voice of an immigrant or a refugee, found either in our own experiences or in the stories of our foremothers. That voice is critical of and baffled by the casual cruelty, unreflective commitments, and self-aggrandizing pre-occupation with personal success of European Americans. The Asian voice knows something of the bewildering struggle to survive and to connect, to make meaning out of what is seen and heard, a meaning that is often elusive.

On the other hand, the assimilated Asian woman's voice speaks through the language and attitudes of Anglo-European American discourse.[7] That culture remains largely ignorant of the diversity of cultures on this continent and reinforces its hegemony by ignoring or squeezing out all but token forms of diversity. While Asian Americans cannot have the full experience of growing up white American, the values, perspectives, and forms of thought of European-American culture are pervasive enough in American society to be learned by those who are not born into it. The voice of assimilation sees Asian immigrants as awkward and unsophisticated, too caught up in willful ignorance, unreasonable paranoia, and fearful self-isolation. This American-born voice is neither sentimental about Asia nor self-pitying about assimilation. It is critical of the class biases, patriarchy, and too-haughty pride of Asian immigrants.

The two come together in a deep and resonant third voice, through which Asian-American women take responsibility for our lives and struggle to make meaning out of the parts. We both reject an authoritarian past, putting the Bible on the floor, and refuse to let it go, dusting it. This third voice leaves out little, not even the painful and problematic, but it speaks neither of nostalgia nor self-hating. The past is embraced, critically and wisely, through the complex discourses of the writers of these stories.

Their meticulous and compassionate writer's voices disclose the complex forces of war and oppression that required us, or our ancestors, to cast our lots with marginalized and suffering people in a hostile new land.[8] Memory of the past as a source of self-awareness and survival is careful, rejecting the oppressive authority of tradition because remembering occurs in a new context that allows more dislocation from the tyranny of tradition. This third voice refuses to blame others or to justify self-righteously the actions of Asian-American women, even as it exposes piercing angers about racism, poverty, and misogyny. Through this third voice, the clarity of insight of Asian-American women writers is guided by an intelligence and a dignity that grant wisdom through the knowledge of life's deep ambiguities. This third healing, integrating voice knows each of the others and decides at which point each voice will speak. The tribal consciousness is not a fixed or constant consciousness. It is a moving center, a flexible observer that listens, reflects, and chooses in a constantly shifting attunement to experiences and relationships. In a fragmented, confusing, and deconstructed world, it constantly reconstructs meaning. The resulting tribal consciousness rejects any intellectual apartheid that forces either/or choices and rejects a cynical fragmentation into total relativism.[9] It guides a democratic clan of voices through its constant work of memory, perception, feeling, and thinking. It struggles to create, from cacophonies, chords of ripening wisdom. The struggle provides trivial resources—trivia, three ways toward self-understanding, survival, and wholeness.

THE BIBLE AND
THE HERMENEUTICS OF WISDOM

The hermeneutics of wisdom offers an approach to biblical texts that helps us understand our relationship to the canon in an ambiguous and nuanced way.[10] My approach parallels the tribal consciousness of Asian-American women in the above stories, which helps them understand their relationship to the past and patriarchal traditions. The Asian immigrant women in the above novels relate differently to the traditions of their native countries because they develop a greater attunement to their own suffering. In addition, their geographical dislocations, after they emigrate, enhance the emergence of a critical distance. With the critical distance that comes with a new context, tradition no longer becomes authoritative because the mechanisms to enforce that authority are to some extent weakened. In an analogous way, the worlds of feminist and womanist activism, consciousness raising, and women's communities empower us to listen to our own suffering and provide us with an alternative to religious patriarchy, undermining the authority of its sexism. That alternative empowers a critical stance. Yet those of us who seek also to maintain a sense of cultural and religious identity in the midst of a secularized, individualistic, technologically fixated society must struggle to find self-understanding and identity in our religious traditions in the midst of that critical stance, which rejects — for the sake of justice and wholeness — the authoritative claim of tradition. The hermeneutics of wisdom may be helpful to women who choose to maintain their commitments to Christian community, as we seek to pass on a sense of culture, hope, and continuity through generations, without being victimized by those commitments.

A tribal consciousness helps us understand our relationship to the Bible and its traditions as akin to belonging to a difficult and troubling circle of kinship. Because we have been given it, whether we willfully choose to love it or not, its discourses and voices are embedded within us. We must engage the voices in dialogue and take responsibility for their presence, even as we fight with them and refuse to tolerate their abusive aspects. The Bible does not speak to us simply as an authority outside ourselves, even as we criticize the patriarchal assumptions and ideologies of the texts based on the experiences and reflections of women. We care about the outcome of our challenges and criticisms because we are not simply outside or separate from what we are criticizing.

Those who understand the Bible as authoritative choose a hierarchical relationship of obedience to it, one edged with passivity, control, and fear. They must obey religious authorities and accept an arbitrary principle of revealed truth in relationship to them perhaps because they assume that authorities speak with a singular, consistent, unified voice.

Demystifying authority opens doors to the critical reclamation of the past that retains it for meaning and identity without granting it authoritative status. We must come to understand through attention to our actual experiences and voices the important aspects of a community to which we belong. For that reason the Bible carries a claim for our attention that other sacred canons do not, but it does not command us to obey it or to draw our theological insights from it when we believe it reinforces suffering and oppression. A tribal consciousness empowers us to understand the voice of authority as part of a system of control, dominance, and the exploitation of those with little power. Without that consciousness we cannot resist the abuse of that authoritarian voice except through apathetic passivity or polemical reaction. A tribal consciousness helps us recognize the danger in language about conformity and obedience and to look for stories of holy disobedience that mirror our own resistance. At the same time we can see our own needs for control and authority in the text.

While sometimes useful politically as the tool of anger and outrage, the urge to reject the Bible and its traditions completely assumes the polemical either/or, win/lose dualistic mentality of Western patriarchy, a mentality that is obsessed with policing boundaries and eliciting loyalty. Polemics and policing are not finally nourishing or nurturing because polarizations keep us off balance. I suggest we examine the Bible as a source of mirrors that sharpen our view of what our past has been, of what we believe and do not believe, of what we must transform, and of who we are to become. Like the relationship of Asian-American women to the past, we can understand the Bible not as authoritative for our sense of ourselves, but as a resource for understanding our identities.

The second aspect of a hermeneutics of wisdom involves the rejection of innocence, which means finding ways to be ethical agents of our own survival and taking responsibility for the complex voices we carry within us. In a patriarchal culture, one of those voices is hierarchical. Knowing that hierarchical voice can help us see how we participate in the oppression of others and thwart our own best aspirations. We can also embrace our role in the transformation of our societies toward justice and wholeness. The multiple voices of a tribal consciousness enable us to hold all the voices inside us and examine each one.

In the same way, we can acknowledge that the Bible also has many voices. Even the patriarchal aspects of a text—those elements that protect hierarchy, authority, and privilege—are not useless to feminists and womanists if they help us see how the text reinforces structures and attitudes in which we are embedded and from which we also benefit, structures such as heterosexism, racism, imperialism, classicism, and the hierarchical and authoritarian structures of higher education, ministry, and business. When we participate with some success in such structures, we must be aware that we cannot participate naïvely, assuming that our status as women prevents us from abusing others. Our criticisms and deconstructions are not solely aimed at those structures that oppress us but also those from which we benefit. Hence, we can use any text to look at the multiple voices inside us and speak with more than the voice of innocent victim. For empowerment comes with taking responsibility for our lives, as well as understanding our need for others.

Since I am not an essentialist in my thinking, I do not believe the Bible is inherently patriarchal. It contains a multitude of voices. To identify it uniformly as hopelessly patriarchal gives too much credit to a few elite men. I know that throughout history women have spoken up against patriarchy and the abuse and oppression of women, have talked to their husbands, sons, and friends, and have influenced the ideas and histories of all communities. In addition, not all men in patriarchal societies grow up thoroughly misogynist. The alternative voices and influences of these women and men are probably not totally absent from the biblical text, even though the dominant voices are overwhelmingly patriarchal and the social-political matrix of the theological perspective is male-dominant.[11]

The biblical text has many authors and many voices. In addition, it may also be helpful to think of individual authors as having several voices, of speaking from several perspectives that they struggle to hold together. For example, Paul, who is a product of the crossroads of several cultures, reappropriates them when he struggles to understand himself and his theological ideas. Rather than trying to decide whether he was sexist or liberating in his attitudes toward women, it may be more honest to say he was both, as he was by turns egalitarian and authoritarian. The search for the historical Jesus also imposes the assumption of a singular voice, as if the conflicts presented in the Gospels could only have been created by an early church and that Jesus himself had a singular voice. If we look for multiple voices in a text, accepting them all, we draw different uses for the text and different theological insights than we would if we expect consistency and singular principles. Beginning with a tribal consciousness allows us to see the text as a resource for exploring theological questions provoked by the text's many voices and compels us to use our own experiences and those of others to create new reflections, rather than relying on the text to tell us.

For a tribal consciousness to be affirmed, it is important to avoid the tendency to read stories about biblical women and men as examples of role models, as those who tell us how to be women and men. This tendency to find models often seems to happen especially to female characters, whose infrequent appearance as actors in the text seems to encourage elevating them, even when the biblical text does not present them as models. Making them such tends to sanitize them and to limit what they can tell us. The full ambiguity of their stories gets lost when we reduce them to heroes, searching for messages or moral principles to guide our actions. The desire to make Jesus a model shares the same limitations. When Jesus becomes the model for human behavior, we must ask, "What would Jesus do in this situation?" This question leads us away from the complexities of our own experiences and feelings, which compel us to ask, "How do I feel now; how are others feeling; and what can I do to lessen pain and suffering and empower survival, justice, and wholeness?"

The whole-making power of a story comes through its ability to mirror and thereby to heighten our sense of reality. A story provides resonances, images for understanding the ambiguities and struggles of our own lives, allowing us to see our lives more fully, more honestly. These resonances are reduced when we search for guidelines for our behavior or for clear, unequivocal messages. The more we search for heroes and guidelines, the more we are interested in controlling behavior, rather than in discovering insight, opening dialogue, and empowering wisdom.

In the constantly shifting power structures and contexts of patriarchal societies, it is up to each of us to break new ground. We must each, in this chaos of the postmodern age, find ways to assess the past critically and to take responsibility for our lives, which have their own distinctive characters. Listening to complex resonances in stories and within ourselves is an important path toward finding resources for creative problem solving — for minimizing evil without surrendering ourselves to simplistic dualities.

A tribal consciousness embraces all the voices that connect us to others, creating a hermeneutics of wisdom. As we journey through life, we accumulate voices from our relationships. These voices are resources for wholeness if we are able to be discriminating and are able to use our own and others' experiences as tools for creating liberation, for healing woundedness, and for sustaining connection.

In using a hermeneutics of wisdom, we accept that the Bible tells us something about the people whose imaginative story we admit in part is ours, but we acknowledge that although the Bible is not an arbitrarily revealed authority it may mirror truths that must be found through our own experiences and those of people we love. In that acknowledgment, we begin dusting the Bible on the floor. We recognize the multiple perspectives that give layers of meaning to our interpretation of the text, and we accept responsibility for our myriad voices. We choose to be agents that nurture life, heal brokenness, and struggle against oppression. The wise voice that is born is the one, worn and soaring, that sings in chords of our brokenness and our wholeness; it sings of the whole and compassionate being. And so, let us lift every voice and sing.

NOTES

1. The term "Asian-American" fuses many diverse cultures and ignores the complex differences among Asians in the United States. Nonetheless, a new hybrid culture, grounded in the affirmation of difference and mutual appreciation, as well as in the acknowledgment of tensions, is emerging in the United States as members of various Asian-American groups increasingly interact. This essay identifies certain issues that emerge in the works of Burmese, Japanese, and Chinese American women.

2. There are parallels to the Hebrew concept of wisdom, which stresses human agency and intelligence in problem solving and coping with life, a more "secular" orientation thought to have emerged as the Hebrews developed a more settled, agricultural society. See Wayne Sibley Towner, "The Renewed Authority of Old Testament Wisdom for Contemporary Faith," in *Canon and Authority: Essays in Old Testament Religion and Theology*, ed. George W. Coats and Burke O. Long (Philadelphia: Fortress Press, 1977). Gerald T. Sheppard argues

that a wisdom orientation evolved from a heightened sense of redactoral canon-consciousness as a late process in the shaping of the Hebrew Bible (*Wisdom as a Hermeneutical Construct* [BZAW 151; Berlin and New York: Walter de Gruyter, 1980]).

3. Cynthia Kadohato, *The Floating World* (New York: Penguin Books, 1989); Wendy Law-Yone, *The Coffin-Tree* (New York: Alfred A. Knopf, 1983); Amy Tan, *The Joy Luck Club* (New York: G. P. Putnam's Sons, 1989); and Maxine Hong Kingston, *The Women Warrior* (New York: Random House, 1975). For a more detailed discussion of the stories by Law-Yone and Tan, see my essay, "Dusting the Bible on the Floor: The Loss of Innocence and the Power of Wisdom in Asian American Women's Writings," *Hamline Review* 15 (Spring 1991): 1–21.

4. One could say that Jesus' role is not as role model, but as one who cancels the need for Christians to be like him. However, the lines between Jesus as model for behavior and as unique soteriological event become extremely confused in the Christian tradition, especially with regard to martyrs and to women's prescribed behavior. In addition, even as a unique event, I think it does not help to see Jesus as innocent victim because such thinking structures our orientation toward and expectation of other victims. For a discussion of the relationship between theological ideas in American Protestantism and its relationship to the abuse of children, see Philip Greven, *Spare the Child: The Religious Roots of Punishment and the Psychological Impact of Physical Abuse* (New York: Alfred A. Knopf, 1991).

5. Nel Noddings, *Women and Evil* (Berkeley: University of California Press, 1990). Noddings does not include an explicit race and class analysis in her work. Nonetheless, as she addresses the consequences of poverty, pain, war, and torture, the implications of her analysis for most women become clear, and the expectations of women she discusses are often used to judge all women. Ideologies about middle- and upper-class white women rest on assumptions about the dichotomy between innocent white women and "other" women who are evil. Her analysis indicates the skills required of all women to survive racism, poverty, sexism, and homophobia. For a study of the nineteenth-century preoccupation with the spiritual superiority of the pure "feminine soul" and its implications for feminist theory, see Marilyn Chapin Massey, *Feminine Soul: The Fate of an Ideal* (Boston: Beacon Press, 1985).

6. The colonialist term "tribal" has been used to identify communities that organize their societies by kinship and clan structures. It was used to refer to people who were "primitive and savage," against whom were set the peoples of "enlightened" Christian Western Europe. More accurate, recent anthropological work on tribal people, including the native peoples of the Americas, demonstrates the inaccuracies of Western assumptions. If one is to find examples of egalitarian, flexible social organizations that tolerate high levels of ambiguity and individual freedom, one is more likely to find such structures in tribal societies. See, e.g., Paula Gunn Allen, *The Sacred Hoop* (Boston: Beacon Press, 1986); Marla Powers, *Ogalala Women* (Chicago: University of Chicago Press, 1986); and Jack Wastherford's *Indian Givers: How the Indians of the Americas Transformed the World* (New York: Fawcett Columbine, 1988).

7. I prefer to use the terms Anglo or European-American because I am referring to cultural realities. The use of the term white tends to imply that the issues have to do with race, which they do to some extent. However, racial questions are not limited to the color of one's skin but include deep cultural differences. In addition, terms like Asian, Latin (or Hispanic), and African American imply cultural roots located in a place where those cultures emerged and from which they were brought to North America as foreign imports. The parallel term to these is European American, not white.

8. For the best comprehensive history that presents the adversity encountered by Asian Americans, as well as our successes, see Ronald Takaki, *Strangers From a Different Shore: A History of Asian Americans* (New York: Penguin Books, 1989).

9. Han Suyin uses the term intellectual apartheid to describe the choices forced on her because she is biracial. See *Between Worlds: Women Writers of Chinese Ancestry* (New York: Pergamon Press, 1990), x.

10. This move toward inclusiveness, evidenced in a tribal consciousness, is similar to the kind of inclusiveness of African-American women described by Henry Louis Gates, Jr., in his introduction to *Reading Black, Reading Feminist: A Critical Anthology* (New York: Meridan, 1990). He states, "Perhaps they have learned from some of the early missteps of both the black nationalist and women's movements. In any event, having been excluded from representational authority for so long, black feminists have declined to respond with a counter-politics of exclusion. They have never been obsessed with arriving at any singular self-image; or legislating who may or may not speak on the subject; or policing boundaries between 'us' and 'them.'"

11. The focus in feminist/womanist biblical scholarship on the stories of women and on the hidden, implicit presence of women is women-centered scholarship. For example, Savina Teubal explores an alternative matrilineal perspective in the Genesis narratives. See *Sarah the Priestess: The First Matriarch of Genesis* (Athens, OH: Swallow Press, 1984) and *Hagar the Egyptian: The Lost Tradition of the Matriarchs* (New York: Harper & Row, 1990).

RECOMMENDED READINGS

Brock, Rita. "Dusting the Bible on the Floor: The Loss of Innocence and the Power of Wisdom in Asian American Women's Writings." *Hamline Review* 15 (Spring 1991): 1–21.

———. *Journeys By Heart: A Christology of Erotic Power.* New York: Crossroad, 1988.

———, and Naomi Southard. "The Other Half of the Basket: Asian American Women and the Search for a Theological Home." *Journal of Feminist Studies in Religion* 3/2 (Fall 1987): 135–49.

Collins, Adela Yarbro, ed. *Feminist Perspectives on Biblical Scholarship.* Atlanta: Scholars Press, 1985.

Kadohato, Cynthia. *The Floating World.* New York: Penguin Books, 1989.

Kingston, Maxine Hong. *The Woman Warrior.* New York: Random House, 1975.

Ling, Amy. *Between Worlds: Women Writers of Chinese Ancestry.* New York: Pergamon Press, 1990.

Massey, Marilyn Chapin. *Feminine Soul: The Fate of an Ideal.* Boston: Beacon Press, 1985.

Noddings, Nel. *Women and Evil.* Berkeley: University of California Press, 1990.

Schüssler Fiorenza, Elisabeth. *In Memory of Her: A Feminist Theological Reconstruction of Christian Origins.* New York: Crossroad, 1983.

Tan, Amy. *The Joy Luck Club.* New York: G. P. Putnam's Sons, 1989.

Teubal, Savina. *Hagar the Egyptian: The Lost Tradition of the Matriarchs.* New York: Harper & Row, 1990.

———. *Sarah the Priestess: The First Matriarch of Genesis.* Athens, OH: Swallow Press, 1984.

5

◆ Feminist Interpretations
in Africa

Teresa Okure ◆

FEMINIST INTERPRETATIONS OF SCRIPTURE, or feminist hermeneutics, constitute part of the human revolutionary movement termed feminism. Mercy Amba Oduyoye describes feminism as a "shorthand for the proclamation that women's experience should be an integral part of what goes into the definition of being human. . . . [It] emphasizes the wholeness of the community as made up of male and female beings."[1]

As in other walks of life, biblical interpretation up to the last three decades of our century was dominated by white, male, clerical scholars. The "accepted" method of this interpretation was the historical-critical method, termed the scientific method, which grew out of European sociopolitical and national interests. Today, in the wake of feminism, women and some men have, as biblical scholars, sought in different ways to include the women's viewpoint and approach in this "biblical science." The aim is to give women a place in the story and thus bring about a more complete and balanced, hence fully human and truly liberating, understanding of the word of God. This is all the more necessary since over the centuries the Bible has been used or abused to legitimize sexism, even as it was used to legitimize racism and classism.[2]

Contemporary women's interpretation of the Bible has received different names in different racial and cultural contexts. From its inception, it was tagged "feminist." Since this sustained pioneering work was undertaken by white North American and European women, feminist hermeneutics became identified with white women theologians' approach to reading the Bible. Black and Hispanic minority women who felt that the white women's approach addressed the issue of sex but not sufficiently those of class and race coined the terms "womanist" and "*mujerista,*" respectively, to describe their interpretation.[3]

African women theologians, to my knowledge, have not coined a terminology for their interpretative efforts. They freely use the term feminist but give it their own particular content, as we shall see in the ensuing discussion. African women (and men for that matter) do not as a cultural rule start with the issue of methodology. Their primary consciousness in doing theology is not method but life and life concerns, their own and those of their own peoples. Second, Africa cannot as yet boast of many "professionally" trained women biblical scholars. As a result, the description of their methodology, its characteristic features, and the areas of application must be culled for the most part from Bible study records and general theological works and reflections. In the discussion that follows I shall address first the issue of methodology and then examine its application in select areas of interpretation.

THE ISSUE OF METHODOLOGY

From the literature available, if one were to coin an expression that would best describe African women's distinctive approach to biblical interpretation, it would be "doing theology from women's perspective." This approach has the distinctive characteristic of inclusiveness. It describes the efforts of women *and* men to interpret the scriptures as they relate to women, in a common search for new inclusive meanings. In this respect, it differs from the strictly feminist approach, which excludes the possibility of men being able to offer a valid interpretation of scripture as it relates to women.[4] The African women's approach is inclusive of scholars and nonscholars, the rich and the poor; it is inclusive of the "scientific," the creative, and the popular methods.

In contrast to the traditional male, individualistic, hierarchical, and competitive approach, doing theology from African women's perspective emphasizes solidarity among the sister theologians, irrespective of their theological status and formation. This is the basic inspiration behind the formation of the "Circle of Concerned African Women Theologians" spearheaded by Mercy Oduyoye. It has already borne rich fruit both in terms of publications and in terms of discovering hidden theological voices and building up potential professional theologians.[5]

The reasons for this inclusiveness are fourfold: First, African women working within the general framework of EATWOT (Ecumenical Association of Third World Theologians) seek to bring about through their doing of theology the existence of the new humanity redeemed by Christ (Gal 3:28; Col 3:11; 1 Cor 12:12–13). For this to happen men need to struggle alongside women in the efforts to read the scriptures "with new eyes."[6]

African women are aware that the Bible is fundamentally a community book. Its message is addressed to both men and women, who together form the community of the people of God and who together must form the community of its interpretation. This message is ultimately not about gender but about life and the relationship of human beings to God, to one another and to creation. A predominantly matriarchal reading of the Bible would be as distorting as the patriarchal one has been over the centuries. If the new creation is to become a reality in our times, "both men and women must reexamine [together] Christian tradition and confront those aspects that justify the domestication of women."[7] This inclusive approach enables one to fix attention not on the gender of the theologian, important as this may be, but on the rights of women and their indispensability in the field of theology and life, if humanity is ever to attain fully its divinely intended status (see Gen 1:26–28).

Second, in the African context, the comprehensive framework for doing theology is the survival of the peoples of the continent. Life problems on the continent of Africa are rooted not only in gender but also in race and class. The problems include "underdevelopment," hunger, and disease; political, economic, and religious exploitation, which is effected by colonialism, neo-colonialism, and that cultural stripping which E. Mveng calls "pauvreté anthropologique." Of this both men and women are victims.[8] Rose Zoe-Obianga and other African women theologians rightly believe that African women cannot afford to divorce their legitimate quest for a liberating theology from the wider quest of liberation for the African peoples. For as Anne Nasimiyu-Wasike notes, "African women together with their African brothers suffer hunger and thirst continuously. Their main struggles are against the forces which rob them of control over their destiny and which do not enable them to fulfill their God-given potential."[9] African women theologians, who with their sisters the world over are by God's special grace "covenanted with life,"[10] feel a special responsibility to foster and sustain the reconciliation (2 Cor 5:18) of all God's children. This awareness underscores their desire to carry the men along with them in their search for a liberating and life-giving theology.

Third, in traditional African contexts, fully human undertakings are done conjointly by men and women. The traditional priesthood, for instance, embraces both women and men, each in his/her own right as a person—notwithstanding the shortcomings voiced by Oduyoye.[11] This perhaps best explains why African men have been relatively prominent in encouraging women to do theology.[12] The issue of sex apart, they suffer with African women the discrimination based on race and color, which in its own way can be as oppressive as that based on sex.

Our brothers in apartheid South Africa have lived this intensely in their flesh. Their experience of blackness in this system becomes a vantage point for dialogue; it enables them to feel paradigmatically the effect of society's pervasive discrimination against women.[13] This common undertaking then gives birth to a new meaning of the scriptures, one that is neither masculinist nor feminist but is truly Christian, leading to the establishment of God's new creation (2 Cor 5:17). It empowers African men and women theologians to overcome the many externally imposed divisive forces that are currently plaguing the continent.[14]

My own consistent experience in running annual seminars on women in the New Testament for the past eight years, at the Catholic Institute of West Africa (CIWA), at present an all-male clerical graduate theological institution, proves the validity of this approach. This experience has revealed that men are in their own way as oppressed as women by the conditioning weight of antifeminist seminary traditions, based largely on Thomistic Aristotelian theology. Through their own research on women in the New Testament and traditional African cultures, the priest graduate students have come to see the need to reevaluate in the light of the Gospel the anti-feminist rhetoric and negative traditions about women which they received in the seminary and to some extent in the culture.

The theological orientation of our institute is inculturation and con-textualization. This requires among other things that each course and topic for discussion be situated firmly in the African context and cultures with a view to bringing about a marriage between the Gospel and the culture. In this way, the students have had to offer a genuine critique of the discrim-inatory practices against women found in the scriptures, the church, and the culture. Issues treated cover a wide range of areas including fundamental equality of the sexes in Christ, widowhood practices, marital status of women, cultural and religious taboos, and women's ministry in the church. The critiques at times turn up quite embarrassing information; for example, in some cultures, like the Ewe culture of Ghana, women enjoy a much higher status and respect than they do in the church which is supposed to proclaim and be God's agent of liberation in and through Christ of all oppressed and marginalized persons.[15]

Feedback received when the students return to their parish ministry has proved the effectiveness of their "feminist reading" of the Bible. Genuine changes occur in attitudes toward women and in pastoral methods; programs of awareness are designed to expand the effect. Though the exer-cise may not make the students feminists—if by that is meant women reflect-ing on women's issues—it does make them better Christians and more faithful preachers of the good news of Jesus of Nazareth.

Fourth, and most significant, this approach to theology from women's perspective is inspired by the methodology of Jesus himself as recorded in the Gospels. His approach to controversial issues (and biblical hermeneutics is one such issue) was never partisan but transcendent.[16] He dialogued freely with his opponents and accepted their invitation to meals, even when this was done in bad faith (cf. Luke 7:44–46); in this way he sought their liberation through communion with them.[17] Pharisees and publicans, women and men, the rich and the poor, the healthy and the sick, nationals and foreigners — all were subjects of his creative, innovative, and even daring theological methodology. A theology that aspires to achieve his liberating results for humanity must adopt his liberating theological methodology.

While being inclusive, reading the Bible from women's perspective recognizes and safeguards women's distinctive approach to doing theology. This method of reading describes any theological efforts of women, done consciously as women, irrespective of the nature of the subject. It extends its scope to the whole of biblical and theological interpretation, not only to issues that deal specifically with women. This applies to method as it does to meaning. Women are by nature creative, intuitive, and comprehensive in their perception of reality. Interpreting scripture from women's perspective requires that their creative approaches be applied and recognized as a valid way of searching the scriptures even as the historical-critical method has been over the years.

The reason for this is self-evident. To state that women are not men is to state the obvious. What may not be so obvious is to accept that women have a distinctive way of viewing reality which differs from but is as valid as that of men. A key problem surrounding the Bible itself and its interpretation is that of patriarchy. By this I mean that the Bible was written most likely only *by* men and, for the Hebrew Scriptures, most specifically *for* men ("my son," "your wife") in male-dominated cultures. Over the centuries, it has also been officially interpreted and applied only by men.[18] Since men are not women, this traditional theologizing could offer only the male viewpoint. Today the female viewpoint is required for a balanced and fully human meaning.

APPLICATION OF THE METHODOLOGY

Given the restricted scope of this chapter, I can mention only in broad outline the areas in which these underlying methodological principles manifest themselves in studies by African women. We find them in works that are predominantly theological in scope, in studies of a sociocultural nature and in those that deal with women's place in the church.

Predominantly Theological Works

The last point made under methodology is important. Most people do not believe that a woman is engaged in "feminist" interpretation unless she is dealing with women's issues. Thus, despite the clearly new and creative discoveries that emerged in my doctoral study of John 4:1–42, the first critique leveled against the work was that it ignored the feminist perspectives of the passage.[19] Interestingly, a woman was also the first to recognize the freshness and innovativeness of the discoveries made in the study.[20] Conversely, in a survey of "feminist literature" from Africa published in *Concilium*, a male colleague here at CIWA left out *The Johannine Approach to Mission* while including my minor works.[21] The implications of this are clear. But it would be a major mistake, worse than the past exclusion of women from the doing of theology, and a serious impoverishment of the word of God, if women were to be restricted to addressing only women's issues in their interpretation of the scriptures. This would still leave the field largely to men.

Within the methodological framework described above, I see the following discoveries as part of my contribution as a woman to the understanding of John 4:1–42 and John's Gospel as a whole: (1) the very application of the contextual method in reading the passage as opposed to the reigning historical-critical approaches; (2) the view of the passage and the Gospel as dealing comprehensively with mission; (3) the identification of the comprehensive rhetorical framework underlying the Gospel; (4) the recognition that Jesus' exchanges with the woman form a real dialogue, that he is not simply using the woman as a pretext to make a theological point; (5) the emphasis on the vital role of the audience as subject, not object, of mission as is still the case in so-called mission territories, and that for John mission embraces those already converted; and (6) the recognition that the Samaritan woman is in every sense a missionary whom Jesus proposes to his male disciples as a model and a lesson. Indeed, with very few exceptions, most of my studies of the scriptures follow this theological approach. In my view this approach has a vital place in doing theology from women's perspective.[22]

WORKS OF SOCIOCULTURAL NATURE

This phrase is coined for want of a better one. Most interpretations by African women follow this approach, which consists principally, though with variations, in identifying a woman's situation in African culture and society, describing and critically analyzing it, then looking at the Gospels to see how Jesus and the women of his time handled similar situations. Implications are then drawn from this Gospel evidence for addressing the contemporary women's situation. Often the application goes beyond the specific situation and becomes symbolic for the woman's plight in society.

A cherished passage here is the woman with the issue of blood (Luke 8:40–56). It is treated by M. Kanyoro in *Talitha Qumi!,* and by Elizabeth Amoah in *New Eyes for Reading.* Both works emphasize the woman's courage in breaking with the crippling cultural taboos imposed on her so as to reach Jesus directly and be fully restored and integrated as a person with full rights in her society. T. Okure uses the same passage to image the conditions from which African women theologians must arise if they are to attain the necessary will to do a life-giving theology.[23] Similarly, T. Hinga and A. Nasimiyu-Wasike address African women's experiences from the standpoint of Christology. They underscore how women see in Christ a liberator, savior, personal friend and healer, and draw strength from this Christology in their struggles for liberation.[24]

WOMEN'S PLACE IN THE CHURCH

The approach adopted here is similar to that just described above. But the focus here is on the experiences of women in the church. Prescribed roles and status of women in the church are studied against the background of culture, Gospel, and early catholicism. In many instances, the church and the culture are found to form a coalition against women and Jesus' attitude to them in the Gospels. This evidence encourages women to reach out to Jesus in the Gospels and gain unfailing strength in their struggle for self-inclusion in all aspects of the church's life. Studies in this area are also numerous, but one may mention those of L. Tappa, R. Edet, B. Ekeya, L. Fanusie, and M. Owanikin, to cite but a few.[25]

To conclude this introductory study on feminist interpretations in Africa, I may refer the reader to Mercy Oduyoye's *Hearing and Knowing: Theological Reflections on Christianity in Africa,* cited many times in this study. In many ways, this work, especially chaps. 6 to 12, sets forth in detail various aspects of what has been described in this study as doing theology from African women's perspective. The reader will also have noticed that the study deliberately made little distinction between African women biblical scholars and theologians. This lack of distinction is itself an aspect of feminist interpretation in the African context.

Finally, the quest for liberation through the Bible in Africa is not a special preserve of women. Men and the poor also have recourse to the same book and believe firmly in it. Traditionally a people of the word, not of the book, Africans see the "word of God" as being most capable of fulfilling what it promises. Respect for the book as the word of God often leads to a certain fundamentalism, backed by traditional interpretation and practice, especially where it makes statements concerning the subjection of women to men. It therefore becomes most necessary to assure a correct understanding of this word so as to be firmly committed to its liberative truth: the full liberation of women and men in, by, and through Christ (John 8:31–36). Feminist hermeneutics is a reliable tool for achieving this.

NOTES

1. M. A. Oduyoye, *Hearing and Knowing: Theological Reflections on Christianity in Africa* (Maryknoll, NY: Orbis, 1986), 121; see also eadem, "The Search for a Two-Winged Theology: Women's Participation in the Development of Theology in Africa: The Inaugural Address," in *Talitha Qumi: Proceedings of the Convocation of African Women Theologians* (Ibadan: Daystar, 1990), 27–48.

2. See T. Okure, "Women in the Bible," in *With Passion and Compassion: Third World Women Doing Theology*, ed. V. Fabella and M. Oduyoye (Maryknoll, NY: Orbis, 1989), 47–59, esp. 47.

3. On white women's feminist literature, see M. Daly, *The Church and the Second Sex* (1968; rev. ed., Boston: Beacon Press, 1985), with a New Feminist Postchristian Introduction by the Author in 1975); eadem, *Beyond God the Father: Towards a Philosophy of Women's Liberation* (Boston: Beacon Press, 1983). The manifesto of white women's feminist theology, in my view, is E. Schüssler Fiorenza's *In Memory of Her: A Feminist Theological Reconstruction of Christian Origins* (New York: Crossroad, 1983), especially chapters 1 and 2 (pp. 3–67). On the womanist and *mujerista* approaches, see, e.g., J. Grant, *White Women's Christ and Black Women's Jesus: Feminist Christology and Womanist Response* (Atlanta: Scholars Press, 1989); and Katie Cannon et al., *Inheriting Our Mother's Gardens: Feminist Theology in Third World Perspective* (Louisville: Westminster/John Knox, 1988).

4. See Ingrid R. Kitzberger, "Love and Footwashing: John 13:1-20 and Luke 7:36-50 Read Intertextually," a paper presented to the Seminar on the Role of the Reader in the Interpretation of the New Testament, at the SNTS Annual Meeting, Madrid, 27–30 July, 1992.

5. For full information on "The Circle," see M. A. Oduyoye, *Talitha Qumi!* 1–26. Another important publication of the Circle is *The Will to Arise: Women, Tradition, and the Church in Africa*, ed. M. A. Oduyoye and M. R. A. Kanyoro (Maryknoll, NY: Orbis, 1992).

6. The phrase is from *New Eyes for Reading: Biblical and Theological Reflections by Women from the Third World*, ed. John. S. Pobee and Barbel von Wartenberg-Potter (Oak Park, IL: Meyer Stone Books, 1987). Pobee is obviously one of the African men who encourages a "feminist" reading of the Bible.

7. Oduyoye, *Hearing and Knowing*, 121, 133.

8. E. Mveng, *L'Afrique dans l'Eglise: Parole d'un Croyant* (Paris: Harmattan, 1985), 120.

9. R. Zoe-Obianga, "Les femmes africaines et la liberation de l'Afrique," *Bulletin de Théologie Africaine* 6/12 (1984): 319–23; A. Nasimiyu-Wasike, "Christology and an African Woman's Experience," in *Faces of Jesus in Africa*, ed. R. J. Schreiter (Maryknoll, NY: Orbis, 1991), 70–81, esp. p. 71; see also Oduyoye, *Talitha Qumi!* 44.

10. See Okure, "Women in the Bible," 51; eadem, "Biblical Perspectives on Women: Eve, the Mother of All the Living (Gen 3:20)," in *Voices from the Third World*, Philippine Edition 8/2 (1985), 17–24, esp. p. 23; Oduyoye, *Hearing and Knowing*, 101.

11. See J. S. Mbiti, "Flowers in the Garden: The Role of the Woman in African Religion," *Cahiers de Religions Africaines* 22 (1988): 69–72; R. M. Owanikin, "The Priesthood of Church Women in the Nigerian Context," in *The Will to Arise*, ed. Oduyoye and Kanyoro, 206–18; Oduyoye, "Women and Ritual in Africa," in *The Will to Arise*, 9–24, esp. p. 10; eadem, *Hearing and Knowing*, 123.

12. A classic example of African men's encouragement of women to do theology is the communiqué issued at the first Pan-African EATWOT conference, Accra, 17–23 December 1977, which declared war on "sexism" and the "exclusion [of women] from past theological endeavors," *African Theologies en Route*, ed. K. Appiah-Kubi and S. Torres (Maryknoll, NY: Orbis, 1979), 194.

13. Interestingly, South African men encountered at Pan-African conferences demonstrate a greater sensitivity to women's issues than do their counterparts in the rest of Africa, especially in Muslim North Africa, where patriarchy is deeply entrenched in the culture and religion.

14. See Oduyoye, *Hearing and Knowing*, 85–86, 88–89.

15. Once their interest in women's issues is aroused, the students often choose to write their Master's theses on these issues; they do so from the biblical, dogmatic, pastoral, moral, and canonical perspectives, that is, in all the current areas of specialization in the Master's program.

16. See further T. Okure, *The Johannine Approach to Mission: A Contextual Study of John 4:1–42* (Wissenschaftliche Untersuchungen zum Neuen Testament 2/31; Tübingen: Mohr-Siebeck, 1988), 96, 100.

17. Jesus knew from the beginning that Judas would betray him; yet he chose him among the Twelve and sought through this close association to wean him away from his crime, even calling him "friend" at the very moment of his betrayal (cf. Matt 26:23, 50).

18. I say "officially" because all through history, women, like Juliana of Norwich and Elizabeth Cady Stanton did interpret the Bible, but their interpretations were hardly taken into account in the organization of the church's life.

19. Robert Morgan's review of *The Johannine Approach to Mission* in *Theological Book Review* 1/3 (1989): 13.

20. Judith Lieu, "John and Mission," a review in *Expository Times* 11 (1989): 431.

21. J. S. Ukpong, "Theological Literature in Africa," *Concilium* 199/5 (1988): 67–75, especially pp. 71–72 ("Feminist Theology").

22. Indeed, most of my studies in the scriptures take this "theological approach"; see further, "Leadership in the New Testament," *Nigerian Journal of Theology* 1/5 (1990):

71–92; "Justice with Compassion: A Biblical Perspective," *SOURCE* 16 (Winter 1987): 5–18; "The Significance Today of Jesus' Commission of Mary Magdalene," *International Review of Mission* 80/322 (1992): 177–88; and "A New Testament Perspective on Evangelization and Human Promotion," in *Evangelization in Africa in the Third Millennium: Challenges and Prospects: Proceedings of the First Theology Week of the Catholic Institute of West Africa, Port Harcourt, Nigeria, May 6–11, 1990*, ed. J. S. Ikpong, T. Okure, et al. (Port Harcourt: CIWA Publications, 1992) 84–94, to cite but a few.

23. M. Kanyoro, "Daughter, Arise, (Luke 8:40–56)," in *Talitha Qumi!* 54–62; E. Amoah, "The Woman Who Decided to Break the Rules," in *New Eyes for Reading*, ed. Pobee and von Wartenberg-Potter, 3–4; T. Okure, "The Will to Arise: Reflections on Luke 8:40–56," in *The Will to Arise*, ed. Oduyoye and Kanyoro, 221–30.

24. T. Hinga, "Jesus Christ and the Liberation of Woman in Africa," in *The Will to Arise*, ed. Oduyoye and Kanyoro, 183–94; Anne Nasimiyu-Wasike, "Christology," in *Faces of Jesus*, ed. Schreiter.

25. Louise Tappa, "God in Man's Image," in *New Eyes for Reading*, ed. Pobee and von Wartenberg-Potter, 101–6; R. Edet, "The Nigerian Theologian at the Service of the Church," *Nigerian Journal of Theology* 1/1 (1985): 43–53; eadem, "Leadership in the New Testament: Resurrection/Feminist Perspective," *Nigerian Journal of Theology* 1/5 (1990): 94–101; B. Ekeya, "Woman for How Long Not?" in *New Eyes for Reading*, 59–67, especially pp. 65–67; L. Fanusie, "Christianity and African Rituals," in *Talitha Qumi!* 84–88; Owanikin, "Priesthood of Church Women," in *The Will to Arise*, ed. Oduyoye and Kanyoro.

RECOMMENDED READINGS

Oduyoye, M. A. *Hearing and Knowing: Theological Reflections on Christianity in Africa.* Maryknoll, NY: Orbis, 1986.

———. *The Will to Arise: Women, Tradition, and the Church in Africa.* Maryknoll, NY: Orbis, 1990.

———, and Musimbi R. A. Kanyoro, eds. *Talithi Qumi! Proceedings of the Convocation of African Women Theologians 1989.* Ibadan: Daystar Press, 1990.

Okure, Teresa. "Conversion-Engagement: Une Perspective Africaine." *Spiritus* 130 (1993): 34–43.

———. "Inculturation: Biblical Theological Bases. In *32 Articles Evaluating the Inculturation of Christianity in Africa*, edited by Teresa Okure, Paul van Thiel, et al., 112–14. Eldoret: AMACEA Gaba Publications, 1990.

———. "Jesus, der Mann, der in der Art der Frauen wirkte." *Jahrbuch Mission 1993*, 53–62. Hamburg: Missionshilfe Verlag, 1993.

◆ *La Palabra de Dios en Nosotras* — The Word of God in Us

ADA MARÍA ISASI-DÍAZ ◆

> I never read the Bible. Once in school I had a Bible class, and it was just like any other subject, like you read a history book. I only know the passages that are read at Mass on Sundays. And I do not have the least idea of what the Old Testament is. Bible to me is an unknown subject. . . . I remember my Bible, they made us buy it one year, and we read it a couple of times. . . . All that about reading the Bible is very American. In Cuba the Bible was not important.[1]

THOUGH THERE ARE Hispanic women whose relationship to the Bible is different from this Latina's, she is representative of how the majority of Hispanic women relate to the Bible.[2] The actual way in which Hispanic women regard the Bible, no matter how peripheral it is, provides the starting point for an articulation of a *mujerista* biblical interpretation.

MUJERISTA BIBLICAL INTERPRETATION

Elsewhere we have begun to articulate the main elements of a critical *mujerista* interpretation of the Bible.[3] We present them here briefly. First, there exists a Hispanic *mestizo* Christianity, heavily influenced by the Catholicism of the *conquistadores,* a religious practice with little biblical content.[4] To this were added religious understandings and practices of African and Amerindian religions. As Protestant and evangelical traditions are now becoming part of the religious understandings and practices of an increasing number of Latinas, we need to find a way to appropriate into our *mestizo* Christianity the central elements of these traditions as they are understood and practiced by Hispanic women. The centrality of the Bible in these faith traditions, the influence they have in the dominant culture, and the number of Latinas who are becoming members of Protestant and evangelical churches indicate the urgency of articulating a *mujerista* biblical interpretation.[5]

Second, Hispanic women's experience and our struggle for survival, not the Bible, are the source of our theology and the starting point for how we should interpret, appropriate, and use the Bible.[6] A great number of Latinas do not consult the Bible in our daily lives. The complexity of the biblical writings, the variety of messages, and the differences in socio-historical and political-economic context make it difficult for us to use the Bible. When we need help we find it not in the Bible but in praying to God, Mary, the saints — all part of the divine — to whom Hispanic women have the direct access they do not have to the Bible, which needs interpretation.[7]

Third, the critical lens of *mujerista* theology is liberation. For us liberation is synonymous with survival, both physical and cultural. As *mujerista* theology struggles to discern how to appropriate and use the Bible, we must apply to it the same liberative lens that we use in all our theological work. Therefore, from the start we can say that *mujerista* biblical hermeneutics accepts the Bible as part of divine revelation and as authoritative only insofar as it contributes to Hispanic women's struggle for liberation.[8]

Two caveats are in order here. For the great majority of Hispanic women, the marginal way they deal with the Bible is not intentional. We do not reject the Bible; we simply do not use it or we use it very sparingly and selectively. Second, since Hispanic women's lived experience is the source of *mujerista* theology, the task of *mujerista* theologians is to articulate the religious practice of Hispanic women. We do this to help our communities understand how their religious beliefs operate in our daily lives. Our task is to analyze those practices through a liberative lens and to evaluate them in view of the liberation of Hispanic women. Because *mujerista* theologians are an integral part of the Latina community, part of our task is to participate with the community in deciding how Hispanic women will relate to and use the Bible from now on.

There are three important elements in *mujerista* biblical interpretation. First, the mostly unarticulated criterion that has guided the Hispanic women's usage of the Bible has been *need*. We have used the Bible when we have needed it, for what we have needed it for, in the manner we have needed it. Second, the struggle for liberation has to be the critical lens of our biblical hermeneutics. Third, Latinas' interpretation of the Bible is central to identifying and struggling for our *proyecto histórico,* our preferred future, which we believe is an intrinsic part of the unfolding of the kin-dom of God.[9]

NEED: HISPANIC WOMEN'S GUIDE
TO THE BIBLE

How have and how do grassroot's Hispanic women approach and use the Bible? The majority of Hispanic women know the Bible mostly from hearing it read on Sundays in their churches; they know the Bible through oral tradition rather than through reading and studying the biblical text.[10] They listen and tell biblical stories. They refer to the Bible in their discussions and struggles not because they believe or do not believe that it is the word of God and that as such it tells them what to do or not to do. Latinas use Bible stories hoping to find someone in the story who will be a source of hope: others have survived similar circumstances, so will I. Hispanic women have traditionally listened to and told Bible stories as a source of strength, in order to understand what is happening to us.

Recently at a national conference of Latinas, the speaker was trying to find a way of explaining how Hispanic women need to insist on our rights. She decided to use a Bible story and in doing so mixed elements of two different biblical pericopes.

> The woman in the Bible needed help. She realized Jesus could help her and nothing was going to stop her. It was not very nice, as a matter of fact, it was terrible of Jesus to tell her that she could not eat from the bread that was on the table. She could only have crumbs. If it had been me, I would have answered him that I have every right to eat from the bread on the table. We do not want just the crumbs, no. (Applause) Well, she insisted on her right; she took it without Jesus giving it to her. Jesus knew that power had gone out of him; that she had taken power in her own hands because she and her daughter were in great need.[11]

No one seemed to notice that the speaker had confused two stories, or, if they noticed, it did not matter, for what gave authority to that text was not the way it was written in the Bible but the way it had been appropriated by this Hispanic woman and the way it could be of help to the rest of us.

Those in the Bible who struggled for survival, including Jesus, are one of the few "reality checks" that Latinas have. Society questions our reality and makes us question it by objectivizing us, instrumentalizing us. Society alienates us unless we are willing to participate in it on the terms of the dominant culture.[12] Anyone, including biblical persons, who has gone through situations similar to ours encourages us to believe in ourselves and our communities and helps us know that we are not imagining things, that though we are often rendered invisible by those who have power we do not cease to exist.

That the people of *our* Bible stories—stories that come from a book we know is important—can understand us because they have also had to struggle for survival is important to Hispanic women. Bible stories become *ours* when we use them because we need them. To make them helpful in a given situation we change even central elements of the story itself, highlighting perhaps nonessential elements.[13] It is not that the integrity of the text is not important; it is that the need to survive takes precedence.

Being linked to the people of *our* Bible stories extends our community to include those of ages past. We know our struggle is an ancient one; *our* Bible stories help us realize that as a community of struggle we have existed for many, many centuries. *Our* biblical stories put us in contact with the communities of our forebears and teach us that though we must struggle with all our might against oppression, we must not grow weary.[14] By making us part of a much wider community of struggle, biblical stories help us hold on to the belief that *se hace lo que se puede,* one does what is possible. It helps us continue to understand that though we may not be able to solve problems or remedy the terrible situation in which we live, we can make a positive contribution. Partial solutions are elements of the transformative change because the struggle to bring them about provides inspiration and can indeed provide the favorable conditions our children will need to be able to continue our struggle for liberation.[15]

APPROPRIATING THE BIBLE
AND LIBERATIVE PRAXIS

For Hispanic women the *palabra de Dios* is not necessarily what is written in the Bible, but refers to the unflinching belief that God is with us in our daily struggles.[16] Years ago in Lima, Perú, where I was living at the time, I used to go to a church in one of the poor *barriadas* that surround the capital; in the church was a huge banner that read: *La palabra de Dios tiene fuerzas y da vida.* These words, taken from Hebrews 4:12, had become very meaningful in the life of the community. For them *la palabra de Dios,* the word of God, referred not to what is written in the Bible but to their understanding that their religious beliefs and practices could help them in their struggle for survival, and that the church, represented for them by the parish priest, was willing to participate with them in that struggle.

This community understood the *palabra de Dios* similarly to the way Latinas do. Such understanding must be the critical lens through which *mujerista* theologians look at the Bible. How do we interpret and appropriate the Bible so that it becomes an effective tool in the struggle for liberation? We start by asserting that in order to survive, to be liberated, we have to develop and strengthen our moral agency as Hispanic women. Liberation for Hispanic women, as well as for all oppressed people, revolves around the process of becoming agents of our own history, *sujetos de nuestra historia,* and this cannot be achieved unless one becomes a strong moral agent capable of making choices, of acting, of challenging, and of creating meaning for ourselves in the midst of the oppressive structures in which we live.[17]

The interpretation, appropriation, and use of the Bible, therefore, for Hispanic women has to enable and enhance Latinas' moral agency. To do this we have to be aware of three concerns about the growth of the role of the Bible in the life of Latinas. First, at present those Hispanic women who use the Bible have little or nothing to say most of the time about the way the Bible is interpreted. This results in accepting as authoritative an interpretation of the Bible and an understanding of its importance and usage that is outside ourselves, not of our own making, not controlled by us and therefore something that will control us. Second, a nonbiblical Christianity has been a good vehicle for the inclusion of Amerindian and African beliefs and practices in our *mestizo* Christianity, an inclusion that is at the heart of popular religiosity. It is questionable whether this process of *mestizaje* will be able to continue if Hispanic women do not have a say in how to interpret, apply, and use the Bible.

From the perspective of moral agency, popular religiosity enables Hispanic women to claim a Christianity that they, and not the church authorities (largely made up of non-Hispanic males), determine. Most Latinas who use the Bible at present do so under the tutelage of priests and pastors, who intepret it and control its interpretation and use in the Hispanic churches. If we do not have a say, the Bible will be imposed on us as the only or the definitive revelation of God to the exclusion of the ongoing revelation of God in our lives and the revelation of God in non-Christian religions.

The third concern we have regarding appropriation of the Bible is how to deal with it when it already plays a role in the life of a growing number of Hispanic women—mainly those who are evangelical, charismatic, whether Roman Catholic or Protestant, and those who are pentecostals.[18] These Latinas use the Bible almost exclusively in an individualistic and pietistic way. Though we consider this usage of the Bible questionable insofar as development and enhancement of moral agency are concerned, we find that it could be an appropriate starting place. But Hispanic women must insist on rejecting a fundamentalist interpretation of the Bible. Nor, given the reality of the oppression of Hispanic women, can our appropriation and usage be only pietistic and individualistic, concerned only with a private sense of salvation and used for the consolation of the individual. Such usage has to be denounced whenever it oppresses Hispanic women or supports and promotes understandings and structures that oppress us. As *mujeristas* we are concerned with the way the Bible is interpreted and used by pentecostals, evangelicals, and charismatics to reject or ignore an understanding of structural sin, the social implications of personal salvation, and the intrinsic relationship between struggle for survival and salvation—between struggling for justice in this world and salvation and life everlasting. The Bible should help us to understand the oppression we suffer because of injustices in our world; the Bible should call us as a community of faith to struggle for justice so as to participate in the unfolding of the kin-dom of God.[19]

For *mujerista* theology the enablement and enhancement of moral agency go hand in hand with a process of conscientization, an ongoing process of critical reflection on action that leads to a critical awareness of oppressive structures and their interconnectedness.[20] In this critical process the Bible should be used to learn how to learn—to involve the people in an "unending process of acquiring new pieces of information that multiply the previous store of information."[21] The Bible is a rich resource of "new information": stories of valiant women, of struggles against unbelievable odds, of communities of resistance, of women who found ways to survive in the midst of the worst oppression. This "new information" helps to make obvious problems that may have existed for a long time but ones we have failed to recognize. This usage of the Bible does not apply what the Bible says directly to our situations. But the Bible is seen as an important element in the formation of the moral character of Hispanic women. The Bible could play an important role as Hispanic women reflect on who we are as Christians and what our attitudes, dispositions, goals, values, norms, and decisions are.[22] But in the end our ethical principle, the source of moral values for Hispanic women, is not the Bible but the struggle to survive.

LIVING INTO OUR PREFERRED FUTURE: NUESTRO PROYECTO HISTÓRICO

An element of liberation-salvation that needs elaboration because it impinges on *mujerista* biblical hermeneutics is our preferred future, our *proyecto histórico.* Before discussing our *proyecto histórico,* two preliminary points need to be made. First, our insistence on liberation carries with it a rejection of equality within the present social-political-economic structures. We believe these structures are based on an oppressive understanding of power: power as domination and control. These structures necessitate a group in need, unemployed, considered as a diminished sector of humanity, that can be used to maintain the privileges of the few. If Hispanics "move ahead" in society, necessarily another group of people will have to take our place as "the diminished sector of society" within the system. Our goal, therefore, is not to partake of the privileges of those who now control and dominate us. Instead we seek to change radically present oppressive structures so nobody will be diminished.

Second, an in-depth analysis of the way oppressive structures work makes it evident that oppressed groups are set against each other for the benefit of those with power. As we struggle to make our *proyecto histórico* a reality, we are committed to denouncing and not participating in horizontal violence; we will not act against other exploited groups around the world. Our liberation as Hispanic women cannot be at the expense of anyone. Though our strategies may be different from those of other racial/ethnic groups, we cannot have goals and strategies that contradict or act against the legitimate struggles of other oppressed groups for liberation. But neither will we allow ourselves to be used, as we have done in the past. We will not postpone our struggle for liberation any longer.

Our *proyecto histórico* relates to and shapes our articulation of *mujerista* biblical hermeneutics in four concrete ways. First, theology, including biblical exegesis, is for us a praxis. The study and interpretation of scripture by Hispanic women are a revolutionary act, for neither our churches nor the academy considers us capable of doing it or considers that we have something to contribute in this field. Therefore, doing biblical exegesis is a way of claiming our right to think, to know critically—it is an element in our self-definition. We must also insist on theology, biblical exegesis included, as a communal task. The values and needs of the community must play a central role in *mujerista* biblical hermeneutics, and the only way to make sure this is so is by doing theology as a community of faith and struggle.[23]

The second way is best illustrated by the example of three women. Talking to Maria a few years ago, I found out that she attends a Protestant church. But she also had her daughter baptized in the Catholic Church, because, "I'm still a Catholic." Margarita is a Catholic who goes to Mass weekly. "But I also go to other churches with my friends," she adds. Doña Inés was a stalwart member of a Lutheran church. Her pastor visited her on her deathbed. Doña Inés asked the pastor to pray with her, and then, in an almost inaudible voice, she prayed, *"Dios te salve, María,"* a Roman Catholic prayer to Mary that Doña Inés had learned when she was small.

These and other Hispanic women's functional religious pluralism, "grassroots ecumenism," moves beyond traditional doctrinal purity, embraces diversity, and emerges as a religious solidarity that becomes a source of motivation and strategies in our daily struggles.[24] The amplification and extension of this experience of ecumenism among Hispanic women are an intentional element of our *proyecto histórico*. For this to happen, we all have to overcome the prejudices we have against Hispanics of different faith traditions; we have to stop discriminating against one another because of race, nation of origin, and economic status.

A third element of our *proyecto histórico* is linked to the previous one: reconstituting church structures. If we are to live into our preferred future we have to demand that our churches give concrete and obvious witness not only by what they say but also by the kind of institutions they are. Most of the institutional structures of our churches respond mainly to the exigencies of the status quo instead of effectively serving the community of faith. Specifically there are two elements which we insist must change. One is the hierarchical self-understanding of our churches that is reflected in the way the ministers of the churches are organized, in how they relate to the laity, in the churches' understanding of truth, relationship, and "fullness of being." The other element that has to be changed concerns the privileges the churches have and what they do with them. Churches must admit having these privileges, enjoying them, and benefiting from them. Those who benefit from these privileges should be accountable to the community for how they use them.[25] Hierarchical understandings and structures as well as ecclesiastical privileges are at the heart of elitism. These are the greatest temptations that churches have yielded to historically. Hispanic women have suffered too much and too long because of elitism not to demand its elimination from our preferred future.

A fourth element to consider as we struggle to live into our preferred future has to do with the social-political-economic reality in which we live. The particularities of this reality are beyond the scope of this article, but we need at least to enumerate the main ones. First, we reject a split between the personal and the political because moral agency requires us to take responsibility for social as well as for interpersonal life. Second, social theories used to explain and construct society must respect the self-determination of the person—person being always understood as a human being in relation to a community. Third, an analysis and redefinition of power are essential if we are to participate in the development of a just society. Fourth, moral criteria for evaluating public policy have to include in a prominent way the understanding of liberation and the right of all groups to struggle to achieve liberation. Fifth, achieving the common good must be the central goal of societal structures, institutions, and policies. By common good we understand at the very least a society in which all have access to what they need to achieve dignity and meaning in life as members of a community to which they are accountable. To assure this we need, among other things, a national commitment to full employment and an adequate minimum wage; redistribution of wealth through redistributive inheritance and wealth taxes; comparable remuneration for comparable work regardless of sex, sexual preference, race/ethnicity, age, etc.; economic democracy that would transform an economy controlled by a few to the economy of a participatory community; health care— particular emphasis being needed on preventive health care—available to all; changes in the economics of the family that will encourage more "symmetrical marriages, allow a better balance between family and work for both men and women, and make parenting a less difficult and impoverishing act for single parents," the majority of whom are women;[26] access to political office for Hispanic women and men so as to ensure adequate representation of our community; restructuring of the educational system so that our children and all those interested can study Hispanic culture and Spanish; restructuring the financing of public education so that its quality does not depend on the economics of those who live in the neighborhood served by a given school but is the responsibility of the whole community of that area, region, or state.

Mujerista biblical hermeneutics, our biblical interpretation, has as its goal the survival—the liberation—of Hispanic women. Therefore, our biblical interpretation, appropriation, and usage are tools in our struggle for survival. We have to be clear that for us Latinas, as members of a community engaged in a process of conscientization, committed to enhancing our moral agency, and claiming our right to be agents of our own history, the final word on the interpretation, appropriation, and use of the Bible in our struggle for survival and liberation is ours. If not, the Bible can indeed become or continue to be a weapon in the hands of those who benefit from the oppression of Hispanic women.[27]

NOTES

1. Words of a Cuban woman living in Miami who considers her way of life "the most Christian she can be." Cited in Ada María Isasi-Díaz and Yolanda Tarango, *Hispanic Women: Prophetic Voice in the Church* (Minneapolis: Fortress Press, 1992), 27–28.

2. There is no agreement among Hispanic/Latina women which of these appellatives to use. Among ourselves we use neither of them, referring to ourselves according to our or our ancestors' country of origin: Cuban, Chicana, Puerto Rican. In this article I will take turns using Hispanic and Latina.

3. See my article "The Bible and *Mujerista* Theology," in *Lift Every Voice: Constructing Christian Theologies from the Underside,* ed. Susan Brooks Thistlethwaite and Mary Potter Engel (San Francisco: Harper & Row, 1990), 261–69; also Isasi-Díaz and Tarango, *Hispanic Women.*

4. Because of the centrality of *mestizaje* to our self-understanding and the negative connotation ascribed to the term "syncretism," we now use *"mestizo* Christianity" to refer to Christianity as practiced by Hispanic women.

5. In 1986 the Religion Gallup Poll found that 19 percent of Hispanics identify themselves as Protestants. Using data gathered by the University of Chicago's National Opinion Research Center, sociologist Andrew Greeley concluded in 1988 that about 23 percent of all Hispanics were Protestants and that approximately sixty thousand Hispanics join Protestant denominations every year. See Roberto Suro, "Switch by Hispanic Catholics Changes Face of U.S. Religion," *The New York Times,* May 14, 1989.

6. It is my experience that even those Latinas who claim the Bible as the starting point of their theology in reality use *their* reading of the Bible, obviously influenced by their experiences, as the basis of their theological enterprise.

7. As a *mujerista* theologian I am an insider/outsider: an insider because I am a Hispanic woman; an outsider because of my formal education and economic status. This sense of insider/outsider is reflected in what could be considered an inconsistent use of "I/we/they/my/our/their" throughout this article.

8. Given that for the majority of Latinas this is a "first" moment in using the Bible, stressing that we accept as authoritative only biblical texts that are liberative to us, we hope will be an effective guide for Hispanic women. We recognize that it will be a long time before our refusal to accept oppressive parts of the Bible as "the word of God" is heard by those who use it to control us. But using the Bible to enhance the moral agency of Latinas will certainly weaken its power as an oppressive tool.

9. We use "kin-dom" instead of "kingdom" because the latter is obviously a sexist word that presumes that God is male; second, the concept of kingdom is both hierarchical and elitist—that is why we do not use "reign." "Kin-dom" makes it clear that when the fullness of God becomes a reality, we will all be sisters and brothers—kin to each other.

10. This element of orality is present also in the African-American community. See Vincent Wimbush, "The Biblical Historical Study as Liberation: Toward an Afro-Christian Hermeneutics," in *African American Religious Studies: An Interdisciplinary Anthology,* ed. Gayraud Wilmore (Durham, NC: Duke University Press, 1989), 140–54. Illiteracy is not necessarily the main reason for Hispanic women not reading the Bible. See my article in *Lift Every Voice,* especially pp. 263–65; see also Isasi-Díaz and Tarango, *Hispanic Women,* 67–70.

11. Since whenever I relate events like this one, non-Hispanics always seem to take for

granted that I am talking about a Latina who has little formal education, let me say that the speaker is a professor and has a Ph.D. in literature from a reputable university in the United States.

12. For an important explanation of this point, see María Lugones, "Playfulness, 'World'-Travelling, and Loving Perception," *Hypatia* 2/2 (Summer 1987): 3–19.

13. Though reader-response theories have helped us understand and explain how we relate to the text, they do not do so fully. In reader-response theories the text is central, or at least the person is always seen in relation to the text. In our appropriation of biblical stories the text disappears as an element per se leaving only some of its elements present but always mediated through the need and usage of Hispanic women. For an overview of reader-response theories, see Jane P. Tompkins, *Reader-Response Criticism* (Baltimore: John Hopkins University Press, 1980).

14. My mother's understanding that to struggle is to live, *la vida es la lucha,* expresses this sense of ongoing resistance as a good and effective strategy in our struggle.

15. On this subject, see Sharon Welch, *A Feminist Ethic of Risk* (Minneapolis: Fortress Press, 1990), 74–81.

16. To the accusation that this places us in the neo-orthodox ranks, we answer that Hispanic women have not been part of the "modern experiment"; that the kind of belief in the divine that for the enlightened, scientific mind signifies lack of autonomous, critical, rational thought, for us is a concrete experience that we can use as a key element in the struggle for liberation. See Christine Gudorf, "Liberation Theology's Use of Scripture: A Response to First World Critics," in *Interpretation* (January 1987): 12–13.

17. For a thorough explanation of the relationship between liberation and salvation, see Gustavo Gutiérrez, *A Theology of Liberation* (Maryknoll, NY: Orbis, 1988), 83–105. See Isasi-Díaz and Tarango, *Hispanic Women;* see also Ada María Isasi-Díaz, *En la Lucha: A Hispanic Women's Liberation Theology* (Minneapolis: Fortress Press, 1993).

18. Mainline Protestant Latinas use the Bible much more than do Catholic Latinas, but following the tradition of mainline Protestant churches, their approach to the Bible is not a fundamentalist one.

19. I believe dialogue among Hispanic women who interpret, appropriate, and use the Bible in very different ways is possible if we are able to meet without the interference of priests and pastors. This has been my experience, necessarily limited.

20. For a fuller discussion of conscientization, see Isasi-Díaz and Tarango, *Hispanic Women,* 94–110. For a different but not contradictory understanding, see Justo González, *Mañana: Christian Theology from a Hispanic Perspective* (Nashville: Abingdon Press, 1990), 75–87.

21. Juan Luis Segundo, *The Liberation of Theology* (Maryknoll, NY: Orbis, 1982), 121.

22. Charles Curran, *Catholic Moral Theology in Dialogue* (Notre Dame, IN: Fides, 1972), 70.

23. For what "doing theology," including biblical exegesis, in community looks like, see Isasi-Díaz and Tarango, *Hispanic Women,* particularly chapter 5.

24. For another perspective on ecumenism from a Hispanic viewpoint, see González, *Mañana,* 55–74; also the foreword to that book written by Virgilio Elizondo.

25. For the task of those who have privileges, see Ada María Isasi-Díaz, "Solidarity: Love of Neighbor in the 1980s," in *Lift Every Voice,* ed. Thistlethwaite and Engel, 31–39.

26. Teresa L. Amott and Julie A. Matthaei, *Race, Gender & Work* (Boston: South End Press, 1991), 346–48.

27. I am most grateful to Angela Bauer for her scholarly critique of this paper, to Ann

Patrick Ware whose giftedness as an editor helps me keep my Cuban flavor when I write in English, and to Yolanda Tarango, who is a central part of the "we" in this paper.

RECOMMENDED READINGS

Cavalcanti, Tereza. "The Prophetic Ministry of Women in the Hebrew Bible." In *Through Her Eyes: Women's Theology from Latin America,* edited by Elsa Tamez, 118–139. Maryknoll, NY: Orbis, 1989.

González, Justo. *Mañana: Christian Theology from a Hispanic Perspective.* Nashville: Abingdon, 1990.

Isasi-Díaz, Ada María. "The Bible and Mujerista Theology." In *Lift Every Voice: Constructing Christian Theologies from the Underside,* edited by Susan Brooks Thistlethwaite and Mary Potter Engel, 261–269. San Francisco: Harper & Row, 1990.

———. *En La Lucha: A Hispanic Women's Liberation Theology.* Minneapolis: Fortress Press, 1993.

Isasi-Díaz, Ada María, and Yolanda Tarango. *Hispanic Women: Prophetic Voice in the Church.* Minneapolis: Fortress Press, 1992.

Mestres, Carlos. *Defenseless Flower: A New Reading of the Bible.* Maryknoll, NY: Orbis, 1989.

Tamez, Elsa. "Women's Rereading of the Bible." In *With Passion and Compassion,* edited by Virginia Fabella, M.M., and Mercy Amba Oduyoye, 173–180. Maryknoll, NY: Orbis, 1988.

PART TWO

Changing Patriarchal Blueprints: Creating Feminist Frames of Meaning

7

❖ Racism and Ethnocentrism
  in Feminist Biblical Interpretation

KWOK PUI-LAN ♦

THE BIBLE EMERGED from the rich cultures of different races and peoples living in Palestine, Mesopotamia, Africa, and the Mediterranean world. In the history of the Christian church, the Bible has largely been interpreted from a white, male, and clerical perspective. As a result, the subtleties of the historical encounter between different cultures, the politics of racial relations, and the hidden voices of women in the biblical account were either overlooked or interpreted from a very biased standpoint. The Bible has been used to legitimize racism, sexism, and classism, as well as to condone colonialism and cultural imperialism.

This chapter examines the related issues of racism and ethnocentrism in feminist biblical interpretation. The questions of race and ethnic identity both in the diverse biblical accounts and in the politics of interpretation will be explored from a Third World women's perspective. The aim is to clarify how the Bible has been constantly used to oppress women, especially Third World women and minority women in the First World, and to demonstrate how these marginalized women can help to recover the liberating potential of the Bible for the salvation of all.

I would like to present ten theses which will help us to address racism and ethnocentrism in biblical interpretation. These theses were developed from a careful and attentive reading of the writings of Third World and African-American female theologians, biblical scholars, and women in the church. My observations will be chiefly based on my experience as an Asian Christian theologian, drawing also on insights from conversations with women of color in professional gatherings, in the ecumenical movement, and in the Ecumenical Association of Third World Theologians.

*Thesis 1:   The politics of biblical authority must be carefully exam-
ined from a feminist liberational perspective.*

The Bible has been understood as one of the most important foundations
of faith for the Christian church. The authority of the Bible is based on
the belief that it is the revealed Word of God. During the missionary era,
the Bible was introduced to peoples around the globe at the same time
as their lands were taken from them. This was understood to be "the white
man's burden" for the "uncivilized heathens." The centuries of colonial conquest of peoples and cultures and the recent Gulf War make it absolutely
clear that such naïve understanding of the Bible and biblical faith is fatal
to peaceful coexistence of people of different faiths.

The Bible is doubly problematic for Third World women because it has
been used not only against their cultures but also against women. In places
such as the Philippines and African societies such as Ghana, the biblical
religion introduced by the colonizers challenged indigenous beliefs and
communal living in which women enjoyed greater status and freedom. In
other East Asian societies, such as China and Korea, the androcentric
elements of the Bible were used to reinforce patriarchy in church and society.

Third World women theologians have begun to reexamine the issue of
biblical authority from their own reality. Teresa Okure, a biblical scholar
from Nigeria, tries to distinguish timely truth in the Bible from its cultural
underpinnings. She writes: "rereading the Bible as a patriarchal book
demands that sustained efforts be made to discern between the divine and
the human elements in it. For while the former embodies timeless truth
for our salvation, the latter inculcates practices that are socioculturally conditioned, hence inapplicable universally."[1] Elsa Tamez, who teaches theology
in Costa Rica, affirms that the central message is essentially liberating
although there are antifemale texts in the Bible. She goes a step further
than Okure in saying that "a time has come to acknowledge that those
biblical texts that reflect patriarchal culture and proclaim women's inferiority
and their submission to men are not normative; neither are those texts that
legitimize slavery normative."[2]

Mine is the most radical view. I grew up in the nonbiblical culture of
Asia, and I do not believe that we can abstractly speak about the divine
elements or the central message of the Bible without historical specificity.
I am also aware that the concept of the "authority of the Bible" does not
have any meaning or might even sound offensive to the majority of Asians
who are non-Christians. For me, the critical principle lies not in the Bible
itself, but "in the community of women and men who read the Bible and

who through their dialogical imagination appropriate it for their own libera-tion."[3] The authority of the text and canon of the Bible in itself must be thoroughly demystified and deconstructed so that they cannot be con-tinuously used against marginalized women.

Thesis 2: *The historical-critical method of interpretation, which grew out of a Eurocentric culture, must be critically judged from the experiences of local interpretive communities.*

The historical-critical method of biblical interpretation emerged from a particular religious and intellectual milieu in Europe. On the one hand, there was a religious need after the Enlightenment to examine and critique the doctrinal use of the Bible by the church. On the other hand, biblical scholars lived in an intellectual climate with heightened historical con-sciousness. They shared a modern concept of history that was "the ideo-logical product of an emergent bourgeois liberal society."[4] The historical-critical method, considered to be fact-finding and value-free, has been taken as the standard for biblical scholarship.

The historical-critical method is perhaps the most suitable praxis for white, male, and middle-class academics, because they alone can afford to be "impartial," which literally means "non-committed." Oppressed women and men of all colors find that the historical-critical method alone cannot help them to address the burning questions they face. Illiterate women in the Third World churches care more about daily survival than any critical method. For Third World and African-American biblical scholars, the method is helpful, yet too limiting, because it does not allow certain ques-tions to be raised or certain perspectives to be entertained.[5] Renita J. Weems, an African-American scholar of the Hebrew Scriptures, powerfully points out that the negative result of the historical-critical method has been "to undermine marginalized reading communities by insisting that their ques-tions and experiences are superfluous to Scripture and their interpretations illegitimate, because of their failure to remain objective."[6] The "aural hermeneutic" of African-American women, about which Weems speaks, will have no place in this method; the Gospel in Solentiname as told by the peasants of Nicaragua will be taken as interesting "stories" but not biblical commentaries.[7]

Many Asian and indigenous Christians live in cultures that understand history and historiography in a totally different way. The Eurocentric positivist approach must not be taken as the sole norm for historical quest. The Bible is too important to be subjected to *only* one norm or model of interpretation. The fruits of the historical-critical method must be tested and challenged by the local religious communities who are daily reading the Bible anew and who have tried to weave their own stories and struggles with the biblical narratives.

Thesis 3:   It is not enough to tell the history of how white women have developed a feminist critique of the Bible, without simultaneously telling the parallel story of women of color. Our common heritage is our shared power.

Many women trace the development of a feminist critique of the Bible to the nineteenth century, when the first wave of feminism in America raised the consciousness of women sitting in the pew. They recount the courageous remarks of Sarah Moore Grimké and hail the publication of *The Woman's Bible* by Elizabeth Cady Stanton as a groundbreaking event. While the contribution of these white forerunners must not be forgotten, we should also remember that women of color at the same period also tried to look at the Bible through their darker eyes.

The story of how the grandmother of Howard Thurman, an ex-slave woman, rejected the white minister's interpretation of slavery is of critical importance for African-American women.[8] Similarly, Jarena Lee and Julia Foote, both preachers of the American Methodist Episcopal Church, challenged Paul's teachings that circumscribe women's roles. Jarena Lee's famous speech illustrates this very well:

> For as unseemly as it may appear now-a-days for a woman to preach, it should be remembered that nothing is impossible with God. And why should it be thought impossible, heterodox, or improper for a woman to preach? seeing the Saviour died for the woman as well as the man. If man may preach, because the Saviour died for him, why not the woman? seeing he died for her also. Is he not a whole Saviour, instead of a half one?[9]

In nineteenth-century China, a Christian woman whose name has not been recorded by the missionary used a pin to cut out from her Bible Paul's teachings that wives should be submissive to their husbands. At the turn of the century, a medical doctor Zhang Zhujun, reportedly the first Chinese woman to preach from the pulpit, challenged Paul's prescription that women should keep silence in the church.[10] The stories of these and other women of color must be told and remembered so that our heritage of courageous women will be expanded to empower us in our present struggle.

Thesis 4: *Feminist interpretation of the Bible must take into serious consideration simultaneously the multiple oppression of women in terms of class, gender, and race.*

Feminist theorists have clearly demonstrated that women's experience is not determined by female biology alone but is largely shaped by powerful cultural and social forces. In other words, there is no such thing as "universal" women's experience. Patriarchy is experienced in varied ways according to different social and political situations. As Elisabeth Schüssler Fiorenza has rightly pointed out, patriarchy should not be construed as "a universal transcultural binary structure," but should be understood as "a historical political system of interlocking dominations."[11]

Women in biblical times were shaped by their particular race, class, and social location, just as are women today. Biblical women who were at the lowest stratum of society helped us to understand the multiple oppression of women in a most vivid way. The story of Hagar, the Egyptian slave girl of Abram and Sarai, has been taken as paradigmatic to show the intersection of racism, classism, and sexism by women of color in different continents.

In the United States, where slavery was abolished only in the mid-nineteenth century, the story of Hagar is especially poignant and relevant. Hagar was given by her mistress as a concubine to her husband; her body was sexually exploited, and she was humiliated and ridiculed by her mistress. For African-American women, whose ancestors were slaves and whose mothers and relatives have worked as domestics, the story of Hagar is just too familiar. "It is a story that also exposes the many hidden scars and ugly memories of the history of relationships between racial ethnic and white women in America."[12]

For Latin American women, Hagar is "the woman who complicated the history of salvation." Elsa Tamez observes that people tend to focus on Deborah, Esther, Sarai, and Mary when speaking about women in the Bible; seldom do they talk about Hagar, who is a "negative model." Latin American women see important parallels in the Hagar story: her extreme poverty caused her to be sold into slavery; she struggled as a single mother abandoned by her husband; and powerful people around her tried to erase her from historical memory. What is important, according to Tamez, is that God instilled hope in her, and it was this slave woman who gave God a name, the God who sees (Gen 16:13).[13]

For African women, the Hagar story is read from a context where polygamy still exists. Hagar, a foreigner and a slave, was not given the full status of a wife in Hebrew society because she was not eligible. Both Hagar and Sarai were valued only as "containers" of Abram's seed in their society. For Musimbi R. A. Kanyoro of Kenya, Sarai "sees Hagar as an instrument for meeting her own needs—in today's idiom, one may say a disposable instrument. It is an issue of women struggling against each other in order to fulfill what society has designed for them."[14] For Anne Nasimiyu-Wasike, the stories of polygamous marriages in the Hebrew Scriptures bring out "the consequences of polygamous family life—for example, rivalries, jealousies, envies, favoritism, quarrels over inheritance, succession feuds, injustices, hatred, and murders. These realities are the experiences of African polygamous families as well."[15]

As an Asian, what interests me most in the Hagar story is how she conducted her life as she struggled to survive in a Hebrew family. Philo observed that Hagar was "an Egyptian by birth, but a Hebrew by her rule of life" (*De Abrahamo* 251).[16] The removal of Hagar's own cultural identity and the imposition of a new one speak not only to people under slavery but also to the vast number of Third World people living for centuries under the threats of colonial and neocolonial powers.

From the above discussion, it seems that African-American women focus on Hagar as a slave woman, the Latin Americans stress that she was poor, the Africans underscore the fate of Hagar in polygamy, and Asians emphasize the loss of cultural identity. Each group observes a certain analogy between the oppression of Hagar and their own situation. Third World women and minority women who are under multiple oppression help us to look at the Bible from the underside, because as the contemporary oppressed they are more likely to "make the analogy between their own experience and similar social relationships reproduced in the biblical texts."[17]

Thesis 5:   *Anti-Semitism in feminist interpretation must be condemned and the Hebrew Scriptures must be interpreted in solidarity with Jewish feminists.*

The greatest irony in the history of biblical interpretation is that the Hebrew Scriptures have been appropriated as the Old Testament of the Christians and used against the Jews. The Holocaust should forever remind us how anti-Semitism led to the genocide of the Jews, the horrible human tragedy in the twentieth century. Christian feminists must honestly deal with the ethical issue of how to appropriate Jewish myths, stories, and scriptures, without repeating the mistakes of the past. Judith Plaskow, a Jewish feminist theologian, has cautioned Christians to guard against anti-Semitic prejudices in their interpretation of the life and significance of Jesus.[18]

Asian Christians have always been aware that the Hebrew Scriptures grew out of a culture fundamentally different from their own. The Asians have their religious classics, but they do not understand religious writings as Torah (sacred teaching representing divine revelation) as the Jews do. For me, the Hebrew Scriptures represent one story of the slaves' struggle for justice in Egypt, the tension in building a just and caring community, the fight for survival of refugees in Babylon, and the continual struggles of small ethnic minorities living among powerful nations. Instead of treating these writings as revelation from God, I understand them to be one significant religious resource of humankind which illuminates human capacity to love, to struggle, to repent, and to cry in joy.

Plaskow, in *Standing Again at Sinai,* has called for a reinterpretation of the concept of Torah, so that it would not be used as an androcentric text, shaping the sacred memory of the Jewish people. The Torah should be expanded, Plaskow says, so that it can include Jewish women's words, teachings, and history. Her understanding of the Torah as "the partial record of the 'Godwrestling' of part of the Jewish people"[19] is very liberating and helpful not only for Jews but for Christians as well. It allows room for Christian feminists to discuss and critique patriarchal elements of the Hebrew Scriptures, without being labeled as "anti-Semitic." But this feminist critique must be done in a spirit of solidarity with Jewish feminists, and not in spite of them.

Thesis 6:   The Bible should not be used to oppress or discriminate against any race or ethnic group.

Besides oppressing the Jews, the Bible has been used to discriminate against other races and ethnic groups. The exclusion of "the Other" is closely connected to the concept of election. According to Cain Hope Felder, an African-American biblical scholar, the explicit concept of Yahweh's preference for Israel over other nations and peoples developed relatively late. It became a religious ideology only in the period of Deuteronomic history toward the end of the seventh century B.C.E. Even so, scholars debated whether one should look at the election of Israel strictly from a racial and ethnic point of view or as a symbol of "universalism" which emphasizes Israel's role as service to the nations.[20]

Although there might be nuanced meanings in the Jewish understanding of election, Christians have taken over this concept indiscriminately to oppress the Jews, the blacks, and all Gentiles. The Jews, who are blamed for the death of Jesus, are said to have lost their status as a chosen people, which is taken over by the Christians. The blacks are discriminated against specifically because of their skin color. Such discrimination is traced back to the ancient myth of the curse of Ham and God's blessing of his brothers. The Gentiles are despised because they worship other gods and it is assumed that, unless they are brought into the Christian fold, they have no hope of salvation. These discriminations are rooted in the politics of "the Other," but there are also differences in their historical and cultural specificities.

African-American scholars have identified four principal ways in which the Bible has been used against the black people. First, the curse of Ham has been used as a religious ideology to justify the belief that blacks are innately and permanently inferior. Treating black women and men as chattel was accepted as the necessary fulfillment of the curse.[21] Second, there is the politics of omission, which minimizes the significance of black presence in the Bible. For example, Clarice J. Martin has documented how the ethnicity of the Ethiopian convert (Acts 8:26–40) as a black-skinned person has been played down by exegetes.[22] Third, there is an anachronistic tendency to read back into the Bible racial relationships as we experience them in modern times. The Bible, in fact, contains many favorable references to black people, such as the allusion to the Ethiopian king Tirhakah, who, it had been hoped, would save the Israelites from the Assyrians.[23] Fourth, the existence of slavery in biblical times was used as a rationalization for modern slavery. The fact that neither Jesus nor Paul opposed slavery openly was used by white people to legitimize the enslavement of other races.

The Bible has also been used against the Gentiles who stand outside the Jewish and Christian traditions. The condemnation of the cultures, religions, and peoples in Canaan can be seen as a forerunner of discrimination against all peoples who do not share the beliefs of Jews or Christians. The Canaanites were portrayed as worshiping idols, as promiscuous, and as having a lower moral standard. The conquest of Canaan has often been seen from the perspective of the chosen people of Israel. Recently, Naim Stifan Ateek, an Arab Palestinian Christian, has raised the pointed question: "How can the Old Testament be the Word of God in light of the Palestinian Christians' experience with its use to support Zionism?"[24] Similarly, Native Americans also identify with the Canaanites, the people who already lived in the promised land. Robert Allen Warrior, a member of the Osage Nation of the American Indians, charges that even those articulating theologies of liberation often overlooked the Canaanite side, especially those stories that "describe Yahweh's command to mercilessly annihilate the indigenous population."[25] He further argues that "the Canaanites should be at the center of Christian theological reflection and political action. They are the last remaining ignored voice in the text, except perhaps for the land itself."[26]

Thesis 7:   *The Bible is the product of complex interaction between many different cultures. Discovering the cultural dynamics shaping the biblical account opens new horizons to see how the Bible functions cross-culturally today.*

The Jews and the early Christians lived among neighbors with different languages, cultural codes, thought patterns, and religious practices. The encounter between cultures in the Bible was never one-dimensional. It was often very complex and subtle, involving not only rejection and resistance but negotiation and adaptation as well. In the Hebrew Scriptures, the Jews were severely warned against interracial marriages and adopting the cults and practices in Canaan. Yet these warnings were repeatedly overlooked, indicating that it was often difficult to uphold one's cultural and religious purity in a pluralistic world.

In the New Testament, the cross-cultural encounter was even more complicated, as Christianity emerged from Judaism to live in the Hellenistic world. According to Lamin Sanneh, this historical development involved a dual process of relativization of the Judaic roots, and the destigmatization of Gentile culture as a "natural extension of the life of the new religion."[27] A better understanding of this process will enable Third World Christians to grapple with the issues surrounding the process of translating the gospel message, religious syncretism, and the function of Christian symbolism in a different cultural milieu.

Given this complex background, the stories of Jesus meeting Gentile women in the Gospels are particularly illuminating. I shall discuss Jesus' encounter with the Syrophoenician woman (Mark 7:24-30) as an example. The story has often been symbolically interpreted as the admission of the Gentiles to the Christian church. But a study of the cultural "worlds" in the border region between Tyre and Galilee reveals more subtle dynamics at work. According to Gerd Theissen, the Syrophoenician woman was a hellenized Phoenician who belonged to the Greek-speaking upper class. In the story, she ran into a Galilee prophet in the rural territory belonging to Tyre.[28] The meeting was between two persons of different cultures, religions, classes, and sexes.

Biblical scholars in the past have emphasized the faith of the Gentile woman which led to the healing of her daughter. For Theissen, the miracle did not "consist in healing someone far away, but in the overcoming of an equally divisive distance: the prejudice-based distance between nations and cultures." He credits the woman with the ability to break through walls that divided peoples.[29] Third World women and minority women interpret this story not from a Christocentric perspective but from the point of view that it was a Gentile woman who dared to challenge Jesus. Rita Nakashima Brock, a Japanese-American theologian, points out that the Syrophoenician woman shatters Jesus' view of religious exclusivity: "It is the courageous work of the 'other' that shatters his view of power and privilege. That courage challenges the structures of benign paternalism that would give Jesus the power from above to fix the power inequities involved."[30]

While the Syrophoenician woman belonged to the elite urban class which exploited the Galilee hinterland, she was also despised by the Jews and oppressed as a woman. She took her Gentile and female identity seriously when she challenged Jesus. Women in the Third World must take their identities seriously too when appropriating the Bible in a cross-cultural context.

Thesis 8:   The Bible must also be read from the perspective of other faith traditions. Multifaith hermeneutics looks at ourselves as others see us, so that we may be able to see ourselves more clearly.

Asian Christians live in a continent populated by adherents of all major historical religions of humankind. For them, the central hermeneutical question is how to interpret the Bible to people of other faith traditions. In our modern world, religious pluralism is not just a phenomenon in Asia, but increasingly in many parts of the world. The Bible is not just read by Christians. Biblical scholarship is not meant for Christians only, but must be accountable to the wider human family. The development of a multifaith hermeneutics must be given more serious attention.[31]

The first step toward a multifaith hermeneutics is to recognize that the majority of the world's population live in a cultural world not shaped by the biblical vision. Asia alone comprises more than half of the world's population, and the Christian population makes up less than three percent. People of other faiths have their own religious practices and sacred writings. The Confucian classics have been read and reread for more than two thousand years by the Chinese; the *Bhagavad Gita* is revered as the "supreme book for the knowledge of Truth"[32] by the Indians. While the issues of the authority and the canon of the Bible might be crucial for Christians, they seem to be parochial for the vast majority of humankind.

Living in our multifaith context, the Bible can be studied in comparison with other sacred writings to bring out the common themes and divergent emphases. Kim Sang Hae, a Korean Catholic nun, has compared the sages in the Confucian tradition to the wise men in the Hebrew Scriptures. Others have compared the *Bhagavad Gita* with the New Testament and studied the wisdom of the Hebrew Scriptures in the context of world religions.[33] Apart from these more descriptive comparisons, the Bible can also be interpreted from another religious perspective. Seiichi Yagi, a Japanese Buddhist, has examined the words of Jesus from a Buddhist perspective.[34] Gandhi has also helped us to look at the Bible through the eyes of his own Hindu spirituality.

The most difficult task for multifaith hermeneutics is how to reinterpret the Bible after seeing it through the lens of other faith traditions. It requires intellectual humility and radical openness to divine disclosure in other faiths and cultures. This *kenosis* and inclusivity demand radical changes in biblical scholarship, which cannot be carried out in the same old manner, as if we have learned nothing from decades of religious dialogue. Biblical scholars are burying their heads in the sand if they continue to study the Bible as if it were a book of the past, without bringing out its potential to address contemporary issues. On the other hand, it must be recognized that the insights and wisdom found in the Bible are but one religious resource of humankind, and they must be shared, tested, and corrected in the wider community of the human family.

Thesis 9:   Women under multiple oppression have multiple identities, and they help us to interpret the Bible in a multidimensional way.

Third World women and minority women emphasize that they have multiple and simultaneous identities as women under multiple oppression. According to Renita J. Weems, African-American women cannot afford to read the Bible simply with the eyes of an "oppressed" man, but have to negotiate their multiple identities when reading.[35] The same is true for Third World women.

From her experience as an Asian American, Rita Nakashima Brock describes a person with multiple identities as having the capacity to search for multiple voices that affirm complex cultural meanings and identities, thereby creating a fluid, multilayered self. This fluid self has a "tribal consciousness" which is "a moving center, a flexible observer that listens, reflects, and chooses in a constantly shifting attunement to experiences and relation-ships." It is able to hold all the voices and examine each one. It seeks to construct meaning in a fragmented world and to experiment with different voices and try out versions of the stories.[36]

We have already seen how these multiple identities are brought to bear on the interpretation of the Hagar story. Other examples elucidate the com-plexities involved when one identity is at odds with another when reading the Bible. The Syrophoenician woman would be a good model for Gentile Christian women because she dared to challenge the Jewish identity of Jesus. But she also belonged to the elite class. Ruth, the Moabite daughter-in-law of Naomi, could be considered a woman of great faith. Yet she entered into a dubious relationship with Boaz, which is quite unimaginable accord-ing to Asian sensibilities.

The multiple identities of women enable them to maintain a critical distance when reading the Bible. As oppressed women, they interpret the Bible differently from oppressed men. For example, in her study of the household codes in the New Testament, Clarice J. Martin asks "Why is the African American interpretative tradition marked by a forceful critique and rejection of a literalist interpretation of the slave regulations in the *Haustafeln,* but not marked by an equally passionate critique and rejec-tion of a literalist interpretation regarding the subordination of women to men in the *Haustafeln?*"[37] In Africa, there are men who try to keep the polygamous tradition as "the touchstone of genuine indigenization" of Christianity into Africa. But many African women strongly object to polygamy based on their rereading of the biblical stories on polygamous marriages.[38]

The Bible itself is a document of multiplicity and plurality. Women with multiple identities appropriate it in a multidimensional and multilayered way. It is like many mirrors with varied sizes and surfaces assembled at angles to one another, creating and reflecting images in different directions and proportions. There is infinite potential in such fascinating reading and rereading.

Thesis 10:   Racism and ethnocentrism are issues for all biblical scholars and not for Third World women or minority women only. The politics of "difference" in biblical hermeneutics must be examined.

People sometimes ask African-American women why they always dwell on the story of Hagar and do not talk about other women in the Bible, such as Mary, the mother of Jesus.[39] Similarly, the question can be posed to pagan converts to Christianity why they always talk about the Syrophoenician woman or the Samaritan woman at the well. This is a catch-22 question. If you do not focus on these multiply-oppressed women, you risk being accused of missing your "unique" contribution to biblical hermeneutics. If you focus on slave and Gentile women, people wonder whether your biblical scholarship is too narrow in scope.

Third World women and minority women focus on the multiple oppression of women in the Bible because these stories speak to their reality and shed light on their existence. But their concern is not just limited to the texts on women or on marginalized women in particular. They seek to use these specific texts to uncover the interlocking oppression of racism, classism, and sexism in the past and in the present, thereby helping all of us to liberate ourselves from bondage. They wish to develop a biblical hermeneutics that addresses the liberation of all peoples, and not women alone. This concern should be shared by all biblical scholars, and men and women reading the Bible for insights. Everyone should participate in the search for a liberating hermeneutics from one's particular social and historical location, while listening to the voices of others. It is morally dubious and intellectually dishonest to wait until the most oppressed women speak out and then appropriate their ideas and insights for one's own consumption.

Studying the Bible with integrity is a radical demand. Many Third World Christians, both women and men, gave up their lives, suffered under torture, or spent years in jail while seeking to live out what the Bible has taught them. Their question for all of us is, What price have you paid in your study of the Bible?

NOTES

1. Teresa Okure, "Women in the Bible," in *With Passion and Compassion: Third World Women Doing Theology,* ed. Virginia Fabella and Mercy Amba Oduyoye (Maryknoll, NY: Orbis, 1988), 56.

2. Elsa Tamez, "Women's Rereading of the Bible," in *With Passion and Compassion,* ed. Fabella and Oduyoye, 176.

3. Kwok Pui-lan, "Discovering the Bible in the Non-Biblical World," *Semeia* 47 (1989): 37.

4. Sheila Briggs, "Can an Enslaved God Liberate? Hermeneutical Reflections on Philippians 2:6–11," *Semeia* 47 (1989): 140.

5. See *Voices from the Margin: Interpreting the Bible in the Third World,* ed. R. S. Sugirtharajah (Maryknoll, NY: Orbis, 1991); and *Stony the Road We Trod: African American Biblical Interpretation,* ed. C. H. Felder (Minneapolis: Fortress, 1991). See also Vincent L. Wimbush, "Historical/Cultural Criticism as Liberation: A Proposal for an

African American Biblical Hermeneutic," *Semeia* 47 (1989): 43–55; and Elisabeth Schüssler Fiorenza, *Bread Not Stone: The Challenge of Feminist Biblical Interpretation* (Boston: Beacon Press, 1984), 128–36.

6. Renita J. Weems, "Reading *Her Way* through the Struggle: African American Women and the Bible," in *Stony the Road We Trod,* ed. Felder, 66.

7. Ibid.; and Ernesto Cardenal, *The Gospel in Solentiname,* 4 vols. (Maryknoll, NY: Orbis, 1976, 1982).

8. See Jacquelyn Grant, *White Women's Christ and Black Women's Jesus: Feminist Christology and Womanist Response* (Atlanta: Scholars Press, 1989), 211–12; and Weems, "Reading *Her Way,*" 61–62.

9. Jarena Lee, "The Life and Religious Experience of Jarena Lee," in *Sisters of the Spirit: Three Black Women's Autobiographies of the Nineteenth Century,* ed. William L. Andrews (Bloomington: Indiana University Press, 1986), 36, quoted in Clarice J. Martin, "The *Haustafeln* (Household Codes) in African American Biblical Interpretation: 'Free Slaves' and 'Subordinate Women,'" in *Stony the Road We Trod,* ed. Felder, 222–23.

10. See "The History of Ms. Zhang Zhujun," in *Jindai Zhongguo nüquan yundong shiliao* (Historical Materials on Modern Chinese Feminist Movement) (Taibei: Biographical Literature Publisher, 1975), 2:1380.

11. Elisabeth Schüssler Fiorenza, "The Politics of Otherness: Biblical Interpretation as a Critical Praxis for Liberation," in *The Future of Liberation Theology,* ed. M. H. Ellis and O. Maduro (Maryknoll, NY: Orbis, 1989), 316.

12. Renita J. Weems, "Do You See What I See? Diversity in Interpretation," *Church and Society* 81 (September/October 1991): 40.

13. Elsa Tamez, "The Woman Who Complicated the History of Salvation," in *New Eyes for Reading: Biblical and Theological Reflections by Women from the Third World,* ed. J. S. Pobee and B. von Wartenberg-Potter (Oak Park, IL: Meyer Stone Books, 1987), 5–17.

14. Musimbi R. A. Kanyoro, "Interpreting Old Testament Polygamy through African Eyes," in *The Will to Arise: Women, Tradition, and the Church in Africa,* ed. M. A. Oduyoye and M. R. A. Kanyoro (Maryknoll, NY: Orbis, 1992), 95.

15. Anne Nasimiyu-Wasike, "Polygamy: A Feminist Critique," in *The Will to Arise,* ed. Oduyoye and Kanyoro, 110.

16. As quoted in Gerd Theissen, *The Gospels in Context: Social and Political History in the Synoptic Tradition* (Minneapolis: Fortress, 1991), 69.

17. Briggs, "Can an Enslaved God Liberate?" 142. Her article has an excellent discussion on the use of analogy in historical reconstruction (pp. 139–42).

18. Judith Plaskow, "Blaming Jews for Inventing Patriarchy," *Lilith* 7 (1980): 12–13; see also chapter 8 in this volume.

19. Judith Plaskow, *Standing Again at Sinai: Judaism from a Feminist Perspective* (San Francisco: Harper SanFrancisco, 1990), 33.

20. Cain Hope Felder, "Race, Racism, and the Biblical Narratives," in *Stony the Road We Trod,* ed. Felder, 137–38.

21. Katie Geneva Cannon, "Slave Ideology and Biblical Interpretation," *Semeia* 47 (1989): 11-13.

22. Clarice J. Martin, "A Chamberlain's Journey and the Challenge of Interpretation for Liberation," *Semeia* 47 (1989): 105–35.

23. Felder, "Race, Racism, and the Biblical Narratives," 136–37. See also Charles B. Copher, "The Black Presence in the Old Testament," in *Stony the Road We Trod,* ed. Felder, 146–64.

24. Naim Stifan Ateek, "A Palestinian Perspective: The Bible and Liberation," in *Voices from the Margin,* ed. Sugirtharajah, 283.

25. Robert Allen Warrior, "A Native American Perspective: Canaanites, Cowboys, and Indians," in *Voices from the Margin,* ed. Sugirtharajah, 289.

26. Ibid., 293.

27. Lamin Sanneh, *Translating the Message: The Missionary Impact on Culture* (Maryknoll, NY: Orbis, 1989), 1.

28. Theissen, *Gospels in Context,* 68–72.

29. Ibid., 79–80. In his scholarly work *The Gospels in Context* Theissen focuses on how the Syrophoenician woman "restructures" the cynical image of a "dog" to overcome the barrier between Jesus and herself. Portraying the woman as persistent and loyal, he says, "she behaves like a 'devoted dog'" (p. 80). But in a sermon on the same passage, Theissen presents the woman as actively challenging Jesus' own prejudice. Thus he asks: "If even Jesus depends on someone else to rid him of prejudices, who wouldn't also be ready to help themselves get rid of prejudices?" (Theissen, "Dealing with Religious Prejudices: The Example of the Canaanite Woman," in *The Open Door: Variations on Biblical Themes* [Minneapolis: Fortress, 1991], 42). Why is this kind of wisdom suppressed in more scholarly work? What is at stake here?

30. Rita Nakashima Brock, *Journeys by Heart: A Christology of Erotic Power* (New York: Crossroad, 1988), 84.

31. The term "multifaith hermeneutics" is suggested by R. S. Sugirtharajah; see *Voices from the Margin,* 5.

32. C. F. Andrews, ed., *Mahatma Gandhi: His Own Story* (London: George Allen & Unwin, 1930), 31, quoted by R. S. Sugirtharajah, "Inter-Faith Hermeneutics: An Example and Some Implications," in *Voices from the Margin,* ed. Sugirtharajah, 352.

33. Ishanand Vempeny, *Krsna and Christ: In the Light of Some of the Fundamental Themes and Concepts of the Bhagavad Gita and the New Testament* (Pune: Ishvani Kendra, 1988); and John Eaton, *The Contemplative Face of the Old Testament in the Context of World Religions* (London: SCM Press, 1989).

34. Seiichi Yagi, "'I' in the Words of Jesus," in *The Myth of Christian Uniqueness,* ed. J. Hick and P. Knitter (Maryknoll, NY: Orbis, 1987), 117–34.

35. Weems, "Reading *Her Way,*" 71.

36. See Rita Nakashima Brock, "Dusting the Bible on the Floor: A Hermeneutics of Wisdom," chapter 4 in this volume.

37. Martin, "The *Haustafeln,*" 225.

38. Nasimiyu-Wasike, "Polygamy: A Feminist Critique," 114–15.

39. Weems, "Do You See What I See?" 28.

RECOMMENDED READINGS

Cardenal, Ernesto. *The Gospel in Solentiname.* 4 vols. Maryknoll, NY: Orbis, 1976–82.

Cannon, Katie G., and E. Schüssler Fiorenza, eds. *Interpretation for Liberation. Semeia* 47. Atlanta: Scholars Press, 1989.

Fabella, Virginia, and Mercy Amba Oduyoye, eds. *With Passion and Compassion: Third World Women Doing Theology.* Maryknoll, NY: Orbis, 1988.

——, and Sun Ai Lee Park, eds. *We Dare to Dream: Doing Theology as Asian Women.* Maryknoll, NY: Orbis, 1990.

Felder, Cain Hope, ed. *Stony the Road We Trod: African American Biblical Interpretation*. Minneapolis: Fortress, 1991.

Oduyoye, Mercy Amba, and Musimbi R. A. Kanyoro, eds. *The Will to Arise: Women, Tradition, and the Church in Africa*. Maryknoll, NY: Orbis, 1992.

Plaskow, Judith. *Standing Again at Sinai: Judaism from a Feminist Perspective*. San Francisco: Harper SanFrancisco, 1990.

Pobee, John S., and Bärbel von Wartenberg-Potter, eds. *New Eyes for Reading: Biblical and Theological Reflections by Women from the Third World*. Oak Park, IL: Meyer Stone Books, 1987.

Sugirtharajah, R. S., ed. *Voices from the Margin: Interpreting the Bible in the Third World*. Maryknoll, NY: Orbis, 1991.

Tamez, Elsa. *Bible of the Oppressed*. Maryknoll, NY: Orbis, 1982.

Weems, Renita J. *Just a Sister Away: A Womanist Vision of Women's Relationship in the Bible*. San Diego: LuraMedia, 1988.

❖ Anti-Judaism
in Feminist Christian Interpretation

JUDITH PLASKOW ❖

IN 1885, ELIZABETH CADY STANTON presented a series of resolutions to the Annual Convention of the National Woman Suffrage Association criticizing Christian theology for its teachings about women. Finding her wording too strong and pointed, the convention leadership substituted different language—language that, as Stanton put it, "hand[ed] over to the Jews what [she] had laid at the door of the Christians":

> WHEREAS, The dogmas incorporated *in religious creeds derived from Judaism* . . . *are contrary* to the law of God (as revealed in nature), and *to the precepts of Christ.* . . .
> *Resolved,* That we call on the Christian ministry . . . to teach and enforce the fundamental idea of creation, that man was made in the image of God male and female. . . . And, furthermore, we ask their recognition of the scriptural declaration that, *in the Christian religion, there is neither male nor female.* . . .[1]

While it was the intent of the convention committee to make Stanton's resolutions less controversial so that they would pass without dissent, some of the Jewish women at the meeting vigorously repudiated the criticisms of their tradition, precipitating the debate the committee had hoped to avoid.[2]

Whether or not this was the first time Christian feminists "hand[ed] over to the Jews" faults that could equally well be attributed to Christianity, the incident indicates that feminist anti-Judaism has a long history. The impulse to vindicate Christianity by laying its patriarchal elements at the feet of Judaism seems to have emerged along with Christian feminist interpretation and to have been given new currency and direction with the second wave of feminism. The hundredth anniversary of *The Woman's Bible* provides an excellent opportunity to examine the continuing failure of feminist thought to deal with the enduring legacy of Christian anti-Judaism.

FEMINISM AND CHRISTIAN ANTI-JUDAISM

Anti-Judaism in feminist interpretation signifies both a failure of feminism to include all women within its vision and an often unconscious appropriation of anti-Jewish themes and strategies that are as old as the New Testament itself. In *Beyond God the Father,* Mary Daly characterized the patriarchal ethic as the "failure to lay claim to that part of the psyche that is then projected onto 'the Other.'"[3] Defining women's oppression as the oldest and most fundamental form of oppression, Daly assumed that the liberation of women from male projections would lead to the disappearance of all other forms of domination. Recent studies of racism and nativism in the woman suffrage movement and recent critiques of feminist theory by racial/ethnic feminists make clear, however, that a single-issue focus on sexism and women's experience does not automatically encompass or address other forms of dominance.[4] On the contrary, in the absence of an explicit commitment to ending the multiple, interstructured forms of oppression that shape women's lives, feminist theory and institutions continue to support dominant racial, religious, class, and sexual perspectives.

Feminists are certainly not the first Christians to make use of anti-Jewish arguments in order to forward a particular agenda. Rather, feminist interpretation adds a new complication to a mode of projective discourse thoroughly embedded in Christian thought. The ancient, deeply rooted, and tenacious character of anti-Jewish themes in Christian writing has been extensively documented.[5] In fact, these themes enter into feminist thought largely through the mediation of popular works in Protestant biblical interpretation, works that communicate the inferiority of Judaism through various subtle and not-so-subtle strategies.[6]

Anti-Jewish motifs in Christian discourse can be schematized and understood in a variety of ways. Katharina von Kellenbach, in her dissertation "Anti-Judaism in Christian-Rooted Feminist Writings," offers a typology that is especially useful for analyzing anti-Judaism in feminist interpretation. Von Kellenbach suggests that "three rules of formation of the anti-Jewish myth define the Christian representation of Judaism."[7] (1) The rule of formation as *antithesis* sets up a set of dualistic oppositions and identifies Judaism with the negative side, Christianity with the positive side of each dualism. Oppositions such as letter versus spirit, works versus faith, and particularism versus universalism are deeply ingrained in Christian language and remain fundamental to Christian writing and preaching about Judaism, including New Testament scholarship. (2) The rule of formation as *scapegoat* builds on these antitheses to blame Jews for the evil in the world. The idea that the Jews are responsible for a long trail of crimes culminating in the death of Jesus has its roots in the Gospels and remains central to many contemporary accounts of Jesus' trial and crucifixion. (3) The rule of formation as *prologue* identifies Judaism with the religion of the "Old Testament" and thus with Christian prehistory. Insofar as Judaism continues to exist, it is only an empty relic, because God's promises to Israel have been transferred to the church as the new elect. Scholarly use of the phrase "late Judaism" to refer to Judaism in the first century is a good example of the persistence of this theme.[8]

Von Kellenbach points out that while these rules of formation have definite theological content in traditional Christian discourse, they are also remarkably flexible, adapting themselves to the "specific needs of particular countries, classes, and ideologies." In the last two centuries, for example, both right- and left-wing political movements have made use of anti-Jewish myths in order to gain adherents.[9] It is thus possible for Christian feminists to use the same classical anti-Jewish framework to set up a new antithesis: Judaism equals sexism, while Christianity equals feminism. Moreover, while discussion of post-Christian feminism is beyond the scope of this chapter, post-Christian feminists also have drawn on this tradition to replace the traditional charge of deicide with the new charge that Jews killed the Goddess.[10]

JESUS AS FEMINIST AND JUDAISM AS ANTITHESIS

While each "rule of formation" discussed by von Kellenbach finds its way into Christian discourse,[11] the rule of antithesis is most characteristic of feminist New Testament interpretation. Indeed, feminist interpreters who want to prove the feminist credentials of Jesus or Paul or the nonsexist nature of the Christian vision are dependent on the rule of antithesis for the cogency of their position. The claim that "Jesus was a feminist" — a claim first articulated by Leonard Swidler and then taken up by numerous feminist interpreters — can be argued persuasively only on the basis of a negative view of Judaism.[12] This is so because, while no sexist saying is attributed to Jesus, while women were present among his disciples, and while he appeals to women's experience in some of his parables, the New Testament provides no evidence that Jesus was a champion of women's rights in the contemporary sense. He is never portrayed as arguing for women's prerogatives, demanding changes in particular restrictive laws that affect women, or debating the Pharisees on the subject of gender.[13] The argument that Jesus was a *feminist,* then — rather than simply a Jewish man who treated women like people—rests on "the rule of antithesis," on contrasting his behavior with his supposed Jewish background. Indeed, Swidler says quite clearly, "there are two factors which raise this negative result [i.e., the fact that Jesus does not treat women as "inferior beings"] exponentially in its significance: *the status of women in Palestine at the time of Jesus,* and the nature of the Gospels."[14]

In order to depict Jesus as a man who stood over against his Jewish upbringing and environment, Christian interpreters select from Jewish sources the most negative and restrictive statements about women and present these as the reality of Jewish women's lives in the first century. As one feminist scholar puts it, "At the historical moment when Jesus was born into the world, the status of Jewish women had never been lower."[15] The composite portrait of Jesus' religious background that emerges from a number of feminist texts includes the following elements: Jewish women were exempt from fixed prayer and "grossly restricted" in public prayer. They were not allowed to study scripture. Men were forbidden to converse with women in public. Polygamy was legal in the time of Jesus, although probably not widely practiced. Men could divorce their wives easily by giving them a writ of divorce, but women were not allowed to divorce their husbands. Women were limited to the private sphere, where they were under the domination of fathers or husbands. Women were unclean during menstruation and after childbirth. Women were viewed by the rabbis as light-minded, dirty, greedy, and gossipy, and girl children were seen as a bane to their parents.[16]

This portrait of Jewish women's situation is then contrasted with Jesus' attitudes toward women in such a way as to make his statements and gestures appear deliberately rebellious. While Jewish men did not normally speak even to their wives in public, Jesus spoke to a Samaritan woman stranger. While men avoided contact with women who were ritually unclean, Jesus healed the woman with a twelve-year flow of blood. While women were not permitted to study Torah, Jesus praised Mary over Martha for choosing "the good portion." While adulterous women were supposed to be stoned, Jesus refused to stone the woman brought before him without her male partner. And so on.

The issue of divorce provides a particularly nice illustration of this method of antithesis, for, using this method, feminist interpreters are able to take a problematic ruling and depict it as largely positive. On the surface, Jesus' prohibition of divorce would seem at best ambiguous for feminists. In a social context in which patriarchal marriage is the expectation and norm, it is hardly in women's undivided interest to have no possibility of exit from it. Yet when Jesus' teaching on divorce is set over against the supposed

Jewish position, it suddenly appears as liberating for women.[17] This argument from opposition is implicit already in *The Woman's Bible* and is more fully developed by a number of contemporary writers.[18] Thus Rosemary Ruether, after warning that Jesus' iconoclasm toward women's subordination should not be used as the basis of a new anti-Judaism, continues as follows:

> Even Jesus' pronouncements on divorce should be seen in the context of a society where a woman, who had no means of support, could be cast out by her husband on the slightest pretext. The stricter attitude toward divorce in Jesus' time had the purpose of providing women with greater respect and security in marriage. . . .[19]

Evelyn and Frank Stagg, discussing Jesus' equation of remarriage with adultery, comment, "Whatever the harshness here, at least there is no double standard for husbands and wives."[20] Leonard Swidler paints the opposition between Jesus and Jewish practice in sharp terms:

> [Jesus' position on marriage] presupposed a feminist view of women; they had rights and responsibilities equal to men's. . . . It was quite possible in Jewish law for men to have more than one wife. . . . Divorce, of course, also was a simple matter, to be initiated *only* by the man. In both situations, women were basically chattel. . . . Jesus rejected both customs by insisting on monogamy and the elimination of divorce.[21]

There are a number of problems with this overall approach to Judaism in the time of Jesus, and with the example of divorce in particular. First of all, the approach assumes that rabbinic literature is the product of the time of Jesus, when in fact the rabbis came to power only after the destruction of the Temple (in 70 c.e.), and the Mishnah and Talmud were redacted centuries after Jesus' death (200 and 500 c.e. respectively). Second, this approach selects from rabbinic materials precisely those customs and sayings that tend to support the uniqueness of Jesus, neglecting both positive sayings and legal rulings that seek to protect women's rights. Thus in presenting the position of women in Jewish marriage, Christian feminists never discuss the commandment of *onah*—a law that protects the sexual rights of women in marriage by defining the marital dues a *husband owes his wife*. In discussing divorce, they assume rabbinic attitudes as normative but do not mention the *ketubah*, or marriage contract, an important rabbinic innovation that had as its purpose the protection of women against hasty divorce.[22] Third, the statements and gestures of an itinerant preacher are compared to a prescriptive literature formulated in the rarefied atmosphere of rabbinic academies. It is simply assumed that this literature corresponds to the total reality of Jewish women's lives, when, as I will discuss more fully below, there is significant evidence that it does not. Fourth, part of the evidence for Jewish women's complex status and roles comes from the New Testament itself. For the purposes of the "rule of antithesis," however, Jesus' attitudes toward women are seen as evidence of his distance from his "Jewish background" rather than as evidence of Jewish attitudes and practices.

At the same time that Jesus' positive attitudes toward women are depicted as un-Jewish, Paul's negative attitudes toward women are defined as the product of his Judaism. Katharina von Kellenbach points out that in Paul's case, the rule of antithesis is developed as a division within the apostle, so that Paul's feminist/Christian side is presented as at war with his sexist/Jewish upbringing.[23] This strategy is already found in *The Woman's Bible*, which dismisses Paul's injunction that women should cover their heads when they pray (1 Cor 11:10), commenting that it lacks authority because it is based on an absurd Hebrew legend. According to Louisa Southworth of the revising committee, "Paul merely repeats this warning [that women should cover their heads], which he must often have heard at the feet of Gamaliel."[24] In other words, because it is the Jewish Paul and not the Christian Paul who speaks in this passage, Christian women can simply ignore it.

In the contemporary discussion, the dichotomy between a Jewish and a Christian Paul is developed more fully and used to elucidate the many contradictions that plague Paul's work. Robin Scroggs, in his "Paul and the Eschatological Woman," describes the social context of Pauline thought about women in terms of a spectrum of Jewish attitudes. Palestinian Judaism constituted one end of the spectrum, he suggests, with women being accorded few privileges outside the family. While Jewish women's situation was more varied in the diaspora, Scroggs feels Paul's views are probably closer to those of Philo, Josephus, and Palestinian Judaism than to those of freer communities like Elephantine.

> The remarkable contrast between Paul's mature Christian views towards women and his probable early ideals says something important about the continuing tension in which he must have lived and worked, as well as about the transforming power on his own life of the gospel he preached.[25]

Paul Jewett develops the tension between the two Pauls into an opposition that can scarcely be contained in one person:

> To understand [Paul's] thought about the relation of the woman to the man, one must appreciate that he was both a Jew and a Christian. . . . So far as he thought in terms of his Jewish background, he thought of the woman as subordinate to the man. . . . But so far as he thought in terms of the new

insight he had gained through the revelation of God in Christ, he thought of the woman as equal to the man in all things. . . .

Because these two perspectives—the Jewish and the Christian—are incompatible, there is no satisfying way to harmonize the Pauline argument for female subordination with the larger Christian vision of which the great apostle to the Gentile was himself the primary architect.[26]

To criticize this perspective is not to deny the apparent contradictions in Paul's attitudes toward women, contradictions that need to be explained. But the division between a Jewish and a Christian Paul purifies Christianity from the charge of sexism by coding all arguments for women's subordination as "Jewish" and then dismissing them as no longer authoritative. As *The Woman's Bible* puts it a bit naïvely, "We congratulate ourselves that we may shift some of these Biblical arguments that have such a sinister effect from their firm foundation."[27] This position elevates Christianity at Judaism's expense in two ways: it makes it difficult to see the "good, i.e. nonsexist Paul" as learning anything from Judaism—even though, as Virginia Mollenkott points out, Paul's famous parenthetical remark in 1 Corinthians 11 (v. 11) exactly parallels a passage from *Genesis Rabbah*.[28] And it makes it unnecessary to look at those aspects of the Christian tradition that are compatible with or foster sexism.

The creation of a division between a Jewish and a Christian Paul brings the theological agenda of much feminist anti-Judaism clearly into view. It is not the direct intention of feminist interpreters to prove the superiority of Christianity to Judaism. Indeed, while some Jewish feminists have objected to the use of the locution "anti-Judaism" as simply a polite version of anti-Semitism,[29] one value of the distinction between the two terms is that it allows for the fact that feminists who are not social or racial anti-Semites still make use of anti-Jewish literary and theological motifs. Where this happens, the negative depiction of Judaism is not the result of deliberate hostility but of a political liberalism yoked to a theological conservatism that sees the New Testament as a source of role models for contemporary Christian behavior. If Jesus and/or Paul was a feminist, then surely the church must repent of its sexism and bring its policies and structures into line with their example. This mode of interpretation assumes, in Krister Stendahl's phrase, that contemporary Christians are called on to "play 'First Century Bible-Land'" and to do as Jesus and Paul did, however their teachings are understood.[30] Since, in fact, however, Paul was deeply ambivalent about women's status, and Jesus acted respectfully toward women without ever explicitly defending their cause, the two men can be turned into unambiguous feminist role models only if first-century Judaism is depicted as unrelievedly misogynist. Deeply embedded patterns of

Christian anti-Judaism are thus uncritically appropriated to aid the feminist program.

There are other ways too in which the "Jesus was a feminist" argument adopts conservative theological or interpretive principles for a liberal social purpose. Though this argument does not depend on explicit claims about Jesus' unique ontological status, such claims are often quietly presupposed in order to give feminism religious legitimacy. Thus after six pages of historical argumentation for Jesus' feminism, Leonard Swidler concludes his original article with the words, "Jesus was a feminist, and a very radical one. Can his followers attempt to be anything less—*De Imitatione Christi?*"[31] In another vein, Christians who contrast Jesus with his Jewish background to bolster his feminist credentials simultaneously acknowledge and negate the fact that Jesus was a Jew. He was sufficiently Jewish that his supposed difference from other Jews is significant and noteworthy, yet he was not a Jew if that means his behavior should count as evidence for the nature of first-century Judaism. Clearly the dilemma for feminist interpreters is that acknowledging the Jesus movement as a movement within Judaism would undercut claims about Jesus' *Christian* uniqueness. If he was simply a Jew, his attitudes toward women would represent not a victory *over* early Judaism but a possibility *within* it.

TOWARD A MORE CRITICAL FEMINIST HERMENEUTIC

Anti-Jewish themes in Christian writing are deep-rooted and tenacious, but there are ways in which feminists can address, rather than reproduce, this sorry aspect of Christian self-understanding. With prodding from women of color, feminists are beginning to grapple with the idea that racism and classism are dimensions of texts and social structures that must be confronted if feminism is to become a movement committed to the liberation of all women. Given the continuing presence of anti-Semitism as a structural element in Christian culture, this insight must also be extended to anti-Judaism in a thoroughgoing way.

1. The first step in eradicating anti-Judaism is becoming aware of its existence, and this means becoming educated about the dimensions of the problem. Fortunately, there are a number of good general histories of anti-Semitism, and also narrower studies of anti-Judaism in Christian history, thought, and practice. The critical discussion of anti-Judaism taking place in the feminist community has antecedents in many Christian scholarly

works. The bibliography at the end of this chapter recommends a number of relevant sources, each of which contains other bibliographic suggestions.

2. Once Christian feminists recognize anti-Jewish patterns, it is essential that they begin systematically to problematize anti-Judaism in the Christian tradition *as part of a feminist analysis* of Christian texts. Again, just as womanist scholars have taught white feminists that looking at racism and race relationships between women is a feminist task, so feminists must analyze "women's relational history" in terms of anti-Judaism and religious difference.[32] This means that it is not enough for feminist interpreters to avoid allying themselves with the anti-Judaism in Christian sources or even to raise in general terms the problem of anti-Judaism in feminist interpretation. Rather, it is necessary to signal the existence of anti-Judaism in Christian texts *wherever it appears* so that the problem of traditional Christian anti-Judaism becomes a dimension of feminist consciousness, and feminists begin to examine the dynamics of the relationship between sexism and anti-Judaism in Christian sources.

Explicit discussion of anti-Judaism is a task for feminist writers, but it is also important in the context of the classroom. Feminist teachers of New Testament can raise questions about the anti-Jewish story line of the Gospels, just as they would raise questions about the roles and status of women in those texts. They can help students to reflect on the anti-Jewish "rules of formation" present in Christian historical materials, and their continuing impact on Christian self-understanding. Sometimes with a class that is resistant to feminist issues, it is tempting to gain student attention by claiming that "Jesus was a feminist" or was especially open to women. Teachers' attempts to avoid negative comparisons with Judaism in this context, however, cannot prevent students from appropriating such material in the framework of an anti-Jewish heritage. That is why, in discussing women in the early Christian movement or Jesus' attitudes toward women, it is essential to raise the problem of anti-Judaism explicitly and to examine its strategies and effects.

3. Addressing the anti-Judaism in Christian sources, because it is consciousness-raising for all parties, is probably the most important next step Christian feminists can take in dealing with the problem of feminist anti-Jewish interpretation. But sensitivity to anti-Judaism cannot of itself effect a transformation of anti-Jewish attitudes. The long history of anti-Judaism will finally be transcended only on the basis of an appreciation of Judaism as an autonomous, changing, and diverse tradition. In the specific context of feminist New Testament interpretation, this means it is impossible fully to discuss or evaluate the Jesus movement in relation to women without knowledge of feminist approaches to first-century Judaism.

Feminist exploration of Jewish women's history is a very new field. Just as feminist scholars have moved from addressing the sexism in Christian sources to recovering the complex reality of women's lives within Christian history, so they have begun to reconstruct the history of women within Judaism. While it is impossible to discuss here all the methodological issues the new feminist scholarship raises for Christian interpretation, probably its most important finding is that rabbinic literature is not an accurate reflection of the diversity of women's roles within first-century Judaism. To cite just two examples: the "Jesus-was-a-feminist" argument maintains that women played no role in the ancient synagogue, contrasting this exclusion with women's discipleship in the Jesus movement. But inscriptions from diaspora synagogues referring to women as elders, leaders, and synagogue presidents suggest that women could have played liturgical or administrative roles in the synagogues of Jesus' time. This inscriptional evidence is particularly significant when combined with the absence of any ancient literary or archaeological evidence for special women's sections or galleries in the synagogues of this period.[33] Second, the assumption that only men could initiate divorce in Judaism is challenged by a number of documents from the first centuries C.E. that depict individual women as divorcing their husbands or reserving the right of divorce in their marriage contracts. These documents suggest that there were two strands of thought and practice concerning divorce in ancient Judaism. One—which became normative Jewish practice—accorded only men the right of divorce, but the other also allowed women to initiate divorce.[34]

4. Two pieces of evidence for this second strand of Jewish practice are Mark 10:11–12 and 1 Cor 7:10–11. This fact points to another important strategy in overcoming anti-Judaism in feminist New Testament interpretation: reading the New Testament not as the antithesis or refutation of "Judaism," but as an important source for Jewish women's history.[35] If the Gospels are seen as reflecting part of the continuum of first-century Jewish practice with regard to women, they tell a very different story about Jewish women's lives than if they are read oppositionally. The absence of any overt challenge to Jesus' treatment of or teachings about women suggests that his relation to women and gender norms might not have been so different from the relations of his contemporaries. Perhaps Jewish women sometimes divorced their husbands, moved freely in the streets and conversed with strangers, were visible in the synagogue and temple, and paid visits and received visitors.[36] Such a reconstruction may not provide a simple warrant for contemporary Christians to become feminists, but it both avoids perpetuating Christian anti-Judaism and yields a more nuanced and interesting picture of women's religious lives in the ancient world.

5. Finally, it is important to mention an institutional dimension to the persistence of anti-Judaism in Christian feminist interpretation. While feminists often celebrate the ways in which women's criticism and reconstruction of religion have opened up new areas of interreligious dialogue, the reality is that much Christian feminist work takes place in isolation from the Jewish feminist agenda. Christian institutes, workshops, panel discussions, and other projects deal with key feminist issues, either without including Jewish feminists working on the same questions or inviting Jewish participation on Christian terms. Whatever the rationale for this institutional isolation, it would seem to reflect and perpetuate a lack of awareness of the Jewish "Other" that necessarily makes it more difficult to recognize and grapple with anti-Judaism in a scholarly context. Appreciation of Judaism as an independent tradition must include an openness to Jewish feminist concerns — concerns that in their similarities and differences from Christian feminism challenge Christian feminists to develop a more critical perspective on a hegemonic tradition.

NOTES

1. Elizabeth Cady Stanton, *Eighty Years and More: Reminiscences 1815–1897* (1898; reprint, New York: Schocken Books, 1971), 381 (emphasis mine).

2. Ibid., 280–82.

3. Mary Daly, *Beyond God the Father* (Boston: Beacon Press, 1973), 10.

4. Two examples from a much larger literature are: Barbara Hilkert Andolsen, *"Daughters of Jefferson, Daughters of Blackboots": Racism and American Feminism* (Macon, GA: Mercer University Press, 1986); and bell hooks, *Feminist Theory: From Margin to Center* (Boston: South End Press, 1984).

5. For one important example, see Rosemary Radford Ruether's *Faith and Fratricide: The Theological Roots of Anti-Semitism* (New York: Seabury, 1974).

6. Charlotte Klein, *Anti-Judaism in Christian Theology,* trans. Edward Quinn (Philadelphia: Fortress, 1975).

7. Katharina von Kellenbach, "Anti-Judaism in Christian-Rooted Feminist Writing: An Analysis of Major U.S. American and West German Feminist Theologians" (Dissertation, Temple University Graduate School, 1990), 57.

8. Ibid., chap. 2; Klein, *Anti-Judaism,* chaps. 5 and 2.

9. Von Kellenbach, "Anti-Judaism," 58.

10. Ibid., chap. 4; Annette Daum, "Blaming Jews for the Death of the Goddess," *Lilith* 7 (1980) 12–13; and Susannah Heschel, "Anti-Judaism in Christian Feminist Theology," *Tikkun* 5:3 (May/June 1990): 26–27.

11. Von Kellenbach's thesis thoroughly documents the use of each of these rules in feminist scholarship.

12. Leonard Swidler, "Jesus Was a Feminist," *Catholic World* 212 (January 1971): 177–83.

13. Von Kellenbach, "Anti-Judaism," 85, 88.

14. Swidler, "Jesus Was a Feminist," 177–78 (emphasis mine).

15. Virginia Ramey Mollenkott, *Women, Men and the Bible* (Nashville: Abingdon, 1977), 10.

16. Swidler, "Jesus Was a Feminist," 178–79 (quotation from p. 178); Mollenkott, *Women,* 10–12; Constance Parvey, "The Theology and Leadership of Women in the New Testament," in *Religion and Sexism: Images of Women in the Jewish and Christian Traditions,* ed. Rosemary Radford Ruether (New York: Simon & Schuster, 1974), 120; Elisabeth Moltmann-Wendel, *Liberty, Equality, Sisterhood* (Philadelphia: Fortress, 1977), 12–21. These sources are examples, not an exhaustive list.

17. Bernadette Brooten discusses this issue in "Early Christian Women and Their Cultural Context: Issues of Method in Historical Reconstruction," in *Feminist Perspectives on Biblical Scholarship,* ed. Adela Yarbro Collins (SBL Centennial Publications 10; Chico, CA: Scholars Press, 1985), 73–74.

18. See Elizabeth Cady Stanton and the Revising Committee, *The Woman's Bible,* 2 vols. in one (Seattle: Coalition Task Force on Women and Religion, 1974), 2:130.

19. Rosemary Radford Ruether, *New Woman New Earth: Sexist Ideologies and Human Liberation* (New York: Seabury, 1975), 64–65.

20. Evelyn and Frank Stagg, *Woman in the World of Jesus* (Philadelphia: Westminster, 1978), 135.

21. Leonard Swidler, *Biblical Affirmations of Woman* (Philadelphia: Westminster, 1979), 174 (emphasis in the original).

22. For a Jewish feminist discussion of *onah* and *ketubah,* see Rachel Biale, *Women and Jewish Law: An Exploration of Women's issues in Halakhic Sources* (New York: Schocken Books, 1984), chapters 3 and 5.

23. Von Kellenbach, "Anti-Judaism," 89–92.

24. *The Woman's Bible,* 2:158–59.

25. Robin Scroggs, "Paul and the Eschatological Woman," *Journal of the American Academy of Religion* 40 (1972): 290. See also Elaine Pagels, *The Gnostic Gospels* (New York: Random House, 1979), 61–63.

26. Paul Jewett, *Man as Male and Female: A Study in Sexual Relationships from a Theological Point of View* (Grand Rapids: Eerdmans, 1975), 112–13; cf. von Kellenbach, "Anti-Judaism," 89–90.

27. *The Woman's Bible,* 2:158.

28. Mollenkott, *Women,* 98; *The Woman's Bible,* 2:158.

29. For example, Asphodel Long, "Anti-Judaism in Britain," *Journal of Feminist Studies in Religion* 7 (1991): 126.

30. Krister Stendahl, *The Bible and the Role of Women* (Philadelphia: Fortress, 1966), 40.

31. Swidler, "Jesus Was a Feminist," 183.

32. The term "women's relational history" is Delores Williams's ("Women's Oppression and Lifeline Politics in Black Women's Religious Narratives," *Journal of Feminist Studies in Religion* 1 [Fall 1985]: 69; see also Clarice Martin, *Journal of Feminist Studies in Religion* 6 [1990]: 41–43).

33. Bernadette Brooten, *Women Leaders in the Ancient Synagogue: Inscriptional Evidence and Background Issues* (Brown Judaic Studies 36; Chico, CA: Scholars Press, 1982); Brooten, "Early Christian Women," 89.

34. Bernadette Brooten, "Could Women Initiate Divorce in Ancient Judaism? The implications for Mark 10:11–12 and I Corinthians 7:10–11" (The Ernest Cadwell Coleman Lecture, School of Theology at Claremont, April 14, 1981); and Brooten, "Early Christian Women," 73.

35. Brooten, "Could Women Initiate Divorce in Ancient Judaism?" esp. 9–12.
36. Von Kellenbach, "Anti-Judaism," 87–89.

RECOMMENDED READINGS

Brooten, Bernadette J. "Early Christian Women and Their Cultural Context: Issues of Method in Historical Reconstruction." In *Feminist Perspectives on Biblical Scholarship*, edited by Adela Yarbro Collins, 65–69. SBL Centennial Publications 10. Chico, CA: Scholars Press, 1985.

——. "Jewish Women's History in the Roman Period: A Task for Christian Theology." In *Christians Among Jews and Gentiles: Essays in Honor of Krister Stendahl on His Sixty-Fifth Birthday,* edited by George W. E. Nickelsburg with George W. MacRae, S.J., 22–30. Philadelphia: Fortress, 1986.

Heschel, Susannah. "Anti-Judaism in Christian Feminist Theology." *Tikkun* 5/3 (May/June 1990): 25ff.

Journal of Feminist Studies in Religion 7/2 (Fall 1991). "Special Section on Christian Feminist Anti-Judaism," 95–133.

Klein, Charlotte. *Anti-Judaism in Christian Theology.* Philadelphia: Fortress, 1975.

Plaskow, Judith. "Christian Feminism and Anti-Judaism." *Cross-Currents* 33 (Fall 1978): 306–9.

Ruether, Rosemary Radford. *Faith and Fratricide: The Theological Roots of Anti-Semitism.* New York: Seabury, 1974.

von Kellenbach, Katharina. "Anti-Judaism in Christian-Rooted Feminist Writing: An Analysis of Major U.S. American and West German Feminist Theologians." Dissertation, Temple University Graduate School, 1990.

9

❖ Native American Women, Missionaries, and Scriptures

CAROL DEVENS-GREEN ♦

GENDER AND RACE are basic analytical categories in my reading of primary documents, my assessments of the literature on history and religion, and my writing. As a feminist historian, I think it crucial that scholarship on women examines how cultural and racial visions and experiences affect women's roles and interactions with one another. Although women are now more frequently incorporated into historical studies and feminist scholarship focuses directly on women and on gender, in general, "women" is understood to refer to European Americans and occasionally African Americans. Native women have been ignored or seen as secondary players in larger movements in most studies of women and religion by non-native writers. Native women's analyses of religion and history are essential to feminist scholarship; and, although non-native scholars cannot claim to know the experiences of native women, they must be careful to produce knowledge that is inclusive of native perspectives, actions, and concerns.

MISSIONARY OUTREACH

Few Native American women had any contact with Christianity before the nineteenth century. During the colonial and early national periods, British, and later American, Protestants made only fitful attempts to gain converts, establishing the occasional "praying village" or mission. Roman Catholic missionaries worked diligently to evangelize New France (present Canada) and Spain's southwestern colonies, but their efforts were limited by small numbers and vast territories. In the early 1800s, however, the evangelical fervor of the Second Great Awakening and budding nationalism created a new systematic missionary effort, which carried Christianity to a larger, distant audience through the interdenominational American Board of

Commissioners for Foreign Missions (ABCFM, 1810) and a variety of denominational organizations. Their missions introduced Native American women in the central and western United States and Hawaii to the message, and the bearers, of the Christian scriptures.[1]

Throughout the century, young Americans, inspired by the Great Commission "Go into all the world and preach the gospel to the whole creation" (Mark 16:15), flocked to mission boards.[2] They yearned to bring the light of the Gospels to "heathens" who, they assumed, would gratefully accept both the Word and the culture that accompanied it. Believing that Christianity and "civilization" were synonymous, they were convinced that native ways must be abandoned to achieve salvation. Indeed, evangelicals maintained that the spread of scriptural truths depended on native adoption of middle-class, European American values. One area in drastic need of reform, they insisted, was gender relations.[3]

NATIVE AMERICAN GENDER ROLES

Although there was no uniform aboriginal culture, generalizations can be made about Native American gender roles, both Indian and Hawaiian. Unlike European Americans, most groups did not have an institutionalized gender hierarchy. Many were egalitarian, and women's and men's roles were complementary rather than ranked. Women frequently controlled their own sexual activities within and outside of marriage, and easy divorce was an almost universal option. Women participated in communal ritual practices as well as in separate female rituals, and they played a central and positive role in the creation stories and cosmology of virtually all groups. Women's contributions to their communities through horticulture, food gathering and preparation activities, and childbearing provided them with status, economic power, and often political influence.[4]

With few exceptions, such gender roles shocked nineteenth-century missionaries.[5] Protestants and Catholics alike were products of a society that celebrated the domestication of middle-class women. They extolled the virtues of piety, purity, and submissiveness even while consigning countless women to the factory or slavery. Prescriptive literature, women's organizations, and clergy promoted "True Womanhood" as a biblical ideal, and many women subscribed to it as a goal. Whether many achieved it is doubtful. Certainly women missionaries, who eventually constituted the majority of those working with Native American women, did not fit the mold, having chosen adventure among the heathens over sedate family life.

Nonetheless, True Womanhood became the standard against which Native American women were measured, and found wanting.[6]

MISSIONARY ASSAULT ON NATIVE MARRIAGE

The attack on women's roles targeted marriage, where, it seemed, native women most flagrantly violated both scriptural mandate and true womanhood. Several issues particularly provoked missionaries. They vigorously objected to the sororal polygyny (sisters marrying the same man) found among groups with a larger female than male population. Unmoved by the expediency of the practice, missionaries roundly censured it, maintaining that polygyny degraded women rather than benefited them. Although Samuel Parker recognized that the polygyny he observed among Plateau tribes in the 1840s was not unlike that described in the Old Testament (e.g., Gen 16:3–16), he nevertheless condemned it. Like Father Peter John DeSmet, who also worked among Plateau peoples at mid-century, most missionaries tended to view polygyny as extramarital sex. The male and female polygamy practiced by Hawaiian chiefs fared no better. As part of their efforts to eradicate the custom, missionaries regularly instructed women on the seventh commandment's injunction against adultery (Exod 20:14). An ABCFM primer for Osage children, for example, included in its moral lessons Moses' laws of marriage prohibiting adultery (Lev 18:18). And a scriptural reader compiled by Jesuits for the Kalispel in Montana presented the story of the Samaritan woman at the well (John 4) in a lesson entitled "The adulteress," or "Lu Smeem lu Espkuneel," apparently in reference to the six men with whom the woman had lived.[7]

What most perturbed missionaries was women's authority within marriage. Pauline doctrine seemed clear on the importance of womanly subjection within the family. True Womanhood held as well that women were weak, submissive to male authority, and best suited for domestic activities and childcare. Native American women, however, often not only lived in non-nuclear familes but were oblivious to the injunctions that should have been regulating their behavior (e.g., 1 Pet 3:1–7, Col 3:18, Eph 5:22). Their autonomy offended both Protestant evangelicals and Roman Catholics, who deemed women's independence of male authority to be unnatural and ungodly. As one missionary ruefully commented when discussing women's participation in native Hawaiian government, "Paul's injunctions are not observed."[8]

Native women's right to divorce their husbands was yet another instance of their inappropriate freedom. Although missionaries rarely mentioned citing chapter and verse to prospective converts, they clearly drew on scriptures to justify their attempts to change native social organization. They claimed that only the Gospels gave women honor and dignity within the family or could lift native women from their autonomous, and thus degraded, condition. Women therefore were to turn their attention to the concerns of the household, as defined by scriptures. The power and value of Christian religion, they insisted, should find expression in clean homes and holy lives.[9]

SCRIPTURES IN THE EDUCATION OF NATIVE CHILDREN

Because of the difficulties encountered in convincing adults to convert and "civilize," missionaries often focused their efforts on children. By the mid-1850s they had targeted girls — future mothers — as the hope of the race. They saw the rising generation as the promise of the future, providing that children were removed from traditional influences and introduced to Christianity at a malleable age. To this end, day and boarding schools became a mainstay of mission organizations. Initially, the Bible in native languages was the main textbook, even in Quaker schools. The curriculum at an ABCFM Choctaw female boarding school in the 1820s had girls reciting the historical parts of Genesis, Exodus, and the New Testament. At the Presbyterian Iowa School, girls routinely memorized scriptural verses; in 1854 the best girl had mastered 359 verses, while the best boy came in a poor second at 241.[10]

Denominational scriptural readers and catechisms in native languages soon followed. However, despite their concern for bringing women into the fold, missionaries did not attempt to appeal to them with readings about women. Most publications paid scant attention to women or ignored them altogether. In *Washashe Wagerena pahugreh tse: The Osage First Book*, published for the ABCFM in 1834, the only lessons directed to girls instructed them in appropriate domestic behavior for Christian women. The implicit message of these readings was that traditional Osage gender roles were wrong: "It is fatiguing to women to work in the field"; and "If we could plant cotton, and get spinning wheels, the women could make plenty of cloth for all." No direct scriptural justification was provided for the criticism. Students were reminded, however, that "people without the scriptures are in darkness," and that they were to follow Moses' law of marriage.[11]

The Peep of Day or, A Series of the Earliest Religious Instruction the

Infant Mind is Capable of Receiving (1836), a collection of scriptural lessons for Ojibwe children, was another publication that gave women short shrift. Although it contained brief entries ostensibly about women, such as the widow of Nain (Luke 7:11) and Jairus's daughter (Mark 5:22), only one lesson really was a woman's story. Rather than the stirring example of Ruth or Judith, however, "The Sinner and Simon" related the story of a poor woman "who had been very naughty." Following Jesus into a rich man's house, she "began to cry for all her naughtiness," then washed Jesus' feet with her tears and was comforted by him (Luke 7:36–50). The study questions that followed asked the children: "What did the naughty woman do to Jesus?" "Why did Jesus forgive her naughtiness?" "Will Jesus forgive you your naughtiness, if you are sorry?" An Ojibwe girl using this book learned that Christian women were "naughty" and needed to be humble to be accepted, unlike the strong females in native cosmology.[12]

In the Jesuits' Kalispel scriptural reader, only nine of 177 entries pertained to women: Mary [Miriam], sister of Moses; Judith; Elizabeth; the Samaritan woman; Jairus's daughter and the woman with an issue of blood; Mary Magdalen; the woman of Canaan; the adulteress; and Mary and Martha. Similarly, a primer for Ojibwe children named only three women in its illustrated alphabet lesson: Eve (naked and picking an apple), Hagar (standing near Ishmael), and Rebekah (unillustrated). A Mohawk hymnal for adults and children contained no songs that mentioned women.[13]

NATIVE WOMEN'S USE OF SCRIPTURES

The decisions that native women made about the significance of scriptural teachings for their lives varied. Although missionary women often held women's Bible and sewing classes to attract women, they generally reported limited success. Maria Chamberlain (ABCFM), for example, was pleased to announce that a Hawaiian woman had told her "we wish to obey the word of God to live together with love to take care of our children and have them wear clothes."[14] And Edmund Ely, a young ABCFM missionary in Minnesota, pointedly reported the occasional evening spent with Ojibwe girls and women, singing, discussing hymns, and looking at scriptural engravings.[15]

Some women, such as Elizabeth Winyan, Helen Aungie Williams, Ellen Spotted Bear and others (in this instance, Lakota) adopted Christianity and became lay missionaries themselves, believing that "without the Bible our people will die."[16] Winyan, for example, trained ABCFM and later American Missionary Association women missionaries in Lakota language and culture, and proselytized with them in the Dakota Territory in the 1870s and 1880s. A few such women were mentioned in missionary pamphlets or memoirs, but in general the written record seldom contained native women's own words about their understanding of scriptural teachings or their experiences as Christians.

A rare exception was Sarah, an elderly Cherokee. In *Poor Sarah: or, The Indian Woman,* she reportedly recounted her path to conversion and her love of the Bible to an unidentified narrator whom she met when begging for food. Sarah was attracted to Christianity by the hope that Jesus would be her comfort in an abusive marriage. She made and sold brooms to purchase a Bible, despite her husband's objections, and prayed that the Holy Spirit would make her heart "all clean and white like Jesus." Alone and penniless in her old age, she remembered Jesus' temptation in the desert when she was hungry and tempted to steal food (Luke 4:1–13). She longed for release from her suffering and was sure that she had a place in heaven, "for my Father's house has many mansions" (John 14:2). Whether Sarah's story is apocryphal or accurate, it is apparent that her humble acceptance of a lowly position in life rendered her the ideal "heathen convert." Sarah's story became a popular Bible tract, especially for use among European-American and African-American children.[17]

An origin story of the Ojibwe Midewiwin (Grand Medicine Lodge) suggests that women sometimes made creative use of scriptures to suit their own needs. The Midewiwin, a society organized around curing rites, recognized women's ritual and social importance in Ojibwe culture. In an evocative inversion of the Jewish creation myth in Genesis, this story related how the Great Spirit made the first Indian, a woman, from a handful of dirt. Wondering why she was all alone when other creatures were in pairs, she requested that the *manitos* (supernatural beings) create a companion for her.

> A spirit was named to meet this wish. As the woman slept, he moved around her to see if he could detach a part of her body from which to shape another Indian. Finally he removed the woman's lower rib. So on wakening, the woman found herself lying with another person, made like herself. That is why a woman has fewer ribs, on both sides, than a man.[18]

Women whose communities were relatively stable socially and economically often resisted or ignored missionaries' attempts to force new values and practices on them. In groups where pressure from European Americans was increasing, women frequently converted or chose to adopt certain aspects of Christianity and ignore others, or accommodated to missionaries' demands only enough to convince them to diminish their attacks.[19]

Nineteenth-century Native American women's understanding or acceptance of scriptural teachings, then, reflected their personal situation, the status of their communities, and the manner in which missionaries introduced Christianity to them.

In short, until recently, Native American women have been relegated to the margins in studies of United States religion, history, missionary activity, and women's religion and history. Scholars either have disregarded women, focused on friendly "heroines" such as Pocahontas or Sakakwea, or considered them only in terms of their relations with European-American missionaries. The written primary sources make it difficult to do otherwise, because few native women left any written record of their experiences, and their oral histories have been reserved for their own communities. Nonetheless, by examining written sources with a cross-cultural feminist perspective one can speculate on, and sometimes determine, the past experiences of native women. If the women's movement in religion is to be truly inclusive, native women's history must be incorporated into the critique of women and religion and native women must take their place within the center of the movement itself.

NOTES

1. In *The Invasion Within: The Contest of Cultures in Colonial North America* (New York: Oxford University Press, 1985), James Axtell examines early conversion efforts. For general discussions on the growth of missionary activities in the nineteenth century, see Robert F. Berkhofer, Jr., *Salvation and the Savage: An Analysis of Protestant Missions and American Indian Response, 1787–1862* (2nd ed.; New York: Atheneum, 1976); Henry Warner Bowden, *American Indians and Christian Missions: Studies in Conflict* (Chicago: University of Chicago Press, 1981); Charles L. Chaney, *The Birth of Missions in America* (South Pasadena, CA: William Carey Library, 1976). William R. Hutchison provides a detailed examination of the ABCFM (*Errand to the World: American Protestant Thought and Foreign Missions* [Chicago: University of Chicago Press, 1987]).

2. All scriptural citations are from the Revised Standard Version.

3. Margaret Jewett Bailey was one of many nineteenth-century missionaries who articulated the urgency of this commission in her autobiographical novel *The Grains, or Passages in the Life of Ruth Rover, with Occasional Pictures of Oregon, Natural and Moral,* ed. Evelyn Leasher and Robert J. Franke (Corvallis: Oregon State University Press, 1986). Berkhofer, *Salvation and the Savage,* 15, 35; Chaney, *Birth of Missions,* 259.

4. For discussion of native gender roles, see Lillian A. Ackerman, "The Effect of Missionary Ideals on Family Structure and Women's Roles in Plateau Indian Culture," *Idaho Yesterday* 31:1–2 (1987): 64–73; Paula Gunn Allen, *The Sacred Hoop: Recovering the Feminine in American Indian Traditions* (Boston: Beacon Press, 1986); Karen Anderson, *Chain Her By One Foot: The Subjugation of Women in Seventeenth-Century New France* (New York: Routledge, 1991); Judith Brown, "Iroquois Women: An Ethnohistoric Note,"

in *Toward an Anthropology of Women,* ed. Rayna R. Reiter (New York: Monthly Review Press, 1975), 235–51; Carol Devens, *Countering Colonization: Native American Women and Great Lakes Missions, 1630–1900* (Berkeley: University of California Press, 1992); Patricia Grimshaw, *Paths of Duty: American Missionary Wives in Nineteenth-Century Hawaii* (Honolulu: University of Hawaii Press, 1989); Ramón A. Gutierréz, *When Jesus Came, the Corn Mothers Went Away: Marriage, Sexuality, and Power in New Mexico, 1500–1846* (Stanford: Stanford University Press, 1991).

5. One such exception was Elaine Goodale Eastman, who greatly admired the Lakota (Sioux) women among whom she taught, although she too believed that their way of life must be left behind. See *Sister to the Sioux: The Memoirs of Elaine Goodale Eastman, 1885–1891,* ed. Kay Graber (Lincoln: University of Nebraska Press, 1978).

6. Barbara Welter, "The Cult of True Womanhood: 1820–1860," *American Quarterly* 18 (1966): 151–74; see also Michael C. Coleman, *Presbyterian Missionary Attitudes Toward American Indians, 1837–1893* (Jackson: University Press of Mississippi, 1985); Carol Devens, *Countering Colonization,* chaps. 4–5; Julie Roy Jeffrey, *Converting the West: A Biography of Narcissa Whitman* (Norman: University of Oklahoma Press, 1991), 122–23.

7. Ackerman, "Missionary Ideals"; Berkhofer, *Salvation and the Savage,* 61; Grimshaw, *Paths of Duty,* 162–64; John Gilmary Shea, *History of the Catholic Missions Among the Indian Tribes of the United States, 1529–1854* (New York: T. W. Strong, 1854), 472. The story of the woman at the well is cited as John 4:42 in Joseph Giorda, *Lu Tel Kaimintis Kolinzuten Kuitlt Smiimii: Narrative from the Holy Scripture in Kalispel,* comp. by the Missionaries of the Society of Jesus (St. Ignatius Missions, MT: St. Ignatius Print, 1879), 90.

8. Grimshaw, *Paths of Duty,* 165.

9. Ackerman, "Missionary Ideals"; Berkhofer, *Salvation and the Savage,* 35, 76–77; Coleman, *Presbyterian Missionaries,* 89, 93–94, 127; Grimshaw, *Paths of Duty,* 161–62; John McLean, *James Evans: Inventor of the Syllabic System of the Cree Language* (Toronto: Methodist Mission Room, 1890), 45; Diane Rothenberg, "The Mothers of the Nation: Seneca Resistance to Quaker Intervention," in *Women and Colonization: Anthropological Perspectives,* ed. Mona Etienne and Eleanor Leacock (New York: Praeger, 1980), 63–87.

10. Berkhofer, *Salvation and the Savage,* 25, 31. See also Coleman, *Presbyterian Missionary Attitudes;* and Carol Devens, "'If We Get the Girls, We Get the Race': Missionary Education of Native American Girls," *Journal of World History* 3/2 (1992): 63–78.

11. William B. Montgomery, *Washashe Wageren pahugreh tse: The Osage First Book (for the ABCFM)* (Boston: Crocker & Brewster, 1834), 17, 20, 24, 90.

12. *Iu pitabvn: gema gaie okikinoamaquziuiniva igiu abinqiua: The Peep of Day or, A Series of the Earliest Religious Instruction the Infant Mind Is Capable of Receiving,* part 2, rev. ed. (New York: B. Waugh & T. Mason, 1836), 38–41. Interestingly, by the 1880s women's missionary organizations were insisting that meek Sarah was no longer the ideal role model for women and that she should be replaced with women like Esther, Anna, Mary Magdalen, and Joanna. They even suggested that it was time to challenge Pauline doctrine. See Patricia R. Hill, *The World Their Household: The American Woman's Foreign Mission Movement and Cultural Transformations, 1870–1920* (Ann Arbor: University of Michigan Press, 1985), 73–75, 78.

13. *Narrative of the Holy Scripture,* 16, 35, 41, 54, 64, 73, 88, 90, 96; *Scripture A.B.C. Book: Ojebwa kiya Sha yah gah nah she momah guk. A.B.C. Mahzenahegun* (Toronto, S. S. Marie, Ont: The Algoma and North-West Colportage Mission, n.d.), 4–5, 6–7, 8–9; *A Collection of Hymns for the Use of Native Christians of the Mohawk Language,* to

which are added a Number of Hymns for Sabbath Schools: Ne Karoron ne Teyerihwakwatha ne Enyonstste ne Yagorihwiyoghstonn Kanyengehaga Kaweanovidahkoga (New York: D. Fanshaw, 1835).

14. Quoted in Grimshaw, *Paths of Duty,* 178.

15. Edmund F. Ely, Writing Book, Ely Family Papers, Minnesota Historical Society, e.g. 14 October 1833, 21 September 1835.

16. *Elizabeth Winyan's Addresses* (Montevideo, MN: Chippewa County Historical Society, n.d.), pamphlet, Center for Western Studies, Sioux Falls. South Dakota Conference of the United Church of Christ Archives, Oahe Mission Collection, MLIR 13:6, 44.20-b; 13:6–9, 44.13, 19.

17. [Elias Boudinot?] *Poor Sarah: or, The Indian Woman* (New Echota, GA: privately printed, 1817; reprint, Philadelphia: American Baptist Publications Society, n.d.), 6–7, 9–14, 15 (quotation). See John F. Freeman, "The Indian Convert: Theme and Variation," *Ethnohistory* 12/2 (1965): 113–28, for a discussion of common themes in nineteenth-century conversion narratives.

18. Ruth Landes, *Ojibwa Religion and the Midewiwin* (Madison: University of Wisconsin Press, 1968), 91. The Midewiwin may have represented a revitalistic response to Europeans, based in traditional shamanistic practices which, by the nineteenth century, had incorporated some aspects of the Christian tradition into Ojibwe mythology. See Harold Hickerson, "Notes on the Post-Contact Origin of the Midewiwin," *Ethnohistory* 9 (1962): 406.

19. On women's reluctance or lack of interest in conversion, see, e.g., Berkhofer, *Salvation and the Savage,* 46; Coleman, *Presbyterian Missionaries,* 105; Devens, *Countering Colonization,* chaps. 4–5; Fr. Anthony Maria Gachet, "Five Years in America (Cinq Ans en Amerique): Journal of a Missionary Among the Redskins 1859," trans. Joseph Schafer, *Wisconsin Magazine of History* 18 (1934–35): 66–76, 191–204, 345–59; Charlotte J. Frisbie, "Traditional Navajo Women: Ethnographic and Life History Portrayals," *American Indian Quarterly* 6 (1982): 11–33; Gutierréz, *When Jesus Came;* Albert Keiser, *Lutheran Mission Work Among the American Indians* (Minneapolis: Augsburg, 1922), 64–68, 73–74. The following mention women's classes: Jeffrey, *Converting the West,* 120–21; Devens, *Countering Colonization,* 103; Grimshaw, *Paths of Duty,* 171–76.

RECOMMENDED READINGS

Berkhofer, Robert F., Jr. *Salvation and the Savage: An Analysis of Protestant Missions and American Indian Response, 1787–1862.* 2d ed. New York: Atheneum, 1976.

Bowden, Henry Warner. *American Indians and Christian Missions: Studies in Conflict.* Chicago: University of Chicago Press, 1981.

Chaney, Charles L. *The Birth of Missions in America.* South Pasadena, CA: William Carey Library, 1976.

Coleman, Michael C. *Presbyterian Missionary Attitudes Toward American Indians, 1827–1893.* Jackson: University Press of Mississippi, 1985.

Devens, Carol. *Countering Colonization: Native American Women and Great Lakes Missions, 1630–1900.* Berkeley: University of California Press, 1992.

Etienne, Mona, and Eleanor Leacock, eds. *Women and Colonization: Anthropological Perspectives.* New York: Praeger, 1980.

Grimshaw, Patricia. *Paths of Duty: American Missionary Wives in Nineteenth-Century Hawaii.* Honolulu: University of Hawaii Press, 1989.

Hutchison, William R. *Errand to the World: American Protestant Thought and Foreign Missions.* Chicago: University of Chicago Press, 1987.

Shea, John Gilmary. *History of the Catholic Missions Among the Indian Tribes of the United States.* New York: T. W. Strong, 1854.

◆ Unity of the Bible, Unity of the Church: Confessionalism, Ecumenism, and Feminist Hermeneutics

MELANIE A. MAY AND LAUREE HERSCH MEYER ◆

THE TWENTIETH-CENTURY SEARCH for the visible unity of the church has again and again turned to the question of the interpretation of scripture.[1] When the World Council of Churches was constituted in 1948, ecumenical leaders were on the whole confident that the Bible could be the basis for church unity. This was the era of "biblical theology," an era during which scholars spoke about the unity of the biblical message or of the content of the Gospel. Ecumenists took this conception of the unity of the Bible as the starting point and norm for their search.[2]

But before two decades had elapsed, ecumenists had to wrestle with two disturbing dynamics. First, attention was increasingly drawn to the diversity and even divergence between and among biblical writers. Second, awareness of the ways in which ecclesial traditions themselves have defined different interpretations of scripture sharpened.[3] From the perspective of some ecumenists, these recognitions undermined the *raison d'être* of the ecumenical movement, inasmuch as they made talk about the unity of the Bible increasingly impossible. From the perspective of others, an awareness of diversity within the Bible was an invitation to refocus the search for unity from preoccupation with recovery of a pristine past to receiving new possibilities for the future.

This debate was most pronounced in a pivotal exchange between Raymond Brown and Ernst Käsemann at the Fourth World Conference on Faith and Order, held in Montreal in 1963. Each delivered an address on "Unity and Diversity in New Testament Ecclesiology." Käsemann declared that one "simply cannot speak of an unbroken unity of New Testament ecclesiology" and accented "differences, dilemmas and antitheses" among New Testament churches and Christians as profound as those today.[4] By contrast, Brown argued that "if New Testament ecclesiology cannot be oversimplified in the direction of theological uniformity, neither can we neglect a *unity in belief* that is present in all stages of New Testament thought about the Church."[5]

An attempt to chart a way ahead appears in the Montreal report entitled "Scripture, Tradition and Traditions." Therein the crucial differentiation between traditions and Tradition was clarified. Tradition was conceived as "the Tradition of the Gospel (the *paradosis* of the *kerygma*) testified in Scripture, transmitted in and by the Church through the power of the Holy Spirit."[6] Tradition was said to be "not an object which we possess, but a reality by which we are possessed," the content of which "not only looks backward to its origin in the past but also forward to the fulness which shall be revealed."[7] Particular ecclesial or confessional traditions were viewed as "historically conditioned forms,"[8] limited in their points of view. It was hoped that this distinction between Tradition and traditions, which included the understanding that scripture *is* Tradition in its written form, would prepare the way for an understanding of unity not predicated on denying diversity, but on appreciating the richness of a scriptural heritage held in common.[9]

Thirty years later diverse incarnate expressions of the Gospel are becoming increasingly visible and vocal, and talk among seasoned ecumenists is turning to the limits of acceptable diversity. It is also becoming clearer that confessionalism, as it was configured at Montreal in terms of traditions, has functioned as a counterpoint to a particular and still prevalent understanding of church unity. On the terms of this confessionalist understanding of church unity, racial, sexual, class, and cultural diversity is suspect, indeed subversive. The tensive distinction between the living Tradition and limited traditions, which was an invitation to churches to interpret scripture in a wide scope of new situations, instead collapsed into ecumenical confessionalism. The reality that church-dividing matters as well as loyalties now run across traditional confessional lines was and is not recognized.[10] As a result, talk of unity has become a cover for a bent toward exclusive uniformity in the image of the so-called classical white male ecclesial theology.

It has been argued that these traditional confessional lines writ large — namely, Protestant, Catholic, Orthodox, Jewish — are also barriers between and among feminists.[11] But we believe there is a more basic question. We believe that feminists in many traditions have more in common as women committed to women's bodily, spiritual, intellectual healing and wholeness than the contrasts among hermeneutical methods or confessional alignments may suggest. From our perspective, this is to say, the question of women's loyalty[12] is more basic than whether women who are members of different confessional traditions interpret scripture accordingly. More basic to the ways in which women interpret scripture is whether women are aligued with one of the man-made methodological or confessional traditions or with one another.

Our thesis is, therefore, that the particularity of numerous feminist hermeneutical methods, which may of course be correlated with and accounted for in terms of confessional alignments, is not fractious for women but signals our way forward. Precisely the pronunciation of our particularity can renew the tensive vitality of the Montreal distinction of the living Tradition actualized in limited traditions, and can thereby give birth to ecclesial realities that bear witness to unity that is invitational rather than exclusive.

We elaborate this thesis as follows. First, we focus on three ways in which feminist hermeneutics work to enflesh the fullness of the living Tradition, namely: reconstruction of the past, recognition of contextual dynamics cutting across divisions to which we have become accustomed, and the creation of new texts. We engage three women authors, an Anglo-American Jew, a Pakistani Christian, and an African-American womanist, to illumine the ways in which feminist hermeneutics enflesh the fullness of the living Tradition. Then we consider unity and diversity, particularly addressing questions regarding the nature of textuality and of authority, with an eye to the further work of both feminists and ecumenists. We write together, one a biblical and one an ecumenical theologian, as an exercise to incarnate our conviction that women belong to one another more basically than to the norms of our ecclesiologies or disciplines. We do not write out of a particular theoretical framework so much as in the hope that others will join this multidimensional conversation committed to liberating life for women and all peoples marginalized by fixed frames of reference.

INCARNATE WORLDS

Savina J. Teubal draws on scholarly traditions rarely central to the exegesis of scriptural texts in order to excavate the world in which Sarah and Hagar were at home.[13] Using anthropology and exploring the literary clues remaining in these women's texts, Teubal discovered that these women, whose stories are at the heart of the Hebrew Bible, were at home in a world where a life-revering goddess was the known divine power. Sarah's and Hagar's actual life, denied and demeaned by their scriptural presentation, had a reality and meaning including ritual practices and spiritual experiences quite unlike that given it by the patriarchal tradition in which these women's stories were set in scripture.

The lost tradition of Sarah's and Hagar's stories shows that these women were profoundly significant, able, strong. Sarah was no barren and blasphemous wife to Abraham the patriarch but an important priestess. In keeping with her position in relation to the life-revering tradition of the goddess, Sarah chose to be childless, as her later history makes apparent. Nor was Hagar a servant or slave, but Sarah's handmaid. Hers was an office as the contracted companion of a priestess. Upon request she would bear a child to "be" the priestess's descendant and heir. Hagar thus bore Sarah a child upon agreement between the two women, not as a mandate from Abraham the patriarch.[14]

For women, Teubal's work raises the question of what counts as tradition. How far back in human history do our traditions seek the legitimate beginnings of Tradition? What authority do we grant traditions that destroyed a partnership Tradition in order to establish a patriarchal dominator Tradition?[15] Women are finding it life-giving to reconstruct our rich past since our different ecclesial traditions base themselves on redacted canonical texts whose Tradition is marked by authority secured by subjugation. Women are finding that the fullness of the living Tradition is greater than the redacted texts of our canon and the established authority of our ecclesial bodies.

The subjugation of ranking threatens the enormous variety of cultural and human experience with factional narrowness and sterile separation. Thus feminists doing biblical hermeneutics have increasingly recognized the rich diversity that cuts across customary divisions. We illustrate this recognition with Christine Amjad-Ali's reflections on the apostle Paul's words concerning head coverings in 1 Corinthians 11:2-16. Like women across ages and continents, Amjad-Ali speaks amid the specific realities of her culture as she examines her tradition and the biblical canon with eyes and values not circumscribed by context. Because her questions and loyalties are global, she is free to question the effect upon human life of scriptural interpretation. So Amjad-Ali wonders whether Paul, like Benazir Bhutto when she was prime minister of Pakistan, "*functionally* disregards the traditional, cultural and religious understanding of the subordination of women" and on the other hand "*symbolically* acknowledges and validates the traditional view that women are subordinate."[16]

Amjad-Ali argues that Paul's justification of traditional beliefs about the subordination of women reifies a particular cultural practice *through* his scriptural interpretation.[17] She sees that Paul's limited defense of cultural symbols of women's deference and subordination, stating that women should cover their heads when they lead in worship, was soon used to justify prohibiting women from assuming any leadership roles in the church.[18] So Amjad-Ali challenges Paul's conception of the equality of men and women only "in the Lord" with a perception at once specific to her Pakistani situation and also able to call all cultures and traditions into question. For in virtually all cultures today, whether or not they are strongly shaped by Christianity, it is common to insist that women are of equal value as men *while* ignoring facts that show the contrary. So long as cultural presuppositions preserve men's unique exercise of power and authority, the differences across ecclesial and cultural contexts will continue to divide women less deeply than our mutual subjugation unites us.

Women are taught, indeed urged, to view, define, and rank one another by how we fit into our specific traditions and cultures rather than by considering our common place in contemporary life. When women attend to our commonality, we find we share a significant circumstance with a host of peoples we are urged to view as "other": Africans, Asians, Pacific and Caribbean Islanders, and South Americans, and peoples of racial minorities, native peoples as well as the poor living among male-dominated white societies of North America and Europe. What we have in common is that we all dwell at the margins of or are excluded from traditional structures of political, economic, social, or religious power. Women's faces are among the "others" against whom powerholders in the prevailing order of things define the positions and possessions they then defend.

We who are defined as "other" are becoming more and more conscious of ourselves and our connections. By articulating our "other" voices, we create new texts. As women believers attend to new texts — even more, as we authorize them when they speak from and to our experience — the limits of any previously accepted canons come into view. It is hard to imagine how the canon of scripture, Jewish or Christian, might be formally reopened. Vested institutional interests, accompanied by constant vying for control over authority, are daunting realities with which to reckon. But there is another reality with which to reckon. Whether or not the biblical canon is formally reopened, newly created texts are daily being added to the canon by which God's people actually live and know life abundant.

Indications abound that new canonical texts already exist among women, texts "adaptable for life"[19] and able to nurture generations to come. Thus, though she does not speak about "canon," Katie G. Cannon considers the emergence of the black woman's literary tradition as an expression of the moral wisdom of black women and as a source for ethical decision making. Cannon focuses on the life and literature of Zora Neale Hurston and shows ways the womanist Tradition partakes of the storytelling so characteristic of the black community. Thus Hurston's texts are canonical because they convey the faith that forms future generations.[20]

Similarly, Rosemary Radford Ruether is clear that her collection of texts, *Womanguides,* is intended to be a contribution to the creation of "a new textual base, a new canon," for feminist theology.[21] Ruether sets texts from the margins of Christian tradition side by side with patriarchal texts that have defined women as subordinate and silent, or as absence. This juxtaposition jars the reader by shaking standard readings of sacred reality. We are invited into this turmoil among ancient texts and, amid this chaos, to create "new stories, new parables, new *midrashim* on the old stories,"[22] examples of which are enfolded in the collection.

A collection of texts becomes a canon as a community acknowledges that these texts free all members for living a truthful and liberating life. There may be no clearer example of a text that is now canonical for the North American feminist community than one from Sojourner Truth. Probably the most familiar text in the life-giving canon of Truth's words is her spontaneous rejoinder at a Women's Rights Convention in 1851. Events at the conference took a painful turn as male ministers claimed superior rights and privileges for men on the basis of several theses. The white women, unaccustomed to speaking in situations of public debate, were silent. Then slowly, the nearly six-foot frame of Sojourner Truth unfolded and went forward to the platform. She lay her old bonnet at her feet, and a profound hush came over the crowd as she wove her words in and through the refrain—"and ar'n't I a woman?"[23]

Sojourner Truth then singled out the men and their theses:

"Den dey talks 'bout dis ting in de head—what dis dey call it?" "Intellect," whispered some one near. "Dat's it honey. What's dat got to do with women's rights or niggers' rights? If my cup won't hold but a pint and yourn holds a quart, would n't ye be mean not to let me have my little half-measure full?" . . .

"Den dat little man in black dar, he say women can't have as much rights as a man, cause Christ want a woman. Whar did your Christ come from? . . . Whar did your Christ come from? From God and a woman. Man had nothing to do with him." . . .

. . ."if de fust woman God ever made was strong enough to turn the world upside down, all 'lone, dese togedder [and she glanced her eye over us], ought to be able to turn it back and get it right side up again, and now dey is asking to do it, de men better let em."[24]

Truth's life and her words disregarded and thus broke down the dividing walls of hostility defined by class, race, and sex. Her life and words are a witness to the existence of a life-giving canon for all who are willing to acknowledge and, finally, authorize it with our own lives and words.

It is important to notice that women who hear and heed the witness of Truth and others like her are not arguing for reopening the canon. The texts by which we *already* live and know life abundant are not restricted to those in the biblical canon. We are in fact creating a new canon. Were women to insist on reopening the canon, we would mimic an effort we have found life-denying: identifyng certain texts as life-giving for all people in all ages and places. Indeed, the Montreal conference had already clarified that the scriptural canon was an inadequate basis for church unity. But the reality that an agreed-upon canon cannot assure unity still awaits recognition by ecumenical leaders.[25]

Texts accepted as canonical, and traditional interpretations of them, have long shaped our actions and differing understandings of Tradition. Yet what we accept as Tradition is itself built upon another Tradition whose foundations it covered over in order to establish itself. Fortunately, traces remain to give evidence that our forebears recast texts to reflect their perspectives in each epoch about divine presence and the meaning of life experiences.[26] Unfortunately, commonly held understandings of Tradition, as of the canon, discourage us from being active participants in this ongoing dialogue between experience and tradition, a dialogue that could result both in re-interpretation and in new creation.[27] We are discouraged, at least in part, inasmuch as we accept prevalent perspectives on textuality and authority. Thus we turn to discuss these, hoping to see a way ahead.

OUR LIVES AS TEXTS, OR NEW AUTHORIZED VERSIONS

Despite contemporary North American fascination with visual imagery, at least as indicated by our consumption of television and videotapes, our culture is still textbound. Anthony Ugolnick, writing about the Russian Orthodox Church and the role of icons, observes: "The Western mind is just as 'image-producing' as the mind of any other culture, yet Westerners think differently about the images they produce. The act of understanding in the West has tended to be bound within the context of the book."[28] While Ugolnick traces this textual fixation to the story of Augustine's conversion— "Take and read, take and read," repeated a voice to which Augustine responded[29] —we believe that this mindset is part of a more massive and pervasive shift from orality to textuality that is a mark of modernity. In this shift, says Arnold Krupat: "Texuality was new, advanced, and male; orality was old, backward, and female. Not only female, of course, for the backwardness of the oral encompassed the 'primitive' as well: the unlettered red savage or black slave."[30] Here it is important to recall that the roots of the black woman's literary tradition that Katie Cannon has recognized are in the oral narratives of the black community.[31]

It is also important to attend to the resonance of Cannon's recognition of other than textual tradition in the voices of many feminist hermeneuts today. For example, Letty Russell emphasizes the distinction between the Word of God and the biblical texts. She speaks of a "process of new hearing," a process in which "the story of these [biblical] texts" may become God's Word "when it is heard in communities of faith and struggle as a witness to God's love for the world."[32] Nelle Morton's understanding of God's Word also focused on hearing and orality. She said: "We began hearing one another to speech. We experienced, as Spirit, hearing human beings to speech—to new creation. . . . The creative act of the Spirit was not Word speaking, but hearing—hearing the created one to speech."[33] Morton was clear that this process of "hearing one another to speech" is the word "becoming visible flesh."[34] This word is not the Word, "the word from the sky or from the patriarchal interpreter," but "the word was ourselves."[35]

Chung Hyun Kyung, of Seoul, Korea, says:

> The text of God's revelation was, is, and will be written in our bodies and our peoples' everyday struggle for survival and liberation. . . . The location of God's revelation is our life itself. Our life is the text, and the Bible and church tradition are the context which sometimes becomes the reference for our own ongoing search for God. We should unfold the ever-growing truth of God in history as the text of God's revelation through our lives.[36]

In short, Chung says of women: ". . . *we are the text*. . . ."[37]

Taken together, these feminists' reflections illumine two perspectives on textuality that may renew our understanding of scripture and Tradition. First, they point to the age-old tendency to see what is written—particularly if canonized as text or book or scripture—as true, authoritative, unchangeable. Yet we are reminded that what is written is not "inertly given," as Edward Said has said. To the contrary, writing "derives from . . . a desire to *tell* a story much more than . . . for telling a *story*.[38] While the desire to *tell* a story is demonstrated within biblical texts, it is also in dormancy because of the biblical texts. Women are again actualizing the desire to *tell* stories. We are all invited to tell our stories, to create new oral traditions, new texts, new canonical traditions that sustain one another in this ongoing outpouring of the human spirit. Women are recognizing and realizing a fluidity of form that matches the variegated content of our lives. Women welcome multiplicity joyously, for, with Said, we know that every new story translated into tradition or text or canon can be a "new parochialism."[39]

The second perspective on the nature of textuality, then, illumines the way a text's ability to bear meaning is part and parcel of its acute particularity, its circumstantial and contingent character. This specificity of a text's situatedness and sensibility points to the limits of interpretation.[40] Although interpretation may loosen a text from its originating context and liberate a superabundance of meaning,[41] not all texts are able to bear life-giving meaning for all people in all times and places. And certain texts are frankly life-denying and irredeemable.[42] The significance of women telling our stories and creating textual traditions out of the rich diversity of our lives is once again highlighted.

These perspectives on the nature of textuality pose the question of authority with new urgency, certainly for people committed to cultivating conversation between ecumenists and feminists. Today women of faith often think about the *structure* of authority in terms of partnership, not domination; about the *source* of authority as experience rather than decree or doctrine; about the *spirit* of authority with images that press into God's future rather than being restrained by the past.[43] While many ecumenists agree with feminists' concern for the abuse of authority as it has been exercised,[44] the attention of many ecumenical leaders is focused on reconciling already established structures of authority.[45] Again, the Montreal insight that the authority of traditions and scriptures should be seen as limited in light of the living Tradition seems lost. Instead, the present predisposition is to preserve the Tradition in forms familiar to the dominant culture and leaders, whether or not those forms still receive and generate life-giving renewal.

A crucial choice is before us: whether we will continue to invest authority in already written texts and already established confessional traditions as if they were the Tradition, or whether we can recognize authority whenever and wherever the divine Word finds flesh.[46] Can we rekindle desire to tell our own stories and weave our own texts and traditions for the sake of a liberating, life-giving future for all people? R. S. Sugirtharajah also speaks the challenge to us:

> In all faith traditions, including Christianity, the original authority is not the text but the word that is heard. Hindus classify their scriptural texts into two categories — *Sruti* (that which is heard) and *Smrti* (that which is remembered). For them *Sruti* has more authority than *Smrti*. Thus the oral word takes precedence over the written word. It also has the power to sensitize a people. When the Jesus movement wrote down the words of Jesus, the prime purpose was to read them aloud publicly to assembled gatherings, and they

were not meant to be read privately in a closed study. So also with the letters of Paul and other compositions of the Jesus movement.[47]

The hermeneutical question for feminists and ecumenists alike is whether we will support the birth of a new orality among all peoples whose voices have been silenced or stifled by our focus on written forms of the Word. Dare we commit ourselves to cultivating continual conversation among oral experiences and written expressions, recognizing the authority appropriate to each? Are we bold enough to authorize diverse life-giving words in our day as new expressions of God's Word? Can we affirm the image of the creator coming to voice in all people, even those by whom we are challenged and with whom we find ourselves at odds?

How we embody our concern for the unity of the church is itself a matter that divides or unites. If we attempt to establish the acceptable limits of diversity with reference to an already given deposit of faith, we serve a dominator tradition. Each of us will then seek to set the terms for unity in our own image and tend to identify the Tradition with our own tradition. When we instead choose to commit ourselves to God's liberating and life-giving presence among all peoples and in all creation, we are linked to all whom God creates and loves. This unity we seek is not an exclusive club but a call for everyone to participate as God's presence transforms all into a new creation.

NOTES

1. For a compendium of the most pertinent documents, see *The Bible: Its Authority and Interpretation in the Ecumenical Movement,* ed. Ellen Flesseman-van Leer (Faith and Order Paper No. 99; Geneva: World Council of Churches, 1983).

2. See, e.g., Suzanne de Dietrich, "The Bible, a Force of Unity," *The Ecumenical Review* 1 (1949): 410–16.

3. See, e.g., *Biblical Authority for Today: A World Council of Churches Symposium on 'The Biblical Authority for the Churches' Social and Political Message Today',* ed. Alan Richardson and W. Schweitzer (Philadelphia: Westminster Press, 1951).

4. Ernst Käsemann, "Unity and Diversity in New Testament Ecclesiology," *Novum Testamentum* 6 (1963): 295.

5. Raymond E. Brown, S.S., "The Unity and Diversity in New Testament Ecclesiology," *Novum Testamentum* 6 (1963): 302.

6. *The Fourth World Conference on Faith and Order, Montreal 1963,* ed. P. C. Rodger and L. Vischer (Faith and Order Paper No. 42; London: SCM Press, 1964), 52.

7. Ibid., 54.

8. Ibid., 55.

9. Ibid., 57ff. The question raised but not adequately addressed at Montreal was "the question of criterion for the genuine Tradition." This question in turn raised the question of "right interpretation" of scripture, since in "the history of the Church the criterion has

been sought in the Holy Scriptures rightly interpreted" (ibid., 53). The World Council of Churches Commission on Faith and Order continued this consideration in a study process that first focused on hermeneutical issues and then on the issue of authority. See "The Significance of the Hermeneutical Problem for the Ecumenical Movement," in *New Directions in Faith and Order, Bristol 1967, Reports-Minutes-Documents* (Faith and Order Paper No. 50; Geneva: World Council of Churches, 1968), 32–41; "The Authority of the Bible," in *Faith and Order, Louvain 1971, Study Reports and Documents* (Faith and Order Paper No. 59; Geneva: World Council of Churches, 1971), 9–23.

10. See Robert Wuthnow, *The Restructuring of American Religion: Society and Faith Since World War II* (Princeton, NJ: Princeton University Press, 1988), esp. 71–99.

11. See Mary Ann Tolbert, "Protestant Feminists and the Bible: On the Horns of a Dilemma," in *The Pleasure of Her Text: Feminist Readings of Biblical and Historical Texts,* ed. Alice Bach (Philadelphia: Trinity Press International, 1990), 5–23.

12. No one in the twentieth century has raised the question of women's loyalty more pointedly or poignantly than Virginia Woolf. She called women to be free from "unreal loyalties," loyalties springing from pride found in religious, educational, political, family institutions, all of which are dominated by the fathers and their sons (*Three Guineas* [London, 1938; Harmondsworth, Middlesex, England: Penguin Books, 1977], 90). Tragically, Woolf found no way to incarnate her real loyalties; her vision of a society informed by women's values and voices was limited to an "anonymous and secret Society of Outsiders" (ibid., 126). It was, finally, not a habitable vision for her.

13. Savina J. Teubal, *Sarah the Priestess: The First Matriarch of Genesis* (Athens, OH: Swallow Press, 1984) and *Hagar the Egyptian: The Lost Tradition of the Matriarchs* (San Francisco: Harper & Row, 1990).

14. See Teubal, *Sarah the Priestess.*

15. We are referring to Riane Eisler's distinction between dominator and partnership cultural behavior. Dominator behavior ranks people, basing its power on the establishment and enforcement of domination. Partnership behavior links people, basing its power on generating and nurturing life. See *The Chalice & the Blade: Our History, Our Future* (San Francisco: Harper & Row, 1987).

16. Christine Amjad-Ali, "The Equality of Women: Form or Substance (I Corinthians 11:2–16)," in *Voices from the Margin: Interpreting the Bible in the Third World,* ed. R. S. Sugirtharajah (Maryknoll, NY: Orbis, 1991), 212.

17. An earlier feminist hermeneut, Henriette Visser't Hooft, whose husband was the first General Secretary of the World Council of Churches, exclaimed to Karl Barth with regard to this text: "It seems to me too cheap simply to say here that Paul was stuck in the prejudices of *his* time, the usual argument. Even then, it would be shocking that a person like Paul could so wantonly damn half the human race" ("Aus den Briefwechsel mit Karl Barth 1934," in Gundrun Kaper, Henriette Visser't Hooft, et al., *Eva wo bist du? Frauen in internationalen Organisation der Okumene: Eine Dokumentation* (Gelnhausen, Berlin: Burckhardthaus-Laetare Verlag, 1981), 14 (our translation).

18. Amjad-Ali, "Equality of Women," 212.

19. See James A. Sanders, *From Sacred Story to Sacred Text* (Philadelphia: Fortress, 1987). Sanders, however, also insists: "Only the traditional can become canonical . . . in crisis situations only the old, tried and true has any real authority. . . . A new story will not do; only a story with old, recognizable elements has the power for life required, because it somehow can pierce beneath the immediate and apparent changes taking place to recover the irreducible core of identity left unthreatened, that which can survive the crisis" (p. 21).

While Sanders addresses the way in which texts attain canonical status, he does not attend to the political questions of what structures of power the canon sacralizes. Robert B. Coote and Mary P. Coote, in contrast, show how, from the outset, the canon was dedicated to the legitimation of monarchical rule, and to the interests of an educated economic elite. See *Power, Politics, and the Making of the Bible: An Introduction* (Minneapolis: Fortress, 1990).

20. See Katie G. Cannon, *Black Womanist Ethics* (Atlanta: Scholars Press, 1988).

21. Rosemary Radford Ruether, *Womanguides: Readings Toward a Feminist Theology* (Boston: Beacon Press, 1985), ix.

22. Ibid., xii.

23. Sojourner Truth, *Narrative and Book of Life,* reprint (Battle Creek, MI, 1878; Salem, NH: Ayer Company, 1988), 133–34.

24. Ibid., 134–35.

25. Geoffrey Wainwright, for example, laments the dissolution of "the whole notion of a literary, artistic, cultural canon," as well as feminist tampering with the scriptural canon, complaining: "Excisions of the offending, the hegemony of a single and narrow hermeneutical principle, the addition of matter believed to have been neglected—all has been attempted without a communal consensus" ("Canon," in *Dictionary of the Ecumenical Movement,* ed. Nicholas Lossky, Jose Miguez Bonino, John S. Pobee, Tom F. Stransky, Geoffrey Wainwright, Pauline Webb [Geneva: World Council of Churches, 1991], 118). Of course, Wainwright does not address the ways in which establishers of these canons themselves excised the offensive, privileged interpretive principles notably narrow, and added what affirmed their position and power. Nor does he wonder whether early church councils really represented "a communal consensus," if by communal he means the whole people of God.

Moreover, as James Sanders has pointed out, "there were numerous 'final' forms" of the canon (*Canon and Community: A Guide to Canonical Criticism* [Philadelphia: Fortress, 1984], 25). Ironically, Sanders goes on to say, *not* that the search for visible church unity depends on a unity of the scriptural canon, but that the "ecumenical movement has raised our consciousness to see that there is a plurality of canons in the several Christian communions" (ibid., 15).

26. For example, see Jacob Neusner, *Self-Fulfilling Prophecy: Exile and Return in the History of Judaism* (Boston: Beacon Press, 1987) for a history of biblical "Judaisms," this is to say, of how "Israel" reconceived itself in each situation in which it existed.

27. As Judith Plaskow contends, the living memory of a people is created by their experience-tradition dialogue. Plaskow argues that, as information is transformative only when it "becomes part of the community's collective memory," Jewish collective memory itself must be reshaped for women's experience to have a full and authoritative place ("Jewish Memory from a Feminist Perspective, in *Weaving the Visions: New Patterns in Feminist Spirituality,* ed. Judith Plaskow and Carol P. Christ [San Francisco: Harper & Row, 1989], 44).

28. Anthony Ugolnick, *The Illuminating Icon* (Grand Rapids: Eerdmans, 1989), 48.

29. Ibid. Cf. *Confessions of St. Augustine,* trans. F. J. Sheed (New York: Sheed & Ward, 1943), 178.

30. Arnold Krupat, *Voices in the Margin: Native American Literature and the Canon* (Berkeley: University of California Press, 1989), 46.

31. See Cannon, *Black Womanist Ethics,* esp. 84ff.

32. Letty M. Russell, "Introduction," in *Feminist Interpretation of the Bible,* ed. Russell (Philadelphia: Westminster, 1985), 17.

33. Nelle Morton, "Toward a Whole Theology," in *The Journey Is Home* (Boston: Beacon Press, 1985), 82.

34. Nelle Morton, "A Word We Cannot Yet Speak," in *The Journey Is Home,* 99.

35. Ibid.

36. Chung Hyun Kyung, *Struggle to be the Sun Again: Introducing Asian Women's Theology* (Maryknoll, NY: Orbis Books, 1990), 111.

37. Ibid. It could be argued that Chung falls into the trap into which Ugolnick thinks Calvin fell. Although Calvin privileged the preached Word, he conceptualized the natural world as a text and employed reading as a central metaphor. For Ugolnick, this is but another version of the Protestant tendency to be textbound. See Ugolnick, *Illuminating Icon,* 56.

38. Edward W. Said, *The World, the Text, and the Critic* (Cambridge, MA: Harvard University Press, 1983), 131–32.

39. Ibid., 143.

40. See Umberto Eco, *The Limits of Interpretation* (Bloomington and Indianapolis: Indiana University Press, 1990).

41. See Paul Ricoeur, "The Logic of Jesus, The Logic of God," *Christianity & Crisis* (December 24, 1979), 324.

42. See, e.g., Phyllis Trible, *Texts of Terror: Literary-Feminist Readings of Biblical Narratives* (Philadelphia: Fortress, 1984).

43. See, e.g., Madeleine Boucher, "Authority-in-Community," *Mid-Stream: An Ecumenical Journal* 21(3); Letty M. Russell, "Authority and the Challenge of Feminist Interpretation of Scripture," in *Feminist Interpretation of the Bible;* eadem, *Household of Freedom: Authority in Feminist Theology* (Philadelphia: Westminster, 1987); eadem, "The Authority of Scripture," in *In God's Image: Reflections on Identity, Human Wholeness and the Authority of Scripture,* ed. Janet Crawford and Michael Kinnamon (Geneva: World Council of Churches, 1983).

44. See Margaret O'Gara, "Ecumenism and Feminism in Dialogue on Authority," in *Women and Church: The Ecumenical Challenge of Solidarity in an Age of Alienation,* ed. Melanie A. May (Grand Rapids: Eerdmanns; New York: Friendship Press, 1991).

45. See, e.g., *Growth in Agreement: Reports and Agreed Statements of Ecumenical Conversations on a World Level,* ed. Harding Meyer and Lukas Vischer (New York/Ramsey, NJ: Paulist Press; Geneva: World Council of Churches, 1984); *Building Unity: Ecumenical Dialogues with Roman Catholic Participation in the United States,* ed. Joseph A. Burgess and Brother Jeffrey Gros, FSC (New York/Mahwah, NJ: Paulist Press, 1989).

46. Writing about biblical authority in relation to her study of Paul's use of rhetoric, Antoinette Clark Wire affirms: "If we take on the role of the reader that Paul sets up and locate the Bible's authority not in given dogmas or individual authors but in the event where the persuasive word meets conviction, this event may occur where we do not expect . . . voices from outside the canon may speak with authority" (*The Corinthian Women Prophets: A Reconstruction through Paul's Rhetoric* [Minneapolis: Fortress, 1990], 11).

47. R. S. Sugirtharajah, "Postscript," in *Voices from the Margin,* ed. Sugirtharajah, 439.

RECOMMENDED READINGS

Bach, Alice, ed. *The Pleasure of Her Text: Feminist Readings of Biblical and Historical Texts*. Philadelphia: Trinity Press International, 1990.

Coote, Robert B., and Mary P. Coote. *Power, Politics, and the Making of the Bible: An Introduction*. Minneapolis: Fortress, 1990.

Flesseman-van Leer, Ellen, ed. *The Bible: Its Authority and Interpretation in the Ecumenical Movement*. Faith and Order Paper No. 99. Geneva: World Council of Churches, 1983.

Ruether, Rosemary Radford. *Womanguides: Readings Toward a Feminist Theology*. Boston: Beacon Press, 1985.

Russell, Letty M., ed. *Feminist Interpretation of the Bible*. Philadelphia: Westminster, 1985.

Sugirtharajah, R. S., ed. *Voices from the Margin: Interpreting the Bible in the Third World*. Maryknoll, NY: Orbis, 1991.

Teubal, Savina J. *Hagar the Egyptian: The Lost Tradition of the Matriarchs*. San Francisco: Harper & Row, 1990.

——. *Sarah the Priestess: The First Matriarch of Genesis*. Athens, OH: Swallow Press, 1984.

◆ Feminist Theological Hermeneutics: Canon and Christian Identity

CLAUDIA V. CAMP ◆

THE TITLE of this essay already contains five terms—feminist, theological, hermeneutics, canon, and Christian identity—each of which could be, and has been, the subject of volumes of contentious discussion. Moreover, even the most cursory attempt to deal with them generates at least three more terms—authority, Christ, and church—that are equally problematic. I would suggest, in fact, that the question of authority is the central question of this whole complex of ideas.

Let me begin by offering (at least) minimal definitions of the title's terminology or, in certain cases, by raising questions that prevent me from offering even a minimal definition. By "feminist" I mean (at least) an approach to culture that understands and analyzes gender relations in structural terms, with particular attention to the structural disempowerment of women. By "theological" I mean (at least) reflection that is determined by the assumed experience of self-transcendence. Thus, by definition, theology must address those areas of life that are not discernible or testable by standards of objectivity. By "hermeneutics" I mean (at least) the process of conscious reflection on how interpretation is done and who does it. The major difficulty with respect to these three terms lies not so much in defining them individually as in determining their relationship to each other. Is all interpretation hermeneutical? Is all hermeneutics theological? Must all theology be feminist?

The terms "canon" and "Christian identity" are less easy to specify briefly. Within Protestantism (and in most current popular usage) "canon" has referred to the sacred writings of Christianity, the Bible with its two testaments. The word "canon" has, however, a more general meaning—"rule"—and has been so used within Catholicism ("canon law"). While feminists agree with the need for a canon, in the sense of standards of judgment, the question of where that rule is to be located remains open. We may thus ask: How will a feminist theological hermeneutics define "canon"?

To ask about *identity* is to ask: Who authorizes, who authors our lives? To say that one's identity is "Christian" has generally meant counting as important at least three things: Christ, the church, and the Bible. But it is precisely the authority of Christ, church, and Bible that is called into question when a person identifies herself also as "feminist." What is the nature of biblical authority in the life of a feminist? Is the notion of the authority of an androcentric text relevant at all to what Elisabeth Schüssler Fiorenza calls a "self-identified woman"? The question, however, is not only one of how a feminist relates to the Bible, but further of how a feminist relates to other Christian women who also claim a place in the church, and who are willing to accept more traditional understandings of "biblical authority." That is to say, can a feminist hermeneutics be both critical *and* inclusive?[1] Our investigation must consider, then, both the general issue of women's relationship to the Bible and the more specific, critical concerns of feminist scholarship, as well as how these arenas interrelate.

FEMINISM, THEOLOGY, AND HERMENEUTICS

The questions raised above about the relationship of interpretation, hermeneutics, and theology only become problematic in the context of modern historical scholarship. In an earlier era, it was taken for granted that interpretation was done to serve the needs of the church of that day and that it would be done by men of faith for whom the world of the text was transparently their own world. It was only with the rise of historical methods and questions in the last two hundred years that consciousness arose of the distance between the text and the contemporary world. With the awareness of distance came as well two other, competing demands. One was the imperative of historical science for objectivity, seeking the facts of the past untainted by beliefs and attitudes of the present. The other was the concomitant need for people of the church to overcome this distance, in order that the Bible might remain relevant to the present.

The struggles and unconscious compromises of imagined objectivity entailed by these competing imperatives have been well elaborated by Schüssler Fiorenza, as has a programmatic alternative which rests in a new view of history, not as "that which happened" but rather as "that which is remembered."[2] Endemic here, not secondary, is the act of interpretation. This perspective abandons the illusion of objectivity in favor of the realization that all interpretation is constrained by the questions of the contemporary interpreter. Granting this perspective, then, indeed, all interpretation necessarily involves a hermeneutics: even that sort of interpretation that purportedly seeks only "the facts of the past" will have access to those "facts" only in the form that fits the question asked. The better part of intellectual credibility is to acknowledge at the outset the factors motivating one's questions.

Even more to the point, from the perspective of feminist liberation theology, is the acknowledgment that the work of interpretation is always engaged either for or against the struggle of the oppressed for liberation. Schüssler Fiorenza presses this issue a step further. In challenging biblical scholarship to become more critical of "its own professed objectivism and value-free stance," feminist theology

> also challenges biblical scholarship to become more theological in the precise sense of the word. If Christians understand the Bible as divine revelation, then biblical interpretation is a theological task in the strictest sense. Insofar as the Bible as Holy Scripture speaks about God, biblical scholarship must develop a critical method and hermeneutics that does not "render God" as a God of patriarchal oppression.[3]

Thus, while the biblical scholar *is* engaged in a hermeneutical process that is aware of the inevitable interaction between "what the text meant" and "what the text means," Schüssler Fiorenza does not envision a simple consensual circle of text and interpretation engaging in mutual self-correction. A patriarchal text read in a patriarchal culture will never self-correct! The role of biblical scholars must, then, be more like that of "culture critics who subject both the historical-critical interpretations of their colleagues and of 'ordinary' believers and preachers to a critical evaluation and hermeneutics of liberation."[4]

DEFINING CANON: CRITICAL PERSPECTIVE AND INCLUSIVITY IN FEMINIST HERMENEUTICS

AN INCLUSIVE PERSPECTIVE

One of the most inclusive understandings of feminist theological hermeneutics is the five-part typology of Carolyn Osiek. She poses the following question:

> When women today in Christian communities become aware of their situation within a patriarchal religious institution and, moreover, when they

recognize that the Bible is a major implement for maintaining the oppression of patriarchal structure, what are the ways in which they respond and adjust to that situation?[5]

The five ways she identifies are rejectionist, loyalist, revisionist, sublimationist, and liberationist. Certain feminists, from Elizabeth Cady Stanton to Mary Daly, have lived out the *rejectionist* model, finding not only the Bible itself but the whole of both Judaism and Christianity to be so corrupted by patriarchalism as to be irredeemable. Fully counter to this is the *loyalist* mode. Osiek's definition here is both subtle and important. In defining loyalists as feminists, she is *not* referring to those women who simply accept the traditionally understood biblical mandate of female inferiority and submission. Although their argumentation varies, feminist loyalists assert both the reality of the Bible as divine revelation, the Word of God, *and* the validity of the notion that God wills women and men to live in "true happiness and mutual respect."[6] The third model, the *revisionist* hermeneutic, represents a midpoint between the first two, holding that "the patriarchal mold in which the Judeo-Christian tradition has been cast is historically but not theologically determined."[7] This mode looks to reform from within by reading the Bible for positive role models for women and by depatriarchalizing the interpretation of texts. The work of Phyllis Trible is often cited as a classic example of this mode. A fourth alternative, the *sublimationist* hermeneutic, posits an essential distinction between the masculine and the feminine. Rather than denigrating the feminine, however, as androcentric interpretation would do, it exalts what it takes to be female traits as equal to or higher than the male. This mode tends to focus on the world of symbols, and is not typical of biblical scholars: even feminist biblical scholars usually maintain some allegiance to their textual and historical training. *Liberationist* feminism, the fifth mode identified by Osiek, defines salvation as liberation in this world. It consciously adopts an advocacy position, using the struggle of women against oppression as its hermeneutical key, and thus striving toward a "transformation of the social order."[8]

Part of the value of Osiek's approach, aside from the usefulness of its typology, is the fact that she too works from an admitted "advocacy position," one that might be defined as advocacy of inclusivism. She believes that these five positions are all "truly alternatives, that is, within the limits imposed on us by our experience and human conditioning, we really are free to choose our own hermeneutical direction."[9] The urge to include a wide range of women's interpretive experiences must confront, however, the challenge of critical rigor, both in an intellectual and in a political sense.

Are all these positions equally capable of coherent argumentation? Do all of them deal equally well with the sources of oppression (including classism and racism, as well as sexism), and do they all provide equally adequate means to combat such oppression? Such critical questions are posed most forcefully in the work of Elisabeth Schüssler Fiorenza, whose work on feminist theological hermeneutics, because of both its quantity and its sophistication, has virtually defined the field.

A CRITICAL PERSPECTIVE

Schüssler Fiorenza is identified by Osiek as one of several liberationist feminists, but Osiek's discussion elides the fact that Schüssler Fiorenza has directed serious criticism at fellow liberationists Letty Russell and Rosemary Radford Ruether, categorizing both as neo-orthodox![10] These three feminists share a commitment to "women-church," a woman-centered Christian praxis oriented toward transforming the structures of both church and world. What distinguishes Schüssler Fiorenza from the others is precisely her approach to the use of scripture. Both Russell and Ruether, she argues, search for "a critical universal principle or normative tradition from particular historical texts and specific cultural situations."[11] Ruether identifies in the Bible what she calls its "liberating-prophetic critique." Russell cites the biblical witness to "God's liberating action on behalf of God's creation."[12] According to Schüssler Fiorenza, however, a feminist theological hermeneutics that relates to the Bible in these ways is problematic because it "still adheres to the archetypal biblical paradigm that establishes universal principles and normative patterns" and does not "seriously take into account the androcentric character of biblical language on the one hand and the patriarchal stamp of all biblical traditions on the other hand."[13] The hermeneutics of Russell and Ruether—because they distinguish language from content, patriarchal expression from liberating tradition, and androcentric text from feminist "witness"—"seems to rely on an untenable linguistic-philosophical position that divides form and content, linguistic expression and revelatory truth."[14]

In a move indicative of her Roman Catholic heritage, Schüssler Fiorenza alters the typical Protestant understanding of canon, shifting from the sense of canon as written scripture to canon as definitive measurement: feminist critical hermeneutics will follow "Augustine, Thomas, and the Second Vatican Council in formulating a criterion or canon that limits inspired truth and revelation to matters pertaining to the salvation, freedom, and liberation of all, especially women."[15] The source of this canon, moreover, is not scripture but rather the community, specifically, the community of women struggling against oppression. Feminist theological hermeneutics is, then, a *critical* hermeneutics, which does not regard the Bible as a mythical archetype (the critique lodged against Ruether and Russell, as well as against more traditional interpreters), but as a "historical prototype, or as a formative root-model of biblical faith and life." As against the ideal and unchanging form of an archetype, a prototype is understood to be open to the possibility of transformation. The vision of liberation and salvation in this hermeneutics "is *informed* by the biblical prototype but is not *derived from it. It places biblical texts under the authority of feminist experience* insofar as it maintains that revelation is ongoing and takes place 'for the sake of our salvation.'"[16]

On occasion, Schüssler Fiorenza slips into the more conventional usage of canon-as-scripture,[17] but these are exceptions that prove the rule. Scripture is canon in the sense of being a "root-model," and what is modeled is precisely a "multiform" understanding of Christian church and life. The fact that the Bible includes many interpretations of faith does not, however, mean that all are equally valid today. Christian *teaching* must preserve all traditions, precisely to preserve the multiformity of the written canon. Christian *preaching*, however, must discern between oppressive texts and liberating ones: only the latter deserve a place in proclamation.[18]

The work of Schüssler Fiorenza challenges the critical adequacy of much of what Carolyn Osiek would call feminist hermeneutics. In practice, a good bit of the enterprise to which Schüssler Fiorenza exhorts feminists is not unlike that of the "neo-orthodox" revisionists and liberationists she criticizes. It involves searching for the "lost coin" of "traditions and visions of liberation among [our] inheritance of androcentric biblical texts and their interpretations."[19] We recover maternal God-language; we restore the elided history of women's leadership in ancient communities; we identify the people of God according to the Bible's own inclusive norm in beginning with creation and ending with the new creation. What makes Schüssler Fiorenza different, and it is an important difference, is her insistence on the authority of women over the Bible. We must understand the background of this assertion not simply in terms of the desire of feminism to advance the cause of women but also in terms of a critical theory that refuses to validate its claims by appeal to a "transcendent other." If there are biblical texts that support women's struggle against oppression, they do so because women claim them in this struggle, not because God (or any other transcendent, de-historicized ideal) says so.

TENSION AND COMPROMISE

In my own wrestling with the ways, means, and effects of biblical interpretation, I have come to a position in full accord with Schüssler Fiorenza's
critical stance, perhaps in some measure even more critical: I find it hard
to speak at all of "revelation," for example. On the other hand, I partake
of both a past experience and a present context that lead me to ask further questions and to imagine the activity of feminist theological hermeneutics in some different, though complementary, ways.

The past experience to which I refer is that of having been led in part
by scripture to my current critical faith, which holds so much against this
same scripture. I have had the experience of relating to Hebrew scripture
in a way that feels "personal" and, indeed, to some extent personifies the
text, an intellectual sin of which Schüssler Fiorenza finds Phyllis Trible,
for example, guilty.[20] This sense of "relationship" was part of the beginning of the raising of my feminist consciousness. I cannot say that scripture alone made me a feminist: I was studying the Bible in an academic
context that was influenced by feminism, and that raised this agenda in
conversation with the Bible. Yet the Bible did also provide an energy and
a motivation for pursuing feminist concerns. It did so by means of another
interpretive model criticized by Schüssler Fiorenza, namely, Ruether's idea
of the prophetic principle of justice. Like Ruether, I saw this principle as
applicable to women today, in spite of the prophets' own tendency to sub-
merge it in sexism.

Today, on the one hand, I assent to Schüssler Fiorenza's critique of these
positions: they are indeed apologies for scripture. Yet they are not only
that. Such apologias derive from a commitment (even if an insufficiently
critical one) to the cause of women. To embrace them is to embrace critical
compromise. It may also be to embrace effective pedagogy, beginning where
the learner is, and thus to claim a source of power in educating Christian
churches toward a theological feminism. My past experience poses for me
the question of the relationship between a feminist hermeneutics that holds
itself accountable to rigorous critical standards and a feminist pedagogy
that finds value in the art of compromise.

In my present context, moreover, I find that an analogous tension between
critical rigor and efficacious compromise also exists in the conversation
between feminist hermeneutics and feminist politics. I am a member of
a congregation of the Christian church (Disciples of Christ), a reputedly
"liberal" congregation with, nonetheless, a strong resistance to facing
feminist issues directly. This congregation, though almost entirely middle
economic bracket Caucasion, participates in a countywide grassroots

political organizing group that crosses racial, economic, and denominational lines. Although the member congregations show varying degrees of resistance to practicing gender equality within their churches, the organization itself provides an unparalleled context for women (as well as men) to receive leadership training, acquire political power, and make an identifiable difference in their communities' quality of life.

Both my immediate and my community-wide church contexts reinforce my sense of the necessity of hermeneutical compromise, not because all versions of feminist hermeneutics are equally valid, as Osiek seems to suggest, but because the facts of religious-political life in the twentieth-century West are what they are. For most Christians with whom I come in contact, the Bible simply *is* authoritative. For change to come in my congregation, critical hermeneutics has to be adapted for conversation to take place with women who still interpret their lives in traditional ways. The same is true, for different reasons, within my political organizing group. There the Bible functions as a source of empowerment for political action. Although it is indeed used against women on one level, it also motivates women and men together to become agents of social change. In the area of the country in which I live, I know of no more effective movement toward improving the actual lives of women, especially poor women, than this one in which I participate, even though it is woefully inadequate in terms of feminist hermeneutics or rhetoric.

What is at issue here, I believe, is the need for reconceptualizations of biblical authority, re-visions that embrace Schüssler Fiorenza's focus on the authority of biblical *people* but also take into fuller account the work of the Bible in defining those people. Assuming Schüssler Fiorenza's model of scripture as historical prototype, I offer here three complementary models for scriptural authority that expand on and nuance her work.

THREE MODELS OF BIBLICAL AUTHORITY IN FEMINIST HERMENEUTICS

The Dialogical Authority Model

The first model begins with the experience, still formative for many women, of the fundamentally "nonintellectual commitment to scripture as somehow determinative for the personal and communal identity of Christians."[21] The model envisions an educational effort to clarify the nature of *authority* in this commitment, and especially to distinguish authority from *coercion*, on the one hand, and from *influence*, on the other. To experience scripture as *coercive* is to experience it as threatening one with its inherent ability to carry out its warnings and promises. Fundamentalists who construe scripture as the literal word of God may experience it as having such coercive power. The experience of scriptural *influence,* on the other hand, is one of its persuasive potential, the sense that it provides information about our environment and may help in the decision-making process, but that it has no more inherent value in such a process than any other worthwhile source of information or guidance. Susan Brooks Thistlethwaite correlates these perspectives with the "conservative" and "liberal" views on authority in general: "The conservative view is that authority is always exercised through coercion and therefore that an authoritarian order must be hierarchical. The liberal view has been that authority is vested in an order of persuasion by reason and therefore must be egalitarian."[22]

In distinction from coercion and influence, *authority* is defined here as a free surrendering to the jurisdiction of scripture. What it means to live within the jurisdiction of scripture will vary from person to person. What is constant is that an uncoerced acknowledgment of this authority has been made. Once authority is granted, one attempts to live in alignment with its source without need of threat, promise, or argumentation. Thus, obedience to true authority involves no loss of freedom.

But what induces such granting of authority and, most importantly, what keeps such an orientation from becoming mindless obedience? Political theorist David V. J. Bell suggests that the answer lies in a shared set of values or beliefs held by both the one who gives and the one who takes authority.[23] Such "credenda" authenticate authority. Thus, one might ask, what credenda might women looking toward the beginning of the twenty-first century hold in common with an ancient and androcentric text? I offer these reflections.

Within scripture itself, the authority of text is always understood in relation to the authority *of persons.* Whether in Moses or Huldah, in David or Esther, in Solomon or Woman Wisdom of Proverbs, the authority of the text is always an embodied authority: persons must authorize the text, even as it authorizes them. Thus, true authority has a *dialogical* quality. Paradoxically, in order to grant authority to someone or something else, one must first *have* the authority to do so. Legitimate and uncoerced granting occurs from a position of strength, not of weakness. This granting is, moreover, reciprocal. For a text to have this dialogical authority, it must continually create new persons to participate in this ongoing interaction. In other words, a truly authoritative text will have a generative, life-giving quality.

Many Christian women, including feminist women, whose lives and vocations have been shaped by scripture, have been "created" by the text in this way. The life-giving quality of scripture provides a powerful, experiential point of departure to encourage others to participate in this dialogical exchange of authority. The act of interpretation becomes the bringing together of the biblical traditions with present circumstances to create life for the present and future, a process that Schüssler Fiorenza envisions in her discussion of the hermeneutics of remembrance and of creative actualization.[24]

Precisely this celebrative identification with scripture may prepare the ground for the more painful aspects of remembrance and also for what Schüssler Fiorenza calls the hermeneutics of suspicion and of proclamation, the recognition that the Bible's patriarchal, androcentric character must be named and condemned.[25] For sometimes the authority of scripture that is embodied in persons will call for the destruction of the existing, coercive institutions that have usurped authority. In fact, the first example of such a call occurs the very first time anyone is reported to have interpreted scripture, and that interpreter was a woman. In 2 Kings 22, the prophet Huldah proclaims the message of the newly found book of the covenant to be the destruction of Judah. Working from her example, we can imagine further that the process of dialogical authority entails that the woman whom scripture authorizes will sometimes have occasion to de-authorize scripture itself. Thus, *the authority of women over scripture becomes a primary credendum of scriptural authority.*

This model of biblical authority suggests one way of transcending the polarity of the critical versus the inclusive in feminist theological hermeneutics. It presupposes both that persons are created by their traditions, and that individuals may take up liberated subject positions in a generally oppressive discourse, presuppositions that are supported by a poststructuralist feminist theory that resists idealization of a unified conception of women's (or even feminist) "experience."[26] This model potentially withholds—or at least delays—a thoroughgoing critique of the tradition, but it does so in the interest of remaining in conversation with women who may yet be empowered to make a fuller acknowledgment of their own biblically grounded authority with respect to the Bible, the church, and society.[27]

THE METAPHOR MODEL

In three books, theologian Sallie McFague has elaborated the structure of a metaphorical theology. The purpose of this theological model is to carve

a third way between religious language that is idolatrous, regarded by its
users as having the capacity to refer literally to God, and language that
is irrelevant, so skeptical of making valid claims about God that it seems
meaningless. Over against these alternatives, metaphor perceives similarity in dissimilarity, sees "this *as* that," without confusing "this *for* that."
A metaphorical theology, then, will be one that sees connections between
God and the world, but sees them as "tensive, discontinuous and surprising," one that "insists on the dialectic of the positive and the negative, on
the 'is *and* the is not.'"[28]

Although McFague's project as a whole involves a constructive theological
task, a significant part of her argument has to do with the authority and
use of scripture. There is no language more likely either to become idolatrous or seem irrelevant than that of the Bible! McFague's proposal to transcend these two undesirable possibilities is to view the Bible as a "poetic
classic" and a "classic model" for Christianity.[29] The word "classic" in each
phrase points to the Bible's proven ability, across many times and places,
to make itself relevant as a discloser of reality. Its "classic" quality points
to its intrinsic authority. The word "classic" also, however, indicates the
Bible's conservative character. It requires qualification by the terms "poetic"
and "model," which suggest its "reforming and revolutionary power."[30] "As
model, the distance between the Bible and the reality it is attempting to
express is always maintained. A model or metaphor is . . . never identifiable
with its object; the Bible as model can never *be* the word of God. . . ."[31]
By the same token, as a poetic text, the Bible's greatness is defined by its
ability to say many things, its intrinsic demand to be interpreted always
anew. The multivocal rhetoric of poetry and the is/is not conceptuality
of the model are aligned in metaphorical thinking. Precisely because of
the Bible's metaphorical characteristics, "tension, dialectic, openness,
change, growth and relativity must be intrinsic to a proper understanding
of its authority"; further, the Bible calls *inherently* for a questioning of
its linguistic distortions and false consciousness.[32]

McFague's construal of the Bible as a classic model/poetic classic
provides, in one sense, an elaboration on Schüssler Fiorenza's concept of
the Bible as historical prototype or root-model (see above). McFague's focus
on language, however, as well as her orientation to a larger constructive
theology, also provides a different, though complementary, set of possibilities for actualizing a feminist hermeneutics. Work by McFague and others
has contributed numerous examples of metaphors whose affective depth
and structural power often derive from their classic source in scriptural
traditions, but whose authority is grounded in their capacity to generate
new and liberating structures in the contemporary world. McFague regards

"the kingdom of God" as the root metaphor of Christianity. As a root metaphor, it is both "supported and fed by many extended metaphors, the various parables," which leave its meaning "ambiguous, multileveled [and] imagistic"; it also generates "translation languages" into more conceptual discourses, which lend it "precision and consistency."[33] McFague's emphasis here on *parable,* a form of extended, narrative metaphor, is characteristic of her work and is evident also in her discussion of the life and death of Jesus as a "parable of God":

> In order to understand the ways of God with us—something unfamiliar and unknown to us, about which we do not know how to think or talk—we look at that life as a metaphor of God. What we see through that "grid" or "screen" is at one level an ordinary, secular story of a human being, but also a story shot through with surprise, unconventionality and incongruities which not only upset our conventional expectations (for instance, of what a "savior" is and who gets "saved"), but also involve a judgment on our part—"Surely this man is the Christ."[34]

This metaphorical perspective on classic theological loci—kingdom and Christ—in the biblical tradition is complemented in McFague's work by attention to other, more peripheral images by means of which she seeks to open and augment theological discourse—for example, the universe as God's body, and God as lover, mother, and friend.[35] The present author has followed McFague's lead in analyzing a Hebrew Bible metaphor, Wisdom as Woman in the book of Proverbs, as a theological root metaphor.[36] In the context of feminist theology, the metaphor of Woman Wisdom affirms the priority of human experience, especially women's experience, in the development of theology, as well as articulating a human relationship with God as Goddess. Woman Wisdom, furthermore, both reinforces and undercuts the concept of an authoritative scripture, defining this authority as personal, relational, and liminal. One final example of the fruitfulness of metaphorical theology can be found in Susan Brooks Thistlethwaite's *Metaphors for the Contemporary Church.*[37] Thistlethwaite proposes that what we see the church "as," how we metaphorize it, is crucial to the kind of church it will be. She commends the metaphors "Body of Christ" and "the Poor" as appropriate metaphors for the North American context.

The concept of metaphor, then, can provide both a theoretical perspective on the nature of scriptural authority itself and also a methodological tool for allowing liberating seeds of the tradition, heretofore scattered and fallow, to blossom forth with possibilities for new structures of reality. In this process, the metaphor model serves two other purposes for a feminist hermeneutics. First, by emphasizing the poetic, it taps into the power of imagination, a crucial source of energy and vision for creating a new future. Second, by emphasizing interpretation, it allows us to experience both our distance from the past, as we seek to understand a given metaphor's function in ancient times, and our connection with that past, as we meditate on the metaphor's meaning and power today. The written canon will be one, though not the only, source for such seeds. The authority of the metaphor will derive, moreover, not only from its source but also from its capacity to empower the transformation of individuals and society toward wholeness and inclusivity.

THE TRICKSTER MODEL

A third model for a feminist theological hermeneutics is more radical than the first two, yet still remains in touch with the experience of empowerment through conversation with the text. I shall call this hermeneutical stance that of "reading as a trickster" or, to use an image at home in the Bible itself, "reading as a strange woman."[38] In the folklore of many traditional cultures, the trickster is a "liminal" figure, that is, one who stands at the margins of authority, who embodies ambiguity and chaos, and who reminds the established orders that such forces of indeterminacy are inescapably present in their midst. The last point is crucial: different cultural worldviews may attempt to "explain" disorder in any number of ways, but they cannot ultimately deny its presence. The trickster figure, by embodying chaos in the guise of humor, allows for its acknowledgment and its embrace within the bounds of order. This embrace of chaos, in turn, imbues a potentially static, deadly order with liveliness and flexibility.

Distinctive yet similar, the biblical image of the "strange woman" may provide a hermeneutical key for the difficult attraction of Christian women and androcentric text. In the book of Proverbs, the Strange Woman is a highly condensed symbol of evil, an evil defined by the chaos of all that lies outside the acceptable system: the foreigner, the adulterer, the prostitute, the ritually impure. Remarkably, the Proverbs texts also develop an equally powerful symbol of all that is good, Wisdom personified as a woman. Though they are evaluated as moral opposites, similarity in vocabulary and imagery links these two figures to a considerable degree: both appear in the public sphere of streets and market; both invite listeners to their houses; both are to be grasped and embraced. This bonding of female-identified good and evil creates a dynamic not unlike that of folklore's trickster, the experience of ambiguity and potential chaos invading orderly oppositions. The tricksterlike ambiguity of the Strange Woman may also be seen in other biblical narratives about foreign women. Tamar (Genesis 38), Ruth, and Delilah, for example, are all figures who render the distinction between good and evil ambiguous by posing the possibility that good—indeed, the will of God—can come from (women's) evil.

To read, then, as a trickster or a strange woman involves, first, claiming identity with those at the margins and, second, willingness to read against the text, to read subversively. Tricksters and strange women recognize that, although the editor of Proverbs united the figures of Woman Wisdom and Woman Stranger by means of female imagery, his intent was to compel his male readers to tell the difference: to embrace Wisdom and avoid the Stranger. A hermeneutics of strangeness teaches us to tell the sameness, to undercut the apparently absolute opposition between good and evil; to illuminate instead their paradoxical, but experientially validated, unity; to affirm the disorder that energizes our struggle against unjust order.

It oppresses women to classify us as ideal wife or evil temptress. Although the Bible is, on one level, androcentric throughout, blatantly sexist passages such as these in Proverbs confront modern readers with unavoidable choices that may be masked elsewhere. It would seem at first glance that the choice is an either–or. Either we choose to accept the text's sexist ideology or, from out of our modern historical consciousness, we argue that such ideas are the product of a prior age, not relevant to us, worthy only of being ignored. But if we will listen only to those parts of the Bible we agree with, where then is its challenge to faith, its ability to make us see the log in our own eye, as we rub at the speck we find in Israel's?

To read subversively, to read as a strange woman, is to take seriously this saying from Prov 18:21:

> Death and life are in the power of the tongue,
> and those who love her shall eat of her fruits.

We are bound, in our humanity, to be lovers of language. The proverb reminds us of the inescapable duality that results, the encounter with both death and life. Every word contains its opposite. Meaning is not just multiple, but always ambiguous, indeterminate. The responsibility is thus ceded to us to find life as well as death in the power of the word and, with the responsibility, also the authority.

Subversive reading goes beyond even this recognition of responsibility in the face of indeterminacy. In a spirit of serious play, it leads us to revalue the oppressive absolutes of the past and the present by re-creating the very terms in which those absolutes are expressed. We thank the tradition which attempted to cast out its strange women for helping us find our name, and

thereby reassert our place in that tradition. As one further example of how
one might read as a strange woman, I offer this reflection on one of the
Bible's most misogynistic comments. Ben Sira, author of the deutero-
canonical book Christians call Ecclesiasticus, opines:

> From woman is the beginning of sin
> and because of her all die. (Sir 25:24)

What would happen if tricky readers were daring enough to embrace rather
than reject this statement? If we said, yes, human reality does include evil
and death? And woman encompasses them, just as she encompasses goodness and life. Woman does indeed represent *all* of human reality. To turn
the text's seemingly ultimate condemnation to the cause of a caricatured
ultimate empowerment is to take a stand in the tradition with a sense of
both humor and justice, the defining traits of the trickster. It replicates,
moreover, the courage of our forebears in claiming the name "Christian,"
initially a derogatory term used against them by the Romans.

Finally, the hermeneutical model of the strange woman, the trickster,
may contribute to mediating the tension between inclusiveness and critical
perspective that runs through feminist hermeneutics. To read the Bible as
a strange woman is to read through it to see the continuing paradox that
persists in the lives of women and men today. In Proverbs, we are met first
by the strong, exalted, almost deified figure of Woman Wisdom, surely
the apex of biblical female imagery. It is good, we nod to ourselves. But
then we confront her opposite, the Strange Woman, and begin to fear that
once again women are being used by male authors to support their own
place of power in the social structure, and the view of reality that supports it. Reading as a strange woman opens yet a third possibility: a positive
valuation of women's power as antistructural, regenerative because of its
liminality. But again we face paradox: What structures are being regenerated
by this liminality? Is it all too convenient for the beneficiaries of an unjust
power structure to give liminality its due in order to draw on its power
for themselves?

The reality is that all of these conflicting forces are at work in the mix
of human life, which is one reason why feminists have no choice but to
acknowledge varied courses of resistance to the patriarchal system, the sum
of which may finally generate real change. Some choose to separate themselves, to live on the margins of patriarchy. Women and men turn their
backs on biblical faith, developing spiritualities that reflect their lives and
serve their needs as persons who condemn the ways of those who own
the center. Christians cannot ignore the challenge of those who have moved
to the margins, though there is danger in this choice. For in removing

liminality from the center of the world, one abdicates the power to transform the world. But perhaps a new world is possible. Others choose to work within the system, to become pastors and lay leaders of churches, to teach in seminaries, sculpting a new reality within the old. This again is a valid choice, but only paradoxically so: the power that might transform the world also helps to support its present form. But perhaps the gain will outweigh the loss. In either case, there is an energy for change that comes when strange women seize the paradox of our existence, draw on the power of our liminality for ourselves, read the Bible as tricksters, and teach others to do so also.

NOTES

1. For earlier formulations of this question, see Dorothy Bass, "Women's Studies and Biblical Studies: An Historical Perspective," *JSOT* 22 (1982): 6–12; and Katharine Doob Sakenfeld, "Feminist Uses of Biblical Materials," in *Feminist Interpretation of the Bible*, ed. L. Russell (Philadelphia: Westminster, 1985), 55–64.

2. Elisabeth Schüssler Fiorenza, *Bread Not Stone: The Challenge of Feminist Biblical Interpretations* (Boston: Beacon Press, 1984), 93–115.

3. Ibid., 118.

4. Ibid., 135.

5. Carolyn Osiek, "The Feminist and the Bible: Hermeneutical Alternatives," in *Feminist Perspectives on Biblical Scholarship,* ed. A. Y. Collins (Chico, CA: Scholars Press, 1985), 97.

6. Ibid., 99.

7. Ibid., 100.

8. Ibid., 103.

9. Ibid., 104.

10. Elisabeth Schüssler Fiorenza, *In Memory of Her: A Feminist Theological Reconstruction of Christian Origins* (New York: Crossroad, 1983), 14–19; eadem, *Bread Not Stone,* 12–13.

11. Schüssler Fiorenza, *Bread Not Stone,* 13.

12. Letty Russell, "Feminist Critique: Opportunity for Cooperation," *JSOT* 22 (1982): 68.

13. Schüssler Fiorenza, *Bread Not Stone,* 13.

14. Ibid.

15. Ibid., 14.

16. Ibid. (emphasis added).

17. Ibid., 36.

18. Ibid., 37.

19. Ibid., 16.

20. Phyllis Trible, *God and the Rhetoric of Sexuality* (Philadelphia: Fortress, 1978); Schüssler Fiorenza, *In Memory of Her,* 19–21.

21. Claudia V. Camp, "Female Voice, Written Word: Women and Authority in Hebrew Scripture," in *Embodied Love: Sensuality and Relationship as Feminist Values,* ed. P. Cooey, S. Farmer, and M. E. Ross (San Francisco: Harper & Row, 1987), 97.

22. Susan Brooks Thistlethwaite, *Metaphors for the Contemporary Church* (New York: Pilgrim, 1983), 155.

23. David V. J. Bell, *Power, Influence and Authority* (New York: Oxford University Press, 1975).

24. Schüssler Fiorenza, *Bread Not Stone*, 19–22.

25. Ibid., 15–19.

26. See Chris Weedon, *Feminist Praxis and Poststructuralist Theory* (Oxford: Basil Blackwell, 1987).

27. See Schüssler Fiorenza, *Bread Not Stone*, 84.

28. Sallie McFague, *Metaphorical Theology: Models of God in Religious Language* (Philadelphia: Fortress, 1982).

29. Ibid., 54–66.

30. Ibid., 63.

31. Ibid., 62.

32. Ibid., 64–65.

33. Ibid., 26–27.

34. Ibid., 18.

35. Ibid., 182–92; eadem, *Models of God: Theology for an Ecological, Nuclear Age* (Philadelphia: Fortress, 1987).

36. Claudia V. Camp, "Woman Wisdom as Root Metaphor: A Theological Considera-tion," in *The Listening Heart: Essays in Wisdom and the Psalms in Honor of R. E. Murphy*, ed. K. Hoglund et al. (Sheffield: JSOT Press, 1987).

37. See n. 22.

38. See Camp, "Wise and Strange: An Interpretation of the Female Imagery in Proverbs in Light of Trickster Mythology," *Semeia* 42 (1988).

RECOMMENDED READINGS

Bass, Dorothy. "Women's Studies and Biblical Studies: An Historical Perspective." *JSOT* 22 (1982): 6–12.

Camp, Claudia V. "Female Voice, Written Word: Women and Authority in Hebrew Scrip-ture." In *Embodied Love: Sensuality and Relationship as Feminist Values*, edited by P. Cooey, S. Farmer, and M. E. Ross, 97–114. San Francisco: Harper & Row, 1987.

———. "Wise and Strange: An Interpretation of the Female Imagery in Proverbs in Light of Trickster Mythology." *Semeia* 42 (1988): 14–36.

———. Woman Wisdom as Root Metaphor: A Theological Consideration." In *The Listen-ing Heart: Essays in Wisdom and the Psalms in Honor of R. E. Murphy*, edited by K. Hoglund et al., 45–76. Sheffield: JSOT Press, 1987.

Cannon, Katie Geneva, and Elisabeth Schüssler Fiorenza, eds. *Interpretation for Libera-tion. Semeia* 47. Atlanta: Scholars Press, 1989.

Chopp, Rebecca. *The Power to Speak: Feminism, Language, God.* New York: Crossroad, 1989.

Duck, Ruth C. *Gender and the Name of God: The Trinitarian Baptismal Formula.* New York: Pilgrim Press, 1991.

McFague, Sallie. *Metaphorical Theology: Models of God in Religious Language.* Phila-delphia: Fortress, 1982.

———. *Models of God: Theology for an Ecological, Nuclear Age.* Philadelphia: Fortress, 1987.

Osiek, Carolyn. "The Feminist and the Bible: Hermeneutical Alternatives." In *Feminist Perspectives on Biblical Scholarship,* edited by A. Y. Collins, 93–106. Biblical Scholarship in North America 10. Chico, CA: Scholars Press, 1985.

Cooperation." *JSOT* 22 (1982): 67–71.

Russell, Letty, ed. *Feminist Interpretation of the Bible.* Philadelphia: Westminster, 1985.

Sakenfeld, Katharine Doob. "Feminist Uses of Biblical Materials." In *Feminist Interpretation of the Bible,* edited by L. Russell, 55–64. Philadelphia: Westminster, 1985.

Schüssler Fiorenza, Elisabeth. *Bread Not Stone: The Challenge of Feminist Biblical Interpretation.* Boston: Beacon Press, 1984.

Thistlethwaite, Susan Brooks. *Metaphors for the Contemporary Church.* New York: Pilgrim, 1983.

Tolbert, Mary Ann. "Defining the Problem: The Bible and Feminist Hermeneutics." *Semeia* 28 (1983): 113–26.

Trible, Phyllis. *God and the Rhetoric of Sexuality.* Philadelphia: Fortress, 1978.

Weems, Renita. "Reading Her Way through the Struggle." In *Stony the Road We Trod: African-American Biblical Interpretation,* edited by Cain Hope Felder, 57–80. Minneapolis: Fortress, 1991.

Williams, Delores S. *Sisters in the Wilderness: The Challenge of Womanist God Talk.* Maryknoll, NY: Orbis.

◆ The Face of Transcendence as a Challenge to the Reading of the Bible in Latin America

IVONE GEBARA ◆

THE IMPORTANCE OF THE BIBLE
IN LATIN AMERICA

THE BIBLE ENTERED LATIN AMERICA through religious instruction. As an accessory to the colonialist project of the sixteenth century, it has made its oppressive or liberating way in our history. Five centuries are not five years, and we must acknowledge the extent to which the mingling of cultures, religions, creeds, and biblical readings has become part of our historical flesh.

In its various interpretations the Bible is a part of our culture, our nationality, even if it must always be resituated in different contexts. The Bible is also part of the tradition of the life of the women of Latin America, especially the poorest, those of the isolated countryside who work in the absolute anonymity of their lives. They bear in their flesh the scars of the rejection of their bodies, of the guilty verdict pronounced on their flesh by the patriarchal system which has formed them. They also bear the desire to be loved, to know the consolation of their suffering and the strength to pursue the sweet or bitter daily struggle.

It is in this perspective that the project of Elizabeth Cady Stanton and her associates to reread certain biblical texts in the cause of the feminist struggles of the last century in the United States continues to retain its extraordinary relevance in different contexts.

For Latin America as well, beginning from a different problematic, we shall attempt to reread in another way the great texts that have stamped the life of our peoples, especially that of women. We shall attempt to show that the world of readers is the fundamental key for understanding a text. A text is subject to life and is capable of inspiring it—if the inspiration comes from history and its challenges. It is our loving passion for liberty, for respect for our differences, for equality, for justice in our relations, that leads us to take the text as a possible "ally." It becomes our ally by our reading, by our attention, by our social and political and anthropological choice, and also by our questions. It is not our ally by itself, given its condition as a "cultural object" which has been produced and which is read and interpreted according to various periods, tendencies, interests, and ideologies. And if it is to become our ally in the enterprise of humanizing our existence, we must reexamine our values and the presuppositions of our theological ideas. It is this critical reexamination that will enable us to see that scripture is an interpretation, and that it is possible to interpret the interpretation. To interpret the interpretation does not mean simply to justify it or to try to see how it might speak to us. To interpret the interpretation is to open a *dialogue* with the text, to enter into conversation with it and to be capable of saying what matters and what does not on the basis of our lived experience and the questions it sets for us.

A hundred years ago Elizabeth Cady Stanton said, "The history of mankind is a history of repeated injuries and usurpations on the part of man towards woman, having its direct object the establishment of an absolute tyranny over her."[1] If this continues to be the case for the greater part of humanity, it must also be said that, in spite of difficulties, we are arriving at a moment of unique richness in our history. Women are beginning to organize against various forms of oppression and in particular against centuries of oppressive interpretations of the Bible.

A new dawn is being heralded for humanity, even if our time is often freighted with a sensation of despair before the growing destruction of our planet—from all points of view.

My reflection, in memory of Elizabeth Cady Stanton, aims to give expression to Latin American women's struggle—pregnant with hope—for the construction of new human relations, for the right of all the beings of the earth to equal happiness and fulfillment, and for the right to praise ceaselessly the transcendence in which we live and move and have our being. This reflection offers three points for consideration: (1) God as a hermeneutical problem in practice; (2) living and thinking transcendence in another way; and (3) resurrection as a key to the feminist reading of the Bible.

GOD AS A HERMENEUTICAL PROBLEM
IN PRACTICE

For nearly fifteen years women from countries in Latin America have been rereading the Bible, seeking to reconstitute their image as subjects of history into something larger than their hearths and domestic labors. I believe that progressive steps have been made, even if in my judgment this reading needs to grow in critical perspective and surpass certain limits.[2] One of these limits, for example, is at times to value woman in our readings of the New Testament because Jesus valued her. This means indirectly that woman has no value in herself but that Jesus, he who is Christianity's greatest authority, endows her with value. In concrete terms, we seem to need a masculine authority to affirm our place in society and in our churches. If Jesus in his time genuinely acted differently with respect to women, this does not justify our retention of the same ways of thinking at the expense of gaining a new understanding of the human being and of theology.

In various contributions based on their readings of the Bible, women have attempted to criticize the androcentric and patriarchal structures of our society, our churches, and ourselves. But even in criticizing them, these readings unconsciously retain and utilize the androcentric and patriarchal basis for their new interpretations. This means that the vision of the cosmos, the practical "anthropovision," and the basic theology continue to be those that understand *God* as a self-contained spiritual being, limitless and independent of the "creature" but at the same time "limited" to God's own being. According to this vision the "spiritual body of God" is separate from and higher than other bodies. God has God's own purpose or plan for humanity, and ultimately the final responsibility for everything that happens is God's.

We often say that this is analogical language, symbolism peculiar to theology, but in practice the symbolism is taken as an independent reality. It is stripped of its own nature, that of transporting us continually beyond what is said, and is made a "materialist" language, since God continues to be experienced as an omnipotent "self-contained being." In Latin America various groups with various ideologies present "plans of God," schemes for salvation, and manipulate the people according to their immediate interests. This touches on a fairly thorny and delicate problem—the efforts of several groups, legitimated by the image of God as liberator, as avenger of the poor, to undertake struggles of liberation to the death.

This reflection is not outside of me. I include myself among those who have struggled and dreamed and still dream of changing the structures of domination in Latin America. If my reflection contains a criticism, it is addressed to me as well, to my writings, in the light of the new moment in our history and of discoveries often made painfully.

I confess that the image of God as liberator presents problems for me and also for the impoverished, who are always the first victims even of just struggles for political, economic, and cultural liberation. We arrive at the paradox of dying and of "living" in a state of mortal armed aggression in the name of the God of life.

As the poor observe the daily massacre of children, women, men, and whole peoples, they begin to have trouble understanding our discourse concerning the plan of God, the love of God, and God's preference for the poor. The liberator God, in spite of the attractiveness of the concept, sometimes seems as dangerous as the God of reason, who governs the world from a throne of glory. In practice this image of God as liberator excludes women as much as does the image of God as "the Other," insofar as women continue to be the *pietás* of war games, accepting on their knees the murdered bodies of husbands, lovers, brothers, sisters, children, parents . . . ; who possess no decisive responses to the "masculine reason" that governs the world; who are accomplices in plans for development by weapons and profits, accomplices in the cold logic in which human tenderness and mercy seem extinguished.

I am suspicious of this omnipotent god, this self-sufficient god, this god beyond the earth and the cosmos, this god beyond humans and at the same time very much like humans, the celestial "double" of powerful men, whether of the right or the left.

The god on high, in heaven, on a throne, the father of men, the god of blind obedience, the god who punishes and saves, is no longer useful — even when he presents a liberator's face — to our world, to the humanization of the human, to women, to the future of the poor. He too is the fruit of an authoritarian religion experienced by the masses, a religion that produces sentimentalism and consolation as faith's response to the nonsense of an existence reduced to survival, the existence today of thousands of humans scrabbling for a wretched loaf to exist.

With Dorothee Sölle I ask the questions "Why do human beings adore a God whose main attribute is power, whose interest is subjugation, who is afraid of equal rights? A being treated as Lord, who has received from his theologians a certificate of omnipotence, simple power being insufficient?"[3]

I think that in spite of our efforts a patriarchal image of God still presides over our feminist readings of the Bible in Latin America. Our anthropological basis has not changed. We have still not understood and experienced the human as a being in communion with all that exists. Our God of life still continues to make war, to buy weapons, to kill in "defense" of life. I am suspicious of this God of life, above life, one more variation of the same father God, creator of the world, the absolute, self-sufficient being who in practice sides with certain lives and destroys others, who also justifies individual and collective murders in the name of life. His ways of fighting for life are very much like the ones used by those who adore the omnipotent God.

It is this same liberator image that leads us to read, for example, the story of Judith as that of a "warrior" capable of killing and of arousing the hatred of oppressors, who uses her weapons and continues to legitimate a certain retaliationism against men, often using the same political weapons, perhaps for want of creativity.

It is the same reclothed image of "liberation" that continues to command human beings from "outside," "from above," like a will above and beyond human beings. It continues to require and to justify sacrifices, to give itself up when the time is right to the cause of the kingdom, to the cause of the people, to the cause of the poor. It issues invitations to become prophets and martyrs, to bear witness to the victory of life by means of death. It is this same image that continues to constitute the basis of all our theology and, in reality, takes seriously neither history nor human responsibility nor our condition as beings sheathed in the mystery of life.

Our theology still begins with God the Father, who sends his only Son as our savior. Jesus continues to come from somewhere outside of history; he continues to be regarded as existing before all the ages; he continues to live an incarnation regarded as a "nearly magic" way for God to enter history. We may wonder why the churches have wished to retain certain theological interpretations of the *Jesus movement* event of the first century, as though these interpretations were the facts themselves, provable material realities.[4] What are the historical conjectures that could have allowed these interpretations to continue? What interests did ecclesiastical authorities have in retaining these interpretations at the expense of others that took history more seriously?

We have still not learned that everything is interpretation and that the "fact," if one can so express oneself, is the existence of a movement given direction by a man from Nazareth who sought to give new life and new identity to people marginalized by the political and religious powers of the time and who welcomed the sick, women prostituted and scorned, slaves, and all sorts of people without effective social recognition. This event within Judaism has had multiple interpretations, especially religious interpretations that have emphasized this "fact" as the result of an intervention of God, as an event that irrupts into history but has its origin beyond history. These interpretations still continue to nourish and legitimate the maintenance of theological "patriarchalism." The feminist readings of the Bible issuing from Latin America retain this same "patriarchalism," even if in a form that is presently a little more mitigated.

To change our understanding of God, to speak of transcendence in another way, necessarily implies going beyond our current dogma, our current Christology and ecclesiology, our reading of the Bible. We are invited to take up the challenge to create an "other" tradition, without denying that the old patriarchal tradition is part of our history; it is also our past, our flesh, but it is high time to create another. To create another tradition in obedience to the history of today signifies the possibility of constructing egalitarian anthropological and theological foundations that respect men and women living in reciprocity and in respect for their differences. To create another tradition also signifies that we welcome the fact that we live in *mystery* and that it lives in us, even though we can speak of this Force, Energy, Breath, Wind, Spirit only approximately, symbolically. In this sense *he* does not have a will for us; *he* does not have a preestablished design or plan; *he* does not take sides; *he* is not a self-sufficient being; *he* is not a person as we are persons. Our entire theology has imprisoned this God, this *he,* in a concept, and has made of it *his* being and *his* place of existence. This prison has also been that of the christianized Latin American masses, who now find themselves prevented from escaping it. It has almost become a part of their being, of their skin, but in spite of everything little pathways have opened up, revealing new possibilities.

To escape the reduction of the concept of the Transcendent solely to God the omnipotent Father signifies a Copernican revolution in our culture and our theology with historical consequences for the next millennium that are not yet foreseeable. This is why feminist theology in Latin America is invited to take bigger steps in order to go beyond the "feminization" of patriarchal concepts. To open the gaps it is not enough to speak of the feminine image of God, the feminine side of the Trinity,[5] the feminine sensibility of Jesus, the leadership of certain women in various churches — even if those things are important.

I believe that we must pass through a moment of purification, in the sense of touching existentially a certain atheism from overly precise images, an atheism necessary for avoiding equivocations and recovering ourselves in another way as humanity. That is the challenge flung our way for the coming years.

LIVING AND THINKING TRANSCENDENCE
IN ANOTHER WAY

Neither the liberation theology fashioned in Latin America nor feminist theology has been able to attain a "Copernican revolution," in spite of the immense steps both have taken. They are revolutionary theologies inside the Western patriarchal Christian tradition. In other words, they have introduced novelties, especially in the effort to reread theology on the basis of love of the impoverished of our continent, and to derive practical consequences from it. But this effort is carried out within patriarchal "orthodoxy" and still retains the same tradition and the same field of religious imagination that have been present for centuries in our culture.

I would like to open a dialogue with tradition, the tradition that belongs to our heritage, to see what possibilities it can welcome for new interpretations generated from the study of different human groups who invoke the Christian faith but wish to live it on the basis of other interpretive foundations. I believe that this effort is a creative and re-creative possibility latent in values at the foundation of our human existence and our Judeo-Christian tradition.

First we must attempt to think of transcendence outside of the patriarchal metaphysical categories to which we are accustomed. We must take the risk of the serpent in chap. 3 of Genesis, which gives an order counter to the one given by God. It urges disobedience of a patriarchal law keeping the human being in childish submission and fear. The serpent, the image of ourselves, of our power of transcendence and liberty, tells us that we must relish this "fruit," conducive to existence, useful for discernment, and attractive as well because full of life. We must even eat it with relish, passion, gluttony, and let it become our new flesh. The transformation is slow and progressive, as was the structuring of our present religious images.

I propose the adventure of attempting to transcend the theological scheme of the self-sufficient God, of the omnipotent being, of God who is creator of all, in order to enter into the mystery of transcendence beyond every image. In this sense, we must reaffirm transcendence as *relation, relation* present to everything, *relation* articulated among all human beings, animals, plants, earth, air, fire, water, cosmos. Everything that exists is *relation* and lives in *relation,* a vital energy in which we exist, a primary mystery that simply *is.* This primary mystery is not a person as we are individual and collective persons, even if we place ourselves in relation to "him," to "her," as though he/she were a person. It is here that the problem of our personal reality appears; in other words, we place ourselves in relation to all that exists as persons. We personalize the world, we speak to the animals, to flowers, to stars, as though they were persons, even as we know that they are not. Antoine de Saint-Exupéry's *Little Prince* is a very rich example for this purpose.

To understand transcendence in another way it is necessary to reinterpret the mysterious reality of the human being, especially in relation to our most profound religious beliefs. At this level we may say that our "divinities" are in a sense "our image," the expression of our desires and fears. They complete us and comfort us. They aid us and sustain us.

We affirm them as being in "the beyond"; this means that through our own human experience we are "beyond," "beyond" ourselves, our daily life, the real that we construct and that constructs us. We are present and future. We exist on the earth as it is, but we dream of the earth that is not yet. We dream of its fruits, of happiness; we dream of healing suffering, hunger, thirst, abandonment. We dream of wiping dry the tears from every face and removing the reproach of the people, as was spoken by the prophet Isaiah (25:8). Our most profound dreams[6] are housed in our divinities, who appear to have realized them; it is this that "divinizes" them for us. Our human dreams become "divine" in our imagination, in our desire, in our being, to the extent that we project them symbolically as realized in our divinities, and even in the stories recounted by our sacred texts. And this is why we invoke them: it is a kind of invocation of ourselves, of our deep energies, so that they may help us maintain hope, so that they may help us keep taut the string of our faith in life. For if it slackens we fall, or walk with difficulty on our daily paths.

This phenomenological consideration of this aspect of our humanity enables us to resituate transcendence beyond all images, beyond the reduction of transcendence to a personal being. This consideration helps us relativize our theological constructions in such a way that we can criticize them to keep them from becoming oppressive idols or alienating theories.

In the reality of our historical condition and according to the present evolution of our humanity, we may speak of transcendence in two interpenetrating ways: (a) Transcendence as *experience* on the basis of the very mystery of our existence, on the basis of lived experience of the unforeseeable, disproportionate, marvelous, and questioning that surround us. We experience the reality of always being larger and smaller than ourselves, of being incapable of dominating life, of understanding it in its wholeness. We are that infinite/finite, that limited/unlimited of which Paul Ricoeur speaks.[7] (b) Transcendence as *ethical experience,* that is, as invitation and summons to live life as an absolute value. This ethical transcendence is experienced on the basis of human relations that "transcend" us, go beyond us, make us move out of our egoism and lethargy. It is an experience that puts us in solidarity, in a state of mercy and love, with those who are different, with neighbors fallen on the byways of life. It is an experience of profound joy, of gracious action for acts of tenderness done in our midst. And it is also an experience of beauty that opens us to larger horizons, inviting and mysterious.

The *experience* of ethical transcendence is that which was experienced by the prophets of Israel, the participants in the Jesus movement, and many others throughout the centuries who have been guided by the passion for life and humanity.

The double plan of transcendence I am emphasizing is really multiple. That is, I explain it in a certain way, but it goes beyond my explanation. It too is based on an anthropology in which equality and difference interpenetrate and intercommunicate and permit a revaluing of human history, the history of men and of women, a revaluing of the creation of meaning, the religious meaning of life, as one of the wonders that characterize us.

This orientation changes everything in the reading of the Bible. Far from denying the patriarchal character of scripture, it allows us to read it as symbolic word, as word that goes beyond itself, that is, beyond even its previous cultural conditioning. That means that the word, read symbolically, allows us to read it by reading ourselves today. We understand ourselves in reading it, and we discover with it the possibility of dialogue between the past and the present, between different cultures and peoples. The Bible, as a human work, is a mediating device for understanding ourselves today. In this perspective, the Bible as a collection of the tradition of a historical faith is a fundamental pole of dialogue for those men and women who identify themselves with the same tradition of values, with the same historical-religious current that continues to the present, in spite of the different stalks issuing from the same root. In this sense the Bible is not the "word of (the patriarchal) God," interpreted on the authority of its patriarchs; instead, it is a "human word," said metaphorically to be of God, because it contains elements without which life would be impossible. This word is justice, love, sharing, pardon, tenderness, mercy, welcome, understanding, respect, solidarity, brotherhood, sisterhood—values so essential that we call them divine.

This attempt to understand transcendence in another way is not part of the popular religious instruction of the churches of Latin America. The churches in general like to speak of the personal plan of God and to moralize, in their way, the life of the poor. The poor themselves find support and consolation in their misfortune or their little blessing in giving thanks to this God. At the level of the great Latin American masses, abandoned to their own kind, there is no way at the moment to make big strides toward rendering them more conscious of the divine images sustaining them. Sometimes the popular world seems a separate world, with its own economy, organization, and supporting religion. But here and there there are clearings, as though to show that the intuition I am presenting is there also — shy, full of fear, but living there, among the poor, among women's groups, among indigenous people, starting to pick up its roots of communion with the earth and the totality of natural forces. I am not alone in this perception; we are hundreds here and elsewhere, who wish to love in another way, to celebrate life, to seek greater happiness and pleasure and the joy of existing in justice and truth. It is communion with other people that makes it possible for me to believe in the coming of a theology with more life, one that can court the erotic excitement of the earth and the intensity of life which arises everywhere in an absolutely unpredictable and mysterious way.

RESURRECTION AS A KEY
TO THE FEMINIST READING OF THE BIBLE

The passage from transcendence "understood" in another way to resurrection as the key to a feminist reading of the Bible follows the same logic of existence.

I would like first to define resurrection and to justify its status as a key to reading. I do not wish to treat the topic broadly, including the study of the resurrection of a people (as, for example, in the beautiful image of dry bones coming to life in Ezekiel 37) or individual resurrection as reward for men and women who lived in fidelity to Yahweh and were cruelly murdered (2 Maccabees). Nor will I take up all the allusions of Jesus and his disciples to resurrection as a return to individual life or as an event following the final judgment or the way in which the churches have theologically developed and taught the resurrection of Jesus Christ, placing the emphasis on resurrection as an event after death marked either by salvation or by condemnation.[8]

On the one hand, I would like to move from an individual and individualist understanding of resurrection to a collective dimension and, on the other hand, to decentralize the experience of resurrection as bound up with a moment after the death of Jesus, in order to emphasize it as practice, that is, as the affirmation that the practice of the Jesus movement was and is an experience centered on resurrection practices.

To speak of resurrection and of resurrection practices in this new perspective enables women to experience in equality with men the work of salvation in history. We are saved for one another; we are responsible to one another for the development of life and its protection against all kinds of enemies that would destroy it. In this sense, the "concept" of resurrection comes to appear more egalitarian and nearer to women's experience than that of the kingdom of God, as we shall see next.

RESURRECTION: FROM THE INDIVIDUAL
TO THE COLLECTIVE—HUMAN, TERRESTRIAL, AND COSMIC

It suffices to look at life around us to take account of vital processes surrounding us, processes from life to death and from death to life in an uninterrupted chain. The human being also lives through this same process but endowed with reality as a thinking being, a being who seeks meaning, incapable of living without creating meaning from that very being and from all that surrounds it. In this case the process takes qualitatively different forms.

Resurrection understood as new life in different senses and situations, as the return to a quality of human life, signifies not a return to life after a total physical death, or an individual life in a contemplated heaven, but a transcendence of situations in which death, murder, injustice, or destruction of a people, a group or a person has been present. To envision resurrection as a vital process is, on the one hand, to valorize human responsibility in the construction or destruction of this world, and, on the other hand, to emphasize the value of the present moment of our historical existence, a unique moment in the search for happiness, a unique moment in paying homage to the life that dwells within us as a provisional eternal abode. It means as well to revalorize the body, our personal and social body; to revalorize our historical temporality; to revalorize the joy and the pleasure of life; to revalorize the earth as the being in which we exist and of which we are part; to revalorize the cosmos to which we belong in a larger way. It is resurrection celebrated as a human-cosmic canticle to the fundamental mystery whose depth we scarcely graze, the mystery that at once frightens and astonishes us. We are not inhabitants of heaven, but of earth; it is our body and our soul.

Resurrection is also an event in the human sphere, an event in our history, an event that situates us in the love of the human within and beyond us, in the love of the earth beyond our local boundaries. And it is in this larger sense that we speak of the resurrection of a person or persons or cultures or nations. This perspective emphasizes the collective ethical character of resurrection in the sense of a continual challenge to respect life, to act for the sake of life, to denounce the murderous forces that menace peoples. Now this action for life, this life in life, is profoundly egalitarian and retains within itself the contribution both of women and of men as locations and agents of resurrection.

To work for life does not have as consequence the acquisition of royal titles or the risk of identifying oneself with a patriarchal kingdom, even a kingdom expressed in egalitarian terms. This is why the category of kingdom engenders a little problem, especially at the level of popular religious imagination. Royalist political experience has not always been a success, and we must always explain this "ameliorated" experience as different from kingdoms of our acquaintance that our faith presents as historical projects. In kingdoms there are often kings, but few queens. Nevertheless, women are often partially eliminated from this project. In kingdoms power is concentrated in the hands of the king and his closest courtiers, and it is they who have responsibility for the life of the "citizens." At the level of the unconscious there results a kind of habit of not genuinely welcoming the fact that a good part of human history depends on our responsibility, even if there exist chance, the unpredictable, the involuntary, natural catastrophes, and so on.

The patriarchal project in society and religion arrived at the end of the second millennium, to slay in part people's responsibility for taking their lives in their own hands, to close the doors to a life of dignity for whole populations, to legitimate violence in the name of progress and to produce misery as the consequence of the concentration of goods in the hands of a minority. To change the image of God and to drop his easily manipulable royalty are to proclaim hope in the human heart, to dare to believe that we can have a different future in which love is not just one more word, but a word of life, a lived experience.

RESURRECTION: THE BEGINNING OF EVERYTHING IN THE JESUS MOVEMENT

To say that *everything* begins with the resurrection is to affirm the fundamental value of life in all its dimensions. It is because of the value of life in each human being that hearts are filled with mercy and that religious movements have sprung up and have expanded. The threat to life is unbearable to a human being. Destruction, lack of liberty, contempt, slavery, and war arrive at certain limits where they become non-sense. Hence the absolute necessity to recover what makes for life, identity, joy, laughter, tenderness, sharing, and meaning.

The Jesus movement is situated within that type of religious humanism, which begins with love for the marginalized, for those with no nation or religion or "god," for those who are impure according to the Jewish regimen of purity, for the sorrowing, the hungry, and the thirsty. It is along this line that I propose an understanding of the Jesus movement, a movement within Judaism that has sought to aid the life of hundreds and hundreds of people. It is a movement of resurrection. Its leader was crucified, murdered like others in that time. This is the paradox of the struggle for life!

Resurrection has therefore been the practice of the Jesus movement, that of the first Christian communities and that of others through the centuries. It is embodied in the personal and collective effort to struggle effectively for the quality of the life of persons, groups, and peoples. In this practice men and women become involved on an equal basis. It is their own responsibility so to act that every form of diminution of life, of threat to life, is denounced. The human being is the great builder and destroyer of humanity. This is the distinctive human reality.

One contribution of religion is situated in the struggle against the forces of destruction within us which can grow to the point of eliminating us all in the name of our own idols, in the name of the omnipotent desire to reign over others, to dominate, to become gods. In this sense the Jesus movement, born in the midst of all kinds of idolatries, is anti-idolatrous. It is the birth of this movement that the author of the Gospel of Luke sought to relate in his account of the birth of Jesus (Luke 2:1–20). The birth of Jesus, the birth of a child, is the theological/symbolic narration of the birth of the Jesus movement. Luke speaks to us of this movement as a re-creation of humanity, a recovery, from within our inward human parts, of mercy, justice, and love—legacies of the prophetic tradition. The empty tomb returns us to the manger, the place of the child, the place of the rebirth of hope. The empty tomb returns us to ourselves, women and men capable of giving birth and rebirth to the divine, the essence of our own flesh.

To read scripture beginning from the resurrection signifies the effort to reclaim a tradition already within us, a tradition more egalitarian and historic, and to give it new life within the great centuries-long Christian tradition.

Today with the growing misery in Latin America, with its destructive consequences for the person, and with the immense need for consolation and tenderness for our peoples, are we capable of contemplating a change in the image of transcendence?

Is it not better to retain the religious heritage as it is, with few changes at the heart of the existing "patriarchalism"? By abandoning it, would we not increase still further the political and religious orphanage of the impoverished, those who are already orphaned from society, from development, from power? These questions sometimes arise among those who work with the people, especially when they are preoccupied with sharing new thoughts with the poor, the fruit of their theological study.

Cultural mutations are not automatic. They take time; they require historical and personal conditions; they require patience and trust in life. It is in this perspective that I share my credo with you: I believe in evolu tion, in change, in maturity of belief, in diversity, in the dynamism of life, in the courage to be, in the desire for happiness, in the unforeseeable. And through this credo I am convinced that we cannot remain silent, that it is necessary to proclaim in different ways the *good news* of the new abode of *transcendence*. And this good news must more and more encircle our reading of the Bible, our theological interpretations, and our ethical outlook in relation to different human activities. It is with this new face of transcendence that I say with the Quebec poet Gilles Vigneault:

> C'est chez toi que je sais mieux
> Donner mon feu et mon lieu
> Et dire à chacun je t'aime.[9]

> It is with you that I know better
> How to give my light and my place
> And how to say to each "I love you."

Translated by Stephen Voss

NOTES

1. Elizabeth Cady Stanton, *The Woman's Bible* (Seattle: Coalition on Women and Religion, 1974), editors' preface, p. 6.

2. Ana Maria Tepedino, *As discipulas de Jesus* (Petrópolis: Ed. Vozes, 1989).

3. Dorothee Sölle, "Pai, Poder e Barbárie," *Concilium* 163 (1981) 83 [Brazilian translation Ed. Vozes].

4. Elisabeth Schüssler Fiorenza, *In Memory of Her: A Feminist Theological Reconstruction of Christian Origins* (New York: Crossroad, 1983).

5. L. Maria Clara Bingemer, "A Trindade a partir da perspectiva da mulher — algumas pistas de reflexão," in *A mulher faz téologia* (Petrópolis: Ed. Vozes, 1986).

6. Rubem Alves, *Variações sobre a vida e a morte* (Sao Paulo: Ed. Paulinas, 1986).

7. Paul Ricoeur, *Fallible Man,* trans. Charles Kelbley (Chicago: Henry Regnery, 1965); idem, *Interpretação e Ideologia* (Rio de Janeiro: Francisco Alves, 1983).

8. See *La résurrection du Christ et l'exégèse moderne,* Lectio Divina 50 (Paris: Cerf, 1969).

9. Gilles Vigneault, *Les Neufs couplets* (Montreal: Nouvelles éditions de l'ARC, 1973), 43–45.

RECOMMENDED READINGS

Boff, Clodovis. *Theology and Praxis.* Maryknoll, NY: Orbis, 1987.

Croatto, Severino J. *Biblical Hermeneutics.* Maryknoll, NY: Orbis, 1984.

Gebara, Ivone. "Women Doing Theology in Latin America." In *With Passion and Compassion: Third World Women Doing Theology,* edited by V. Fabella and M. A. Oduyoye, 125–34. Maryknoll, NY: Orbis, 1988.

——, and Clara Maria Bingemer. *Mary: Mother of God, Mother of the Poor.* Maryknoll, NY: Orbis, 1987.

Johnson, Elizabeth A. *She Who Is: The Mystery of God in Feminist Theological Discourse.* New York: Crossroad, 1992.

McFague, S. *The Body of God: An Ecological Theology.* Minneapolis: Augsburg Fortress Press, 1993.

Pobee, John S., and B. von Wartenberg-Potter, eds. *New Eyes for Reading.* Oak Park, IL: Meyer Stone, 1987.

Ricoeur, Paul. *Fallible Man.* Translated by Charles Kelbley. Chicago: Henry Regnery, 1965.

Sugirtharajah, R. S., ed. *Voices from the Margins: Interpreting the Bible in the Third World.* Maryknoll, NY: Orbis, 1991.

Swimme, Brian. *The University Is a Green Dragon: A Cosmic Creation Story.* Santa Fe, NM: Bear & Company, 1984.

Tamez, Elsa. *Against Machismo: Interviews.* Oak Park, IL: Meyer Stone, 1987.

——, ed. *Through Her Eyes: Women's Theology from Latin America.* Maryknoll, NY: Orbis, 1989.

PART THREE

Scrutinizing the Master's Tools: Rethinking Critical Methods

◆ *Les Belles Infidèles/*
Fidelity or Feminism?
The Meanings of Feminist
Biblical Translation

ELIZABETH A. CASTELLI ◆

> Translation then becomes second nature. It is an ongoing activity with us,
> like breathing. Only occasionally, as during an asthma attack, do we sud-
> denly become aware (sometimes with an excruciating pang) of the ongoing
> process.[1]

As FEMINISTS WORKING in the late twentieth century on the biblical tradition, we are the ambivalent heirs to modes of thought which are not often
aligned with our interests and those of people traditionally marginalized
by Western culture. Many women within Western culture, and most women
and men whose roots are outside of it though they may live within it, can
identify with the notion of translation not simply as a rhetorical or
hermeneutical linguistic gesture but also as a metaphor for their ambiguous
experience in the dominant culture. Sri Lankan writer Ranjini Obeyesekere
captures the experience of the writer-in-exile in the metaphor of translation-
as-natural-as-breathing. Many women who are grounded in the Christian
tradition have spent much of their religious lives in radical acts of translation of the tradition. One might well ask, At what cost? One might also
note that, as we enter into this discussion, more women are feeling more
asthmatic than ever before. Our success will certainly be measured, at least
in part, by the ways in which we are able to offer solace to our sisters'
distress. This paper seeks to raise to the level of consciousness some of
the sources of that distress, rooted in the theoretical and philosophical
problems embedded in the very practice of translation, and to pose some

questions which I believe must be answered as an initial step in a feminist
project of biblical translation.

1.

The metaphors of linguistic difference emerging from the biblical tradition describe the multiplicity of human languages as the result of God's
anger at human arrogance; that we do not speak the mythical original
language of Eden is, according to the biblical narrative of Babel, a sign
of our fallen status.[2] The very need for translation grows out of human
sin, and the practice of translation is coded by this fallenness. Translation
is often figured as a miraculous event, as with the account of Pentecost
and the legends surrounding the creation of the Septuagint; somehow good
translation is only made posssible through divine intervention.

Given this tradition, feminist translators of the Bible rightly pause at
the task they set for themselves.[3] What does it mean for us to take on the
task of translating Scripture for feminist ends? How do we begin to think
about this gesture and our place in the history of translation in the West—in
general, and in relation to the specific texts we are engaging? Will we, in
the process, add to the mythological accretions concerning biblical translation—invoking God's intervention as part of our practice, as has been
done at other moments of transformative translation? How does our practice
relate to that of others? How do we conceptualize it? How do we interact
with the discourse of translation already in place?

In beginning to think about a feminist theory of translation, we must
ask a series of difficult questions about philosophy of language, how meanings are produced, how they are culturally situated. We must ask whether
it is possible to write a translation of the Bible that is a (sub)version of
it.[4] We must think through the philosophical problems in the claims about
androcentric language and the Word of God: is this a simple recasting of
the Romantic idea of progressive movement toward the *logos*?[5] Will there
necessarily be congruence between what we want "the word of God" to
say and what the texts display, as though translation as a constantly
progressive journey toward the very language of God will produce liberating
meanings as a matter of course? Is our feminist practice of translation
guaranteed to produce a text that points ever closer to, attains to, a truth
of translation? Or is our work not always already undercut by uninter-
rogated categories of authority and canonicity? Or, to put the question
another way, does a feminist translation of a text always produce a nonsexist
text?

While some would want to answer this last question affirmatively, such an answer presupposes that translation is a technical process separable from farther reaching interpretive concerns. A feminist method of translation ought not to adopt gender neutral formulae blindly, as though that strategy might answer the challenge of androcentric texts. One model for thinking these issues through may be found in the work of Elisabeth Schüssler Fiorenza who, in her book *Bread Not Stone,* raises a number of crucial hermeneutical issues.[6] In the course of her discussion, Schüssler Fiorenza balances several concerns at once. There is the overarching recognition that biblical texts are written in androcentric language, and that androcentric language embodies shifting nuances at different historical moments. While, for example, androcentric languages might at some other historical moment have been understood to convey generic meanings, this is no longer the case. Therefore, feminist translation must reject the androcentric equivalent in favor of terms that convey inclusivity. Schüssler Fiorenza, however, is quick to point out that translation theory must also take into account historical realities, and not obscure the patriarchal quality of some biblical texts through formulaic use of gender-neutral language. The project is therefore nuanced and delicate, striving not to obscure the nature of the text while at the same time trying not to construct and reify further sexist expectations and assumptions through the used of language that erases, marginalizes, or trivializes women's lives, agency, and contributions.

One of the difficulties in thinking these questions through is that we are caught up in a hermeneutical tension that renders problematic much work on biblical texts in general; a profound tension between treating the text as a cultural artifact accessible to analysis and interpretation, and viewing the text as somehow deeply different from other texts. Translating the Bible is wound up with this same tension, and has been for centuries. While translation has long been understood by many translators as a kind of creative labor performed on the texts of others, the Bible has been seen as the exception to this rule; where translators might boast of their quick and agile work on secular texts, biblical translators would speak of their "long, careful labor" and "consciously based their renderings on those of their predecessors."[7] As one historian of translation has put it, "considering that the *operis lex* of the Bible was determined by its divine authorship, the commitment of Jewish and early Christian translators was that of servitude—what other authority structure but the positional did God exercise?"[8] Here, issues of the relationship of the translator to her predecessors intersect with the overdetermined concerns in biblical writing in general with authorship and authority. To discuss feminist practice of translation is to raise the fundamental question of feminist authorship and authority.

Beyond the question of authority lies the very question of the nature of the language of the text itself. Even a critic like Steiner, who sees language as foundationally and perpetually in flux, sees a difference when one is dealing with religious texts, "preserved in a condition of artificial stasis."[9] One of the issues we need to resolve as feminists translating the Bible is our position on the question of the status of biblical language; it need not go without saying that the text is a static body of language, beyond the reach of decisions we might make about it. Deciding that the text is made up of fluid language, changeable and diffuse is a freeing gesture for the translator; however, it also means that we set into question as well the very concept of "word of God" as it has been used throughout the tradition. This is a radical and risky gesture, one which opens up our own agency in relation to the text while situating our work in a particular theological position that demands further theorizing.

Finally, in relation to these questions of authority and the nature of the texts, on what grounds will we select the texts subject to a feminist translation of the Bible? Will we limit ourselves to the canon as it has historically (politically, and tendentiously) been constituted? Or will our challenge to authority include a reconsideration of the question of which texts belong in a feminist translation of the Bible? As we work here together, another group of biblical scholars is working to produce a new translation of the New Testament that will include the Gospel of Thomas as a text; once the bounds of canon have been stretched, will we wish to fill this new space with new texts? Perhaps more to the point, will we abandon other, ir-redeemable texts? How shall we make such decisions?

2.

When exploring the literature on translation, one is immediately struck by the attempt to find language to describe what the process of translation is. A cursory list does not do justice to the richness of the struggle to speak about translation; translation is variously described:

— as a process of interpretation,[10]
— as not a process of interpretation,[11]
— as a rhetorical exercise,[12]
— as a process of transmission,[13]
— as a process of creation,[14]

— as *mimesis* or *aemulatio,*[15]
— as communication,[16]
— as alchemy,[17]
— as narcissism,[18]
— as a combination of guilt and longing,[19]
— as aggression and violence,[20]
— as representation,[21]
— as access to one's own past[22] (and by implication, as political),
— as crucial to any gesture toward reform,[23]
— as the deperate movement of fallen beings toward the *logos,* and *Ursprache,* the language of God.[24]

The struggle for the words to say it—to speak about the practice of translation—is a suitable analogy for the process of translation itself. All of these metaphors for translation have their alluring qualities, illuminate some aspect of translation; none speaks of translation in a totalizing fashion. None can, for if we take seriously the notion that translation tells us something about the intricacies of language itself, then nothing we say about the process can exhaust it. The impossibility of translation, posited by some theorists, captures the intense philosophical impasse of the "nature of translation."[25]

Some kind of philosophy of language underlies every position on translation; what one thinks about language points to how one thinks about the nature of translation. Epistemologies and assumptions about human nature also come into play,[26] and though these distinctions are rarely rendered explicit in theorizing about the practice of translations and when they are, it is in schematic (usually dualistic) fashion, they nevertheless play a critical role in the process of thinking about translation.

For example, oppositions such as "literal vs. idiomatic,"[27] "form vs. content," "style vs. meaning," "word vs. sense" govern much theorizing about translation; here, the underlying assumption is that meaning exists in some ethereal arena quite apart from its material expression. In this view, there is a kernel of meaning encased within the chaff of expression, and one may easily dispense with the chaff without significant loss. Often theorists of translation will make an exception to this rule in the case of poetic language which, they argue, is markedly different from other kinds of language. Nevertheless, since Jerome, the maxim *non verbum e verbo, sed sensum exprimere de sensu* (not word for word, but rather to express the sense from the sense [the meaning]) has been the order of the day, and has colored many translations.[28] This position often ends up begging the question of meaning itself, for it presumes to know the "sense" (which can only be communicated in language, in words) and to be able to transfer adequately that sense into equivalent words in another language. Yet the slipperiness of such an operation is rarely acknowledged, and the philosophical underpinnings of the practice almost never explicitly articulated.

This is important for feminist translation of the New Testament because it raises questions about movement between languages and between cultural worlds. Some people have criticized projects such as the Inclusive Language Lectionary because their attempts to put Scripture into language for contemporary uses scuttle historical concerns. More often than not, these critics reason that the world of the Bible was relentlessly patriarchal, and therefore to recast the text in nonpatriarchal ways is to rewrite history. One might well argue with such people that the history of such remote periods remains, in large part, still to be written for the first time since we actually possess such a small fragment of it, and to invoke the magic words "historical truth" may in fact be quite a premature gesture which obscures the political interests of those who invoke them.

Nevertheless, we can safely acknowledge, I think, that there are many parts of the biblical text that do reflect patriarchal expectations and modes of thought. Further, we know that the Bible as a whole has been used frequently throughout history toward patriarchal ends. I am uncomfortable with claims about kernels of feminist truth encased in the chaff of androcentric discourse, just as I am wary of what often appear to me to be too simple oppositions between form and content. Androcentric discourse is both form and content, and to the extent that androcentrism is a coherent ideological stance (systematic, lacking in contradictions, albeit politically distressing), it also presents a particularly tangled theoretical problem for a project such as the one pursued by feminist translators.

3.

One of the remarkable aspects of theoretical discourse concerning translation in the West is its highly gendered character. In a fascinating exploration of this rhetorical phenomenon, Lori Chamberlain suggests that the dualistic hierarchy of the original text over the translation (original/copy) is linked with imagery of masculine and feminine, so that translation is figured as the feminine and derivative practice, while producing the original text is seen in masculine (usually paternal) terms.[29] The imagery is not always consistent or constant among various writers, though the writer of the original text is usually understood to be its father.[30] Sometimes the text to be translated is a woman, often one who needs to be tamed. Chamberlain cites the case of the sixteenth-century English translator of

Horace, Thomas Drant, who explains his method of translating the satirist through reference to Deuteronomy 21:12–14, where God commands the Israelites who wish to make captive women their wives to shave their heads and pare their nails in order to remove all signs of beauty.[31] This method for dealing with texts goes back, however, significantly to Jerome who is often seen as the father of biblical translation and who makes reference to the same scriptural citation to explain his work with secular texts.[32] Part of a feminist theory of translation must come to terms with this imagery insofar as it grounds the Western tradition of thinking about translation.

Translation as a process of taming a wild woman of a text is perhaps the most graphic example of engendered theory, but is certainly not the only one. George Steiner, whose work *After Babel* has become a classic on translation, outlines a fourfold process by which the translator recasts the text.[33] The language he uses is worth noting, invoking both gendered and violent imagery. The first step is the act of "initiative trust" in the "adverse text," (296) followed by "aggression"; "the second move of the translator is incursive and extractive. The relevant analysis is that of Heidegger when he focuses our attention on understanding as an act, on the access, inherently appropriative and therefore violent, of *Erkenntnis* to *Dasein*" (297). The imagery continues, as the translator comprehends "by encirclement and ingestion," a gesture "explicitly invasive and exhaustive." "We 'break' a code: decipherment is dissective, leaving the shell smashed and the vital layers stripped." "The translator invades, extracts, and brings home. The simile is that of the open-cast mine left an empty scar in the landscape" (298).

Once one has captured and split open the text, the third gesture of the translator in "incorporative," an "embodiment." To stop here, however, is dangerous according to Steiner "because it is incomplete, if it lacks its fourth stage, the piston-stroke, as it were, which completes the cycle. The a-prioristic movement of trust puts us off balance. We 'lean towards' the confronting text (every translator has experienced this palpable bending towards and launching at his target)." What is required is a gesture of reciprocity, to balance out the process since "[t]he appropriative 'rapture' of the translator—the word has in it, of course, the root and meaning of violent transport—leaves the original with a dialectically enigmatic residue" (300). The work survives the rape by the translator and in fact is "enhanced" for "[b]eing methodical, penetrative, analytic, enumerative, the process of translation, like all modes of focussed understanding, will detail, illumine, and generally body forth its object" (300). It is perhaps not necessary to perform a radical hermeneutical exercise on this rhetoric, as its implications for the practice of translation are fairly self-evident. If Lori Chamberlain is correct that much of what is at stake for translators is the usurping of the paternal role of the writer,[34] then the imagery of sexual violence as crucial to the practice of translation is self-explanatory. Translation is about claims to authorship and authority, and the tradition to which we are ambivalent heirs often finds itself incapable of speaking of these notions except through hierarchies and violence. How we situate ourselves in relationship to such claims is of crucial moment.

4.

In the language of translation theory, a pervasive concern for fidelity expresses itself. The Renaissance aphorism — *traduttore, traditore* — expresses one position in the discussion, that the person who translates also betrays. Ironically, we see the aphorism's "truth" in the practice of its very translation; translating this aphorism is itself an impossibility, as its tight and efficient pun gets lost.

The concern for fidelity, for faithfulness in translation is a dense concern when it interacts with feminist practice of translating the Bible, for faithfulness has a sexual as well as a religious connotation. What does it mean to speak of a faithful feminist translation? To whom is our virtue promised? Is there a double standard in the demands for fidelity in this context, as there is in other arenas where women's fidelity is compared with men's? What kinds of ordeals are part of the test of fidelity?

The concept of fidelity is conventionally bound up with women, as a consideration of the notion of *les belles infidèles* makes clear.[35] Translations, the argument runs, are like women: the faithful ones are homely, while the unfaithful ones are beautiful. Theorists of translation almost always situate fidelity in some relation to women, whether by explicit analogy or underlying structure of their arguments. Steiner, for example, sees fidelity to lie in the last step of his four-tiered path toward translation, a step he calls equilibrium. The restoration of balance is a responsible and faithful gesture, Steiner argues, as ethical as it is economically necessary. Equilibrium can be established through a transaction of exchange "of words, women, and material goods" in accordance with Lévi-Strauss. The text in Steiner's model becomes a woman whose capture calls for recompense (302–3). Here, fidelity is an arrangement between the writer and the translator, an act carried out through the manipulation of the woman, the text.

Fidelity is also aligned theoretically with concepts almost ubiquitous in Western translation discourse — letter and spirit. This polarity has obscured thinking about language in the Christian West since it was made so crucial in that highly problematic conflation of philosophy of language and theology produced by one of Christianity's most undaunted purveyors of polemical dualisms, Paul. When put together with the concept of fidelity, the religious dimension of the term is highlighted, and the language of letter and spirit resonates with a profound religious separation between Jewish and Christian traditional relationships to language.[36] Greenstein points out that it is not at all unusual to see the letter/spirit dichotomy used within the context of the evangelizing purposes of translation, whereby the "new" idiomatic method of translation, translation that adheres to the "spirit" of the text, supplants the "old," literal, Hebrew style.[37] The dangers of such a conceptualization should be obvious. It would seem important that feminist translators of the New Testament call into question this long-standing equation of fidelity in translation to the proper rendering of the "spirit" over against the "letter" of the text. To avoid doing so would, at the very least, further reify Paul's unfortunate formulation at a point in time when our hermeneutics ought to have moved beyond such simplifications.

5.

A very real concern that should enter into the question of feminist translation of the New Testament is the political origins and effects of that work. The tradition of biblical translation has been colored by evangelistic interests at least since Jerome and Augustine, and its evangelistic motives are present in contemporary publications appearing to date. Most theorizing about biblical translation has emerged within the framework of missionary practice, which historically has been aligned with colonizing and paternalistic positions.[38] The purpose here of translating the Bible is to gain new converts for the kingdom, through the pragmatic approach of putting the text into the local language. The relative effects of such a gesture vary considerably, though they are potentially dramatic, particularly in situations where writing the biblical text in the local language becomes the first instance of writing in that culture. It would certainly be naïve to argue that every act of translating the Bible serves colonial interests, though I would not be the first to suggest that women are a colonized people in Western society.[39] It would seem crucial, however, to examine extremely closely the philosophical and ideological underpinnings of theories of translation emerging from such contexts.

Among the assumptions governing these theories is the idea that it is within the capacity of languages to evoke equivalent responses in two historically and culturally divergent contexts, and that the purpose of translation is to cause the reader in the second setting to respond as the reader in the first setting would have.[40] This assumption and goal presuppose a radical sameness of human subjects, a sameness feminist criticism in other arenas has certainly called into question. This approach is also doubly contradictory; it calls upon the translator to let the text speak for itself at the same time as it calls for a radically mediated enculturation of the text in order to evoke similar responses. However, in its critique of attempts at inclusive language—to which its attitude is clear in such phenomena as index entries, where one finds "inclusive (sexless) language"— this position argues that inclusive language is flawed because it "distorts" the text and imposes "anachronistic" standards. At the same time, the position argues for "dynamic equivalence" whereby the reader does not need to know the original context of the text.[41]

Within this position lies the implicit assumption that language is primarily referential, transparent, and always translatable. Such an understanding of language has certainly become problematic in light of a great deal of post-modern criticism, including some feminist literary theory. As feminist biblical scholars, we need at the very least to engage any such simple readings of language with a healthy hermeneutics of suspicion, since the effects of such an understanding tend in conservative and literalist directions and do not tend toward our best interests.

6.

In "Pierre Menard, autor del Quijote," a story invoked frequently by theorists of translation, Jorge Luis Borges recounts the tale of an early twentieth-century French writer who plans to write the Spanish novel, *Don Quijote*. Pierre Menard does not want to write a *version* of *Don Quijote*, for that would be too simple; nor does he want to make a mechanical reproduction of Cervantes' majestic epic. No. "Su admirable ambición era producir unas páginas que coincidieran—palabra por palabra y línea por línea—con las de Miguel de Cervantes."[42] ("His admirable ambition was to produce several pages which coincided—word for word and line for line—with those of Miguel de Cervantes.") The paradox of Pierre Menard, who wishes "*ser* [to be] Miguel de Cervantes," captures for us the untenable and compelling position of the feminist translator of the Bible; she wishes, not to produce a version of the Bible, nor a mechanical reproduction (neither a photocopy nor a machine-assisted translation) of it, but to produce "the

Bible" itself. In wishing to perform such a radical act of writing, she cannot help but encounter numerous obstacles, some of which I have sought to uncover here.

Lori Chamberlain embraces the idea of the feminist translator as collaborator.

> [W]hat is required for a feminist theory of translator is a practice governed by what Derrida calls the double bind. . . . Such a theory might rely . . . on the double-edged razor of translation as collaboration, where author and translator are seen as working together, both in the cooperative and the subversive sense.[43]

The difficulty of taking up the image of feminist-translator-as-collaborator is the here-repressed sense of the term *collaboration*. Collaboration can signify working together, especially in a joint intellectual effort; however, it can also mean cooperating with an enemy who occupies one's own country. If the observation made earlier about certain points of connection between the experience of colonized peoples and the experience of women as colonized subjects in culture has any merit, it would seem that the idea of translation as collaboration is at best an ambivalent one.

At the same time, it occurs to me that, despite certain rather obvious obstacles, feminist translators' work can begin to take on the magical impossibility of Menard's project, and that this magical impossibility embodies both the radical potential of the feminist project as well as its political dangerousness. It is women becoming authors of the text—not collaborating with the original authors, but becoming authors themselves—that makes everyone from local pastors to conservative biblical scholars to *Time* magazine so nervous.[44] Just as Menard's text must hang in the paradox of "same/not same," so must the Bible written/translated by women. And the feminist translator can hope that what is true for Pierre Menard's *Don Quijote* is equally true for her bible—"El texto de Cervantes y el de Menard son verbalmente idénticos, pero el segundo es casi infinitamente más rico."[45] ("The text of Cervantes and that of Menard are verbally identical, but Menard's is so infinitely richer.")

NOTES

This article first appeared in the *Journal of Feminist Studies in Religion* 6/2 (1990): 25–39, in a "Special Section on Feminist Translation of the New Testament," which represented revised versions of papers and responses presented November 19, 1989, at the annual meeting of the Society of Biblical Literature in the section on Women in the Biblical World. The other contributors to the discussion were Clarice J. Martin, Joanna Dewey, Peggy Hutaff, and Jane Schaberg.

1. Ranjini Obeyesekere, "The Art of Translation," *Massachusetts Review* 29 (1988): 763.

2. George Steiner, *After Babel: Aspects of Language and Translation* (London: Oxford University Press, 1975), 57–63, notes that every civilization has some mythology of the primal dispersion of languages.

3. The literature on the issue of feminist translation is widespread, usually engaged with questions of inclusive language in liturgy. See, as some examples, Phyllis A. Bird, "Translating Sexist Language as a Theological and Cultural Problem," *Union Seminary Quarterly Review* 42:1–2 (1988): 89–95; Madeline Boucher, "Scriptural Readings: God-Language and Non-sexist Translation," *Reformed Liturgy and Music* 17 (1983): 156–59; Roger A. Bullard, "Feminine and Feminist Touches in the *Centenary New Testament*," *Bible Translator* 38 (1987): 118–22; Frederick W. Danker, "Gains and Problems in the New Testament Translation," *Dialog* 24 (1985): 49–50; Richard Franklin, "God and Pronouns," in *The Force of the Feminine: Women, Men, and the Church*, ed. Margaret Franklin (Sydney: Allen and Unwin, 1986), 113–19; Nancy A. Hardesty, "'Whosoever Surely Meaneth Me': Inclusive Language and the Gospel," *Christian Scholar's Review* 17:3 (1988): 231–40; Hugh T. Kerr, ed., "Symposium: *Inclusive Language Lectionary*," *Theology Today* 43 (1987): 533–57; Virginia Ramey Mollenkott, "Toward a Unity that Affirms Diversity: An Inclusive Language Lectionary," *Ecumenism* 84 (1986): 14–16; and many others.

4. See one feminist translator's encounter with the problem of translation as subversive practice: Suzanne Jill Levine, "Translation as (Sub)Version: On Translating *Infante's Inferno*," *Sub-stance* 42 (1984): 85–94.

5. See the discussion of this approach in Edward L. Greenstein, "Theories of Modern Bible Translation," *Prooftexts* 3 (1983): 26–27; Steiner, 57–63. These ideas find their expression most fully in the works of Friedrich Schleiermacher, "Über die verschiedenen Methoden des Übersetzens," in *Das Problem des Übersetzens,* ed. Hans Joachim Störig (Darmstadt: Wissenschaftliche Buchgesellschaft, 1969), 39–70; English translation in *German Romantic Criticism* (ed. A. Leslie Willson; New York: Continuum, 1982), 1–30. Also see, with rather different emphases, Walter Benjamin, "Die Aufgabe des Übersetzers," in Störig, 156–169; English translation: "The Task of the Translator," in *Illuminations: Essays and Reflections,* ed. Hannah Arendt, trans. Harry Zohn (New York: Schocken, 1969), 69–82.

6. Elisabeth Schüssler Fiorenza, *Bread Not Stone: The Challenge of Feminist Biblical Interpretation* (Boston: Beacon, 1984). See especially the discussion on 17–18, where concern over adequate translation interacts with a hermeneutics of suspicion.

7. Flora Ross Amos, *Early Theories of Translation* (New York: Columbia University Press, 1920), 50; see p. 51 for specific examples in the history of biblical translation.

8. L. G. Kelly, *The True Interpreter: A History of Translation Theory and Practice in the West* (New York: St. Martin's, 1979), 207. Sharon H. Ringe, "Standing Toward the Text," *Theology Today* 43 (1987): 552–57 raises some crucial issues concerning textual authority and feminist practice.

9. Steiner, 18.

10. Steiner, 28: "*Interprète/interpreter* are commonly used to mean translator. This, I believe, is the vital starting point." Renato Poggioli, "The Added Artificer," in *On Translation,* ed. Reuben A. Brower (Cambridge: Harvard University, 1959; repr. ed. New York: Oxford University, 1966), 137: "That translation is an interpretive art is a self-evident truth."

11. Herbert Cushing Tolman, *The Art of Translating with Special Reference to Cauer's Die Kunst des Übersetzens* (Boston: Sanborn, 1901), 35: "One thing I wish to emphasize strongly—*translation is not interpretation*. The work of the translator is one, the work

of the exegete is another. Very true are the words of Wilhelm von Humboldt: '*Eine Über-setzung kann und soll kein Kommentar sein.*'"

12. Pliny, *Epistle* 7, cited by L. G. Kelly, 79.

13. Kelly, 34–44, which describes translation in terms of the relationship between the translator and the original text (or between the translator and language).

14. Kelly, 44–67, where translation is seen as a relationship between the translator and the author, with the two languages functioning as mediators.

15. Quintilian, as cited by Kelly, 45.

16. Jan de Waard and Eugene A. Nida, *From One Language to Another: Functional Equivalence in Bible Translating* (Nashville: Thomas Nelson, 1986), with chapter titles such as "Translating is Communicating," and "Translating Means Translating Meaning."

17. Poggioli, 143: "The gifted translator is an alchemist who changes a piece of gold into another piece of gold."

18. Poggioli, 139: "It is my contention that, like the original poet, the translator is a Narcissus who in this case chooses to contemplate his own likeness not in the spring of nature but in the pool of art."

19. Rosmarie Waldrop, "The Joy of the Demiurge," in *Translation: Literary, Linguistic, and Philosophical Perspectives,* ed. William Frawley (Newark: University of Delaware, 1984), 42–43, where translation is described as producing at once "the guilt of connivance" and "longing for reparation."

20. Kelly, 109, places "the translator's 'aggression'" in apposition to "his interpretive movement into the text to find what it has to offer and under what conditions." See also Waldrop, 43: "Translating is more like wrenching a soul from its body and luring it into a different one. It means killing."

21. Stephen David Ross, "Translation and Similarity," in *Translation Spectrum: Essays in Theory and Practice,* ed. Marilyn Gaddis Rose (Albany: SUNY Press, 1981), 12–14; Ross here is influenced by E. H. Gombrich, *Art and Illusion.*

22. Steiner, 29–30: "As every generation retranslates the classics out of a vital compulsion for immediacy and precise echo, so every generation uses language to build its own resonant past."

23. Steiner, 245: "Each impulse towards reformation from inside the Church brings with it a call for more authentic, more readily intelligible versions of the holy word."

24. Greenstein, 26–27, characterizes the ideas of Friedrich Schleiermacher, Franz Rosenzweig, and Walter Benjamin all as desiring for careful translation to aid in the movement toward the language of God; see Schleiermacher, "Über die vershiedenen Methoden des Übersetzens"; Martin Buber and Franz Rosenzweig, *Die fünf Bücher der Weisung* (Berlin: Lambert Schneider, 1930); Walter Benjamin, "Die Aufgabe des Übersetzers." See also Steiner, 59–65, for a discussion of the history of this notion, and the conclusions of his book, 474, which returns to this crucial idea; and, finally, Poggioli, 139: "If the translators of the Holy Writ worked only in teams of scholar-priest, searching through the babel of tongues for no other mirror than that reflecting the Word of God. . . ."

25. See Steiner, 239–44, 362–95, 474; Kelly, 214–18 (on the history of ideas about the [im]possibility of translation); Werner Winter, "Impossibilities of Translation," in *The Craft and Context of Translation,* ed. William Arrowsmith and Roger Shattuck (Austin: University of Texas Press, 1961), 68–82; and the most recent discussions by post-structuralists on the problem of "the remainder" in translation; Joseph F. Graham, ed. *Difference in Translation* (Ithaca: Cornell University Press, 1985); Jacques Derrida, "Living On/Border Lines," in *Deconstruction and Criticism* (New York: Continuum, 1979), 755–76; idem,

L'oreille de l'autre (Montreal: Vlb Editeur, 1982); English translation: *The Ear of the Other: Otobiography, Transference, Translation,* ed. Christine McDonald, trans. Peggy Kamuf (Lincoln: University of Nebraska, 1988); idem, "Des tours de Babel," in Graham, 209–48 with English translation, 165–207; Barbara Johnson, "Taking Fidelity Philosophically," in Graham, 142–49; and others.

26. This is true for translation theory at least since the contributions of Romantic critics; see Steiner, 265.

27. But see Greenstein's remarkable rereading of this opposition.

28. See Steiner, 276–78.

29. Lori Chamberlain, "Gender and the Metaphorics of Translation," *Signs* 13 (1987/88): 456–58, 461.

30. But see Jean Paris, "Translation and Creation," in Arrowsmith and Shattuck, 63: "If I dared to phrase it in family terms, I would say that a successful translation should rather be the brother than the son of the original, for both should proceed from the same transcendental Idea which is the real but invisible father of the work."

31. Chamberlain, 460, citing Amos, 112–13: "First I have now done as the people of God were commanded to do with their captive women that were handsome and beautiful: I have shaved off his hair and pared off his nails, that is, I have wiped away all his vanity and superfluity of matter. Further, I have for the most part drawn his private carpings of this or that man to a general moral. I have Englished things not according to the vein of the Latin propriety, but of his own vulgar tongue. I have interfered (to remove his obscurity and sometimes to better his matter) much of mine own devising. I have pieced his reason, eked and mended his similitudes, mollified his hardness, prolonged his cortall kind of speeches, changed and much altered his words but not his sentence, or at least (I dare say) not his purpose." Thomas Drant, *A Medicinable Moral, that is, the two books of Horace his satires Englished according to the prescription of St. Hierome* (London 1566) *To the Reader,* cited by Amos, 112–13.

32. Jerome, *Letter* 21.13 (*PL* 22.385).

33. Steiner, 296–303; further page references are included in the text.

34. Chamberlain, 456–58.

35. See Georges Mounin, *Les belles infidèles* (Paris: Cahiers du Sud, 1955).

36. See Greenstein, 19–20.

37. Greenstein, 17–19.

38. One of the striking aspects of this intersection is the role of the translator in maintaining the notion of the missionized as "other." Eugene A. Nida, father of biblical translation in this century, opens his work, *Toward a Science of Translating with Special Reference to Principles and Procedures Involved in Bible Translating* (Leiden: Brill, 1964), with a perhaps unconscious reference to the political nature and context of translation: "Whether one is dealing with translation in international gatherings, or with the highly publicized efforts to put machines to work translating masses of scientific abstracts, or with the *pioneering* efforts of missionaries translating the Scriptures for *remote, primitive tribes* . . ." p. 1 (emphasis added).

As recently as 1988, there appeared an article in *Christian Century* by a translator whose rhetoric made it clear that he considers the places in which he worked and the languages into which he was translating the Bible to be exotic and strange, other: "In my work as a consultant for the United Bible Societies in West Africa and South America, [I] help[ed] to organize and supervise translation projects in such places as Ouagadougou, Bobo Dioulasso, Timbuktu and Tamale, and check[ed] translations in such languages as Bobo,

Bwamu, Gourma, Pila-Pila and Kabiyé." (Roger L. Omanson, "Can You Get There from Here? Problems in Bible Translation," *Christian Century* 105 [1988]: 605). It was not enough to open his article with such a characterization, but rather he found it necessary to conclude with yet further references to languages (Guarani, Chulupi, Ewe) meant to evoke an image of strangeness in the reader (607). When he goes on to group these languages with "the several thousand languages still waiting to receive an entire New Testament or a complete Bible," the image of the native population hungry for civilization lingers uncomfortably. Compare de Waard and Nida, 20–21, following a claim that at least some part of the Bible has been translated for 97 percent of the world's population: "But those who do not as yet have anything of the Scriptures represent at least another thousand languages *which should have something*" (emphasis added).

The full history of the effects of missionary discourse on indigenous cultures remains to be written. For an evocative discussion of the directions in which such historical work might fruitfully move, see V. Y. Mudimbe, *The Invention of Africa: Gnosis, Philosophy, and the Order of Knowledge* (Bloomington: Indiana University Press, 1988), especially chap. 3, "The Power of Speech."

39. See John McBratney, "Images of Indian Women in Rudyard Kipling: A Case of Doubling Discourse," *Inscriptions* 3/4, *Feminism and the Critique of Colonial Discourse* (1988), 47–57.

40. This is the dominant idea in biblical translation theory produced by Eugene Nida and his school; see as examples, Eugene A. Nida, "A Framework for the Analysis and Evaluation of Theories of Translation," in *Translation: Applications and Research*, ed. Richard W. Brislin (New York: Gardner, 1976), 47–91; Nida, "Principles of Translation as Exemplified by Bible Translating," in Brower, 11–31; Nida, *Toward a Science of Translating*; Nida and Charles R. Taber, *The Theory and Practice of Translation* (Leiden: Brill, 1974); and de Waard and Nida. For a thoroughgoing critique of such positions, see Henri Meschonnic, *Pour la poétique, II: Epistémologie de l'écriture; Poétique de la traduction* (Paris: Gallimard, 1973), 328–49.

41. See de Waard and Nida, 24: "In addition *to letting the Scriptures speak for themselves*, it is essential to accurately *reflect the cultural contexts of biblical times* whether ideological, sociological, or ecological. . . . The biblical culture was also a male-oriented culture, and to try to rewrite the Scriptures in so-called 'inclusive language' introduces cultural anachronisms and serious contextual distortions. To insist that God be spoken of as both 'father and mother' is to create *a bisexual God, not a sexually neutral God*" (emphasis added).

42. Jorge Luis Borges, *Narraciones*, ed. Marcos Ricardo Barnatán (Madrid: Cátedra, 1986), 86.

43. Chamberlain, 470.

44. For some sense of the perceived threat of feminist translation, consider the titles of articles such as James R. Edward, "Toward a Neutered Bible: Making God S/he," *Christianity Today* 27:4 (1983): 19–21 and "Unmanning the Holy Bible," *Time* (December 8, 1980): 128.

45. Borges, 89.

RECOMMENDED READINGS

Biguenet, John, and Rainer Schulte, eds. *The Craft of Translation*. Chicago: University of Chicago Press, 1989.

Chamberlain, Lori. "Gender and the Metaphorics of Translation." *Signs* 13 (1988): 454–72. Reprinted in Venuti, 57–74.

Falk, Marcia. "Translation as a Journey." In *The Song of Songs: Love Lyrics from the Bible,* 89–98. San Francisco: HarperCollins, 1990.

Graham, Joseph, ed. *Difference in Translation.* Ithaca, NY: Cornell University Press, 1985.

Journal of Feminist Studies in Religion 6/2 (1990). Responses to the present article by Joanna Dewey (pp. 63–69), Peggy Hutaff (pp. 69–74), and Jane Schaberg (pp. 74–85).

Levine, Suzanna Jill. "Translation as (Sub)Version: On Translating *Infante's Inferno." Substance* 42 (1983): 85–94.

Martin, Clarice J. "Womanist Interpretations of the New Testament: The Quest for Holistic and Inclusive Translation and Interpretation." *Journal of Feminist Studies in Religion* 6/2 (1990): 41–61.

Niranjana, Tejaswini. *Siting Translation: History, Post-Structuralism, and the Colonial Context.* Berkeley: University of California Press, 1992.

Schulte, Rainer, and John Biguenet, eds. *Theories of Translation: An Anthology of Essays from Dryden to Derrida.* Chicago: University of Chicago Press, 1992.

Venuti, Lawrence, ed. *Rethinking Translation: Discourse, Subjectivity, Ideology.* New York: Routledge, 1992.

14

❖ Historical-Critical Methods

MONIKA FANDER ◆

THE COMMON STARTING POINT of all feminist approaches is a profound suspicion of the results of a patriarchal system of thinking in which women are often excluded from the symbolic, public, and social forms of communication, and by which femaleness has been devalued and frequently reduced to the role of victim. However, while a self-definition in terms of victim status alone excuses personal actions, it can scarcely explain why efforts toward emancipation should not suddenly be interpreted as the result of manipulation. To define oneself exclusively as a victim means to understand one's very being in terms of a dependence on patriarchy. In recent years, the approach of difference developed by Italian feminists, especially the women of the Milan "Libreria delle donne," has become very important to me.[1] They presuppose that every woman possesses an area of freedom, no matter how minimal. In consequence, they speak not of liberation but rather of the way in which female freedom comes about.

They focus on women who function as significant mediators for women's entrance into the order of social symbolism. Until now it has been almost inevitable . . . that women who seek to achieve authority in the public sphere and to assume roles of responsibility have had to subject their difference as women to a masculine understanding of subjectivity. It is important to acknowledge the existence and acceptance of female mediation of reality throughout many generations. It is only from women who represent for one another what is called a source of value, who bestow dignity and authority on one another, that a public discussion can originate, together with a differentiation and resolution of conflicts . . . within the figure of the female sex. We are speaking of the symbolic mother figures, personalities who are advanced beyond others in competence, knowledge, experience, and frequently also in age, whose authority constitutes a basis on which others can critically build.[2]

At the same time, it is important to these Italian women to inject dynamic energy into the system of relations between and among women. Without losing sight of the responsibility of the dominant discourse, and the solidarity among women, they emphasize the differences among women as a group — differences that, in turn, give rise to different historical questions. These differences need not enlarge the gulf between women; instead, they can indicate the multiplicity of possibilities for women's development. The women of Milan describe the dilemma as follows: "The absence of female authority in the world is the consequence of an unfortunate kind of 'mirroring' among women. Other women are my mirror, and what I cannot see in any of them is lost to me."[3] Breaking down this barrier appears to me to be an important goal of feminist historical research.

The anthropological approach sketched here focuses our attention on women themselves. When women are seen exclusively as victims of patriarchy, there is great danger that what men say about women will be given more authority than is appropriate, and that such statements will be regarded all too easily as representative of women's reality. If, instead, I go in search of spheres in which women are free, I will be looking for other sources that may give a different picture of women's situation in a given epoch. I am taking it for granted that patriarchy is not a fixed system but is subject to adaptation. By adopting the approach thus briefly described we will not remain fixated on patriarchal oppression; instead, women themselves will become the center of our interest.

A CRITIQUE OF HISTORICAL CRITICISM

A good deal of criticism has recently been directed at the historical-critical method.[4] That method stands accused of being unfeeling, cerebral, irreligious, and even godless; of being too philological in its interests and less theological. It is said that the effort expended by this method is quite out of proportion to its results, that exegetical studies are too much focused on questions proposed by other scholars and hence are seldom relevant to pastoral praxis. These are only a few of the objections. From the feminist side there is the added accusation that the results of historical criticism are by no means as objective as their proponents say they are, since a great number of androcentric tendencies can be shown to exist in the translations and interpretations produced by such scholarship. Women's questions are seldom addressed by historical-critical analysis, or else the answers proposed are a stumbling block; the result is that the historical-critical method may be and is suspected of serving masculine interests.

In light of such criticism, there is discussion among exegetes — often quite dogmatic in tone — about whether the historical-critical method should be replaced or augmented by literary or structuralist analysis.[5] Whereas historical-critical methods attempt to explain the stages of development through which the text has passed, and how and why what the text says has changed in the course of its transmission, linguistic structuralism works with the final version of the text. While historical-critical methods are interested in the history of a text, linguistic methods inquire about the meaning derived from it by its readers and deny that it is possible to reconstruct the meaning of a text from outside the text itself. However, in the United States (far more than in Europe thus far) there is already an awareness that these two starting points for analysis cannot be treated as ideological opponents. A biblical text must be studied with literary methods, but biblical texts often originated as "usable texts" and therefore presume a particular situation of communication. Hence, in a second step, the social, historical, and ecclesial context must be reconstructed before the text can be understood. Complete rejection of any historical questions would also mean that we would have to abandon the study of the history of early Christianity. Nevertheless, despite this plea for historical research, we cannot overlook the tension between feminist-historical and historical-critical methods.

Is the Historical-Critical Method Unsuitable for Feminist-Historical Research?

The Bible is not *a* book, but a whole collection of books. In them we encounter pious people and doubters, the wise and the critics of wisdom, the powerful and the enemies of power, rich and poor, women and men. They tell us of joy and love, sorrow and suffering, liberation, disappointment, rage, and despair. This variety offers us opportunities for identification and for rejection. It is the purpose of the historical-critical method to discern this variety. Since the historical-critical method is a child of the Enlightenment and of historicism, it is aware of the historical distance between the present and the period in which the biblical texts had their origin. At the same time, it is aware that the answers supplied by biblical texts are fundamentally captive to the situations in which they originated. Consequently, the historical-critical method does not take its starting point from a literal understanding of Scripture, but from the insight that "in the Holy Scriptures, God has spoken to human beings in human fashion" (Vatican Council II, *Dei Verbum* 2, with reference to Augustine). Its concern is with understanding texts historically. This interest is directed both to the history of a text's origins and transmission, and to the world in which the text came to be. In order to reconstruct these developments, we need *critical* investigations of the text. The word "critical" comes from the Greek *krinein* and means "to distinguish." Hence, the historical-critical method attempts (a) to analyze the biblical texts with philological exactness, (b) to reconstruct the historical events that are described in the text or assumed by it, and (c) to interpret the text against that background. Thus it is primarily concerned with capturing the *original* meaning of the text and is less interested in interpreting the text for the present.

We currently include within the historical-critical method a number of submethodologies, distinguishing among textual, literary, form, genre, tradition, and redaction criticism. All these are methods that serve the purposes of an analysis that is immanent to the text. They are augmented, to an increasing degree, by studies of religious, social, and legal history that interpret the biblical texts with the aid of sources drawn from the history of the times and independent of the Bible itself.

I would like to investigate, on the basis of a series of examples, whether the historical-critical method is, in fact, unsuitable for a feminist analysis of the text. In this context, we must also ask whether the method itself is patriarchal, or whether it is the goal and application—that is, the hermeneutical pre-understanding—of the method that should be called into question.

Textual Criticism

The textual tradition of Hosea 11 is relatively complicated: as a result, various translations are possible. Here I would like to compare two such suggested translations, one derived from the German version by Helen Schüngel-Straumann, the other from that by Martin Luther.

Schüngel-Straumann[6]	*Luther*

1 When Israel was a child
   I began to love him,
   out of Egypt I called my son.
	When Israel was a child
	I loved him
	and called my son out of Egypt;

2 But when I called them,
   they turned from me,
   they sacrificed to the Baals,
   and offered incense to images.
	but now if they are called,
	they turn away
	and sacrifice to the Baals
	and offer incense to images.

3 *And yet it was I*
   who nursed Ephraim.
   taking him in my arms.
	I taught Ephraim to walk
	
	and took him up in my arms;

But they did not understand that I *took care of them*.	but they did not know how I *helped them*.
4 I led them with cords of human kindness, with bonds of love.	I let a human yoke be made for them and with cords of love I helped them to walk,
And I was for them like those who bear an infant at the breast. I bent down to him and fed him.	*and I helped them to bear the yokes upon their necks* and gave them nourishment,
5 He must return to Egypt, and Assyria will be his ruler, because they refused to turn back.	so that they need not return to Egypt. But now Assyria must be their ruler; for they refused to turn back.
6 And the sword will rage in his cities and consume the babblers, and they will have to eat up what they have sown.	Therefore will the sword abide in their cities and consume their branches, and devour them because of their own counsels.
7 But my people are bent on turning away from me: They call to Baal, *but he will never nurture them* to adulthood!	My people are bent on backsliding from me, and if anyone preaches to them, *none rises up.*
8 How can I give you up, Ephraim? how can I hand you over, Israel? How can I abandon you like Adma or treat you like Zeboim? My heart recoils within me, *my womb is utterly on fire.*	How shall I give you up, Ephraim? and hand you over, Israel? How can I abandon you like Adma and injure you like Zeboim? My heart is turned within me, *all my compassion is aroused.*
9 I cannot execute my fierce anger, nor can I again turn back (my inmost self), to destroy Ephraim! For I am God *and not a man* holy in your midst and I do not come to destroy.	I will not do as my wrath demands nor again destroy Ephraim. For I am God *and not a human being* and I am the Holy One in your midst and will not come to lay waste.
10 (. . .)	
11 (. . .)	

These texts speak for themselves, and therefore I will not offer an additional interpretation. In vv. 3, 4, and 7, both translations are allowed by the text, but it is absolutely clear that *'îš* in v. 9 refers not to human, but to masculine behavior. When Hosea speaks of human beings or of human attitudes, he always uses the word *'ādām* (Hos 9:12; 11:4; 13:2).[7] Schüngel-Straumann's version is favored by the uniformity of the images, which in the Luther version are shifting. In any case, Schüngel-Straumann's reconstruction of the text reveals a God-image that is quite different from that found in the usual translations.

Form and Genre Criticism

The story of the healing of Simon's mother-in-law appears in Mark as a brief narrative that would originally have read as follows:[8]

> He came to Capernaum and went into Simon's house. Now Simon's mother-in-law was lying sick with a fever. And immediately they told him about her. Then he went to her, took her by the hand and raised her up. The fever left her, and she served him.

Most exegetes are uncertain what to do with this brief, concise narrative. As a result, they often deny that the story makes any independent statement, so that in spite of severe criticism the thesis of the life-of-Jesus researchers still has become firm: namely, that Mark 1:29-31 represents an eyewitness account by Peter that was originally told in the first person plural ("we" form).[9]

Although the narrative contains all the elements of a miracle story, it is striking that the stylistic features that support the christological statement in a miracle story are lacking. This is especially noteworthy since one of the most important purposes of a miracle story is to make a christological statement. I believe this is also the reason why most exegetes deny that this narrative has any independent statement to make. However, it appears that the christological aspect is by no means so important: the primary purpose of the story is not to underscore Jesus' importance and uniqueness. Instead, the healed woman herself takes center stage. What we are hearing is the story of how Simon's mother-in-law entered the service of Jesus. Three elements in the concise narrative catch our attention: the biographical aspect (the indirect indication of name), the place (Capernaum), and the conclusion ("she served him"). This last does not refer to some kind of housewifely activity; in the Greek text it is in the imperfect tense and thus indicates an ongoing activity.

If we include the following verses (32–34) in this story, it presents a remarkable parallel to Acts 28:7-10, which is apparently a narrative of the foundation of the first Christian community in Malta. There Paul is welcomed by the leading figure on the island, a man named Publius. Publius's father is lying in the house, ill with fever and dysentery, and he is miraculously healed by Paul. The result of this healing is that other sick people come to Paul and are also healed by him. Thus in both stories an itinerant man of God is a guest in the house of another man who is mentioned by name, probably an early disciple. In both cases a close relative is lying sick and is healed, whereupon the disciple's house becomes the "base" for further healings. However, there is a decisive difference between the two stories: in Acts 28:7-10 the focus is on Publius's reaction, and nothing further is said about the behavior of the father who has been healed. It is different with Simon's mother-in-law: her healing brings her into Jesus' service, and there is no mention of Simon's reaction. On the basis of this parallel to Acts 28:7-10, we may see in Mark 1:29–34 a community's foundational legend of Capernaum, which in this case is connected with a woman.

Although there are no form-critical criteria by means of which one may test this thesis, the discussion of the *Sitz im Leben* contains some interesting suggestions. According to G. Schille's study, the founding of a community in a particular place or region is often narrated in the form of a miracle story.[10] Through the example of a first disciple, or by the Lord's working a miracle, the great faith of a certain place is described and, in this way, an attempt is made to legitimate the apostolic foundation of a specific community. In this sense, the intention of our story could be the following: we are told how Simon's mother-in-law became a disciple of Jesus as a result of a miracle. At the same time, through its connection with the name of the town, Capernaum, the story serves as a reflection of the beginnings of the Christian community in that place; in this case, the community's origin is connected with a woman.

Redaction Criticism

Mark's redactional work integrates the narrative of the healing of Simon's mother-in-law into the composition of a "first day" of Jesus' public activity (1:21–34).[11] The first chapter as a whole, but especially the strongly redactional unit in 1:21–34, serves as an introduction to the major themes of Mark's Gospel. Hence the first chapter has a programmatic character.

Verses 29–31 introduce the theme of "discipleship." They stand in sharp contrast to the preceding story of the exorcism of a demon. The healing of the mother-in-law is told very briefly and tonelessly, without any spectacular elements of any kind. In contrast, the driving out of the demon is the focus of a sensational narrative. The point of comparison between the two stories, toward which this contrast is aimed, is the difference in the reactions to the healing. After the exorcism, the crowd reacts with shock, then enthusiasm, but they do not understand that the miracles are only signs. The exorcism leads neither to conversion nor to a christological confession, not even on the part of those who have already been called. The crowd spreads the word of the marvel through an enthusiastic activism, describing Jesus as a local miracle-working hero (1:28). What we find here is a lust for sensation rather than discipleship. Simon's mother-in-law reacts differently: her response is apparently calm and sober; she comes to serve Jesus as a result of the event, and she does so in the context of her own unspectacular, unsensational daily life, unmarked by any kind of enthusiastic raptures. Discipleship means understanding what has happened and translating what one has learned into normal daily life.

There is another similar contrast in the scene in Mark 1:35–39. Jesus retreats into isolation, fleeing the misunderstanding of his role as that of a popular wonder-worker. In his retreat there occurs an initial confrontation with his disciples. They, as those first called, Simon in particular, make themselves the advocates for the crowd and seek to bring Jesus back. Jesus has to correct them and explain his true mission. The disciples misunderstand Jesus just as the crowd does; they thus stand in contrast to Simon's mother-in-law. In this first chapter the motif of the disciples' misunderstanding is developed in contrast to the behavior of a woman.

Diakonia is a differentiation of Mark's concept of discipleship. Interestingly enough, this kind of discipleship is attributed only to women (1:29; 15:41). Eduard Schweizer attempts to defuse this explosive finding by interpreting service as "the specific form of women's discipleship."[12] But this is refuted by the usage of *diakonein* in 10:42–45, where Jesus teaches the disciples the true meaning of discipleship. "If one considers as well that [Mark], by introducing the names of the disciples in 1:29, appears to have deliberately shaped this little narrative as a story of discipleship," it would seem to have been his theological intention "in this way to depict service as the duty of a disciple as such and, as in 14:3–9; 15:41, to present a woman as the model of true discipleship."[13]

Preliminary Conclusion

These examples should suffice to show that the method as such is not unsuitable for feminist criticism of the biblical text. It even aids us in working through a number of deficiencies in feminist readings of the Bible and in giving precision to some statements.

In some feminist publications reference is made to Jesus' revolutionary attitudes toward women, and this reference is turned into a historical judgment. However, such a procedure is highly problematic and touches on a central question of exegetical work. The results of the research carried out by the life-of-Jesus movement have already shown that there are only a few texts that may with assurance be traced back to Jesus himself. Historical criticism can make us sensitive to the need to read texts as testimonies of the faith of the Jesus movement or of the first Christian communities. The question of the historical roots of a text is related to a further problem: the historical-critical method calls our attention to the fact that we must distinguish between historical and literary levels. The narratives about Jesus and his followers are not historical sources in the classical sense. It is methodologically correct to draw conclusions from the type of depiction about the use of this piece of tradition in relation to the interests of the community that is handing it on. That is, in terms of form criticism we must ask about the "*Sitz im Leben*," the life situation, and the context in which the text arose.

The historical-critical method makes us aware of the important distinction between tradition and redaction. Redactional emphases reveal problems and points of discussion within the community for which a particular author wrote. A comparison between tradition and redaction can, in addition, reveal a moment in the church's development.

Only a *historical* understanding of the origins and transmission of biblical texts can prevent a biblicistic, fundamentalist misunderstanding. If revelatory character is attributed to every word of the Bible, misogynistic statements can only be accepted, or else the liberation of women can only occur outside Christianity. But the historical-critical method is based on an understanding of scripture according to which God has spoken in the sacred scriptures through human beings and in the way that human beings speak. Such an understanding of scripture is the precondition for any possibility of criticism of biblical texts; for example, the ability to inquire whether the silencing of women (1 Tim 2:11) really has revelatory character or not. And only a historical understanding of the texts makes it possible to distinguish among different traditions, for in the Bible some quite distinct theologies are found check by jowl, often contradicting one another, correcting one another, or expanding the perspective of the other. Historical criticism preserves this variety of theological initiatives, which invites us to identify with them or arouses us to opposition. Another essential service of the historical-critical method is its emphasis on the strangeness and independence of the texts. Only in this way is it possible for the biblical word to change our view of things and to correct present praxis. Thus the method contributes to our critical reappraisal of various traditions and of (church) history.

ANDROCENTRIC OR IDEOLOGICALLY SUSPECT? THE TENSE RELATIONSHIP BETWEEN HISTORICAL-CRITICAL AND HISTORICAL-FEMINIST RESEARCH

Although the historical-critical method appears appropriate for feminist inquiry, the tensions between feminist-critical and historical-critical study are not so easily eliminated. On the feminist side there remains the suspicion that this method is being used against women. On the other side, the results of feminist research appear to many exegetes to be unscientific and are suspected of being ideological and reductionist, because feminist theology begins with the experiences of women and poses contemporary questions to the biblical texts. Toward feminist initiatives, in particular, many exegetes raise objections regarding scholarly validity, seriousness, and objectivity. In such instances, historical inquiry is still being interpreted within exegetical circles in Leopold von Ranke's sense: Ranke supposed that "the historian can 'step out of his own time' and study history 'on its own terms,' 'unencumbered' by questions and experiences of 'his own day.'"[14]

Can the past really be studied as such? Are the results of historical-critical research truly value-free and purely descriptive? Elisabeth Schüssler Fiorenza was the first to introduce the concept of androcentrism into this discussion.[15] In doing so, she described the way in which biblical history and stories are written and interpreted from a masculine point of view and are presented as an objective representation of what really happened.

For example: Bernadette Brooten was able to present persuasive arguments to show that in Rom 16:7 it is not a man named Junias but a woman named Junia who is described as "outstanding among the apostles."[16] She first published this work in 1977. In the seventh revised printing of the twenty-sixth edition of the Greek text by Nestle-Aland, which appeared in 1985 (!), the alternate reading "Junia" has been removed from the text-critical apparatus. Anyone working with this edition of the text will not even be aware that there is a problem.

For another example, see Josef Blank's discussion of Luke 8:1–3. He writes:

> This note, despite its brevity, is a further indication that women were among Jesus's regular companions, and that they had apparently taken over the task

of supplying daily necessities for Jesus and his disciples. We should assume that they were also participants in "discipleship," though not necessarily in preaching; with respect to the message of the reign of God one may also speak of their having "equal rights."[17]

Here it appears that a liberal attitude gives women a status as disciples; still, they are second-class disciples. Susanne Heine hits the mark when she says of this:

> What are we supposed to think of as constituting the supply of daily necessities? Cooking? Where? Washing clothes, when there is no reason for changing them? Care of the body in view of the imminence of the reign of God? Besides, such an interpretation overlooks the fact that the text expressly says that the women supported the group with their money. But Josef Blank prefers to stick to the idea of "daily necessities," and thus gives us a nice example of the way in which individual interests can turn exegesis into eisegesis.[18]

Here the interpretation is dictated by an ancient system of roles, not an attention to history itself.

However, this example illustrates another problem: a search of the concordance reveals that in Luke's Gospel all those who believe in Jesus are his disciples, whether female or male. According to this evangelist, the title "disciple" is not restricted to the Twelve, whom he instead calls "apostles." Luke 8:1–3 is not proof that Jesus had female disciples; instead, in Luke 8:1–3 the women are associated with the apostles. It is true, as Blank insists, that there is no indication whatever of the women's having been active as preachers. But the question remains whether Luke's depiction really reflects the actual situation of women in the Jesus movement, or whether we should here suspect a theological and ecclesio-political intention on the part of Luke — especially since it is striking that Paul knows women who perform duties and functions within the early Christian communities, while Luke, in the Acts of the Apostles, conveys the impression that the beginnings and development of the church were purely the work of men. For example, we may note the interesting changes Luke has introduced, against Matthew, in the listing of criteria for discipleship. In Matthew (10:37–38) we read: "Anyone who loves father or mother more than me is not worthy of me, and anyone who loves son or daughter more than me is not worthy of me. . . ." Luke has inserted the one crucial word: "If anyone comes to me and does not hate his father and mother *and his wife and children* . . . he cannot be my disciple" (Luke 14:26). Thus while the identity of the audience is left open in Matthew, in Luke it is only men who are addressed.

There has been much discussion among exegetes about the historicity

of Luke's concept of "apostles," because it differs markedly from Paul's definition in 1 Corinthians 15. But this discussion appears to be forgotten when
it is a question of women.

> If it is assumed that the New Testament texts mirror the reality of early Chris-
> tian women and give us an accurate picture of their involvement in early
> Christianity, then it is the "scientific" exegete who establishes objectively *"wie
> es am Anfang war"* [i.e., how it was in the beginning].[19]

Schüssler Fiorenza therefore emphasizes that the biblical texts themselves
are not exempt from the suspicion of androcentrism. The Bible was written by men; consequently, it reflects their view of reality. For example, the
strictures regarding the veil in 1 Corinthians 11 tell us in the first place
only what Paul thought about the matter. We do not know whether the
women in Corinth obeyed him unresistingly.

These examples are already sufficient to make us understand why women
are skeptical about the results of traditional scholarship. At the same time,
they make clear that many interpretations fall far short of their own claim
to objectivity. The tensions between representatives of traditional and
feminist exegesis are hermeneutical in character. They rest on the pre-
understanding that consciously or unconsciously shapes the treatment of
the texts, and on the question of the authority that is to be attributed to
those texts. The question remains whether an exegesis free from any pre-
understanding, as Ranke imagined it, is at all possible and what it means,
in a feminist sense, to do historical and critical research.

SCHOLARSHIP WITHOUT PRECONDITIONS
OR PREJUDICES? HISTORICAL CRITICISM AND
THE HERMENEUTICAL CIRCLE

The idea of an exegesis without preconditions was rejected by Rudolf
Bultmann as early as 1957.[20] Historical scholarship in Ranke's sense con-
fuses one's own reconstruction of history with the facticity of historical
events. A glance at Jesus research alone makes it clear that every age in
theology has found its own ideas reflected in Jesus. The historical Jesus
of biblical scholarship has never been identical with the earthly Jesus;
instead, such portrayals are always attempts at a historical reconstruction
of the life of Jesus. Nothing else is possible, since

> in order to make statements of historical fact, scholars must draw inferences
> based in part upon their "data" or "sources" and in part upon their general
> understanding of human behavior and the nature of the world. They not

only deal selectively with their historical sources in order to present a "coherent" narrative account, but also ascribe historical "significance" to their "data" in accordance with the theoretical model or perspective that "orders" their information.[21]

That means that historical scholarship is unable to escape from its hermeneutical circle. But we are dealing not only with the mutual influence of information drawn from source material and the models of interpretation applied to that information; writers write in the context of the dominant scholarly theories that are current at a given time.

Add to this that the New Testament texts depart from the concept of historical criticism in Ranke's sense by the very fact that they do not present a pure recital of facts; they are, instead, human testimonies of faith. If we are to understand the biblical texts as statements of faith, however, we must interpret them *historically,* since they were formulated against the background of a different time and an alien image of the world. At this point we need, for example, the instruments of tradition and motif criticism and the tools of the history of religions, as well as specific studies of contemporary texts.

> Simply stated: they [the texts] must be translated, and that translation is the task of historical scholarship. As soon as we speak of translation, the *hermeneutical problem* arises. Translation means making intelligible, and it presupposes an understanding. Understanding history as a context of connected events presupposes *an understanding of the active forces* that connect individual phenomena. Such forces include economic requirements, social necessities, political grasping for power. . . . Historians differ in their evaluation of such factors, and despite all efforts to achieve a unified view, each historian will always be driven by *a particular approach to the questions, an individual perspective.* This does not imply any falsification of the historical picture, so long as the pre-set approach to questions is not a prejudice, but really an individual approach, and if the historian is aware that this approach is one-sided and looks at the phenomenon, or the text, from a particular perspective.[22]

The approach to the questions, however, is determined by the life context of the researcher. The choice and determination of those things that were important in the past and that therefore are to be studied are always shaped by the personal and social perspective of the scholar, and thus by an interest and an approach that belong to the present time. A particular approach is suspect of being ideological only if the researcher denies that there are other approaches to the analysis of a text. The one who rejects the variety of possible approaches is the one who is beginning to be an ideologue.

From that perspective it is legitimate for Christian women to inquire, regarding the beginnings of Christianity, whether the devaluation that women have experienced in the course of history was intended from the start, or whether the New Testament can serve as a corrective to present practice. After all, history is not done merely as "art for art's sake," and we must therefore ask *why*, in fact, it is done, and *for whom*. It is meant to yield insights into the present, whether as confirmation, contrast, or critique of things as they now are. "Only those can understand history who do not approach it as neutral, uninvolved onlookers, but who are themselves in the midst of history and accept responsibility for it."[23]

An encounter with the history of the past is possible only from within one's own historicity, which is a part of the hermeneutical circle and not a subsequent and detached step: first the explanation of what happened back then, and then its application to today.

Thus, it is not a present-related interest that makes an approach suspect of ideology; the question, rather, is the location of the dividing line between reading-in and reading-out, between wishful thinking and demonstrable result. For example, when someone asks whether Mary Magdalene had an erotic relationship with Jesus, the thesis is dictated by a present-day understanding of sexuality. Even if Mary Magdalene was part of Jesus' closest circle of disciples, she need not have been his lover. The biblical text offers us no basis for answering this question; it simply has nothing at all to say about it. Here our contemporary ideas of sexuality are being projected into the text. Often these are notions that completely ignore the fact that people of other times may have aspired to ideals not of sexual liberalism but of asceticism.

An awareness of the hermeneutical circle does not mean that the conclusions of scholarship are not subject to verification or that they are withdrawn from any kind of control. The exactitude of scholarly work can be tested by the following criteria:

> To what extent have relevant sources been utilized and how much has the present state of research been considered? . . . How much has the account reached an optimal plausible integration of all available historical information? . . . How logically rigorous, consistent, and coherent is the use of explanatory heuristic models, and are they reasonably free from self-contradictions?[24]

A particular piece of research is not rendered false by its pre-understanding. It becomes so only if that pre-understanding is already taken to be the final result, or if the difference between the present and the past situation is overlooked. A historical investigation is never without some pre-understanding, but it must be free of prejudice;[25] that is, the result of a study can be presented in such a way that the theses originally proposed cannot be proved, and the results are disappointing or disagreeable to me. At the same time, the hermeneutical circle makes it clear that the results of historical research must be subject to constant testing and review and that they do not stand fast for all time. Discussion and contemporary questions change, and what today may be incomprehensible and inaccessible may in later years be unlocked by a changed situation or the progress of discussion.

If historical-critical method is applied not on the basis of a positivist idea of scholarship but in terms of the reconstructionist ideas just outlined, feminist scholarship can also work with this method. I believe that feminist exegesis demands not a new scholarly method but a new hermeneutics. This new approach to the question of women's roles in early Christianity, however, requires a considerable shift in perspective. What questions must we ask if we seek to reconstruct the history of women? That history, especially in an era as distant as antiquity, cannot be reconstructed very easily. It cannot simply be tacked onto men's history as the missing half. For the most part, we lack historical sources by and about women. The New Testament texts themselves were written from an androcentric perspective. What does it mean to do research from women's perspective? What is historical-critical research in a feminist sense? I wish to address these questions in the following section, following the work of Elisabeth Schüssler Fiorenza and Bernadette Brooten.[26]

FEMINIST HISTORICAL-CRITICAL RESEARCH

"Critical," in the sense of feminist historical research, includes far more than what is meant by this term in the expression "historical-critical method." It is not simply a matter of reconstructing strands of tradition and of analyzing the historical conditions under which a text was created. Feminist exegesis has succeeded in demonstrating the androcentric tendencies in numerous translations, interpretations, and models of explanation that are commonly used by scholars. Feminist analysis of texts thus works, in the sense of Elisabeth Schüssler Fiorenza's expression, with a "hermeneutics of suspicion."[27] But such a hermeneutic is not applicable only to commonly accepted scholarly conclusions and theories; it also calls into question the authority of the biblical texts themselves. "Since the early Christian sources stand within this historical continuum of androcentric culture and scholarship, it is not surprising that they treat women as marginal figures in early Christian history."[28] This calls for attention to contradictions within the biblical text. For example, there are tensions between the Pauline and Lukan accounts of what women did for the building up of the first Christian communities. Consequently, there need to be differentiated redaction-critical studies, both synchronous and diachronous. Attention must also be paid to the textual tradition itself. For example, Codex D should be examined, since it can be demonstrated that it clearly reduces the role of women, even to a disappearing point.[29]

It follows that studies of men's opinions of women should not be too quickly accepted as reflections of reality. It is of course necessary to investigate, for example, what Paul thought about women, but do we then know whether Junia or Prisca shared his theology, or whether the women of Corinth obeyed his demand that they wear veils? Should not the rhetorical form of a text be examined in order to give a precise description of its *Sitz im Leben*? For example, is it not true that polemic language in a text indicates that what is being described is not an actual situation but rather what the writer thinks *should* be the case? A prescriptive text is not to be confused with a descriptive one.

> Rather than taking Paul's views on women as an accurate reflection of early Christian women's reality, one would analyze Paul's system of thought on its own terms and in the context of male thinking of the time and then ask how women in antiquity were affected by and, in turn, how they affected Paul's views.[30]

The household codes are another good example of the problem we are addressing here. The demands of the household codes, with their strict hierarchy, were at the time of their reception into Christian texts not so much a reality as a situation men considered desirable, and an attempt to counter the emancipatory struggles of Greek and Roman women. In the same time period we find endless moral laments, particularly from Roman men, about the supposed sexual abandon of women and the collapse of the traditional wifely ideal.[31]

Feminist research must bring about a shift in categories. It cannot simply organize its efforts in relation to the significant dates and events of official history. These are mainly military events, councils, edicts, and dogmas — in themselves events and occurrences in which women rarely participated. If we want to know something about the conditions of women's lives, we must look to very different sources. The reconstruction of women's reality, however, cannot be easily accomplished. It demands a very clever and imaginative search for documentation. Interesting in this context are business and private letters; purchase, marriage, and loan contracts; archaeological and architectonic data. This also shows that the traditional division of scholarly fields is too narrow for feminist research. Women cannot simply do exegesis; they must also apply insights from such fields as philology, Jewish studies, the study of the ancient Orient, and so on. Thus it appears from rabbinic sources (*m. Yebam.* 14:1; *t. Ketub.* 12.3; *y. Ketub.* V 1,29c, and *b. Giṭ.* 49b) that only Jewish men had a right to initiate divorce. Marriage contracts and writs of divorce from the fifth century B.C.E. to the twelfth century C.E., however, testify to a parallel legal tradition that granted Jewish women that same right.[32]

The discussion of anti-Semitism in feminist theology has shown that the divorce of cultural contexts, that is, separate studies of the position of women in Judaism and in the Greek and Roman contexts, makes little sense. Prisca and Junia were not only Christian women; they were also Jewish women. It is much more appropriate to investigate the reasons why Christianity was attractive to women and what opportunities for self-development it offered them. Thus, including women's perspectives means shifting our categories in many areas; in others it requires a break with common models of interpretation and a good deal of alteration in our thinking—whether we are women or men.

SUMMARY

It is not the methods of historical criticism as such that are unsuitable for feminist historical research. The tensions between the historical critical method and feminist historical study are hermeneutical in character. From the perspective of a positivist conception of history, feminist research is suspected of being ideological, even though a great many androcentric examples can be adduced to demonstrate that the representatives of the positivist approach to scholarship are by no means as objective as they pretend to be.

It is not any particular present-day question that renders an approach suspect of reductionism. Every scholar addresses a text in terms of a particular pre-understanding that is marked, consciously or unconsciously, by the cultural context and questions of the researcher's own time. Only when the scholar understands her- or himself as existing within history is an encounter with past history possible. For historical research is done not for the sake of the people of the past but for the people of today. No research is without presuppositions, but it must be free of prejudice. That is, it must not take its pre-understanding to be the result of the research; it must be prepared for possible revisions of its initial theses.

Historical-critical research in a feminist sense means analyzing the texts through a hermeneutics of suspicion. This not only applies to current translations, interpretations, and models of explanation, but also inquires whether the text to be analyzed is itself marked by an androcentric point of view. It asks about the theological content of a text and its function in the lives of women then and now. The search for women as historical subjects demands a considerable shift in categories, but all this can be effected by use of the instruments of the historical-critical method.

When feminist scholarship supplies a content to the adjectives "historical" and "critical" that is in accord with its own thinking, it becomes clear that the historical-critical method possesses several advantages: in particular, it defends against any kind of biblicistic fundamentalism. Only when not every word of scripture is regarded as divine revelation, only when it is acknowledged instead that scripture contains revelation, is it possible to criticize particular traditions. The historical-critical method also helps us to avoid hastily projecting our own standpoint into the text, thus confirming what we have always thought to be true. The historical-critical method emphasizes the strangeness and independence of the text. Only in this way is it possible for the biblical word to help us change our way of thinking and our present praxis. In doing so, it contributes to an ongoing analysis of different traditions, and of the church's history as well.

Translation by Linda M. Maloney

NOTES

1. Libreria delle donne di Milano, *Wie weibliche Freiheit entsteht: Eine neue politische Praxis* (2nd ed.; Berlin, 1989); Diotima (Women's Philosophy Group of Verona), ed., *Der Mensch ist Zwei,* Reihe Frauenforschung 11 (Vienna, 1989).

2. Ingvild Birkhan, "Der Mensch ist Zwei: Das Menschwerden im Spannungsfeld der sexuellen Differenz," in *Der Mensch ist Zwei,* 9–10.

3. Libreria, *Wie weibliche Freiheit entsteht,* 151.

4. A short selection of scholarly criticism would include I. Baldermann, ed., "Zum Problem des biblischen Kanons," *Jahrbuch Biblische Theologie* 3 (Neukirchen-Vluyn, 1988); D. Greenwood, "Rhetorical Criticism and Formgeschichte: Some Methodological Considerations," *Journal of Biblical Literature* 89 (1979): 418–26; J. Ratzinger, ed., *Schriftauslegung im Widerstreit,* (Quaestiones Disputatae 117; Freiburg, 1989); E. Drewermann, *Tiefenpsychologie und Exegese,* 2 vols. (Olten, 1984, 1985); Elisabeth Schüssler Fiorenza, *Bread Not Stone: The Challenge of Feminist Biblical Interpretation* (Boston: Beacon Press, 1984); Adela Yarbro Collins, ed., *Feminist Perspectives on Biblical Scholarship,* SBL Centennial Publications 10 (Chico, CA: Scholars Press, 1985); Augustine A. Stock, "The Limits of Historical-Critical Exegesis," *Biblical Theology Bulletin* 13 (1983): 28–31.

5. See, e.g., W. Egger, *Methodenlehre zum Neuen Testament: Eine Einführung in linguistische und historisch-kritische Methoden* (Freiburg, 1987); R. A. Spencer, ed., *Orien-*

tation by Disorientation: Studies in Literary Criticism and Biblical Literary Criticism. Festschrift for W. A. Beardslee, Pittsburgh Theological Monograph Series 35 (Pittsburgh, 1980); L. J. White, "Historical and Literary Criticism: A Theological Response," *Biblical Theology Bulletin* 13 (1983): 32–34.

6. Helen Schüngel-Straumann, "Gott als Mutter in Hosea 11," *Tübinger Theologische Quartalschrift* 166 (1986): 120–21. [Translator's note: The translations given here are from the German texts. Reference has also been made to KJV and NRSV, both of which resemble the Luther text in the crucial verses, rather than the translation by Prof. Schüngel-Straumann. In other words, the tradition of English translation resembles the standard German versions.]

7. See Schüngel-Straumann, "Gott als Mutter," 123–30.

8. Space does not allow a lengthy discussion of the reasoning behind this reconstruction. For details, see Monika Fander, *Die Stellung der Frau im Markusevangelium: Unter besonderer Berücksichtigung kultur- und religionsgeschichtlicher Hintergründe,* Münsteraner Theologische Abhandlungen 8 (Altenberge, 1992), 17–25.

9. See A. Klostermann, *Das Markusevangelium nach seinem Quellenwert* (Göttingen, 1867), 19.

10. See G. Schille, *Die urchristliche Wundertradition: Ein Beitrag zur Frage nach dem irdischen Jesus,* ATh 1/29 (Stuttgart, 1967), 26–27.

11. See Fander, *Frau im Markusevangelium,* 31–34.

12. E. Schweizer, *Das Evangelium nach Markus* (NTD 1; 11th ed.; Göttingen, 1967), 28.

13. L. Schenke, *Die Wundererzählungen des Markusevangeliums,* Stuttgarter Biblische Beiträge 5 (Stuttgart, 1974).

14. Schüssler Fiorenza, *Bread Not Stone,* 96.

15. Cf. E. Schüssler Fiorenza, "Der Beitrag der Frau zur urchristlichen Bewegung: Kritische Überlegungen zur Rekonstruktion urchristlicher Geschichte," in *Traditionen der Befreiung,* ed. W. Schottroff and W. Stegemann (Munich, 1980) 2:60–90; eadem, "Die Frauen in den vorpaulinischen und paulinischen Gemeinden," in *Frauen in der Männerkirche,* ed. Bernadette Brooten and Norbert Greinacher (Munich, 1982), 112–40; see also *Bread Not Stone,* 2–8.

16. See Bernadette Brooten, "Junia . . . Outstanding among the Apostles (Romans 16:7)," in *Women Priests: A Catholic Commentary on the Vatican Declaration,* ed. Leonard Swidler and Arlene Swidler (New York: Paulist, 1977), 141–44.

17. Josef Blank, "Frauen in den Jesusüberlieferungen," in *Die Frau im Urchristentum,* ed. G. Dautzenberg (Sonderausgabe Quaestiones Disputatae 95; Freiburg, 1989), 53.

18. Susanne Heine, *Frauen der frühen Christenheit: Zur historischen Kritik einer feministischen Theologie* (2nd ed.; Göttingen, 1987), 69.

19. Schüssler Fiorenza, *Bread Not Stone,* 97.

20. See R. Bultmann, "Ist eine voraussetzungslose Exegese möglich?" *Theologische Zeitschrift* 13 (1957): 143.

21. Schüssler Fiorenza, *Bread Not Stone,* 99.

22. Bultmann, "Voraussetzungslose Exegese?" 145–46.

23. Ibid., 147.

24. Schüssler Fiorenza, *Bread Not Stone,* 104.

25. Bultmann, "Voraussetzungslose Exegese?" 142.

26. Schüssler Fiorenza, *Bread Not Stone,* 93–94, 106–15; B. Brooten, "Early Christian Women and Their Cultural Context: Issues of Method in Historical Reconstruction," in *Feminist Perspectives on Biblical Scholarship,* ed. Collins, 65–91; eadem, "Methodenfragen zur Rekonstruktion urchristlicher Frauengeschichte," *Bibel und Kirche* 4 (1984): 157–64.

27. See Schüssler Fiorenza, *Bread Not Stone*, 15–18.
28. Schüssler Fiorenza, "Der Beitrag der Frau," 63.
29. See E. Schüssler Fiorenza, *In Memory of Her: A Feminist Theological Reconstruction of Christian Origins* (New York: Crossroad, 1983), 52.
30. Brooten, "Early Christian Women," 82.
31. Cf. K. Thraede, "Ärger mit der Freiheit," in *Freunde in Christus werden*, ed. Gerta Scharffenorth and K. Thraede (Kennzeichen 1; Gelnhausen, 1977), 79–87; Schüssler Fiorenza, *Bread Not Stone*, 77–79.
32. See Fander, *Frau im Markusevangelium*, 200–256; B. Brooten, "Konnten Frauen im alten Judentum die Scheidung betreiben? Überlegungen zu Mk 10,11-12 und 1 Kor 7,10-11," *Evangelische Theologie* 42 (1982): 65–80.

RECOMMENDED READINGS

Blank, Josef. "Frauen in den Jesusüberlieferungen." In *Die Frau im Urchristentum*, edited by G. Dautzenberg, 9–91. Sonderausgabe Quaestiones Disputatae 95. Freiburg, 1989.

Brooten, Bernadette. "Junia . . . Outstanding among the Apostles (Romans 16:7)." In *Women Priests: A Catholic Commentary on the Vatican Declaration*, edited by Leonard Swidler and Arlene Swidler, 141–44. New York: Paulist, 1977.

———. "Early Christian Women and Their Cultural Context: Issues of Method in Historical Reconstruction." In *Feminist Perspectives on Biblical Scholarship*, edited by Adela Yarbro Collins, 65–91. Biblical Scholarship in North America 10. Chico, CA: Scholars Press, 1985.

Bultmann, Rudolf. "Ist eine voraussetzungslose Exegese möglich?" *Theologische Zeitschrift* 13 (1957): 142–50.

Fander, Monika. *Die Stellung der Frau im Markusevangelium: Unter besonderer Berücksichtigung kultur- und religionsgeschichtlicher Hintergründe*. Münsteraner Theologische Abhandlungen 8. Altenberge, 1992.

Libreria delle donne di Milano. *Wie weibliche Freiheit entsteht: Eine neue politische Praxis*. 2nd ed. Berlin, 1989.

Schüngel-Straumann, Helen. "Gott als Mutter in Hosea 11." *Tübinger Theologische Quartalschrift* 166 (1986): 119–34.

Schüssler Fiorenza, Elisabeth. *Bread Not Stone: The Challenge of Feminist Biblical Interpretation*. Boston: Beacon Press, 1984.

———. "Der Beitrag der Frau zur urchristlichen Bewegung: Kritische Überlegungen zur Rekonstruktion urchristlicher Geschichte." In *Traditionen der Befreiung*, edited by W. Schottroff and W. Stegemann, 2:60–90. Munich, 1980.

———. *In Memory of Her: A Feminist Theological Reconstruction of Christian Origins*. New York: Crossroad, 1983.

♦ Toward a Materialist-Feminist
Reading

BRIGITTE KAHL ♦

"NON-IDEALIST" BIBLE INTERPRETATIONS
IN WESTERN EUROPE

POLITICALLY AND THEOLOGICALLY, the 1960s in Europe were a decade of exciting events and developments. With the Second Vatican Council, the emergence of liberation theologies, the World Conference on Church and Society in Geneva in 1966, and the decision of the World Council of Churches to initiate its Programme to Combat Racism in 1969, along with the utopian outburst of social hopes and passions in the student rebellions of 1968 and a few months later the tragic defeat of democratic socialism in Prague, something had changed. The issue of social injustice and economic, political, and racial oppression had been put on the theological agenda of the churches.

It was in this context that new ways of reading the Bible came to the fore in many countries of Western Europe. Quite different with regard to their theological, sociological, and methodological frameworks, they converged in a strong emphasis (1) on a social-critical analysis of the historical backgrounds of the biblical texts and (2) on a political practice of active involvement in current social struggles. They called themselves, variously, "concrete," "political," "social-historical," "nonidealist," or "materialist" exegesis, the last two terms often being used as a sort of collective name to describe the common denominator of these new methods.

The term materialist interpretation of the Bible, which was first introduced in Fernando Belo's *Lecture matérialiste de l'Evangile de Marc* (Paris, 1974), sounds contradictory, even paradoxical.[1] Historical and dialectic materialism going back to Karl Marx seems at first sight rather unsuitable for theological work, not only because of its atheist and anti-religious implications but even more so because of its perversion in the repressive state ideology of the Eastern European countries under state socialism.

Materialist reading of the Bible, however, claimed a different point of access to be theologically productive. Materialism was not taken as a closed philosophical or ideological system, but rather as a scientific methodology and heuristic principle, which may help to expose the idealism of the prevalent academic exegesis. Basically, "materialist," therefore, meant the opposite of "idealist" in the sense of an individualistic, abstract, "other-worldly" interpretation of the Bible which does not consider concrete realities of life such as economic and political power structures, social struggles against oppression, exploitation, discrimination, etc. Nonidealist interpretations of the Bible thus challenged the established historical-critical methods of exegesis to become more critical: first with regard to analysis of the social contexts of biblical texts; second with regard to the social position and economic-political interests of the original author/addressees as well as those of the present reader/interpreter of the text; third with regard to the necessity of turning away from the practice and perspective of the privileged, inasmuch as their position is irreconcilable with the position, practice, and perspective of the biblical God revealed on the cross. The "materialism" of materialist interpretations of the Bible is thus understood as something like an exegetical tool which helps to liberate the Bible from secondary "idealist" traditions and reading habits in order to regain the original message of the gospel for the poor.

It should be mentioned that this understanding of a materialist inter-pretation of the Bible as "non-idealist" was much indebted to the original approach of Karl Marx. He developed his materialist conception in criti-cizing Hegel's idealist interpretation of history and society as based on an Absolute Spirit as their moving force. Marx proposed rather to start from the material basis of life, which he saw primarily under the aspect of human activity. History and the structures and developments of society arise from the human practice of production and reproduction. How human beings manage to survive, how they produce their means of subsistence, and how they reproduce life — these are seen as the material bases for all other human activity, including the production of culture and ideas. This strong accent on the element of praxis stresses the role of the human subject, whereas pre-Marxist materialism saw the human being rather as the object of the determining processes of nature.

"Non-idealist" idealist approaches can be found mainly in three exegetical schools in Western Europe:

1. *The Sociohistorical School in Germany: L. Schottroff, W. Schottroff, F. Crüsemann, and W. Stegemann.*[2] This school departs from the

methodological framework of the historical-critical approach and fundamentally modifies it by introducing detailed questions concerning social contexts. The material conditions of life and the struggles of ordinary people especially, as well as the functioning of domination, exploitation, and discrimination within the economic, political, and ideological framework of society as a whole are carefully explored.

2. *The Amsterdam School in the Netherlands: F. Breukelmann, K. Deurloo, and R. Zuurmond; also T. Veerkamp (in Germany).*[3] Without neglecting the study of historical contexts, this approach puts its main emphasis on the "materiality" of the biblical text itself. Combining traditions of Jewish exegesis with a theological background based on Karl Barth, the Amsterdam school is strongly influenced at the same time by the Bible translation of Martin Buber and Franz Rosenzweig and the hermeneutical principles underlying it. The biblical texts of both the Old and New Testaments are primarily read in terms of their organic unity established by the work of the final redactor, who is called R (that is, *Rabbenu*=our teacher). The Hebrew Bible and the messianic writings (i.e., the New Testament) are strictly perceived as a unity, maintaining the original structure of the Hebrew canon as consisting of Torah, prophets, and writings (*Tenak: Tôrâ, Nĕbî'îm, Kĕtûbîm*). There is an inner-biblical contextuality and structural coherence, specifically materializing itself through language (e.g., mnemonic usage of certain key terms). In a process of permanent self-interpretation, biblical texts refer to each other and to their "burning center" in the Torah, more precisely, in the liberating event of the exodus.

3. *The "Lecture matérialiste": F. Belo, M. Clévenot,*[4] *and G. Casalis in France; K. Füssel in Germany.* This approach is strongly concerned with both biblical texts as such and their historical contexts. For the first time a synthesis of history and linguistics, namely, of French Marxist-psychoanalytical structuralism and linguistic structuralism, was made a program of exegetical work.

Among these non-idealist interpretations only the sociohistorical school centered on Luise Schottroff has been able so far to transform its historical-critical and sociocritical approach into a feminist-critical liberation theology, which has become an influential branch of feminist exegesis in Germany.[5] This chapter, however, will concentrate on the *lecture matérialiste* and a few remarks on the Amsterdam school, both of which are not so well known. Nevertheless, it is assumed that their specific way of defining and handling the materiality of biblical texts could be of potential value for feminist-critical interpretations as well.

Thus in the next section the *lecture matérialiste* and its textual theory will be presented together with certain hitherto undrawn feminist conclusions. In the last two sections the feminist implications of inner-biblical self-interpretation according to the Amsterdam approach will be examined, taking Luke as an example.

THE SYNTHESIS BETWEEN HISTORY
AND LINGUISTICS IN FERNANDO BELO'S
LECTURE MATÉRIALISTE

"C/X": to read Mark (French: *Marc*) by Marx—this was the challenging slogan Fernando Belo used in 1974 to describe the hermeneutical program of his *Lecture matérialiste de l'évangile de Marc*. In that year the Portuguese ex-priest, who had gotten married and who lived as an exile in France for political reasons, published his weighty commentary on the second Gospel. It was the year of the legendary "Revolution of Carnations" in Portugal, and Fernando Belo could now return home. The book clearly reflects the unique political context of post–1968 Europe. Fundamental social change seemed possible and imminent. In a time full of political commitment, hope, and, as it later turned out, illusion, the theological key question for Fernando Belo and many other Catholic and Protestant "activists" was: Is Christian faith as expressed in the Bible an ideology that contradicts a liberating political practice?

With this question in mind Belo starts to look for conceptual tools that might be useful for analyzing biblical texts and contexts. By no means is it Marx alone who helps him to read Mark. He introduces a highly complex linkage between Marxism, structuralism, and psychoanalysis, marked by names like L. Althusser, R. Barthes, J. Lacan, J.-J. Goux, and G. Bataille. This sophisticated theoretical framework, with its specific French flavor, makes Belo's work difficult to digest. Nevertheless, Bible-reading groups all over Europe took up the new method, which was further popularized in France by Michel Clévenot and Georges Casalis and in Germany by Kuno Füssel. International meetings of materialist readings of the Bible took place in Paris, Berlin, and elsewhere.

As already mentioned, the most interesting aspect of the *lecture matérialiste* exegetically is the synthesis it achieves between history and linguistics, thus integrating two approaches traditionally conceived as irreconcilable. The "materialism" of this method is shaped in such a way that it is able to make both ends meet: on the one hand structuralism, which is usually defined as a-historical inasmuch as it deals with the text "synchronically" in its present textual shape and unity, without considering pre-stages of textual development or problems of concrete social and historical contexts, and on the other hand the "diachronic" methods such as historical-critical and sociohistorical ones, which put the main emphasis on the historical analysis of the texts and their respective contexts.[6]

In order to understand how this integrated materialist reading according to Belo functions and how it could be applied in feminist interpretations, three key questions need to be answered: What is a text? What is reading? How does a text relate to its social context?

TEXT AS TEXTILE

It might be helpful to recall the meaning of the Latin word *textilis*, from which both the English "text" and "textile" are derived — something made by weaving. Narrative texts like the Gospel of Mark are seen as a piece of material reality, produced out of the material of language by the labor of writing. This productive work of putting together a text is understood as similar to the weaving of a textile. Out of an endless plurality of sense-bearing elements, which constitute reality outside ourselves, certain "threads" are taken up and interlaced in a specific way, using certain "patterns" to produce a text/textile, that is, a structured fabric. It is the texture of these "threads"—the patterns according to which they are interwoven, the arrangement of colors and knots—which produces the meaning of a text.

READING AS PRACTICE

According to the structuralist theory of the French linguist Roland Barthes, the meaningful "threads" of a literary text/textile are called "codes." Reading a text is something like decoding it; it is a highly complex, creative, and co-creative activity. To understand a text requires studying its code structures or "weaving patterns."

The decoding of a text first requires finding out which "codes" are present in it. This first step demands careful and repetitious reading. All terms relating to one another in a certain way are listed and grouped under relevant codes. Belo uses two main types of codes. On the one hand there are three codes referring to the progress of action inside the text, called sequential codes. They list what is done/thought/intended and by whom (=actional, analytical, strategical codes). On the other hand there are the so-called cultural codes, which connect terms inside the text to contextual realities outside the text: Aside from a geographical and a chronological code, including expressions of place and time, there is a social code comprising economic terms (money, wage, debt, etc.), political terms (Caesar, rule, soldiers, etc.), and ideological/religious terms (clean and unclean, God, pagans, temple, etc.).

After one has disclosed these serial lines or codes, their "pattern" has to be studied: how they are structured in themselves and in their interlacing with other lines, which words serve as "knots" or the "crossing" of different codes (e.g., the term "Caesarea" belongs to the geographical and at the same time to the political code). In order to determine these structural relationships, various operations are accomplished: comparing opposites (e.g., heaven–earth, God of death–God of life); finding out the logical connections between the acting persons (actantial model) of the text or between selected elements of it (e.g., between A, non-A, B, non-B according to the so-called semiotic quadrangle); reflecting the change that has taken place between the beginning and the end of a text or sequence, and so on.

The most significant advantage of these synchronic intratextual operations is that they may help to understand texts in a way they have not been understood before. For a feminist interpretation the methodological equipment of structuralism, which requires and develops a lot of curiosity, sensitivity, and creativity (traditionally understood as "typically feminine" qualities) in dealing with texts, could contribute to reading the Bible "with new eyes." It might help to overcome the "reading habits" of traditional, ruling male exegesis by making available scientific tools for discovering within the biblical texts patterns and structures of meaning not seen before—including, maybe, even a "feminist code."

Text as Part of the Overall Social Texture

By introducing social, geographical, and chronological codes, Belo ties textual and contextual fabric inseparably together, leaving no possibility for interpretation to remain exclusively on the level of an isolated synchronic reading. In order to analyze this social contextuality existing outside and referred to inside the biblical text, Belo basically claims the categories of historical materialism. He takes over the Marxist classification of social structure on the threefold levels of economy, politics, and ideology. At the same time Belo substantially enriches and modifies these categories with theoretical elements from various other sources, like ethnographic and psychoanalytical ones.

Among the influences that should be mentioned is the work of the French Marxist and structuralist philosopher Louis Althusser, who developed a specific concept of human practice which became very important for Belo's interpretation. In order to overcome any mechanistic understanding of the dominant role of economy (according to Marx) in relation to the so-called superstructures (politics, ideology), Althusser redefines the fundamental materialist category of practice: In a threefold inclusive way it is understood as either economic, political, or ideological practice.

The implications of this concept of practice for Belo's theories on the mode of production in biblical Palestine (parts I and II of his book) cannot be discussed here; the consequences for the perception of texts have already been mentioned above: Reading and writing a text are understood as part of an ideological practice of their own. Texts are not a simple reflection of reality; they are a way to form the unstructured "chaos" of the existing things into the structured "cosmos" of a readable and understandable text. Texts may either cement the status quo of society or interfere with it, and thus represent a counterreality. Texts are not only a way to describe, interpret, and understand reality but also a means to change it. In his commentary on Mark, Belo tries to demonstrate how biblical texts can at the same time be part and "counterpart" of the social texture.

THE BIBLICAL TEXT AS COUNTERPART OF THE SOCIAL TEXTURE

One of Belo's codes that is central for his reading of Mark has yet to be mentioned: the messianic code or code of the reign of God. It refers to the powerful messianic practice of Jesus, which fundamentally subverts all other social codes. The tearing of the temple curtain into two pieces, from top to bottom, at the death of Jesus (Mark 15:38) symbolizes this total rupture of the whole social tissue and fabric. In a concluding chapter about a "materialist ecclesiology," Belo describes this messianic practice using the threefold definition of Althusser. This last part best illustrates how Belo succeeds in linking economic, political, and ideological practices closely together, and how he is able to combine social and textual realities, history and linguistics:

The Practice of the Hands

In the Jesus movement bread is given, not bought; sharing leads to multiplication and blessing (e.g., in the feeding of the five thousand in Mark

6:30–44); being touched by Jesus means regaining health. The messianic countereconomy which aims at the reestablishment of bodily integrity is based on the circulation of the spirit rather than on the circulation of money. This aspect of Jesus' practice is symbolized by the "circle"—for example, that of the table where the hungry and poor are fed; the traditional expression for it is "love." In the framework of the textual codes it relates to the code of action and the social/economic code.

The Practice of the Feet

The "Way" of Jesus from Galilee to Judea and from there back to Galilee and subsequently to the ends of the earth transcends not only spatial but also any social borders and lines of demarcation drawn by the existing power structures. The worldwide extension of the table of satiety or fullness and the total absence of any "fathers" and rulers in the new ecclesial communities (Mark 10:30) are the significants of the messianic counterstrategy of the kingdom of God, which subverts the political order of both the Roman Empire and the Jewish ruling system. Traditionally the church has called this aspect of the messianic practice "hope." In the textual analysis it appears as a strategic code and in the social/political and geographical codes.

The Practice of the Eyes/Ears

It makes a difference whether the messianic word, compared to a seed in Mark 4:1–20, falls upon rocky ground, thorns, or fertile earth. The social position of those who read and hear the Gospel determines the way in which they understand it. The opponents of Jesus "read" his practice from the standpoint and with the eyes of ruling values like money, temple, state, Caesar, and a false "God of death"; they are thus unable to understand it. The dominant social codes of power and material greed have a blinding and deafening effect with regard to the healing and bread-giving messianic practice of love ("hands") and hope ("feet"). The messianic practice of the eyes/ears means turning away from the old social positions and hermeneutical patterns. This is what Belo calls "faith." In the textual analysis it refers to the social/ideological and to the analytical code. This breakthrough to new semantic fields means understanding

> that the powerful practice of Jesus always bears fruit in material blessing, whereas the practice of the ruling classes always implies curse. Therefore the text must be read from the materialist perspective of this blessing. The healing of the bodies and the feeding of the hungry has to become the starting point of that reading.[7]

FEMINIST EVALUATION

"Practice" had been defined by L. Althusser as any process by which a given material is changed into a certain product. The threefold messianic practice as perceived by Belo thus transforms the "raw material" of the prevailing social relationships and codes into the new ecclesial relationships and codes of the kingdom of God: a reality free of domination and discrimination, full of bread, health, and community—and without any fathers. Commenting on a passage like Mark 10:28–30, Belo underlines the fact that in the messianic circle houses, brothers, sisters, mothers, children, and lands left by the disciples will multiply according to the deuteronomic logic of blessing (giving and sharing result in receiving a hundredfold). The fathers, however, who have been left, too, do not return. The messianic conversion of patriarchal family and property relations is central to Belo's interpretation of the Gospel.

Nevertheless, in most places he describes this messianic conversion in terms of brotherhood rather than sisterhood: as gathering of the poor without the rich, of servants without lords, of disciples without masters, youngsters without adults, brothers without fathers. The implications that a total and comprehensive subversion of the existing patriarchal order would have for the position of women are occasionally mentioned but never dealt with in detail. Similarly, Belo's consideration of the threefold messianic practice lack any female dimension. The specific consequences of an integral bodily restitution, of a radically inclusive ecumenical community, of new ways of speaking and understanding for a feminist practice of "hands," "feet," and "eyes/ears" are not indicated. Fernando Belo's concept of liberation is a male-centered one.

It should be noted that this deficiency was to some extent recognized by Belo himself. Ten years after his commentary on Mark appeared, Belo provided a kind of self-critical reassessment and reinterpretation.[8] Meanwhile, the carnations of the Portuguese revolution had faded (just as the candles of the East German revolution fifteen years later were not lit for long); basic social change seemed impossible, in Europe and elsewhere. Belo's quasi-messianic hopes for a new type of "integral" revolution that would change economic as well as interhuman relationships had turned out to be illusionary.

Consequently, Belo now redefines the messianic practice of Jesus. It was not a revolutionary practice, aiming at a direct change of social structures, but an indirect one. The objects of messianic transformation were the concrete human bodies who got healed and fed, resurrected and reintegrated into the ecclesial community of the "collective body" which represents the Son of man. Thus, emphasis has shifted from the mode of production (including all the "big" questions of class struggle, state, capital, ruling ideology, mass media) to the reproductive sphere which comprises all the "small" questions of everyday life concerning the concrete bodies of women, men, children (e.g., gender and family relations, sexuality, house, consuming habits, etc.).

According to Belo, human bodies may regain unknown power and abilities if they are freed from oppressive family structures to live under egalitarian and communitarian conditions signifying the "body of Christ." (Out of this specific interest in bodily experiences transcending normal capabilities, Belo already in his book on Mark vigorously defended the dimension of "miracle" against any demythologizing.) Change of the existing power structures now takes place within, possibly through, small ecclesial or quasi-ecclesial communities (*mini-corps-communautaires*), where the liberating messianic experiences of the first followers of Jesus continue as a present reality. It is obvious that this definition of messianic practice is more open to feminist interpretations and modifications, for example, a concept like that of women-church.

BIBLICAL SELF-INTERPRETATION
ACCORDING TO THE AMSTERDAM SCHOOL

Like Fernando Belo, the Amsterdam school departs from the notion of the biblical text(s) as a structured materiality to be analyzed synchronically (i.e., on the level of inner-textual relationships) and diachronically (i.e., with regard to extra-textual sociohistorical realities). Both strongly reject the "decomposition method" of the historical-critical approaches, which by separating the text into single pieces destroys the inner logic of the surface structures: it is strictly the text in its last and present shape that serves as basis for any interpretation.

Moreover, the Amsterdam school widens this principle of inner-textual coherence to make it comprise the whole of biblical contextuality. Any single text can be properly understood only as part of the overall biblical "textile." Reading a biblical passage requires reading the Bible as a whole. In a programmatic way the hermeneutical pattern of the Amsterdam school claims to be canonical.

Contrary to Belo, who sees the canonization of the biblical texts as a basically negative process dominated by the interests of the ruling postexilic priestly class, the Amsterdam school strongly defends the integrity of the Bible as a whole and the work and wisdom of the final redactor R. In a unique way the Bible represents the Magna Carta of the historically oppressed and defeated. Decisively marked by the twofold catastrophe of 587 B.C.E. and 70 C.E., the Bible has liberation as its "glowing center." The variety of biblical stories constitutes the one story of the manifold liberating deeds of God. The final criterion of Bible reading is not to be found outside the Bible—neither in liberating nor oppressive experiences or ideologies of any kind—but exclusively by and within the Bible itself. And no selective reading of the Bible is allowed, playing off, for example, prophetic traditions and sources against priestly and royal ones. The given materiality of the Bible has to be taken with radical seriousness, as the Bible is not a resource but the only and unique source of revelation.

There is no doubt that the hermeneutical principles of the Amsterdam school, which at first sight look like a neo- or even ultra-orthodox revitalization of the Protestant principle of *sola scriptura* (scripture alone), seem highly irritating or irrelevant from a feminist perspective. How does one deal with the problem of biblical androcentrism without evaluating and criticizing, dividing and selecting, biblical texts and traditions, concepts and notions, from the perspective of a feminist-critical point of reference outside the Bible?

Theoretically, the Amsterdam school is taking up the idea of Martin Luther that scripture has to be (and can be) its own interpreter (*scriptura scripturae interpres*). Practically it modifies this idea considerably by being much more centered than Luther was in the Old Testament, namely, the Torah. "Justification by faith alone" is thus inseparably linked to and interpreted by justice and liberation. In this way the Lutheran "canon within the canon" gets a more biblical, less "idealist," foundation.

It has to be asked whether this principle applied in an even more critical way might not produce some helpful and liberating insights for feminist exegesis as well, especially in contexts shaped by Protestant traditions and struggling with fundamentalist influences. This would imply a feminist reinterpretation of the Lutheran principle of biblical self-interpretation together with that of inner-biblical self-criticism (*innere Kanonkritik*).

Just one example might be given to indicate possible directions of such a "canonical" feminist interpretation which would search for the self-interpreting and self-criticizing potential inherent in the materiality of the scriptural "textile."

READING LUKE AGAINST LUKE:
FEMINIST CRITICISM WITHIN THE BIBLE ITSELF?

Contrary to John 4, where the beginning of the Christian mission in Samaria is attributed to an unnamed woman, in Acts 8 a man, Philip, is introduced as the first missionary to this place. One way of handling this problem results from the methodology of historical-feminist criticism, which, behind and against the androcentric perspective of Acts 8, tries to reconstruct the history of women as an integral and constitutive part of the early Jesus and missionary movements. Complementary to this, however, the possibilities of a "canonical-feminist criticism" should be explored, taking the literary unity of Luke/Acts (together with the complete unity of Old and New Testaments) as a methodological principle.

It is well known that Luke's description of the Christian missionary expansion from Jerusalem to Rome has in the end almost completely "lost" the female part. After Easter there are hardly any women's voices to be heard in a predominantly male proclamation of the Gospel. This androcentric version of Christian origins has to be criticized from the external standpoints of historical reality and of women's experiences and interests in past and present times. But, astonishingly, Luke is also contradicted by Luke himself, this feminist criticism of the Gospel being founded fundamentally in Luke 1.

The crucial point in Luke 1 is not simply the fact that the first theologically qualified proclamation of the gospel is attributed to a woman, Mary (Luke 1:46–55). The more decisive fact is that Mary's messianic theology is articulated in the context of a radically de-patriarchalized social reality. At first sight, this fundamental transformation of the patriarchal deep structures is demonstrated in the person of Zechariah. The paterfamilias remains dumb and invisible in his own house, silenced in an ordeal for his unbelief (1:20), while the new language of faith is developed in the community of two pregnant women completely occupying the "father's house." Zechariah will regain his capacity for speech only after publicly recognizing the "naming authority" of his wife (1:60–64).

Moreover, the events occurring between vv. 24 and 59 of chapter in many respects subvert and tear all patriarchal "codes." To mention only one example: In the central part of Luke 1 the female counterchronology of pregnancy replaces the male hierarchical synchronisms. The story told about the very beginnings of Jesus is determined neither by Israelite or Roman imperial time, counting "in the days of Herod, king of Judea" (1:5), of Emperor Augustus and Governor Quirinius (2:1–2), nor by the integrated

Roman-Israelite patriarchal chronology of 3:1–2, which defines the further story of Luke-Acts (the time of Emperor Tiberius, Pontius Pilate, Herod and the other tetrarchs, and the high priests Annas and Caiaphas). When the "genesis" of Jesus happens, patriarchal time stops and is replaced by a completely feminist synchronism which puts events into the chronological order of Elizabeth's pregnancy: five months, in the sixth month, six months, three months, time to be delivered (1:24, 26, 36, 56, 57).

Together with the feminist transformation of patriarchal time, the patriarchal space of the "father's house" is converted for three months into a mothers' house: the two women and the two boys still unborn greet each other with joy (1:41–45). The age-old rivalry between one woman and another woman, between firstborn and younger son, which is inherent in the rules of patriarchy, finally turns into sisterhood and brotherhood: Hagar and Sarah, Leah and Rachel, Hannah and Peninnah as well as Cain and Abel, Ishmael and Isaac, Esau and Jacob finally become reconciled in Elizabeth and Mary, John and Jesus. This close interwovenness of the Genesis narratives with the story of Christian beginnings materializes in a surprisingly dense network of scripture quotations and allusions, one of the main literary features of Luke 1.

For hermeneutical reflection it is of vital importance that in Luke 1 the great song of liberation, the Magnificat, even if it is not explicitly talking about women's liberation, is sung by a woman (just as in the underlying song of Hannah in 1 Samuel 1) and comes out of a radically "matriarchal," that is, feminist-egalitarian and inclusive context. Luke 1 binds the gospel for the poor and the gospel of/for women "genetically" and therefore "in principle" inseparably together. An "archetype" is established that should be used as permanent criterion and criticism of what follows.

Repatriarchalization already takes place in Luke 2. From now on the chronological and spatial order of Caesar is reigning again, and Mary, without saying a word in the entire chapter, simply follows her husband (2:1–5), forgetting that she once rose by herself (1:39). Likewise, the prophet Hannah is merely mentioned (2:36–38) — her words apparently not being worth reporting; the prophet Simeon has already given the decisive theological comment and proclamation. The "natural order of things," promising the "orderly" behavior of Christians within the patriarchal structures of the Roman Empire, is reestablished. From now on the gospel of the mothers will be silenced by the fathers, just as the gospel of the poor will be fully replaced by a socially neutral "gospel for the Gentiles," at the latest by the time Luke's Paul reaches Rome (see Acts 28:28–31).

This feminist-critical reading of Luke against Luke (which would require a much more detailed exegetical explanation)[9] is based on the notion that the totality of the biblical texts constitutes a highly complex and dialectical process of tradition as adaptation and resistance to the given patriarchal contexts. However, there seem to be certain feminist "key structures" that could be perceived as something like a "feminist code" woven into the texture of the biblical "textile." This code may be hidden over long distances but turns up at strategically decisive points like Luke 1, where it functions as a kind of hermeneutical key for what follows. Like the clef and the signatures in a piece of music it doesn't change the notes but indicates how they should be played and interpreted. It is true that in Luke the provocative reality of the gospel for the poor originally proclaimed by women is gradually transformed into and replaced by a universally acceptable, socially indifferent gospel for "the Gentiles and kings and the sons of Israel" (Acts 9:15). Nevertheless, Luke 1 remains as a constant challenge to reinterpret and reanimate the Pauline gospel for the Gentiles by the "original" spirit of an inclusive and ecumenical justice and liberation for poor men and women.

In a similar way feminist key structures may be found throughout the Bible, for example, at the beginning of the exodus story and of the four books of Samuel–Kings. Without doubt the dominant actors of both narratives are male. But how, then, should we interpret the fact that the whole story of Israel's liberation in Exodus 1–2 is inaugurated by a sequence of exclusively female acts of resistance transcending all divisions of family, class, generation, race, and nation? The Hebrew midwives, a mother and daughter of the house of Levi, Pharaoh's daughter and her maiden all collaborate against the murderous decree of Pharaoh in order to save the life of Moses, the coming liberator. Could not Exodus 1:15–2:10, which describes the "female origin" of the exodus be interpreted as something like an *aide mémoire* inscribing women's universal liberation as the ultimate horizon of Israel's liberation?

Or what does it mean if all the male kings' stories telling of royal hopes, illusions, and final disaster are inaugurated in 1 Samuel 1–2 by the story of a woman deprived and discriminated against who resists her marginalization? Hannah, who will be echoed by Mary later on, first proclaims what is going to become the essence of the prophetic witness vis-à-vis the king: "The bows of the mighty are broken, but the feeble gird on strength" (1 Sam 2:1–10). Does this not mean that social justice as the basic goal and criterion of any future king has to stand its final test with regard to women? That to a certain extent feminist standards are applied to the whole story of kingly failure leading finally to exile in 2 Kings 25?

The important point, then, would be not only to read and remember isolated women's stories in the Bible but to discover the network of sisterhood and inter-textual communication that relates them to one another and structures their resistance to the stories of an exclusive, androcentric liberation. Maybe this kind of structural-feminist approach could reveal something like an underground women's church and a feminist-critical commentary within the Bible itself.

NOTES

1. English translation: *A Materialist Reading of the Gospel of Mark* (Maryknoll, NY: Orbis, 1981).

2. See Luise Schottroff and Wolfgang Stegemann, *Jesus and the Hope of the Poor* (Maryknoll, NY: Orbis, 1986); and W. Schottroff and W. Stegemann, eds., *Traditionen der Befreiung: Methodische Zügange* (Munich, 1980).

3. K. Deurloo and R. Zuurmond, eds. *De Bijbel maakt School: Eeen Amsterdamse Weg in de Exegese* (Ten Have, Baarn, 1984); Martin Kessler, ed., *Voices from Amsterdam: A Modern Tradition of Reading Biblical Narratives* (Atlanta: Scholars Press, 1993); T. Veerkamp, *Autonomie und Egalität: Ökonomie, Politik und Ideologie in der Schrift* (Berlin, 1993).

4. Michel Clévenot, *Materialist Approaches to the Bible* (Maryknoll, NY: Orbis, 1985).

5. See Luise Schottroff, *Let the Oppressed Go Free: Feminist Perspectives on the New Testament* (Louisville, KY: Westminster/John Knox, 1993); C. Schaumberger and L. Schott-roff, *Schuld und Macht: Studien zu einer feministischen Befreiungstheologie* (Munich, 1988); and E. Gössmann, ed., *Wörterbuch der feministischen Theologie* (Gütersloh, 1991).

6. In North America this debate had centered on the two poles of literary criticism, on the one hand, and historical criticism and sociological exegesis, on the other. The basic idea of a synthesis insisting on both the literary and sociohistorical integrity of the whole text has been taken up by Ched Myers, *Binding the Strong Man: A Political Reading of Mark's Story of Jesus* (Maryknoll, NY: Orbis, 1988). Myers's "socio-literary" approach to reading Mark acknowledges its debt to the work of Belo, while noting some of its major inconsistencies (Myers, 36, 467).

7. Belo, *Lecture matérialiste de l'Evangile de Marc,* 339.

8. Fernando Belo, "Ceci est mon corps," *Lumière et Vie* 166 (1984).

9. For a fuller treatment, see Brigitte Kahl, *Armenevangelium und Heidenevangelium: "Sola Scriptura" und die ökumenische Traditionsproblematik im Lichte von Väterkonflikt und Väterkonsensus bei Lukas* (Berlin: Evangelische Verlagsanstalt, 1987).

RECOMMENDED READINGS

Barrett, Michèle. *The Politics of Truth: From Marx to Foucault.* Cambridge: Polity Press, 1991.

———. "Words and Things: Materialism and Method in Contemporary Feminist Analysis." In *Destabilizing Theory: Contemporary Feminist Debates,* edited by Michèle Barrett and Anne Phillips, 201–19. Stanford: Stanford University Press, 1992.

Belo, Fernando. *A Materialist Reading of the Gospel of Mark.* Translated by Matthew O'Connell. Maryknoll, NY: Orbis, 1981.

Clévenot, Michel. *Materialist Approaches to the Bible.* Translated by William J. Nottingham. Maryknoll, NY: Orbis, 1985.

Felski, Rita. *Beyond Feminist Aesthetics.* Cambridge, MA: Harvard University Press, 1989.

Hartsock, Nancy C. M. *Money, Sex, and Power: Toward a Feminist Historical Materialism.* Boston: Northeastern University Press, 1985.

Hennessy, Rosemary, *Materialist Feminism and the Politics of Discourse.* New York: Routledge, 1993.

Jameson, Frederic. *The Political Unconsciousness: Narrative as a Socially Symbolic Act.* Ithaca, NY: Cornell University Press, 1981.

Kahl, Brigitte. *Armenevangelium und Heidenevangelium: "Sola Scriptura" und die ökumenische Traditionsproblematik im Lichte von Väterkonflikt und Väterkonsensus bei Lukas.* Berlin: Evangelische Verlagsanstalt, 1987.

Kessler, Martin, ed. *Voices from Amsterdam: A Modern Tradition of Reading Biblical Narratives.* Atlanta: Scholars Press, 1993.

Mosala, Itumeleng J. *Biblical Hermeneutics and Black Theology in South Africa.* Grand Rapids: Eerdmans, 1989.

———. "Bible and Liberation in South Africa in the 1980s: Toward an Antipopulist Reading of the Bible." In *The Bible and the Politics of Exegesis,* edited by David Jobling, Peggy L. Day, Gerald T. Sheppard, 267–74. Cleveland: The Pilgrim Press, 1991.

Myers, Ched. *Binding the Strong Man: A Political Reading of Mark's Story of Jesus.* Maryknoll, NY: Orbis, 1988.

Schottroff, Luise. *Let the Oppressed Go Free: Feminist Perspectives on the New Testament.* Translated by Annemarie S. Kidder. Louisville, KY: Westminster/John Knox Press, 1993.

———, and Wolfgang Stegemann. *Jesus and the Hope of the Poor.* Translated by Matthew J. O'Connell. Maryknoll, NY: Orbis, 1986.

Wainwright, Elaine M. *Towards a Feminist Critical Reading of the Gospel According to Matthew.* Berlin: de Gruyter, 1991.

16

❖ Literary-Critical Methods

ELIZABETH STRUTHERS MALBON AND
JANICE CAPEL ANDERSON ◆

FOR MUCH OF ITS LONG LIFE, the New Testament has been the source of religious dogma and historical reconstruction. In the past thirty-five years there has been a paradigm shift among some of its scholarly readers. We have changed our overall view of the text, what we expect, what we seek. Rather than looking *to* the text for confirmation of articles of faith, or *through* the text for a view of the historical world behind it, we have been looking *at* the text as a medium of communication between author and readers or hearers. Literary critics regard "the text" as an abstraction that represents the center of a communication event: an "author" presents "the text" to an "audience" in a given "context." Historical critics focus on questions about the author and the original audience: What world does the text reflect? Those interested in theology focus on questions about the present audience: What faith does the text project? Literary critics focus on questions about the text as communication: What experience does the text mediate? Cultural critics focus on the context in which communication occurs: How are text and culture interrelated?

In this essay we describe recent New Testament literary methods from a feminist perspective. Feminist New Testament literary critics live at the intersection of feminism and the disciplines of literary and biblical studies. Therefore, we begin with a brief look at literary studies as practiced in American departments of English and Comparative Literature. This is followed by an examination of narrative criticism of the Gospels and reader-oriented approaches, including Pauline rhetorical criticism. We are both middle-class, Anglo-American teachers at state universities and members of mainline Protestant denominations. As feminists we hold that both equality and difference are important. We recognize as critical the challenge of women of color to avoid false universalism and essentialism. At the same time we believe feminists can form coalitions of resistance to the many forms of male domination and affirm the right of women to construct and take responsibility for the various positions from which they act. The story we tell of literary methods reflects our perspectives.

LITERARY CRITICISM IN THE LITERARY GUILD

Literature professors often describe the history of modern literary criticism as a series of moments in which the focus has been on each element of the communication model in turn: author, text, reader, and context. Both nineteenth-century Romantics and philological scholars focused on the author, either in terms of the genius who expressed his or her intuitions and personality in the work or in terms of biography and historical background. With the arrival of the New Criticism of the 1930s through the 1960s, the focus shifted to the text itself (as an aesthetic object) and the internal relations of its elements. In the sixties and seventies structuralism continued New Criticism's focus on the text as a coherent whole, albeit as a system of differences. Structuralism insisted that language—and thus literature and culture itself—is built on difference: /b/ is not /p/; therefore we can meaningfully label a bun as distinct from a pun. Up is not down; order is not chaos—these oppositions and attempts to mediate them are central. Structuralism also marked a turn toward interest in the reader and the role of the reader in creating meaning. Poststructuralist approaches, including various reader response, psychoanalytic, materialist, and deconstructive criticisms, blossomed in the seventies and eighties. Poststructuralism spoke of the death of the author, the death of the subject, the death of positivism, and the death of Truth with a capital T. Poststructuralists took the structuralist discussion of language as a system of differences to heart and began to emphasize difference with no external reality. In the late eighties and early nineties, spurred in large part by feminists and others previously marginalized, criticism has returned (although not full circle) to the context in which communication occurs. Texts are part of the vast signifying system that is culture. A text reflects the culture that produced it, and culture is a "text" to be interpreted. The same is true of subjectivity, of gendered identities. Cultural criticism is currently the center of critical activity.

Feminist literary criticism both developed out of and shaped this history. One of the first moves of feminist literary critics in the sixties and seventies was to study the images of women present in the literary canon. The methods used reflected the training critics had received, including New

Criticism and myth and archetypal criticism. They also began to critique previous interpreters and the canon itself as androcentric and patriarchally determined. Particularly in the United States, there followed an emphasis on *gynocriticism,* the study and recovery of texts authored by women and the ways in which women's writing is constantly in dialogue with male and female literary traditions. The experience of women writers and readers was to be recovered and valued.

As feminist criticism gained a central place in the literary academy, poststructuralism began to permeate the discussion. Among poststructuralists (mostly French or Francophile and influenced by Derrida, Lacan, and Foucault) gynocriticism was sometimes seen as naïvely empiricist and essentialist, a product of liberal humanism. Creating a female counter-canon, for example, simply supported the oppressive notion of a canon itself. More importantly, if reality is constituted by language and language is a system of differences, then there is no such thing as a reality or a subject prior to or independent of language; thus sexual difference is simply a product of language. Yet uncovering the repressed "Female" in texts and culture can play a disruptive role uncovering dominant claims to Truth and Power.

For some, the most disruptive, utopian, antiphallic move to make was to write *écriture feminine,* to write the female body, the pre-rational, the pre linguistic, to write with female fluid—milk, blood, amniotic water— to write multiplicity, multiorgasmically. An obvious question raised by many Anglo-American gynocritics and British materialist theorists was, Who is being essentialist? That is, who is tying women to a universal, biological essence, rather than treating gender as a social construction, a cultural and historical product? They asked, Is *Woman* merely a trope? What about *women* who need maternity leave or who are raped? For a time feminist literary criticism was seen as constituted by two camps: an "Anglo-American" gynocriticism (aligned with British materialist criticism that read male and female texts) seen as representing liberal equality feminism—even though it focused on women—and a "French" poststructuralist criticism or *gynesis* emphasizing female difference and multiplicity—even though it focused on male texts and theorists as well as writing the female body.

Despite the picture painted of two quite different camps, to some they looked more alike than different. Womanist, *mujerista,* Native American, post-colonial, and lesbian critics challenged this two-camp construction of feminist criticism. One of the key points most feminists have made is that patriarchal cultures subsume women under a male norm. To be human is to be male. These other voices challenged a parallel universal category called "woman," which subsumed them under a middle-class white heterosexual norm. This challenge has meant an increasing focus on the writing, reading, and theory of those previously treated as marginal by

male and female Eurocentric critics. It has also meant an increased concentration on cultural context. The social construction of and representation of the multiple variables of race, class, gender, and sexual orientation
in constructing identity, novels, and other cultural artifacts is a central focus
of feminist criticism in the nineties.

Another important development was a shift from a focus on feminism
and women to a focus on gender. Feminists have long recognized the importance of gender as an analytic category. They have noted that "male" and
"female" are defined in relation to one another and that both definitions
underwrite patriarchy. What was usually meant by gender, however, was
the female. The male and masculinity were the unmarked and unstudied
categories. One factor in the shift to the study of both male and female
gender was the question of men in feminism. As feminist criticism became
established in literary studies, female critics were pleased that men were
reading and supporting their work. However, there was a sneaking suspicion
that some men wanted to take over and show women how to do feminist
criticism properly—what Elaine Showalter called critical cross-dressing.[1]
Thus many feminists argued that one of the most helpful tasks male critics
could undertake was to study the embodiment and construction of masculinities in texts and readers. This conclusion was not intended to restrict
women to studying female gender and men to studying male gender. It
was, however, to resist the reinstituting of men's definition and control of
women and their interests. In a similar vein, while many feminists see a
positive value in the move to gender studies from feminist or women's
studies, they see dangers as well. Women's writing, reading, teaching, and
criticism could again be marginalized if the focus shifts to masculinity, and
the connection between academic and political commitments might be
severed.

New Testament literary criticism has been influenced, often with a ten-
to twenty-year lag, by the developments in the wider literary field described
above. It has, however, developed in the light of the particular texts that
constitute its object of study and its own disciplinary and institutional
histories. Thus we now turn to New Testament narrative criticism and
reader-oriented approaches.

NARRATIVE CRITICISM

In many ways literary criticism of the Gospels may be understood as a
reaction to historical criticism taken to its extremes. Historical critics on
a quest for the historical Jesus developed source criticism to identify the
interrelationships of the Gospel accounts and thus the earliest Gospel,
Mark. When the contention that Mark's Gospel was a "historical" account

could no longer be supported, attention turned to "the sources behind the sources," the oral traditions behind the individual units of material in the Gospels—the concern of form criticism. Redaction criticism at first seemed to return attention to the Gospels as wholes, focusing on how the evangelists edited their received materials to reflect their theologies. In practice, however, redaction criticism often meant an increasingly detailed—and increasingly hypothetical—separation of "tradition" (what an evangelist received) and "redaction" (what an evangelist changed or added). The goal was historical reconstruction of the world behind the text, and the technique was fragmentation of the text. In reaction to such fragmentation and historicizing, literary methods focusing holistically on the unity of the text itself were developed. In Gospel studies this took the form of narrative criticism.

The reaction against the extremes of historical criticism of the Bible was given impetus by the New Criticism. The New Critics sought the internal or essential meaning of a poem or a novel, not its external or referential meaning. New Testament literary critics approached the parables with the zeal of the New Critics for poetry, with a renewed appreciation of the metaphoric power of language. They approached the Gospels with the enthusiasm of the New Critics for short stories and novels, with a deepened awareness of the drama of characterization and plot.

Narrative approaches have also been influenced by structuralism. Structuralism's contribution to narrative criticism is the conviction that all meaning is relational. Both denotations and connotations depend on a system of relationships among elements. This insight means that settings, characters, and actions of the plot are all to be investigated as systems of relationships. Only when we appreciate how the elements interrelate are we able to appreciate how the story moves.

For narrative critics, "the text" is not an isolated object but the center of a communication event: author/text/audience. In fact, the author and the audience are implied elements of the text. Literary critics distinguish between the real author and the real audience and the implied author and the implied audience. The implied author and implied audience are creations of the real author that are embedded in the text. The implied audience is the addressee, the one or ones to whom and for whom the story is told. By focusing on the implied author and the implied audience, narrative critics are asserting a certain independence from the presumed intention of the real author and the reconstructed historical circumstances of the original audience in interpreting the work. The chief elements narrative critics investigate are settings (spatial and temporal), characters, plot, and rhetoric. (More work needs to be done linking the study of these elements to gender as an analytic category.) Through the interrelationships of these elements, the implied author communicates with the implied audience; the story unfolds between them.

The way literary critics approach the settings of the Gospel narratives illustrates well the difference between historical and literary approaches. Historical critics sifted through spatial and temporal references for clues that would reveal the biography of Jesus or the community of the evangelist; they constructed a geography and a chronology of Jesus' ministry or a description of the redactor's community. Literary critics, however, are more interested in the connotational or symbolic value of these spatial and temporal markers. Literary critics do not try to locate physically and literally the mountain on which Jesus gave the Sermon on the Mount. (Geographically, there is no "mountain" on the western shore of the Sea of Galilee.) Rather, they observe the association made between Moses as the bearer of *tôrâ* (teaching, law) on the mountain and Jesus as the bearer of new *tôrâ* on the mountain. Similarly, Mark's use of the name "*Sea* of Galilee" (Luke uses the usual "Lake of Gennesaret," 5:1) for the place where Jesus manifests extraordinary power (calming the sea, walking on water) links Jesus' power to God's power over the sea (cf. Psalm 107). The map constructed by literary methods is associative, ideational, and symbolic, rather than literal, physical, and geographic.

Temporal markers are understood similarly. "Forty" is a biblical number indicating a long time. The Hebrew people wandered in the wilderness for forty years. Jesus was in the wilderness tested by Satan for forty days. Here the spatial and temporal settings combine to suggest that Jesus recapitulates the history of the people of God; Jesus passes the test. This story of the prelude to Jesus' ministry is recounted briefly in each of the Synoptic Gospels. All four Gospels relate the story of Jesus' passion, the postlude to his ministry, in some detail. And each of them slows down the narrative at this point. We are given a day-by-day and, finally, an hour-by-hour account of Jesus' end. Literary critics understand this not as more detailed and accurate biography but as rhetorical emphasis on the most startling aspect of the Jesus story: the messiah comes as suffering servant. The storyteller demands attention to this point; the hearer/reader is forced to let it sink in slowly.

The "Jesus" that narrative critics investigate is not "the historical Jesus" that historical critics quest after, but the central character of the Gospel narratives. The audience learns about this Jesus the way it learns about all the characters: through speech and through actions. We learn about characters by what they say and do and by what others (both characters and the narrator) say and do in relation to them. The Gospels reveal their characters more by "showing" than by "telling," more by the unfolding action than by the narrator's direct descriptions. Compared with the complex, psychological characterization of modern novels, the characters of the Gospels are quite simply sketched. Most of them are "flat," that is, one-dimensional, manifesting one character trait. The "Pharisees" in Matthew's Gospel are hypocritical; the "little people" who seek Jesus' help in Mark's Gospel are trusting. Only Jesus and the disciples would appear to be "round" characters, that is, multidimensional, exhibiting at least several character traits and, possibly, change and development. The disciples in Mark illustrate trust and fear, initiative and flight. Feminist narrative critics shed light on previously ignored women characters and female images of God in much the same way as feminist secular critics focus on images of women in the literary canon.

Characters interact within the plot. The plot is an ordered sequence of actions and events. Just as the Gospels do not rely on complex characterization for their stories, they do not depend on intrigue and suspense for their plots. There are unknowns, of course: Will the Markan disciples come to understand? Will the "Jews" in Luke-Acts ever see and perceive? But the main events of the plot have a certain divine inevitability. What is intriguing about the plots of the Gospels is the intertwining of the story lines of two major groups of characters based on their response to Jesus. Jesus' story is the central cord. Around it are wound the story line of the Jewish religious leaders (from the questioning of Jesus' authority by the Pharisees in Galilee to the plotting of his death by the chief priests, scribes, and elders in Jerusalem) and the story line of the disciples (following Jesus, preaching and healing, struggling to understand Jesus, abandoning him at his death, being called again at his resurrection). It is the disciples who experience the most ups and downs (especially in Mark), and it is the disciples with whom the implied author most invites the implied audience to identify. The challenges the disciples experience in the plot are not unlike the challenges the audience experiences in its life and faith.

The ability of the Gospels to pull the audience into the story, to offer critique and encouragement of the disciples as an implicit word to the hearers and readers, is part of the rhetoric of the Gospels. Rhetoric is the art of persuasion. Narrative rhetoric is *how* the story is told. To show the passion story in slow motion is a rhetorical move. To juxtapose Jesus' anointing by an unnamed woman with his betrayal by a named man (Judas), as Mark does in 14:3–11, is a rhetorical move. To imply by careful wording that not Jesus but all who respond to him are on trial, as John does, is a rhetorical move. The rhetoric of the Gospels involves symbolic numbers: in Matthew and Mark, twelve baskets of food are left over from the miraculous feeding of the Jews (representing the twelve tribes of Israel), and seven baskets are left over from the feeding of the Gentiles (representing the seventy nations of the Gentiles). And, of course, there are plenty of rhetorical questions—questions that seem not to demand real answers in their immediate contexts but that linger with the implied audience in broader contexts. The disciples, having seen Jesus calm the sea, ask, "Who then is this . . . ?" (Mark 4:41 // Luke 8:25; Matt 8:27). Jesus, having reviewed the miraculous feedings with the disciples, asks, "Do you not yet understand?" (Mark 8:21). Pilate, having questioned Jesus, asks, "What is truth?" (John 18:38). Literary methods draw attention to these and other rhetorical devices and patterns whereby the implied author persuades the implied audience to follow the story.

READER-ORIENTED APPROACHES

Narrative criticism focuses on the text and the interrelations of its elements. Reader response critics ask what the text *does,* what effects a text has. The focus shifts from the autonomous text to the reader or hearer. Reader response critics ask three related questions: (1) What role does the reader or hearer of a text play in creating the meaning of a text (i.e., does the reader find or make meaning)? (2) Who is the reader/hearer? (3) What is the experience of reading or listening to a text like? In answering the first question critics range from those who speak as if the text guides and molds the reader to those who argue that without the reader no text exists. One key reader response critic (Wolfgang Iser) compares the text to stars in the night sky. One reader draws lines between the stars to form the Big Dipper, another to form a plough. Nonetheless, there are fixed stars. Another critic (Stanley Fish) suggests that without the reader not only are there no constellations, but there are no fixed stars.[2] But whether individual readers are limited by the text or completely free, reader response criticism raises what some view as a specter—multiple interpretations. Yet reader response critics must explain not only differences, variant interpretations, but also agreements about meaning.

The question of interpretative authority is closely related to the second question, Who is the reader? Some critics examine the responses of *actual* flesh-and-blood readers. This may take the form of asking students to share their interpretations of a text or of reconstructing the history of the interpretation of a particular passage by examining sermons, scholarly exegeses, novels, operas, paintings, and other "readings." The latter is termed reception history (the creation of which is itself an act of reading, of interpretation). Other critics are more interested in various *hypothetical* readers, readers proposed by the critic. For those reader response critics closest to narrative criticism, the reader is in the text. The reader is the counterpart of the implied author; the reader is the image of the reader the implied author has created. This *internal* reader is a set of values and a response-inviting structure in the text, a role a real reader must play or resist in reading. *External* readers may be real readers whose interpretations critics examine or a historical audience that the critic constructs from information about readers/hearers at the time the text was written or in subsequent historical periods. Mediating between these two positions are those who view the reader as partly internal and partly external. This *implied* reader exists at the intersection of textual structures and perspectives that control any reading *and* positions outside the text from which the text must be read. Whether the reader is internal or external, a further related question arises: What does the reader know, what competence does the reader possess? Some critics tell the story of reading a text as the story of a *naïve, first-time* reader who is educated by the text and only knows what the text has revealed at any given point in reading time. Others posit an *ideal* reader who knows whatever is necessary to create the fullest possible reading. This informed reader (or perceptive critic) possesses all the information that the entire text supplies and also external data, such as knowledge about social customs, historical events, and literary conventions, that the text presupposes (and/or critics have supplied after years of interpretation).

The variety of ways of construing "the reader" raises our third question: What happens when we read? One of the central aspects of reader response criticism is its focus on reading as an experience, as an event with a linear, temporal dimension. As we read we anticipate what is to come and reflect on what has gone before. We fill in gaps (the omitted or unsaid in the text) and give fixed meanings to indeterminacies. We thus create coherence and consistency wherever they seem to be lacking. Or, we look for inconsistencies, seams, and gaps to challenge a false unity, highlight ideology, and foreground multiplicity, that is, to undermine any reading that claims to be the true and final meaning of a text. We do all these things in the light of the individual experiences we bring to the text, through social competencies, and through learned communal linguistic and literary conventions. This description of the reading experience emphasizes cognitive activity. Some critics also emphasize affective and pragmatic responses, such as being moved to tears or changing one's political party or the way one treats children. Some critics point out that the emphasis on temporal sequence aids in reconstructing the aural experience of the first-century audience who heard New Testament texts read aloud.

Matthew 1–2 can serve as an example of how critics describe the reading process. Matthew begins with a genealogy and the story of Jesus' birth. The genealogy traces Jesus' ancestry through Joseph to King David and Abraham. In the birth story Jesus is threatened (as Moses was) by an evil king who slaughters innocent male babies. Like Moses, Jesus travels to

Egypt and sojourns there before returning to the promised land. One can describe the effect on the reader as the text guiding the reader, leading the reader to view Jesus in a certain light. Or one can say readers use this information to characterize Jesus as the Messiah. They will read the rest of the Gospel in the light of this prologue and look back on it in the course of reading the narrative. Readers supply connections between Jesus and Abraham as the father of the Jewish people and David as the ancestor of the Messiah from associations with Abraham and David they bring to the text. They make parallels between Jesus and Moses, and Jesus and Israel, and view these connections as significant. These connections are supported by their readings of allusions to the Hebrew Scriptures in 1:22–23; 2:5–6; 2:15; 2:23, interpreted as "fulfillment quotations" by scholars. None of the readings offered so far is very controversial in the contemporary scholarly reading community. However, this is not true of readings of the presence of five women—Tamar, Rahab, Ruth, the wife of Uriah (Bathsheba), and Mary—in the genealogy or the tracing of Jesus' genealogy patrilineally through Joseph.

The history of the reception of Matthew 1–2 shows at least three families of readings of the women. Some readers have read the first four women as sinners included in the patrilineal genealogy as an indication that Jesus comes to save sinners. Others have read the first four women as Gentiles (Bathsheba is counted as Gentile as the wife of a Gentile proselyte) foreshadowing the Gentile mission. Still others have tied the first four to Mary, reading them all as instruments of the Holy Spirit who moved the messianic line forward even though scandal was attached to their giving birth.[3] Thus the first four help to normalize Mary's role. None of these readings, however, asks what gender ideologies the text and/or readers construct. They do not ask why women, sin, sexuality, foreignness, *and* the power of birth should be associated and in need of domestication in a patriarchal order where lineage is traced through an adoptive father rather than a birth mother. None asks, What difference does it make if the reader is a woman? What response might a woman who has borne an "illegitimate" child have? What resonances might the entire birth story—with its allusions to Moses, Egypt, and the Babylonian captivity—have for womanists who recall the history of slavery, when maternity was not always a choice and children could be easily killed or sold away by those in power?

With the latter questions we shift from questions about whether texts or readers create meanings to questions about texts and readers exercising power in particular cultural contexts. Whether one tells a story of a text representing and constructing gender ideology, transcribing and inscribing a cultural script, or of a reader creating and reflecting it, the gender and social location of the reader emerge as key issues. What difference does it make if the reader—actual or hypothetical, internal or external, naïve or ideal—is a male or female of a particular race, class, or religion? Feminist critics have pointed out that reader constructs pretending to be gender neutral often mask male interpreters and their reading strategies. Womanists and others have pointed out that reader constructs often mask particular sorts of male interpreters and reading strategies.

But what does it mean to read as a woman or as a feminist? Feminist critics compare and contrast readings of a text by different actual women. They also appeal to the hypothesis of a woman or a feminist reader, constructing what it means to be a woman or a feminist as they read. They have described the process of reading male and female texts. Often a woman reading an androcentric/patriarchal text is *immasculated,* that is, she reads and identifies as male.[4] She identifies, for example, with Joseph's predicament in Matthew 1–2, faced with the affront to his honor posed by the shameless Mary, or with the narrator who seems uncomfortable with female reproductive power outside a patriarchal context. Yet as the reader identifies with the male as universal and dominant, she knows she is a female. She constructs herself as Other. Hers may be the multiple female and racial/ethnic difference of Rahab or Ruth viewed as problematic. Hers is always a female difference and power that must be domesticated. However, that is not necessarily the end of the reading process.

Once a woman is aware of immasculation, she can read as a feminist. As she reads she recognizes the text immasculating her and the particular male reading strategies she uses. She also reads recognizing what the text forbids or tensions within it. She recognizes that she and other feminists can resist or affirm the text, read it against the grain or transform it for feminist use. She may have to do both simultaneously, for even a single verse can serve liberating or oppressive ends depending on the historical and social context. Certainly, that is the case with appeals to the motherhood of Mary. Some critics who emphasize the power of readers even question one of the central tenets of feminist criticism: that the New Testament is androcentric and patriarchal. They argue that androcentrism and patriarchy are created by readers and depend on the historical context and interpretive communities in which the texts are read.

But can a male read as a feminist? What are the roles of men in feminist biblical criticism? Discussions in the literary field suggest that their most useful role may be to examine various masculinities embodied in and/or created by the New Testament and readers, including ecclesiastical and academic interpretive communities.

RHETORICAL CRITICISM

The turn to ancient and modern reader/hearers is seen not only in study of the Gospels but also in rhetorical criticism of the Pauline corpus. Rhetorical criticism arises out of both a study of rhetoric in antiquity and the modern revival of rhetoric as persuasive argument. Scholars study Greco-Roman rhetorical guides to speechmaking and epistolary handbooks. They highlight the power of language to achieve goals in specific situations and how the rhetorical occasion shapes argument. Rhetorical criticism has much in common with narrative criticism in its focus on the internal relations of parts to wholes, the structure of the letters, and particular stylistic devices. It also has much in common with reader response criticism in its focus on the audience and the rhetorical occasion in which emotional, cognitive, and practical effects upon the hearer are a central concern. These two emphases are united in discussion of classical rhetorical genres. Judicial or forensic rhetoric leads to judgment, often taking an accusing or apologetic form in letters. Deliberative rhetoric aims at effecting decision and future action in the form of advising and consoling. Epideictic or demonstrative rhetoric moves the hearer to agree or disagree, frequently praising or blaming values.

Feminist rhetorical criticism is very recent. It centers on 1 Corinthians, especially on the reconstruction of the conflicts and agreements between Paul and the Corinthian women, their location in the rhetorical occasion. It has shaded into social history in the work of Elisabeth Schüssler Fiorenza and Antoinette Clark Wire and intersected with poststructuralism in Elizabeth Castelli. Schüssler Fiorenza employs close rhetorical analysis to bring to light the historical situation of the followers of Chloe (1:11) and thus avoid reconstructing the situation of the Corinthian community as simply the story of Paul. Wire concentrates on the women prophets. She points out how gender influences the social status and rhetorical positions of Paul and the women. Similarly, Castelli finds a place for the "subjugated discourse" of the Corinthians in the history of Christianity. She also uses a Foucaultian analysis of knowledge and power to render Paul's claims as a privileged speaker contingent. Paul's discourse is not a solution to "problems" in the community. Rather it is an attempt to establish his own authority against competing interpretations of power.

Castelli's use of Foucault, along with some reader response criticism, marks the beginning of feminist New Testament critics' use of the post-structuralist and cultural approaches noted above in our discussion of criticism in the literary guild. Feminist biblical critics have seen this most prominently displayed in Mieke Bal's work on the Hebrew Bible.[5]

There have been some important parallels between the insights and goals of feminist criticism and biblical literary criticism. The rejection by literary critics of the positivistic aspects of form and redaction criticism parallels the feminist critique of positivism. Literary critics' respect for the interdependence of the text and the audience parallels feminist respect for "the Other" *and* responsibility for the self. Literary critics' acceptance of a plurality of meanings parallels feminism's acceptance of a plurality of voices. The concern of (especially) reader response critics to make us more aware of how much of ourselves we include in our interpretations shares the concern of feminists to make us (women and especially men) more aware of how gender influences interpretation and action.

There remain significant challenges addressed to biblical literary criticism by feminist perspectives. Feminist critiques of dominant male power as it leads to silencing "the Other" challenge biblical literary critics to give their serious attention to early Christian literature outside the canon—and to support those who are already doing so. Feminism challenges biblical literary criticism to avoid the dualism of traditional androcentrism that sees historical methods and literary methods as opposites. Feminist perspectives discourage either/or thinking and encourage both/and thinking. This is already seen in the work of some biblical literary critics. In its advanced form it might be cultural criticism.

In a related way, literary criticism presents a challenge to feminist historical criticism of the Bible. The historical approach that the literary approach reacted against was concerned with history by, for, and about dominant males, who assumed for themselves universal status. The historical approach from the point of view of women and other dominated groups and classes is still in its early stages, although important foundations have been laid. Feminist historical critics have the opportunity—and the responsibility—to fill out and/or subvert this historical picture of the biblical world with full awareness of the literary nature of the documents, an awareness the traditional male historical critics did not have.

Both literary and historical approaches—in fact, multiple approaches— are called for by feminists reading the Bible. There are important roles for narrative, reader response, rhetorical, poststructuralist, and cultural criticisms. Literary methods are one strand in the complex web being woven anew by women searching the scriptures.

NOTES

1. Elaine Showalter, "Critical Cross-Dressing: Male Feminists and The Woman of the Year," *Raritan* 3/2 (1983): 130–49.
2. See Stephen D. Moore, *Literary Criticism and the Gospels: The Theoretical Challenge* (New Haven: Yale University Press, 1989), 101, 127.
3. Raymond E. Brown, *The Birth of the Messiah: A Commentary on the Infancy Narratives in Matthew and Luke* (Garden City, NY: Doubleday, Image Books, 1979), 71–74.
4. Judith Feterley coined this term in *The Resisting Reader: A Feminist Approach to American Fiction* (Bloomington: Indiana University Press, 1978).
5. Bal's works include *Lethal Love: Feminist Literary Readings of Biblical Love Stories* (Bloomington: Indiana University Press, 1987); *Murder and Difference: Gender, Genre, and Scholarship on Sisera's Death* (Bloomington: Indiana University Press, 1988); and *Death and Dissymmetry: The Politics of Coherence in the Book of Judges* (Chicago: University of Chicago Press, 1988).

RECOMMENDED READINGS

Anderson, Janice Capel, and Stephen D. Moore, eds. *Mark and Method: New Approaches in Biblical Studies.* Minneapolis: Fortress Press, 1992.
Castelli, Elizabeth A. *Imitating Paul: A Discourse of Power.* Louisville, KY: Westminster/John Knox, 1991.
Fowler, Robert M. *Let the Reader Understand: Reader-Response Criticism and the Gospel of Mark.* Minneapolis: Fortress Press, 1991.
Gibaldi, Joseph, ed. *Introduction to Scholarship in Modern Languages and Literatures.* 2nd ed. New York: Modern Language Association, 1992.
Gallop, Jane. *Around 1981: Academic Feminist Literary Theory.* New York: Routledge, 1992.
Jobling, David, and Stephen D. Moore, eds. "Poststructuralism as Exegesis." *Semeia* 54. Atlanta: Scholars Press, 1991.
Moore, Stephen D. *Literary Criticism and the Gospels: The Theoretical Challenge.* New Haven: Yale University Press, 1989.
Powell, Mark Alan. *What Is Narrative Criticism?* Guides to Biblical Scholarship. Minneapolis: Fortress Press, 1990.
Schüssler Fiorenza, Elisabeth. "Rhetorical Situation and Historical Reconstruction in 1 Corinthians." *New Testament Studies* 33 (1987): 386–403.
Tolbert, Mary Ann, ed. "The Bible and Feminist Hermeneutics." *Semeia* 28. Missoula, MT: Scholars Press, 1983.
Warhol, Robyn R., and Diane Price Herndl. *Feminisms: An Anthology of Literary Theory and Criticism.* New Brunswick, NJ: Rutgers University Press, 1991.
Weems, Renita J. "Reading *Her Way* through the Struggle: African American Women and the Bible." In *Stony the Road We Trod: African American Biblical Interpretation,* edited by Cain Hope Felder, 57–80. Minneapolis: Fortress Press, 1991.
Wire, Antoinette Clark. *The Corinthian Women Prophets: A Reconstruction through Paul's Rhetoric.* Minneapolis: Fortress Press, 1990.

❖ Social, Sociological, and Anthropological Methods

MARY ANN TOLBERT ◆

ALL RELIGIONS ARE profoundly social phenomena, whatever their varied claims may be to divine revelation or transcendent knowledge. Religious rituals and beliefs form the basis of group solidarity, determining who is in and who is out; they specify various social roles within a group, indicating who does or who does not have the right to hold power or exercise control; they explain the origin and values of the group, providing the group with a history, a present purpose, and a destiny. Religions, then, rank as one of the most important social institutions of any society and as such have been the subject of sociological and anthropological investigations since the modern beginnings of those disciplines in the nineteenth century.

Scholars of scripture, however, have been slow to adopt these approaches for their studies of early Christianity or Judaism. It was not until the mid-1970s that New Testament scholars began to make explicit use of methods and models from sociology or cultural anthropology. Part of the hesitation of some scripture scholars might have been due to the assumption, undergirding most sociological or anthropological discussions, that religions are socially constructed. The omission or denial of some formative divine agency may be seen by many as a problematic aspect of the adoption of these methods. For a feminist, however, emphasizing the social construction of religious institutions surely has definite benefits, since discriminatory social constructions, unlike claims to "natural" or transcendent forms, are subject to debate and alteration. After a discussion of the definitions of the terms "social," "sociology," and "anthropology," I want to analyze the use of these methods in recent New Testament study from a feminist perspective by outlining briefly some of the current positions in feminist theory that fuel the critiques feminists in sociology and anthropology are making of their respective disciplines. I will then use these critiques as a perspective from which to understand the possible positive and negative values such disciplines might have for feminist study of early Christianity and Judaism.

DEFINITIONS

Absolute divisions between the methodological realms designated by the terms "social," "sociology," and "anthropology" are practically impossible. The terminological confusion is prompted by the similar origins and aims of the perspectives. "Social" generally refers to social description or social history, types of analyses that some scholars want to call "proto-sociology." Social description may range from simply acknowledging the social dimensions of a group under discussion to applying one or more specific sociological categories, like "status" or "sect," in examining the group. Social history attempts a comprehensive social description of a group or society, including its economic, political, and social dimensions. However, the occasional claim that social description is merely the unbiased listing of the social *realia* of a society or group is misleading. The categories of analysis (e.g., class, status,) as well as the selection of areas sufficiently significant to analyze (e.g., the minting of money rather than the cooking of food) evince the presence of value decisions and methodological assumptions. Such assumptions cannot be avoided, of course, but neither should they be denied.

Sociological studies are usually distinguished from social description by their explicit application of established theoretical models to explain the development, stability, or alteration of a group or society, a distinction often clearer in principle than in practice. Furthermore, the division between sociological studies and anthropological studies, or indeed between the disciplines of sociology and anthropology, is even more problematic. Both modern disciplines trace their origins to the same nineteenth-century figures, especially the French sociologist, Emile Durkheim. Durkheim posited a radical demarcation between the personal and the social and focused exclusive attention on the study of the social. Hence, both sociology and anthropology, as studies of the social, address many of the same questions in their investigations. What tends to separate the two disciplines are *what* they choose to study and *how* they go about it. Sociology primarily examines the complex modern social structures of industrial and post-industrial societies, relying heavily on quantitative methods of analysis (e.g., statistical studies, demographics, questionnaires). The goal is to formulate theories of social interaction that are generally predictive in nature (i.e., if certain situations occur, all other things being equal, the following will often result), and the procedure is to propose a theory, design a study to test the theory by verifiable and quantitative means, and then amend the theory according to the results of the study.

Cultural or social anthropology (the two modifiers, the first used primarily in North America and the second in Britain, are basically synonymous) is usually differentiated from sociology by its more comparative and cross-cultural subject matter and its emphasis on field work procedures. Anthropologists attempt to study a society as a whole by face-to-face observation. To accomplish such a goal, the society under analysis must be sufficiently small and its institutions sufficiently rudimentary to be encompassed adequately by a trained observer. The procedure involves the careful recording of the observations by the investigator in a field work situation of sufficient length to assess the dynamics and interactions of the society as a whole, and the goal is generally either the fullest possible interpretation of that society or the comparison of several societies with each other. But anthropological studies almost always manifest some explicit or implicit attempt to arrive at more general conclusions concerning human society-building dynamics or at least to "translate" seemingly foreign patterns into more familiar Western forms.

Since neither statistical analyses and questionnaires nor field observations are possible procedures for studying ancient, culturally distant societies, biblical scholars face serious problems in adopting these methods fully. Even the archaeological evidence employed by anthropologists is denied to Christian historians because Christianity was not a separate and self-contained culture with distinctive archaeological remains in its first centuries of growth. For feminists, other issues of concern in the adoption of these methods also arise.

FEMINIST THEORY

Feminists recognize the systematic oppression and marginalization of women of all different classes, races, ethnic origins, sexual orientations, and physical abilities to be one of the most complex and pervasive injustices of human societies during the past several millennia. Yet the more careful feminists have reflected on the experiences of women, the more intricate the situation of oppression has been seen to be. Because gender is not extricable from other variables of social status like race, class, ethnic origin, or sexual orientation, a thorough analysis of gender discrimination requires the voices of many women and explicit attention to their different experiences and needs. The use of universalizing slogans, like "woman's oppression," tends to name only the discrimination felt by those doing the talking and thus not only omits the experience of the majority of women in the world but also severely underestimates the complexity of the problem and the variety of analyses necessary to understand it.

In recent feminist theory, the recognition that universal categories, totalizing theories, or assertions of "essence" often mask a hidden agenda of privilege, has led many feminists, including some in religion, sociology, and anthropology, to explore their connections to other aspects of contemporary postmodernism. With some oversimplification, postmodernism might be described as the intellectual ferment in science, architecture, art, and the humanities, originating in the late 1960s and early 1970s, that radically calls into question many of the Enlightenment foundations of modern Western thought and society. Specifically under attack are the Enlightenment belief in the supremacy of human reason to transcend historical and cultural particularity in order to arrive at objective, value-neutral assessments of "natural law" or universal "truth"; the belief in a basic dichotomy of thought and life, following the pattern of reason versus emotion, objective versus subjective, public versus private, etc.; and the belief in the transparency of language to some external reality that it serves merely to make present to human consciousness by naming. Instead, the various proponents of postmodernism argue that all human theorizing is culturally constrained and historically limited; that there can be no absolute division between objectivity and subjectivity even in science because the methodological and theoretical assumptions of the observer always shape the outcome of the observation; that methodological and theoretical assumptions, moreover, always involve the privileging of certain values or categories over others; and, perhaps most fundamentally, that language does not merely represent some reality "out there" but itself makes up that reality as it weaves the very fabric of human interaction in historically specific, socially constructed, and thoroughly political ways.

Some postmodernists, following the poststructuralist, deconstructive theories of the French philosopher Jacques Derrida, assert that since all claims to truth or knowledge are partial and contingent, there are no overarching, legitimating structures to support the adoption of one claim over another. Many feminists have been rightly suspicious of this direction in postmodernism since it can be used to undercut the grounding of any specific movement for social reform. In reflecting on the concrete experiences of women, feminists point out that no matter how philosophically unfounded may be the claims of some dominant groups to exercise power and authority over all others, human societies have regularly manifested such structures, and only those who emerge unscathed (i.e., the socially privileged) have sufficient comfort and security to enjoy the free play of difference advocated by some poststructuralists. Most feminists, like other social reformers, function on the belief that the interests and limitations of those holding power in any society may be analyzed and that arguments for better or worse uses of power may be mounted, no matter how contingent or qualified by historical particularity they must be. Furthermore, all reform movements posit some real human agency, again no matter how tenuous, that allows for the possibility of social change. Society does not have to remain as it has been. My own feminist stance, as a white, middle-class North American woman, is one informed by postmodern suspicions concerning objectivity, universals, and referential language, but one that also retains beliefs in the legitimacy of historically specific claims to a more just distribution of power and in the requisite human agency to accomplish that end.

Many of these issues in current feminist theory underlie the critiques feminist scholars in sociology and anthropology are now raising concerning their disciplines. As a context for evaluating the use of sociology and anthropology in the study of scripture, I want to explore briefly both of these disciplines from the perspective of their respective feminist critiques.

SOCIOLOGY FROM A FEMINIST PERSPECTIVE

Although sociological studies of roles, functions, and social situations specifically related to women have increased dramatically in recent years and attempts have been made to chart the differing socialization processes women experience, the fundamental paradigms of sociological analysis have not proved as amenable to challenge and change by feminists as those of some other disciplines, for example, anthropology. Several reasons have been suggested for this "missing feminist revolution in sociology."[1] Among the most important are the canonical status accorded the founding "fathers" of sociology and the profound entrenchment of sociological theory and methods in the positivistic, objectivistic tendencies of the Enlightenment. To illustrate the problem and also to understand contemporary sociology somewhat better, I want to look briefly at the thought of three early "sociologists," Karl Marx (1818–1883), Emile Durkheim (1858–1917), and Max Weber (1864–1920).

KARL MARX

That Karl Marx should be listed as an early "sociologist" would appear to some sociologists as heresy, for sociological theory generally regards Marx with both suspicion and distance. Marx's analysis of the plight of the worker in industrial society represents a classic example of one type of sociological model for society, the conflict model, since it posits the basic dynamic of society to be conflict between social classes. However, Marx's own political advocacy of revolution, a clearly nonobjective stance, and his reliance on psychological rather than solely social motivations, such as the worker's feeling of alienation, have prevented sociologists from claiming him as their own. Yet many of the concepts Marx and his later followers formulated in their development of historical materialism as a method of social analysis have influenced later sociological theory. For example, the Marxist explication of ideology as the "false consciousness" encouraged by the upper classes through their control of education, religion, the media, and so on, in order to justify the inequality of capitalist society and to reconcile workers to it, can be viewed as an early investigation in the sociology of knowledge, which correlates the symbolic systems of a society to the actual social data of daily life.

Nevertheless, Marx is strikingly silent concerning the situation of women. No less a child of the Enlightenment than Durkheim, Marx assumed a basic dualism between public and private that segregated the domestic world of female–male interaction away from the real world of work, economics, capitalism, and private property. Furthermore, Marx, following another cherished Enlightenment dichotomy, assumed that reproduction of the species was part of nature and not society, thus freeing it from any social conditioning. Although Marx's colleague Friedrich Engels related the subordinate position of women in society to the historical development of private property, the general tenor of Marxist theory was that whatever situation of inequality women may experience will disappear when the revolution of the working masses abolishes the class-dominant, capitalist society of private ownership, a conviction that the concrete experience of women in communist or socialist countries has completely refuted. Contemporary Marxist feminists are attempting to stretch Marxist theory to account for the situation of women, but so far their efforts have met with only modest results, since arguments that women form a distinctive "class" or that reproduction can be treated analogously to production are fraught with conceptual and practical difficulties.

EMILE DURKHEIM

The towering nineteenth-century figure for the later elaboration of both sociology and anthropology is Emile Durkheim. Durkheim was the intellectual heir and major proponent of the "positive" philosophy of Auguste Comte. At the beginning of the nineteenth century, Comte, who many argue was the true "father" of modern sociology, proposed the basic premises of what came to be called "positivism," the new scientific rationalism of the age: only statements subject to empirical verification are to be considered valid, thus making art, religion, and any type of metaphysical speculation essentially meaningless; a basic difference exists between statements of fact, which are empirically verifiable, and value judgments, which are not subject to such tests, and hence science with its solely empirical stance is of necessity value-free; and the natural sciences and the new social sciences share a basic unity. Durkheim built his conception of what the scientific study of the social should be on the foundation of logical positivism. His own fondness for the dualisms of Enlightenment logic added additional aspects to his development of sociology. For Durkheim, sociology was to be the science of the social. It was, like the natural sciences, objective and value-free, empirical and verifiable.

Durkheim's own analysis of society emphasized the functions of social institutions and the roles required to fulfill those functions. Societies are organic units, in which the good of the whole is the highest value; thus, societies regularly impose their views and requirements on individuals and not vice versa. The model of social functioning proposed by Durkheim has come to be called structural functionalism. Unlike the conflict model, structural functionalism stresses harmony and maintenance as the essential dynamics of social structures; social functioning depends on consensus with any disagreements viewed as a transitory deviance. Indeed, in Durkheim's analysis societies themselves become almost personified entities, meeting their own needs and ensuring their own futures. In such a system, any real human agency is so constrained as to be nonexistent.

From the standpoint of contemporary feminism the problems with the structural functionalist model of society are many. Attempts at social change are named as deviance and are relatively useless anyway because little or no human agency is possible. Perhaps even more importantly, the personification of society, criticized by many sociologists as well, hides the real sources of power and influence. Who benefits from the maintenance and harmony of the social structure as a whole? Who is represented by this "consensus"? If societies are not organic entities with their own wills and needs, then the identification of whose wills and needs are being socially reinforced is critical to understanding the functioning of the social order. That Durkheim's objective, value-free scientific analysis generates a conservative model of society that protects and preserves the status quo against the revolutionary calls of any deviants provides further evidence for the position of postmodernism — despite his avowed intentions, the values of the interpreter (or, for Durkheim, the interpreter's culture) appear to be inscribed in the resulting interpretation.

MAX WEBER

Although Emile Durkheim is clearly the most significant figure for the disciplinary formation of both sociology and anthropology, Max Weber's explorations of the possibilities of historical sociology have important ramifications for the use of these disciplines in the study of the New Testament. Weber adopted a moderating position in the debate over the radical split between objective empiricism and subjective value judgments. He was critical of Comte's claims for the unity of the natural and social sciences because he believed that cultures consisted of the subjective meanings of individuals and that human social actions could not be understood without the consideration of values. Indeed, Weber's own method of analysis, *Verstehen,* can be described as an empathetic, imaginative interpretation of the social actions and values of another individual. Nor was it necessary in Weber's view for the individual to be around to answer questions, for such empathetic, imaginative understanding could be extended to past historical periods, although the availability of data might limit what could be ascertained.

On the other hand, Weber insisted that subjective empathy alone was insufficient because sociology was a science concerned with social actions, not just with how individuals viewed themselves. The objective moment in Weber's system of inquiry was the establishment of a causal analysis, by which he meant the hypothetical isolation of the decisive factor or cause that led to a certain social situation or action. Moreover, in his theoretical writings, Weber did not recognize the possibility of any disjunction between subjective meanings and objective social actions, perceiving language to be transparent on social reality (unlike Marx's conception of ideology, in which meanings purposely obscure the true nature of social actions). Thus, Weber's sociology was concerned with the individual rather than the group, as in structural functionalism, and its goals were interpretation and causality.

To evaluate the possibilities and problems of historical sociology, Weber's studies of ancient Judaism, Islam, and the religions of China and India are the most significant, even though Weber is probably best known for his not unrelated discussion of the symbiotic connection between the growth of capitalism and the "Protestant ethic," that Calvinistic anxiety attack which drove Christians into the ascetic world of overwork. Weber's sociology of religion employed a tripartite schema of ideal types to analyze the modes of authority, religious roles, and social actions characteristic of each religion. These three ideal types, tradition, charisma, and rationality, were abstractions or analytic conceptions used to organize social data and remained only vaguely defined in Weber's writings. Despite the erudition found in Weber's studies of Buddhism, Confucianism, Hinduism, Islam, and Judaism, his conclusion, which argued that only Judaism, as represented especially by the Hebrew prophets, contained the seed of rationality that could later grow into capitalism and modern secular culture while the other religions remained locked in an inner-directed traditionalism, has been severely criticized. Just to take one obvious example, it is hard to understand why Confucianism, with its agnostic stance and contempt for mysticism, should be characterized as more magical (one of the essential features of traditionalism) than Judaism.

Critics argue that it is Weber's reading back of the Protestant ethic and capitalism into his study of Judaism that makes him highlight some elements there that he downplays in the study of the other religions. Judaism's rationality, thus, becomes a causative factor in the modern development of Western economics, but Judaism can only be viewed in that fashion by starting with the Protestant ethic and selectively reading the past. The fear that such deterministic selectivity is endemic to historical sociology makes many sociologists question its validity. From a feminist standpoint, reading the present situation back into past societies in a causal fashion raises the possibility of granting to patriarchy and the marginalization of women not only an undisputed heritage but also a certain inevitability that relieves each successive generation of its moral responsibility for the particular choices that encouraged the evolution of the pattern.

From this rather superficial review of the founding figures, basic models, and prevalent methods of early sociology, it should be clear why feminists in sociology have had difficulty challenging the fundamental paradigms of the discipline. Since the "canonical" writings of the early sociologists are so profoundly encoded in the rational, dichotomous, positivistic projects of the Enlightenment, any feminist challenge to them must take on the proportions of an entirely new system, with new foundations, models, and methods. Fortunately, feminists in anthropology have had more success in reformulating some of the founding assumptions of their discipline.

ANTHROPOLOGY FROM A FEMINIST PERSPECTIVE

Although anthropology also traces its origin to the work of Emile Durkheim, and indeed some anthropologists see their area as a subdiscipline of sociology, the emphasis on cross-cultural investigations in anthropology worked against the application of rigid Enlightenment dichotomies or the assumption of the historical transcendence of reason. Anthropology in the present argues strongly for the distinctiveness of particular cultural systems and the necessity of exploring social structures within their specific contexts in order to understand them. Some anthropologists argue that the singularity of individual cultural systems is such that comparisons between them are always suspect. Certainly the question of the commensurability of cultures must always be raised in regard to comparisons. Furthermore, whether or not it is even possible to abstract sufficiently from the particularity of each cultural system to be able to establish useful models or types is a continuing debate in contemporary anthropology.

The feminist critique of anthropology began in the 1970s primarily as an indictment of male bias in anthropological studies. These feminist accusations fueled the flames of a growing worry in anthropology over the issue of ethnocentrism. Ethnocentrism is the interpretation of different cultures and peoples in terms of one's own culture and views. Feminists pointed out that assumptions about the role of women in Western countries were being used illegitimately to interpret women in non-Western cultures, and consequently some of the crucial cultural activities of women in tribal religion or tribal affairs were being ignored or misinterpreted. This disclosure of male bias led to a second phase of feminist critique: feminist anthropologists began restudying the situation of women in various societies, arguing for quite different readings of the roles of women.

While such rereadings continue, current feminist work in anthropology, as in many other disciplines, has begun to challenge the basic models and assumptions of the area. In anthropology, feminists are insisting that gender is a major structural factor in the construction of all societies and must be considered in the development of any social model. The homogeneous society of Durkheim's structural functionalism, in which any internal divisions of society such as class, ethnic group, or *gender,* are generally ignored since they fall outside of the model, is thus rendered highly suspect.

The cross-cultural exploration of gender has, moreover, uncovered several important issues. While gender is a major factor in all cultures, how gender roles are defined within cultures may vary radically. Attempts to isolate some universal role that cross-culturally defines "woman" have run into contradictory evidence at every turn. Even the suggestion that "woman" ideally means the physical and/or emotional nurturing of children can be disputed within Western culture itself by the nineteenth-century upper-class British practice of employing a wet nurse and a nanny for such purposes. Anthropological studies have, thus, deconstructed any notion of a universal or essential woman and have, in addition, established beyond question the socially constructed nature of gender roles.

Gender not only varies cross-culturally; it also intersects with class, race, and other variables within cultures to produce a variety of specific gender roles internally. The importance of always considering gender in relation to other factors of status can be illustrated even from ancient Greek culture. Aristotle's understanding of gender is easily misconstrued unless it is examined in light of his discussion of slaves.[2] Aristotle described the proper relation of men to women, of men to slaves, and even of women to slaves, making it clear that men, women, and slaves constituted quite distinct groups. Since it is apparent that slaves included both females and males, for Aristotle only *free* males and females could have gender, that is, be considered "men" and "women," while slaves, male or female, are considered only in relation to their servitude. Consequently, being female is not a sufficient condition for being a woman, if one is a slave; and being male is not a sufficient condition for being a man, if one is a slave. Although women are inferior in status to men, for Aristotle, they are also superior to slaves, including male slaves. Thus, in Aristotle's view, gender must be understood as a *class* privilege, and gender identity and class identity cannot be separated. This kind of analysis underscores the complexity of gender issues, whether the culture be ancient and fairly homogeneous or modern and multi-ethnic.

Finally, feminist anthropological studies indicate that societal gender expectations need to be recognized as the ritualized or highly symbolized accounts of the relations between men and women. These symbolic constructions of gender, or gender stereotypes, though often exerting powerful constraints on the range of choices available to men and women, must not be assumed to describe the actual social relations that exist between women and men in daily life. Concrete social relations may vary considerably from the symbolic constructions of gender upheld by social ideology.

Using the issues raised by these feminist critiques of sociology and anthropology, I now want to review the adoption of sociological and anthropological methods in recent New Testament research.

SOCIOLOGY AND ANTHROPOLOGY IN NEW TESTAMENT SCHOLARSHIP

Several general overviews of the major studies employing sociological or anthropological methods for research in New Testament or early Christian history are available, and that material will not be repeated here.[3] A feminist analysis of the use of these methods, however, reveals some of the same methodological issues raised by feminists in sociology and anthropology. A few examples will illustrate the issues involved.

A number of the initial biblical sociological investigations and some of the current work in anthropology stress the scientific paradigm of the methods. Scholars often explicitly indicate that they will follow the social science procedure of positing a theory, testing it, and then modifying it. Implementing such a procedure on the early Christian sources available is, of course, practically impossible, which the author may or may not admit. There are three primary difficulties with New Testament or other early Christian documents from a social science perspective: (1) The texts are fixed, as are all historical texts, so that what they present is all they present, and the researcher cannot ask additional questions or obtain further clarification on a point. (2) The texts are not intended to supply sociological information, and indeed their general proselytizing or apologetic functions may serve to obscure the actual social realities of the group. (3) Many of the texts are informed by individual rather than typical points of view, as is clearly the case with one of the most common topics for New Testament sociological analysis, Paul's letters, which, by expressing only the opinions of one person, are completely insufficient as a basis for describing an entire community. What scanty sociological information can be teased out of these recalcitrant texts is much too tentative to be used to test any theory or model, and in general, regardless of the initial procedural claims, the main use of the model or theory is to see what it can make of the textual material, not how the material can test the theory. In other words, most sociological and anthropological studies of the New Testament tend to *invert* the social science method: rather than making the theory the conjectural topic of investigation and the social data the arena of proof, New Testament explorations have often made the textual data the topic of investigation and the theory or model the vehicle of proof.

Social science models, however, are not designed to function in this manner.

In his anthropological research on the New Testament, Bruce Malina admits that the predictive function of social science models and the procedures for testing them are ruled out by the nature of early Christian documents. Nevertheless, he goes on to argue that such a lack in New Testament anthropological studies can be addressed by "retrodictive" techniques: since we know how things turned out, that information can be used as a check on the theories. Such a procedure raises the precise problem for which Weber's historical sociology of religion was so severely criticized: reading later history back into the study of an earlier period in a causal fashion. "How things turned out" may rest on any number of totally unpredictable factors, including chance, human psychopathology, or iconoclasm; thus, the present can never function as a check on earlier social dynamics. Using later history to control the social analysis of earlier periods imparts a determinism to social processes that sociological theory itself denies. For feminists concerned with recovering the history of women in early Christianity, reliance on retrodictive checks is disastrous, because it could be argued that since women are not in positions of authority in the present, social realities must have kept them from those positions in the past. Indeed, just such criticisms were voiced at the publication of the pioneering reconstruction of early Christianity by Elisabeth Schüssler Fiorenza. A few male scholars asserted that her depiction of the leadership roles of women in the Jesus movement had to be wrong since women were not in those positions in later centuries, and several agreed that the Jesus movement may have been egalitarian but only in a socially transitory fashion, for Christianity had to institutionalize in order to survive, which necessarily meant the subordination of women, as evidenced by the later situation of the church. Both of these retrodictive responses assume a causal, necessary connection between later social structures and earlier social organization, a thoroughly unjustified assumption from the standpoint of contemporary sociological or anthropological theory.

If the New Testament sources and even the actual procedures followed contradict established social science methodology, why has the citation of that methodology been so prominent in many sociological and anthropological studies? I think the reason has to do with the positivistic underpinnings of such a scientific method. Biblical historical criticism has its roots in the same positivistic Enlightenment mentality as early sociology, and beginning in the late 1970s, it too has been attacked for its rhetoric of rigid separation between objective exegesis and subjective eisegesis. Some scholars may be attracted to sociology and anthropology because they find an affinity between what they have been doing in biblical criticism and what they think the social sciences stipulate. Gerd Theissen's reconstruction of the Jesus movement is a good case in point. He weds a very traditional form-critical analysis of the Gospels and Acts to a structural functionalist model of society to argue for the role of the wandering charismatics in the Jesus movement; sociology in his study is little more than an extension of the form-critical *Sitz im Leben*. Additionally, Theissen's form-critical analysis, like much biblical historical criticism, rests on the Enlightenment view of language as transparent on reality, for he assumes that the reason for preserving sayings about wandering must be the presence of actual wanderers in the early Palestinian period, a rather naïve assumption that also seems to contradict Paul's evidence for the fixed centrality of Peter and the Jerusalem church (Gal 1:18–2:10).

Concomitantly, scholars who emphasize the scientific nature of these new methods may be responding to more than mere affinity. Some appear to be using these approaches as a way of avoiding the mounting critique of historical positivism in biblical studies by feminists and other liberation theologians; yet to do that they must also ignore the mounting critique of positivism in sociology and anthropology. For example, Malina's insistence on the differences between modern North American culture and ancient Mediterranean culture revealed by the use of anthropological models cannot be taken, as it sometimes seems to be, as evidence that the use of such models protects the interpreter from his or her own modern values, concerns, and presuppositions.

From a feminist standpoint, the most serious problem with most social science research into Christian origins is the omission of any consideration of gender. In part at least this omission is endemic to the primary models being adopted. For instance, in their major studies of Pauline Christianity, Theissen and Wayne Meeks both appropriate a somewhat modified form of the structural functionalist model. This model emphasizes harmonious social maintenance by ignoring the differing agenda of the social stratifications of class, race, ethnic identity, and gender. To their credit both Theissen and Meeks add a class analysis to determine to which class or status early Christians belonged, a difficult task given the incommensurability between early Roman class structure and contemporary models for class or status (indeed, even the attempt to use a modern class or status analysis has been criticized as "sociocentrism," the reading of post-industrial society back into antiquity[4]).

In Roman society, the emperor, his family, counselors, and even slaves sat at the apex of the social order; under him three officially recognized classes existed: the Roman senators; the knights or equestrian class, made up of the rest of the Roman aristocracy; and the decurions, the local aristocracy of the towns and villages of the empire. It has been estimated that these three (or four) classes accounted for less than 1 percent of the population of the empire; the other 99 percent were officially classless, just as slaves for Aristotle were genderless. How that 99 percent, from which all of the early Christians probably came, viewed their own social stratification is virtually unknown, making discussions of early Christian status differentiation highly speculative and problematic.

Theissen and Meeks argue that the people most attracted to early Christianity were individuals with status inconsistency, those having a higher achieved status (through the accumulation of wealth, education, etc.) than their status ascribed by birth. For Meeks, status inconsistency led to cognitive dissonance, a disorienting sense that the world was not treating them as they deserved to be treated. Such people would find the egalitarian ethos of early Christianity inviting, since it rejected the disappointing world social order. Neither Meeks nor Theissen raises the issue of gender in his analysis (nor do they fully examine the situation of slaves); the status-inconsistent individual appears to be a free or freed (former slave) man. Yet, as a number of critics have pointed out, it is difficult to understand how joining a group that lowered his prestige in the eyes of the community (after all, women and slaves were equal members) would alleviate, instead of elevate, a man's sense of status inconsistency. When gender is considered, as it has been in a careful and sophisticated study by Antoinette Clark Wire, the picture changes dramatically. Wire suggests that the status inconsistency of wealthy or educated women and slaves would indeed be addressed by the egalitarian ethos of early Christianity, but the status of educated men like Paul would be lowered, posing the question of what additional factors or social impulses influenced free or freed men to enter the group and in what ways they may then have wanted to shape it. Analyzing the social needs that attracted people into early Christian groups and understanding the possible concerns for the social organization of the church they may have brought with them clearly must take account of gender and servitude.

In addition, the information on gender divisions that can be found in the New Testament or other Greco-Roman writings should be read as symbolic accounts and not as depictions of actual day-to-day social relations. The assumption in some texts that women's proper place is in the private sphere of the home is obviously disputed by Paul's occasional references to the travels of early Christian women (cf. Rom 16:1–4; Acts 18:1–3). Such an apparent contradiction simply points to the distance between social stereotypes and real social relations.

Social, sociological, and anthropological investigations of early Christian history provide a genuine heuristic value; that is, they pose new and often interesting questions, opening formerly unexplored avenues of research. Whether or not these methods have or will have substantive value, supplying additional, reliable information about early Christianity is much more doubtful, given the problematics of the methods themselves and the limitations imposed by the sources. To ensure the best possible fit (or the least distortion) between the material being studied and the sociological or anthropological model adopted, the first step in any analysis ought to be the fullest understanding of the historical material in its own Greco-Roman context. If New Testament sociologists accomplish this first step more adequately, the possibility of substantive results might increase. However, no matter how these methods are applied, feminists must always be aware that many of their modern presuppositions promote the invisibility of women, and feminists must always insist that no study be considered adequate without an analysis of gender.

NOTES

1. See the article by the same name by J. Stacey and B. Thorne, "The Missing Feminist Revolution in Sociology," *Social Problems* 32 (1985): 301–17.

2. For this discussion, see Elizabeth Spelman, *Inessential Woman: Problems of Exclusion in Feminist Thought* (Boston: Beacon Press, 1988), 37–55.

3. See Carolyn Osiek, *What Are They Saying About the Social Setting of the New Testament?* (New York: Paulist, 1984); Bengt Holmberg, *Sociology and the New Testament: An Appraisal* (Minneapolis: Fortress, 1990).

4. Richard Rohrbaugh, "'Social Location of Thought' as a Heuristic Construct in New Testament Study," *Journal for the Study of the New Testament* 30 (1987): 113. On the problem of commensurability, see Stanley Stowers, "The Social Sciences and the Study of Early Christianity," in *Approaches to Ancient Judaism V: Studies in Judaism and Its Greco-Roman Context*, ed. W. S. Green (Atlanta: Scholars Press, 1985), 149–81.

RECOMMENDED READINGS

Holmberg, Bengt. *Sociology and the New Testament: An Appraisal*. Minneapolis: Fortress, 1990.

Malina, Bruce. *The New Testament World: Insights from Cultural Anthropology*. Atlanta: John Knox, 1981.

Meeks, Wayne. *The First Urban Christians: The Social World of the Apostle Paul*. New Haven: Yale University Press, 1983.

Moore, Henrietta. *Feminism and Anthropology*. Minneapolis: University of Minnesota Press, 1988.

Nicholson, Linda, ed. *Feminism/Postmodernism*. New York: Routledge, 1990.

Osiek, Carolyn. *What Are They Saying About the Social Setting of the New Testament?* New York: Paulist, 1984.

Schüssler Fiorenza, Elisabeth. *In Memory of Her: A Feminist Theological Reconstruction of Christian Origins.* New York: Crossroad, 1983.

Stambaugh, John, and David Balch. *The New Testament in Its Social Environment.* Library of Early Christianity. Philadelphia: Westminster, 1986.

Theissen, Gerd. *The Sociology of Early Palestinian Christianity.* Philadelphia: Fortress, 1978.

Wire, Antoinette Clark. *The Corinthian Women Prophets: A Reconstruction through Paul's Rhetoric.* Minneapolis: Fortress, 1990.

18

♦ Toward a Multicultural
Ecumenical History of Women
in the First Century/ies C.E.

BARBARA H. GELLER NATHANSON ♦

THE TITLE OF THIS CHAPTER is both a challenge to and a goal of feminist historians. It evokes images of what Elisabeth Schüssler Fiorenza describes as the "ekklēsia of women," characteristics of which include "political equality, economic equality, social equality, religious equality, heterogeneity, inclusivity."[1] It is also a reminder that women's history is the histories of all women, "not just of white, Christian-born, non-poor, U.S.-American and North European women,"[2] and that gender is only one of a number of key factors that define women's opportunities and oppression in a given environment. For example, in discussing the writing of American women's history, Ann Gordon, Mari Jo Buhle, and Nancy Schrom Dye observed:

> The conceptual confusion created by unvarying and undifferentiated use of "oppression" to analyze women in the same period of time can be illustrated by the situation of women on an antebellum plantation. For the slave woman, oppression meant physical cruelty and sexual exploitation. For the leisured, financially comfortable plantation mistress, oppression, realized or not, was not physical hardship but social and legal constriction and oppressive sexuality. Focusing entirely on the bond women share by virtue of sex, the concept of oppression does little to explain the dynamics of either woman's life or of the historical conditions underlying it. It does violence to the lives of black women and men and sidesteps white women's role in that enslavement.[3]

Analogously, the data for women in the Roman Empire suggest that both one's economic status and one's political status, including one's status as slave or free, were decisive in determining how a woman spent her days. (Unlike Europe and the Americas of the past five hundred years, race was not generally a significant factor in determining the status of women in the empire.) As the preceding intimates, this essay focuses on women's history/ies in the Roman Empire. Specifically, it is a brief prolegomenon to the study of Jewish women of the first centuries C.E. in the empire, a topic that demands consideration of broader issues of multiculturalism and ecumenism.

The study of both Jewish and pagan women's history in the Roman era is important in its own right. It is also essential for any understanding of early Christian women's history, which cannot be divorced in its initial phase from its first-century Palestinian Jewish context, and thereafter from the larger context of women, both Jewish and non-Jewish, in the Roman Empire. The extant ancient sources make clear that the boundaries among such categories as "Jewish," "Christian," and "pagan" women were themselves, in varying degrees, according to time, place, and circumstance, blurred and changing during the first centuries C.E.[4]

In her pioneering study of women in early Christianity, Elisabeth Schüssler Fiorenza was emphatic:

> To speak about the Jesus movement is to speak about a Jewish movement that is part of Jewish history in the first century C.E. It is therefore misleading to speak about "Jesus and his Jewish background" as though Jesus' Judaism was not integral to his life and ministry, or to describe the behavior of Jesus' disciples over and against Jewish practice as though the first followers were not Jews themselves. . . . Such historical reconstructions of Christianity over and against Judaism can be continuing resources for Christian anti-Judaism because they perceive Christian origins in light of the historical fact of Christianity's separation from and partial rejection of its Jewish roots and heritage.[5]

As Schüssler Fiorenza notes, "[s]uch an anti-Jewish sentiment and historical misperception is especially deeply ingrained in popular consciousness."[6] In the same vein, it is very troubling to find in some Christian feminist writings a tendency to attribute Christian subordination of women largely to Christianity's Jewish roots, and concomitantly to view the freedom and opportunities offered to women in the early church as constituting a radical innovation and departure from Jewish practice.[7] It is important to note that there are few data which describe the social or economic status of Jewish women in the first century. The corpus of rabbinic literature is itself too late in date to serve as a reliable source for the first century. The New Testament is one of the major sources from which kernels of such information can be gleaned. In other words, the study of women in the New Testament should not be separated from the study of Jewish women's history; rather, it is an important component of such study. Of course, as Christianity made its way into the non-Jewish communities of the empire, the opportunities and limitations of Christian women were shaped in large part by the laws to which they were subject. For example, during the first and second centuries, a woman was more likely to be able to inherit property if she were a Roman citizen than if she were a citizen of one of the Greek cities of Roman Asia, many of which were the sites of long-standing Jewish communities and early Christian communities.

The necessity of situating earliest Christianity in its first-century Palestinian Jewish context can be broadened to make emphatic also the necessity for feminists to resist all efforts to "dehistoricize" the formative texts, both canonical and noncanonical, of the Jewish and Christian religious traditions. When texts are uprooted from their historical contexts, they are more likely to function as potent weapons from an arsenal directed against the "other," most often in early Christanity, the Jews. Two well-known examples will suffice to make this point. The Gospel of John, written almost certainly in the context of a late first-century Jewish Christian community, is both firmly rooted in its Jewish environment and at the same time regarded by many as the most anti-Jewish Gospel. The term "the Jews" appears seventy-one times in the Gospel and functions as a multipurpose designation for the opponents of Jesus. Chapter 8 is especially problematic. In response to the Jews' assertion that they have one father, God, Jesus says, "You are from your father the devil, and you choose to do your father's desires" (v. 44).[8] In its own time, such language probably reflected the anger and pain of the Johannine community, a small minority community within a small minority community in the landscape of the empire, as it became separate—divorced in a sense—from the larger Jewish community, and as it sought to establish its own identity outside of this other Judaism in an empire whose officials were less than receptive to "new religions from the East."[9] However, the ramifications of this and other documents that associated the Jews with the devil and the enemies of God, when loosed from their historical moorings and functioning as the "timeless" voices of the majority community of power and empire, require careful attention.

Consider, similarly, the anti-Judaism in John Chrysostom's homilies to the judaizing Christians of Antioch, an example from the fourth century, an era which Christianity entered as a persecuted minority faith community and exited as the official state religion, a century that witnessed also the breakdown of the Roman–Jewish *entente* that had functioned effectively since the close of the Bar Kokhba War in 135 C.E. and the delegitimization of the pagan religions, which were regarded by Rome's pre-Christian rulers as the sustainers and perpetuators of empire. As Robert Wilken writes in his excellent study *John Chrysostom and the Jews,* Chrysostom's sermons, delivered in 386 and 387, can be understood only in the context of an environment in which such standard-bearers of Nicene Christianity as John could not be sure that the future belonged to them, and in which Judaism remained a vital and attractive social and religious force both to pagans and to Christians, for many of whom the boundaries between Judaism and Christianity were blurred. John drew on his training in classical rhetoric to describe the Jews in the stock images of sickness, drunkenness, licentiousness, and thievery as well as what had become by the fourth century, what Wilken describes as stereotyped anti-Jewish Christian invective. John was also among the first to use the term "Christ-killer" to refer both to first-century and contemporary Jewry. Again, John's sermons, the words of an authoritative church father, would be divorced from their original context to contribute to Christian anti-Judaism of later generations.[10] As many historians have noted, the texts and teachings of the Jew as the demonic "other" were the necessary foundation for the anti-Jewish violence of medieval and modern Europe.[11]

Finally, any multicultural ecumenical history of women in the early empire must have as one of its starting points an acceptance of the legitimacy of its many ethnic and religious communities. Such an acceptance must avoid categories of inferiority and superiority as well as any arguments that one community or another had a monopoly on religious truths or right relationships with the divine. It is especially important in any consideration of Jewish women, since, of course, unlike the pagan religions of the empire, Judaism has survived. This may be challenging to those who juggle ecumenical commitments with a belief that Christianity is the only path for right relationship with God. In this connection, it is important to note that a number of New Testament scholars, including Krister Stendahl and John Gager, argue convincingly that postbiblical Christian exegetes have generally misinterpreted Paul, and that an accurate reading of Romans 9–11 suggests that he envisioned separate paths of salvation for Jews and Christians.[12] One must also remember that for millennia, the many forms of Greco-Roman paganism satisfied a broad range of needs for millions of people, providing them with very effective frameworks for making sense of their lives.

In different ways and to a greater and lesser degree, respectively, both rabbinic Judaism and the religions and governments of pagan Rome can serve as examples of religious tolerance and ecumenism. The formative documents of rabbinic Judaism reflect a consensus that salvation and right relationship with God were available, in separate paths, for righteous Jews and righteous Gentiles. The salvation of the latter depended on the individual's adherence to the six to ten commandments that the rabbis interpreted to be part of God's covenant with Noah.[13] The Roman government itself was generally tolerant of the religious diversity of its many peoples, except in those cases where it believed—to be sure, often mistakenly—that religious communities or associations were challenging the political rule of Rome. Thus the Roman–Jewish wars of the first and second centuries C.E. arose out of a constellation of factors prominent among which were the nationalist aspirations of some segments of the Jewish population. These factors did not include a Roman campaign against Judaism as such. It had been recognized as a licit religion at least since the time of Julius Caesar in the first century B.C.E. and was therefore under the protection of Roman law. The constant fear of political rebellion by Rome's small class of rulers, who administered an empire that at one time extended from Scotland to India and encompassed significant portions of three continents, was the primary reason for the episodic persecution of Christian communities through the early fourth century. Although Christianity was first declared a licit religion in the Edict of Toleration, issued in 313, as noted above, it exited the century as the offical state religion of the empire. Also by the end of the century, the now-Christian Roman emperors promulgated legislation both to close pagan temples and to eliminate pagan sacrifice, as well as to limit severely the spread of Judaism. This legislation, much of which echoed the pronouncements of the fourth-century church councils, sought also to impose group boundaries at a time when most Christians were new Christians and, again as noted above, when the boundaries among Jews, Christians, and pagans, were blurred and fluid.[14]

The groundbreaking studies of Ross Kraemer and Bernadette Brooten have not only put to rest long-held misconceptions about the restrictions in public life of Jewish women relative to their pagan and Christian counterparts, they have also added significantly to the growing understanding of the high degree to which at least some Jews participated in the social institutions and economic activities of the larger communities in which they resided. It should be remembered that a substantial corpus of inscriptions and papyri, as well as passages from the writings of Philo, Josephus, and several pagan authors, makes clear the existence of thriving Jewish communities in many of the urban centers and some of the villages of the Roman Empire. Thus Kraemer begins a study of diaspora Jewish women with an inscription from second-century C.E. Smyrna in Asia Minor:

> Rufina, a Jewess, head of the synagogue built this tomb for her freed slaves and the slaves raised in her household. No one else has the right to bury anyone [here]. Anyone who dares to do [so] will pay 1500 denaria to the

sacred treasury and 1000 denaria to the Jewish people. A copy of this inscription has been placed in the [public] archives.[15]

As Kraemer notes, this inscription is noteworthy for several reasons including the following: it makes no mention of a father, husband, son, or male guardian—that is, Rufina appears to be acting autonomously; Rufina calls herself "head of the synagogue," the Jewish title that appears most frequently in Roman-era inscriptions, usually, although not always, of men; she seems to run a household that includes her slaves and former slaves; she is sufficiently connected both to the Jewish and non-Jewish communities to demand a dual penalty for tomb violators and to deposit a copy of the inscription, perhaps, in the local archive.[16]

Rufina's inscription is one of nineteen Greek and Latin inscriptions that Bernadette Brooten has examined in which women bear the titles "head of the synagogue," "leader," "elder," "mother of the synagogue" "mother," "fatheress," and "priestess." The inscriptions date from the first century B.C.E. to the sixth century C.E., and come from Africa, Asia Minor, Crete, Egypt, Greece, Italy, and Thrace. Only one comes from Palestine, and it is a Greek inscription from the necropolis at Beth Shearim, a burial place for Jews both from the diaspora and from Palestine. Notwithstanding the lack of certainty concerning the functions associated with a given title and the variations in the regional distributions of some titles, Brooten argues convincingly that the inscriptions provide evidence that at least some women served in leadership positions in some synagogues.[17] It is likely that the officeholders, like those who held other Greco-Roman offices, were people of wealth and influence. The older scholarly consensus had assumed a priori that Jewish women could not have possibly served in official positions of authority in the ancient synagogue, and that therefore the titles must have been honorific, a reflection of the position of a father, husband, or son. The same titles, when associated with males, were assumed to be functional.

Although Tessa Rajak maintains that there are good reasons to suspect that for both men and women the titles were "essentially honorific" — especially given the presence of young children among the title bearers in some inscriptions—whether honorific or functional they point to the connection between Jewish communal practices and the larger Greco-Roman phenomenon of euergetism,[18] "the private subsidization of public services and amenities, . . . one of the primary sources of the vitality and stability of Graeco-Roman city-life."[19] Just as some pagan women of the empire were able to control and dispose of their property to make benefactions for which they received honors and which probably also both reflected and added to their influence, given the connections among wealth, philanthropy, and power, so too some Jewish women were able to act similarly and to participate in practices associated with euergetism. Inscriptions provide clear evidence that women were significant donors to synagogues.[20] It appears also that not all women donors to synagogues were Jews. Julia Severa, a high priestess during the reign of Nero, provided funds for the building of a synagogue at Acmonia, a benefaction which suggests the friendly relations between a Jewish community and a non-Jewish patron, and which may reflect the significant degree to which some, probably many, diaspora Jewish communities were connected with the major social and economic institutions of the cities in which they resided.[21] The famous "Godfearers" inscription from third-century Aphrodisias, also in Asia Minor, reveals the fluidity of group boundaries between some Jews and non-Jews, and the good relations between the Jewish and non-Jewish communities.[22] The epigraphic material from Aphrodisias suggests also that the president or patron of the Aphrodisian Jewish association which funded what may have been a soup kitchen was a woman, Iael. As Bernadette Brooten notes, Iael would not have been anomalous in Roman-period Aphrodisias, given the ample inscriptional evidence for women benefactors and officeholders.[23]

To be sure, Jewish women donors and officeholders, like their pagan counterparts, were atypical, both in their wealth and in their probable influence. Unfortunately, the extant data for both Jewish and non-Jewish women yield very little information about the lives of the majority of women who remained poor from the cradle to the grave. Their days were filled with a myriad of activities required to survive, including tasks associated with crop and food production, the production of clothing, and child care. However, the data for the wealthy Jewish women of the diaspora communities of the empire are instructive in a number of ways: they make clear the ability of at least some Jewish women to control and dispose of their property and to assume positions of public power and influence; they reveal significant elements of social and economic continuity between Jewish women and their pagan counterparts; they make clear that one can find models for the leadership positions held by women in the early church both in the Jewish and in the non-Jewish communities, and probably among women, who shared, at least in part, similar opportunities and power.

A consideration of some of the data for the elite Jewish women of the donor inscriptions makes clear the centrality of the study of nonliterary sources for any understanding of Jewish women's history. However, the sources are few in number, are often ambiguous as to whether or not they should be connected with a Jewish individual or community, and yield, at best, very fragmentary information. For example, they yield very little information about the religious practices of Jewish women. Several women from the Jewish community at Rome are described as "pious" in their epitaphs, to be sure a description consistent with that of the "ideal" women of pagan Roman epitaphs. However, one Jewish woman is described as a "lover of the commandments" and another as a "good pupil."[24] In an epitaph dated to the second century C.E., a woman is praised for her marital devotion, piety, love of her people, and observance of Jewish law:

> Here lies Regina, covered by such a tomb, which her husband set up as fitting to his love. After twice ten years she spent with him one year, four months and eight days more. She will live again, return to the light again, for she can hope that she will rise to the life promised, as is our true faith, to the worthy and the pious, in that she has deserved to possess an abode in the hallowed land. This your piety has assured you, this your chaste life, this your love for your people, this your observance of the Law, your devotion to your wedlock, the glory of which was dear to you. For all these deeds your hope of the future is assured. In this your sorrowing husband seeks his comfort.[25]

Although Regina's virtues have earned her a place in the world to come, as Kraemer notes, it is not at all clear how Regina enacted her piety and her love of her people, or what activities may have constituted observance of the law.[26] It should be added, however, that, for both men and women, the nature and range of Jewish religious activities in the communities of the diaspora are generally unclear, even for such practices as Sabbath observance, which is mentioned in a number of Jewish and non-Jewish sources.[27]

The papyri sources from Egypt are also elusive concerning religious practices; however, the "magical" papyri probably reflect religious practices common to both men and women.[28] The term "magic" merits careful consideration, especially since it is often used polemically, both in modern studies and in ancient sources, where it was used at times by religious elites to describe the practices of nonelites and "outsiders" even when the "insiders" engaged in similar practices.

Although the papyri do not provide much information about Jewish women's religious practices, they are very helpful in providing some understanding of broad demographic trends and, relative to most literary and epigraphic sources, yield data on women across a broad economic spectrum, including women of very modest economic means. The papyri give some indication of the range of occupations in which Jewish women were engaged and provide evidence that, like their non-Jewish counterparts, Jewish women in Roman-era Egypt were able to own land and livestock. Further, like those of their non-Jewish counterparts, the business transactions of some, but not all, involved a male legal guardian.[29]

The corpus of Egyptian papyri suggests also that most people, men and women, and Jews and non-Jews, were illiterate. However, Philo, philosopher, statesman, and a member of Alexandria's wealthy and educated Jewish stratum in the first century C.E., describes a community of Jewish monastics located near Alexandria, which included both men and women. The latter, called the Therapeutrides, were very educated and perhaps wealthy women who sought a contemplative life. According to Philo, they were "most of them aged virgins, who have kept their chastity not under compulsion. . . . Eager to have her [wisdom] for their life mate they have spurned the pleasures of the body and desire no mortal offspring. . . ."[30] Although Philo often writes negatively about women and the feminine, he is favorably disposed to the Therapeutrides, who, however, have renounced the traditional roles and activities of women.

It is only recently that studies of Jewish women in late antiquity have not focused almost entirely on the depictions of women's lives in the classical documents of rabbinic Judaism: the Mishnah, Tosefta, Palestinian and Babylonian Talmuds, and midrashic collections. The Mishnah, which covers a broad range of topics of Jewish law, includes legal rulings attributed to rabbis from an era prior to the editing of the Mishnah ca. 200 C.E. The Tosefta, which shares the Mishnah's organizational structure by topic, is a bit later in date and contains some material not found in the Mishnah. The Talmuds consist of mishnaic texts and commentaries on those texts by later generations of rabbis. The Palestinian Talmud was edited in Palestine ca. 400, the Babylonian Talmud, in Babylonia ca. 600. The midrashic collections of roughly the same time period consist of rabbinic scriptural interpretations and commentaries and are arranged by biblical text rather than topic.[31] These documents represent the recorded worldviews and attitudes of a type of late-antique class of male scholars and holy men. It is not at all clear to what degree their teachings were authoritative outside of their own academies and communities, or, indeed, what was their evolving status with and relationship to the larger Jewish population of which they were part, but, at the same time, from which they distinguished themselves in their own writings in various ways, especially in areas having to do with religious practices and observances.[32] It is not unlikely that their teachings were even less authoritative in the diaspora communities of the Roman Empire than they were in Palestine. It is only in later centuries that the documents noted above became the authoritative, formative, and "foundation" texts, in a sense, of what would become the dominant kind of Judaism. It should also be noted that one must be very cautious in generalizing about what "the rabbis say" since the same rabbinic document includes many voices and opinions on a given topic.

Not only is it unclear for whom, to what degree, and in which places the rabbis of Roman Palestine were authoritative; it is also unclear to what degree rabbinic literature reflected the realities of daily life. For example, as Judith Wegner notes, approximately two-thirds of the Mishnah is concerned with practices associated with the Jerusalem temple, which had been destroyed by the Roman army in 70 C.E., more than a century before the Mishnah was produced.[33]

As Jacob Neusner has discussed in his studies of the mishnaic orders of women and uncleannesses, the rabbinic interest in women was confined primarily to those points at which a woman was perceived as threatening the orderly and sanctified world which the rabbis created in their academies — at times of marriage and divorce when a woman and her property had to be transferred from the domain of her father to that of her husband and sometimes back again, and in the woman's capacity as a purveyor of uncleanness through her status as a menstruant.[34] As a mother, wife, or daughter, functioning in the framework of rabbinic law, a woman was to be cared for and honored. However, as a female, outside of the constraints of rabbinic law, she created chaos and disorder and was a source of danger. Thus Neusner writes: "And the goal and purpose of Mishnah's division of Women are to bring under control, and force into stasis all of [the Mishnah's conception of] the wild and unruly potentialities of female sexuality, with their dreadful threat of uncontrolled shifts in personal status and possession alike."[35]

Notwithstanding the overall concerns of the authors of the Mishnah, as Judith Wegner demonstrates in *Chattel or Person?*, her pioneering study of the status of women in the Mishnah, they do not treat all women alike.[36] In a later work, Wegner summarizes:

> The Mishnah recognized three classes of dependent woman: minor daughter, wife, and levirate widow. Each woman is legally controlled by the man who owns the sole right to use or profit from her biological function: her father, husband, or brother-in-law as the case may be. Corresponding to these dependent women are three classes of autonomous women: emancipated [i.e., adult unmarried] daughter, divorcee, and regular widow. In their legal entitlements and obligations, these three subgroups form mirror images of their dependent counterparts.[37]

Whereas, for example, a dependent woman could not arrange her own marriage, an emancipated woman could do so. Similarly, the latter, unlike the dependent woman, could keep her earnings and control and dispose of her property.[38] This suggests that in whatever was the domain of rabbinic authority, some women could accrue wealth. Furthermore, according to the Mishnah, if a husband divorced or predeceased his wife, the property that she had brought into the marriage or had acquired by gift or inheritance reverted to her control.[39]

The Mishnah, Talmuds, and Midrash envisioned women's roles as generally confined to the domestic and private sphere, focusing on such activities as food preparation, child care, and weaving. Thus, the Mishnah states that a woman had to fulfill certain obligations to her husband including grinding flour and baking bread, cooking food, washing clothes, preparing his bed, nursing her child, and working in wool. The same passage is illustrative also of the ways in which economic status shaped the ways a woman spent her days, for the wife's obligations decreased in relationship to the number of servants she brought into the household.[40]

Not surprisingly, rabbinic literature is concerned in large part with the activities of the rabbis, for whom achievement and, indeed, holiness were based on the study of Torah and the performance of commandments. In general, women were exempted from the study of Torah and from all commandments that were positive and time-bound.[41] As Wegner comments:

> Though the Mishnah gives no reason for women's exemption, the likeliest explanation lies in the pervasive androcentrism of the sages. Viewing woman primarily as man's enabler, they wish to avoid situations that may impede that function — above all, to prevent women from exercising a possible preference for some alternative role. To this end they first *exempt* women from precepts whose performance might interfere with domestic duties, and then — in a classic catch-22 — argue that women cannot lead others in the performance of precepts *from which they are exempt.*[42]

Both the Mishnah and the Talmuds yield little information on Jewish women's religious practices. There were no festivals specific to women.[43] However, three precepts were incumbent on women: the lighting of candles at the beginning of the Sabbath; the challah precept, which mandated the separating and burning of a piece of dough prior to baking the bread; and the observance of the laws of the menstruant.[44] Some texts identify these precepts as punishments for Eve's transgressions.[45] Intriguingly, Kraemer raises the possibility that the first and the second may be connected, in some way, with practices associated with the worship of goddesses, both in earlier Israelite communities and in the non-Jewish communities of the Roman Empire.[46]

It is worth noting again that rabbinic literature yields far more information on the roles of women in the intellectual landscapes of the rabbis than on the opportunities, restrictions, and activities of Jewish women in Roman Palestine. The few and fragmentary sources for the latter provide more questions than answers. For example, in reading the Mishnah and Talmuds, one is barely aware of the presence of the Roman court system in Palestine. To what laws were Jewish women subject? Who, when, where, under what circumstances, and at whose bidding did Jewish women make use of the Roman court system? This would seem to be a very important question, especially since Emperor Caracalla's Antonine Constitution of 212, which extended Roman citizenship to most of the inhabitants of the empire, is roughly contemporary with the editing of the Mishnah, the earliest rabbinic document. Did Palestinian Jewish women seek divorces from the Roman courts especially given that rabbinic law enabled only men to initiate divorces? Consider, for example, the possible social context for Josephus's comment, written in the first century C.E., that Salome divorced her husband and sent him a document that was "not in accordance with Jewish law"?[47]

The second-century archive of Babata, a cache of legal documents found in the Judean desert and belonging to a young Jewish widow of not insignificant wealth, is illustrative of the broad questions raised above. The cache consists of thirty-five documents, of which three are in Aramaic, six in Nabatean, seventeen in Greek, and eleven in Greek with Aramaic or Nabatean signatures or subscriptions. They include Babata's property deeds, marriage documents "with their remarkable blend of Roman, Greek, and Jewish elements,"[48] documents concerning lawsuits brought by and against her on matters of property, as well as those concerning litigation she was pursuing to have the guardianship of the son of her deceased husband transferred to her.[49] Many of these documents conform to Roman law and were issued by the regional branch of the imperial bureaucracy at Petra.[50]

Both Jewish literary sources and the growing body of evidence from excavations and regional surveys of Roman Palestine reveal the rapid rate of urbanization in the first centuries C.E., and the presence of Jews and non-Jews who lived in close proximity to one another and who had ongoing business relationships, such that the rabbis legislated concerning those rare instances in which such transactions were prohibited or restricted.[51] Thus Ze'ev Maoz writes:

> Many a Hellenistic polis [in Palestine] had a well-established Jewish community (Caesarea, Scythopolis, Ptolemais, Gadara, Hippos, Gerasa and others), while in Roman times, most predominantly Jewish towns included Gentiles among their inhabitants (Tiberias, Diocaesarea, Diospolis and others). In the Roman-Byzantine period there was a growing tendency towards a mixed urban population due to economic and other factors.[52]

Again, the data raise questions more than provide answers. In what ways did the religious and ethnic diversity of the cities of Roman Palestine affect and shape the lives of the cities' Jewish women? Similarly, how were the lives of Jewish women shaped by an urban architectural and artistic style which represented an evolving, creative melange of Greek, Roman, and local elements? Minimally, the preceding suggests that the environment existed in which one could expect to find Jewish households whose lives were very similar to those of their non-Jewish counterparts.

Finally, it is interesting to note the great similarities among the images of the "ideal" woman of the New Testament household codes, the later rabbinic documents, and the works of the Roman orators, historians, and elegists, as well as those epitaphs for pagan women of the empire which mention more than the name and age of the deceased. The epitaph of a Roman housewife of the first century B.C.E. sums it up: "Here lies Amynome wife of Marcus best and most beautiful, worker in wool, pious, chaste, thrifty, faithful, a stayer-at-home."[53] Some historians, anthropologists, and textual critics link the common images of the "good" and, conversely, the "bad" woman with a long-time "Mediterranean culture of honor and shame" in which men accrue honor or shame, in large part, in response to the sexual conduct of the women in their family.[54] Interestingly, Livy and Tacitus, in their histories of Rome, not only wrote with great admiration about those women who were obedient and loyal to their father or husband at whatever cost to themselves, and who kept their chastity even at the expense of their own lives; they suggested also that the very well-being of the Roman state was dependent on the behavior of such women.[55]

Of course, the image of the "ideal" woman depicted in Amynome's epitaph must be balanced with sources that depict upper-class Roman women attending dinner parties, games, and the theater, and also, Roman women participating in a broad range of occupations including some in the fields of medicine, philosophy, professional athletics, artistry, and trade. So too, as noted above, some Roman women held municipal offices and were honored as benefactors.[56]

Notwithstanding the paucity and ambiguity of the data for Jewish women's history/ies both in Palestine and in the diaspora, the sources make clear that Jewish women of the first centuries C.E., like their non-Jewish sisters, were engaged in a much broader range of activities than what is suggested by the rabbinic equivalent of the "weaver of wool and stayer-at-home." They illustrate also that one cannot speak of Jewish women as if they were a homogeneous group, or divorce them from the larger environments of which they were part. It is perhaps fitting that much of the concluding section of this essay consists of questions — questions which demand continued study of a broad range of literary and nonliterary sources, and which require that we question our own assumptions about group boundaries and categories, both for antiquity and for the present.

NOTES

1. Elisabeth Schüssler Fiorenza, *But She Said: Feminist Practices of Biblical Interpretation* (Boston: Beacon Press, 1992), 119.

2. Bernadette J. Brooten, "Jewish Women's History in the Roman Period: A Task for Christian Theology," in *Christians Among Jews and Gentiles: Essays in Honor of Krister Stendahl on His Sixty-Fifth Birthday,* ed. George W. E. Nickelsburg with George W. MacRae, S.J. (Philadelphia: Fortress, 1986), 30. Brooten's statement of her goals for contemporary Christian theology continues: "Further, Christian theology needs women's history in order to articulate a theology which takes Christian women's experiences into account and which allows non-Christian women to live their lives fully and in peace. Understanding something of Jewish women's past can help us to understand and live together with Jewish women in our society today. The same is true for the history of women of other religious traditions."

3. Ann D. Gordon, Mari Jo Buhle, and Nancy Schrom Dye, "The Problem of Women's History," in *Liberating Women's History: Theoretical and Critical Essays,* ed. Berenice A. Carroll (Urbana: University of Illinois Press, 1976), 86–87.

4. On Jewish group boundaries in the Roman Empire, see Tessa Rajak's insightful essay, "The Jewish Community and its Boundaries," in *The Jews Among Pagans and Christians in the Roman Empire,* ed. Judith Lieu, John North, and Tessa Rajak (London and New York: Routledge, 1992), 9–28.

5. Elisabeth Schüssler Fiorenza, *In Memory of Her: A Feminist Theological Reconstruction of Christian Origins* (New York: Crossroad, 1985), 105.

6. Ibid.

7. See Judith Plaskow's chapter on anti-Judaism in feminist Christian interpretation in this volume. See also Bernadette J. Brooten, "Early Christian Women and Their Cultural Context: Issues of Method in Historical Reconstruction," in *Feminist Perspectives on Biblical Scholarship,* ed. Adela Yarbro Collins (Biblical Scholarship in North America 10; Chico, CA: Scholars Press, 1985), 65–91.

8. John Gager writes similarly in his valuable study *The Origins of Anti-Semitism: Attitudes Toward Judaism in Pagan and Christian Antiquity* (New York: Oxford University Press, 1985), 151–52.

9. Many New Testament scholars offer very plausible arguments that the Gospel of John reflects the expulsion of the Johannine community from some Jewish community and is thus, in a sense, one half of a kind of conversation. However, such a conclusion must be somewhat tentative, especially in the absence of contemporary Jewish texts that might constitute the second half of that conversation. On Roman religious tolerance, see Richard Gordon, "Religion in the Roman Empire," in *Pagan Priests,* ed. Mary Beard and John North (London: Duckworth, 1990), 235–55.

10. Robert Wilken, *John Chrysostom and the Jews: Rhetoric and Reality in the Late Fourth Century* (Berkeley: University of California Press, 1983); see also Barbara G. Nathanson, "Wilken's *John Chrysostom and the Jews,*" *Jewish Quarterly Review* 75 (1985): 408–10.

11. This is not to equate Christian anti-Judaism with racial anti-Semitism. The former

sought the conversion and not the murder of the Jews; the latter eliminated conversion as an option and in its most virulent forms sought the physical annihilation of all Jews. Indeed, racial anti-Semitism was always implicitly, and often explicitly, anti-Christian. However, as Rosemary Ruether has written in her very thoughtful and thought-provoking essay "The 'Faith and Fratricide' Discussion: Old Problems and New Dimensions," in *AntiSemitism and the Foundations of Christianity,* ed. Alan T. Davies (New York: Paulist Press, 1979), "The Church had thought of Jewishness as a religion as a demonic contagion, but the Jew as person as redeemable. But it helped prepare the minds of Europeans for the confusion of the two long before the rise of Nazism. It fomented a popular Jew-hate that did not understand the theological distinctions of Christian anti-Judaism any more than it understood the anti-Christian intentions of Nazi Jew-hate (p. 250)."

12. See, e.g., Krister Stendahl, *Paul Among Jews and Gentiles* (Philadelphia: Fortress, 1976); and John Gager, *Origins of Anti-Semitism.* However, there are also plausible arguments to the contrary. Thus, Daniel Harrington concludes, "it is very difficult to hold anything but the Christological interpretation of Romans 11:25–26. The eschatological salvation of all Israel must have some explicit connection with the saving work of Christ. That, at least, is the logic of Romans" ("Paul and Judaism: Five Puzzles," *Bible Review* 9/2 [April 1993]: 52).

13. See, e.g., in the Babylonian Talmud, *Baba Qamma* 38a, quoted in Alan Segal, *Rebecca's Children: Judaism and Christianity in the Roman World* (Cambridge, MA: Harvard University Press, 1986), 168, and the helpful discussion on pp. 167–71.

14. For example, from the reign of Constantius (337–361), the first Roman emperor who was born and raised as a Christian, see, in the Theodosian Code, 16.8.6 and 16.10.2, 4–6. See also the discussion in Barbara Geller Nathanson, "Jews, Christians, and the Gallus Revolt in Fourth-Century Palestine," *Biblical Archaeologist* 49 (March 1986): 26–36.

15. *CIJ* 741, as translated in Ross S. Kraemer, "Jewish Women in the Diaspora World of Late Antiquity," in *Jewish Women in Historical Perspective,* ed. Judith Baskin (Detroit: Wayne State University Press, 1991), 43.

16. Kraemer, "Jewish Women," 43.

17. Bernadette Brooten, *Women Leaders in the Ancient Synagogue: Inscriptional Evidence and Background Issues* (Brown Judaic Studies 36; Chico, CA: Scholars Press, 1982).

18. Rajak, "Jewish Community," 22–23.

19. Guy Rogers, "The Gift and Society in Roman Asia: Orthodoxies and Heresies," *Scripta Classica Israelica* 12 (1993): 1 (forthcoming). See also Riet Van Bremen, "Women and Wealth," in *Images of Women in Antiquity,* ed. Averil Cameron and Amélie Kuhrt (Detroit: Wayne State University Press, 1983), 223–42.

20. See, e.g., the appendix to Brooten's *Women Leaders,* in which she presents twenty-three inscriptions from Palestine and the diaspora in which women are synagogue donors. See also the valuable discussion in Ross Kraemer, *Her Share of the Blessings: Women's Religions Among Pagans, Jews, and Christians in the Greco-Roman World* (New York: Oxford University Press, 1992), esp. pp. 106–7, 118–23.

21. See Brooten, *Women Leaders,* 158 no. 6, and the helpful discussion in Kraemer, *Her Share of the Blessings,* 119–20.

22. Joyce Reynolds and Robert Tannenbaum, *Jews and God-Fearers at Aphrodisias: Greek Inscriptions with Commentary* (Cambridge: Cambridge Philological Society, 1987).

23. Bernadette Brooten, "Iael Prostatēs in the Jewish Donative Inscription from Aphro-

disias," in *The Future of Early Christianity,* ed. Birger Pearson (Minneapolis: Fortress, 1991), 149–62.

24. *CII* 132; 215, cited in Ross Kraemer, "Non-Literary Evidence for Jewish Women in Rome and Egypt," in *Rescuing Creusa: New Methodological Approaches to Women in Antiquity,* Marilyn Skinner, guest editor, *Helios* 13 (1986): 89.

25. *CIJ* 476, as translated in *Maenads, Martyrs, Matrons, Monastics: A Sourcebook on Women's Religions in the Greco-Roman World,* ed. Ross Kraemer (Philadelphia: Fortress, 1988), 301.

26. Kraemer, "Non-Literary Evidence for Jewish Women in Rome and Egypt," 90.

27. See the helpful discussion in Rajak, "Jewish Community," 14–19.

28. See, similarly, the translation of a tablet of uncertain date in which a woman binds a divine spirit to bring her the man whom she wishes to marry (*Maenads, Martyrs, Matrons, and Monastics,* ed. Kraemer, 108–9).

29. See, e.g., *CPJ* 19, 146, 148, and 183, in *Maenads, Martyrs, Matrons, Monastics,* ed. Kraemer, 81–82, 86–87, 89–90.

30. Philo, *On the Contemplative Life* 68–69, as translated in *Maenads, Martyrs, Matrons, Monastics,* ed. Kraemer, 27; see also Ross Kraemer, "Monastic-Jewish Women in Greco-Roman Egypt: Philo on the Therapeutrides," *Signs: Journal of Women in Culture and Society* 14 (1989): 342–70.

31. See, similarly, Kraemer, *Her Share of the Blessings,* 93–94; and Judith Romney Wegner, "The Image and Status of Women in Classical Rabbinic Judaism," in *Jewish Women in Historical Perspective,* ed. Baskin, 68–69.

32. See the helpful study by Lee Levine, *The Rabbinic Class of Roman Palestine in Late Antiquity* (Jerusalem: Yad Izhak Ben-Zvi; New York: Jewish Theological Seminary of America, 1989).

33. Wegner, "Image and Status of Women in Classical Rabbinic Judaism," 69.

34. Jacob Neusner, "From Scripture to Mishnah: The Origins of Mishnah's Division of Women," *Journal of Jewish Studies* 30 (1979): 143; idem, *A History of the Mishnaic Law of Women Part Five: The Mishnaic System of Women* (Leiden: Brill, 1980), 263.

35. Neusner, *History of the Mishnaic Law of Women,* 271; see also Barbara Nathanson, "Reflections on the Silent Woman of Ancient Judaism and Her Pagan Roman Counterpart," in *The Listening Heart: Essays in Wisdom and the Psalms in honor of R. E. Murphy,* ed. Kenneth Hoglund et al. (Journal for the Study of the Old Testament Supplement Series 58; Sheffield: Sheffield Academic Press, 1987), 259–60.

36. Judith Wegner, *Chattel or Person? The Status of Women in the Mishnah* (New York and Oxford: Oxford University Press, 1988).

37. Wegner, "Image and Status of Women in Classical Rabbinic Judaism," 70–71.

38. See, e.g., Mishnah (M) *Ketubot* 4:4, 6:1, *Kiddushin* 2:1, *Baba Metzia* 1:5, *Niddah* 5:7, cited in Wegner, "Image and Status of Women in Classical Rabbinic Judaism," 71, 74.

39. See, e.g., M. *Ketubot* 4:2; 11:2.

40. M. *Ketubot* 5:5. See also the helpful study by Samuel Morell, "An Equal or a Ward: How Independent is a Married Woman According to Rabbinic Law," *Jewish Social Studies* 44 (1982): 189–210.

41. See, e.g., M. *Kiddushin* 1:7, *Soṭah* 3:4, Tosefta *Berakot* 2:12.

42. Wegner, *Chattel or Person?* 154–55. The emphases are Wegner's. As Wegner notes, there were many exceptions to the principle wherein women were exempted from time-bound positive precepts, especially where such exceptions served to fulfill the woman's role

as the enabler whose actions, for example, prevented her husband from committing transgressions.

43. As Wegner notes, M. *Pesaḥim* 8:7 prohibited women, together with slaves and minors, from forming fellowship groups to sacrifice the paschal lamb at Passover (*Chattel or Person?* 148–49).

44. On the laws of the menstruant in rabbinic Judaism and the issue of menstrual impurity in early Christianity, see the excellent study by Shaye Cohen, "Menstruants and the Sacred in Judaism and Christianity," in *Women's History and Ancient History*, ed. Sarah Pomeroy (Chapel Hill and London: University of North Carolina Press, 1991), 273–91.

45. See, e.g., *Genesis Rabbah* 17:7.

46. Kraemer, *Her Share of the Blessings*, 100–101.

47. Josephus, *Antiquities* 15.259–60. An Egyptian papyrus, *CPJ* 144, from the reign of Augustus may describe the divorce of a Jewish couple by mutual content. See *Maenads, Martyrs, Matrons, Monastics*, ed. Kraemer, 88. On the possibility that some ancient Jewish traditions, perhaps reflected in Mark 10:12, allowed both men and women to initiate divorces, see Bernadette Brooten, "Zur Debatte über das Scheidungsrecht der jüdischen Frau," *Evangelische Theologie* 43 (1983): 466–78.

48. Naphtali Lewis, Ranon Katzoff, Jonas Greenfield, "Papyrus Yadin 18," *Israel Exploration Journal* 37 (1987): 236. See also *Documents from the Bar Kochba Period in the Cave of Letters: Greek Papyri*, ed. Naphtali Lewis (Jerusalem: Israel Exploration Society, 1989).

49. Yigael Yadin, *Bar Kochba* (New York: Random House, 1971), 222–54.

50. Nathanson, "Reflections on the Silent Woman," 263.

51. Nathanson, "Reflections on the Silent Woman," 267; see, e.g., M. *Avodah Zarah*.

52. Ze'ev Maoz, "Comments on Jewish and Christian Communities in Byzantine Palestine," *Palestine Exploration Quarterly* 117 (1985): 64.

53. ILS 8402, as translated in Mary Lefkowitz and Maureen Fant, *Women's Life in Greece and Rome* (Baltimore: Johns Hopkins University Press, 1992), 17.

54. See, e.g., Claudia Camp's essay on honor and shame in the book of Ben Sira, "Understanding a Patriarchy: Women in Second Century Jerusalem Through the Eyes of Ben Sira," in *"Women Like This" New Perspectives on Jewish Women in the Greco-Roman World*, ed. Amy-Jill Levine (Atlanta: Scholars Press, 1991), 1–39.

55. See, e.g., Livy, *History of Rome* 1.58, on the suicide of Lucretia.

56. Nathanson, "Reflections on the Silent Woman," 270. See the very valuable collection of sources in Lefkowitz and Fant, *Women's Life;* see also Sarah Pomeroy, *Goddesses, Whores, Wives, and Slaves* (New York: Schocken, 1975); Eva Cantarella, *Pandora's Daughters: The Role and Status of Women in Greek and Roman Antiquity* (Baltimore and London: Johns Hopkins University Press, 1987); Jane Gardner, *Women in Roman Law and Society* (Bloomington and Indianapolis: Indiana University Press, 1986).

RECOMMENDED READINGS

Brooten, Bernadette. *Women Leaders in the Ancient Synagogue: Inscriptional Evidence and Background Issues*. Brown Judaic Studies 36. Chico, CA: Scholars Press, 1982.

Cantarella, Eva. *Pandora's Daughters: The Role and Status of Women in Greek and Roman Antiquity*. Translated by Maureen B. Fant. Baltimore and London: Johns Hopkins University Press, 1987.

Kraemer, Ross Shepard. *Her Share of the Blessings: Women's Religions Among Pagans, Jews, and Christians in the Greco-Roman World.* New York and Oxford: Oxford University Press, 1992.

———, ed. *Maenads, Martyrs, Matrons, Monastics: A Sourcebook on Women's Religions in the Greco-Roman World.* Philadelphia: Fortress, 1988.

Lefkowitz, Mary R., and Maureen B. Fant. *Women's Life in Greece and Rome: A source book in translation.* 2nd ed. Baltimore: Johns Hopkins University Press, 1992.

Nathanson, Barbara Geller. "Reflections on the Silent Woman of Ancient Judaism and Her Pagan Roman Counterpart." In *The Listening Heart: Essays in Wisdom and the Psalms in Honor of Roland E. Murphy, O. Carm.* Edited by Kenneth Hoglund et al., 259–79. Journal for the Study of the Old Testament Supplement Series 58. Sheffield: Sheffield Academic Press, 1987.

Pomeroy, Sarah B. *Goddesses, Whores, Wives and Slaves: Women in Classical Antiquity.* New York: Schocken, 1975.

———. *Women in Hellenistic Egypt: From Alexander to Cleopatra.* New York: Schocken, 1984.

Schüssler Fiorenza, Elisabeth. *In Memory of Her: A Feminist Theological Reconstruction of Christian Origins.* New York: Crossroad, 1983.

Wegner, Judith. *Chattel or Person? The Status of Women in the Mishnah.* New York and Oxford: Oxford University Press, 1988.

❖ Reconstruction of Women's Early Christian History

KAREN JO TORJESEN ◆

METHODOLOGICAL ISSUES: THE MEDITERRANEAN GENDER SYSTEM

THE EARLY TRADITIONS out of which Christianity constructs its history were formed in the cultural milieu of patriarchal Mediterranean society. Thus the literary legacy of the first generations of Christian intellectuals is distorted by the cultural assumption that male activity is normative. Elisabeth Schüssler Fiorenza in *In Memory of Her* provides a critical analysis of the way androcentric selection of traditions and androcentric translations have suppressed the memory of women's contribution to formative Christianity.[1] The androcentrism of ancient Mediterranean societies had a particular configuration; it was constituted by patterns of gender beliefs which distinguished sharply between male and female honor and between public and private space. In terms of the ancient public–private social theory, the public sphere of the state was inherently superior to the private sphere of the household and constituted the only arena of freedom and civilized culture. It was the primary locus of male identity. The domestic sphere was the locus of female identity. The gender ideology that described the *polis* (city) as a male domain and the *oikos* (household) as a female sphere segregated women from public, political life but gave them a great deal of power in the private sphere.

The public–private gender ideology was supported by a system of cultural values that differentiated sharply between male and female honor. Honor was equivalent to reputation, an acknowledged claim to social worth. Although both men and women strove to enhance their public persona of honor and evinced the same concern for their reputations in the eyes of others, a man achieved honor through challenging another man's honor successfully and by avenging any loss of honor of his own. In contrast, a woman's honor consisted in her reputation for chastity, understood as a sense of shame. Shame, the defining quality of womanhood was manifested in passivity, subordination, and seclusion within the household. Since Christian writers viewed women's activities through the lens of their society's beliefs about gender, their accounts of women's activities and their polemic against women leaders must be interpreted critically in the light of the system of sexual politics current in the ancient Mediterranean.

Consequently, although women's words, women's achievements, and women's lives were an integral part of the fabric of every Christian community, women's contributions to formative Christianity have been largely suppressed or ignored. Although women such as Mary Magdalene were prominent in an early tradition, their importance was muted through the ongoing process of reworking those traditions to make them conform better to contemporary beliefs about gender. As the varied ministries of the church became institutionalized and as the context of Christian worship shifted from house-churches to a more public space, the role of women leaders became increasingly controversial. Furthermore, the long process of canonization, which began in the middle of the second century and concluded in the early fourth century took place concurrently with a struggle over women's leadership. Consequently, books celebrating women's apostolic activity (*Acts of Thecla*), containing women's words (collections of oracles of women prophets), and transmitting women's teachings (*Gospel of Mary*), which had nurtured the religious life of many churches, were not included in the canon, which was defined in terms of male authorship.

Nevertheless, women made considerable contributions to the development of Christianity during the first four centuries and provided leadership for communities of Christians throughout the Mediterranean. Schüssler Fiorenza warns that "women's actual social-religious status must be determined by the degree of their economic autonomy and social roles, rather than by ideological or prescriptive statements."[2] Only through a "hermeneutic of suspicion" can the actual contributions of women be discerned behind the gender rhetoric of male writers. Furthermore, she shows that the theological foundations for women's leadership were laid in the Christian vision of the reign of God (*basileia*) in which God's wholeness was extended to all, making women and men equal.[3] Despite the androcentric retelling of women's stories, treatises from this formative period reveal that women were apostles, prophets, and teachers; that they exercised a diversity of ministries including baptizing, disciplining, and presiding over the

Eucharist; and that they held the full range of church offices — bishop, presbyter, widow, deacon, and virgin.

METHODOLOGICAL ISSUES: SOURCES

A twentieth-century reconstruction of women's roles in the formation of Christianity depends on two kinds of sources, literary and documentary. Both were formed in the patriarchal cultural milieu of the ancient Mediterranean; however, the Mediterranean beliefs about public and private and honor and shame impacted them differently. Although literary sources are attractive for their rich detail, emotional nuances, and intellectual content, they speak in terms of "generic woman." In patriarchal societies generic woman is a reified notion of woman expressive of male interests in controlling them. Generally, the appeal to generic woman functions to minimize woman's power and to circumscribe her sphere of activity. These literary sources, comprising letters, gospels, apocalypses, acts, histories, and theological treatises written by men, not only provide a report of women's activities; they also illuminate the tensions created when women's leadership intersected with Mediterranean beliefs about male honor and female shame and public male space and private female space.

These literary sources yield valuable clues about women's activities when they are read with a critical awareness of the dynamics of the Mediterranean gender system. Often it is the case that we gain an insight into women's activities only through a polemical attack on women's leadership. For example, much can be learned from an injunction against widows baptizing in the *Didascalia,* a third-century church order.

> We do not advise that a woman baptize, nor that anyone allow themselves
> to be baptized by a woman, for it is a transgression of the commandment
> and a great danger for the one who is baptized and the one who baptizes.
> (*Didascalia* 15)

It is clear not only that women were baptizing but also that converts sought out women to baptize them. Women in the order of widows were counted as members of the clergy and enjoyed high regard in Christian congregations, since new converts sought out these powerful women ministers for baptism.

In the course of the same polemic the writer tries to dissuade widows from exercising public ministries by urging them to return to private spaces:

> Let a widow know that she is the altar of God. And let her constantly sit
> at home. A widow must not therefore wander or run about among houses,

for those who are roving and have no shame cannot stay quiet even in their houses. (*Didascalia* 15)

Only by staying in private space could a widow preserve her honor, that is, her reputation for chastity. This writer uses inflammatory terms, "wandering and running about," to characterize widows involved in public ministry and to raise questions about their chastity. His innuendos imply that widows in public ministry are shameless because their presence in public male space shows that they have no concern for their sexual reputations.

On the other hand, documentary sources for women's activities such as dedicatory inscriptions, funerary epitaphs, statues, and portraits function to enhance the honor of a family through highlighting the achievements of an individual woman. Instead of speaking about "generic woman" in the interests of controlling her, these sources record the name, family relations, benefactions, offices, and public honors of a particular woman in order to honor her. Since these works were commissioned by devoted family members or grateful communities, they provide us with the details of an individual woman's achievements in a context in which the legitimacy of these activities is not being contested.[4]

Bernadette Brooten has demonstrated the importance of documentary sources for reconstructing the history of women in Judaism. By studying Jewish inscriptions, she demonstrates that Jewish women held important offices, including ruler of the synagogue, elder, priest, and mother of the synagogue.[5] An inscription from Smyrna, for example, reads, "Rufina a Jewess, Head of the Synagogue"; another from Crete reads "Sophia of Gortyn, Elder and Head of the Synagogue." Inscriptions from Rome (Sara Ura), Italy (Beronike, Mannine, and Faustina), Thrace (Rebeka), Malta (Eulogia), and Africa (Makaria) testify to the presence of Jewish women who were elders in their communities.[6] Among Jewish epitaphs are three that commemorate Jewish women who held the title of priestess, one from Rome (Gaudentia), one from Israel (Lady Maria), and one from Egypt, which reads "O Marin priestess, worthy one and friend to all."[7] It is striking how widespread the documentary evidence for women's leadership in Jewish communities is. It is found around the Mediterranean and spans six centuries.

Although no comprehensive study of inscriptions for Christian women has been done, preliminary studies of documentary evidence present a similar picture of women's leadership. Epitaphs from Egypt (Artemidoras), Phrygia (Ammio), Greece (Epiktas), and Sicily (Kale) honor Christian women who were presbyters in their congregations.[8] Evidence for women holding the office of deacon is equally impressive, although more complex since the office of deacon changed more dramatically in function than other offices. It evolved from that of leader of the congregation in the first century to assistant to the bishop in the third century. During the first three centuries the office of deacon was ungendered, meaning that both men and women held the office and performed the same functions. By the fourth century the office of deaconness appears as a woman's office whose ministry was exclusively to women. Deaconesses assisted in the baptism of women catechumens, regulated women's conduct in church, and visited women when they were sick. Women deacons were known in Asia Minor (Phoebe), Cappadocia (Maria), Achaia (Aggripiane), Melos (Agliasis), Macedonia (Matrona), Delphi (Athanasia), Bithynia (Kirazalia), and Jerusalem (Sophia). From the geographical spread of these inscriptions, it is clear that the office of deaconess was common among the Greek-speaking churches of the eastern Mediterranean.[9] Since the Latin cultures of the western Mediterranean did not insist on gender segregation during Christian worship, the special functions performed by deaconesses for the women of Greek congregations were not considered necessary. Therefore a specialized female order of deacons does not appear in the Latin sources for this period.

Documentary evidence also includes works of art, such as mosaics, paintings, and statues. These also offer tantalizing clues about women's roles in early Christian communities. In the labyrinthian catacombs under the streets of Rome are paintings that portray women in ministry. One scene shows seven women seated around a semi-circular table on which loaves of bread are set.[10] The central woman seems to be presiding over this eucharistic ritual. In a Roman basilica dedicated to two women saints, Prudentiana and Praxedis, is a mosaic portraying the two saints, Mary, and a fourth woman. A carefully lettered inscription identifies the figure on the far left as Episcopa Theodora, Bishop Theodora.[11] Do we have here documentary evidence for women bishops?

Women's roles in Greek and Roman religions provide a framework for interpreting the documentary evidence for women's leadership in Jewish and Christian communities. In Greek society women's roles in public religion were well established. In Asia Minor Tata of Aphrodisias served as priestess of Hera and at the same time as a priestess of the imperial cult. Aba of Histria in Thrace was a high priestess of Cybele; Berenice of Syros served as priestess of Demeter and Kore.[12] Women also served as priestesses of Isis. Depending on the size of temple and town, priestesses were responsible for a wide range of activities: the performance of purification rites for the temple, care and protection of temple facilities (statues, temple treasures, cultic equipment), leading processions, presiding over rituals, and sponsoring banquets in honor of the deity. In larger towns and for larger temples these functions would be divided among temple staff.[13]

In Rome, priests for the official cults were organized into colleges, many of which were male. Nevertheless, the most important college, the College of Vestal Virgins, was made up of priestesses of Vesta whose residence was situated at the administrative heart of the Roman Empire—the Forum. These women priests enjoyed some of the rights and privileges of male magistrates—the right to be accompanied by lictors (a retinue for state officials) and the right to commute a death sentence. Further, they possessed some of the rights of male citizens—the right to bequeath property and the right to represent themselves in court. Roman matrons celebrated the Matronalia, a festival in honor of Juno Licinia, as well as the Veneralia, which celebrated Venus. The rites of the Roman goddess Bona Dea were celebrated in the home of a magistrate by Roman matrons. Roman freed-women held the official state office of priestess for Bona Dea.[14]

Women's extensive participation in both Greek and Roman religious rites reveals that neither of these societies considered women's gender an impediment to religious leadership. In fact, Valerie Abrahamsen has suggested that pagan women who held religious offices in their civic communities may well have expected to hold religious office in their newly adopted Christian communities.[15]

Christian literary sources corroborate the evidence of the documentary sources that women participated in a wide variety of ministries and were recognized as leaders in their local congregations. Although the documentary sources show that women held the familiar church offices of bishop, presbyter, and deacon, these sources do not record the functions that these women actually performed. We must turn to the literary sources for accounts of women's ministries.

EVANGELISM

One of the earliest leadership roles was that of missionary-evangelist-apostle. For the earliest period there is no stable terminology for this role, which included teaching, preaching, and sometimes prophesying. Christian missionaries, women and men, followed in the footsteps of philosophers, prophets, traveling sorcerers, and itinerant preachers, who carried new religious ideas from the East to the urban centers of Greek and Roman culture. Schüssler Fiorenza identifies Paul's "co-workers" who were evangelizing and teaching as such itinerant missionaries: Mary, Tryphaena, Tryphosa, and Persis, who are mentioned in his letter to the Romans; and

Euodia and Syntyche whom he greets in his letter to the Philippians.[16] The work of the itinerant evangelist could be dangerous; a popular outcry in a strange city could provoke an intervention by the local authorities, and an evangelist could find herself or himself in prison. In fact, it was in prison that Paul met the famous woman evangelist Junia, whom he called (along with her husband) "foremost among the apostles."[17] Three centuries later John Chrysostom held up this Junia as an apostolic model for his women parishioners (*Homilies on Romans* 31.2).

Women and men traveled together as missionary couples, Prisca and Aquila, moving from Rome to Corinth, and Junia and Andronicus, traveling from Tarsus to Antioch, then to Rome. Philologos and Julia, and Nereus and his sister, mentioned in Paul's letter to the Romans, were probably also missionary couples.[18] Clement of Alexandria, writing in the second century, commends the early practice of missionary couples because the women evangelists would have had access to the women's quarters, which would have been closed to strange men. Clement even claims that Paul himself considered traveling as a missionary couple with the woman companion he greets in one of his letters. Clement thinks Paul is referring to this woman when he protests "Have we not the right to take about with us a wife that is a sister like the other apostles" (*Stromateis* 3; see 1 Cor 9:5).[19]

The most dramatic story of a woman evangelist is found in the second-century book the *Acts of Thecla*. In this story Thecla's calling as an evangelist was legitimated by her ascetic renunciation and her experiences of martyrdom. After hearing Paul's teachings on ascetic Christianity, she rejected her fiance, renounced marriage, and refused to continue her family's line by producing heirs. Twice she endured martyrdom, once by burning at the stake (she was miraculously rescued by a downpour) and again by being thrown to the beasts. (They were all females of the species and refused to eat her.) In both cases her resounding rejection of male suitors in order to pursue the ascetic life precipitated these events. In the final scene she declares her apostolic mission to evangelize Iconium and Paul confirms her mission saying, "Go preach the gospel and baptize."[20] A century later the women of Carthage appealed to the story of Thecla to defend their right to baptize. Tertullian, who was trying to suppress women's public ministries claimed that the *Acts of Thecla* (also called the *Acts of Paul and Thecla*) was a forgery and that a presbyter admitted he had written them out of a love for Paul. By the third century women's leadership was so well entrenched that women were appealing to literary sources to defend their authority. Simply attacking women's ministries on the grounds that they did not conform to gender roles was not enough, Tertullian must also contest the literary sources that underwrote women's ministries.

Baptism was closely associated with evangelism, for those who made a convert to Christianity would often act as a sponsor for that person during the process of catechetical training and then perform the rite of baptism. Tertullian's polemic against women baptizing is itself evidence that women exercised this ministry in Africa. As we have seen, another third-century treatise, the *Didascalia,* reveals a conflict over women's ministries of evangelizing and baptizing. Because the writer of the *Didascalia* is attempting to consolidate all the ministries of the church in the hands of a monarchial bishop he must wrest these ministries from the widows in order to bring them under the control of the bishop. So he warns the widows that if they continue in their work of evangelism, they will be guilty of blasphemy and in danger of God's judgment. If they are the ones who preach the Christian message that God became flesh, pagans will mock and jeer and fail to believe the Christian message because they heard it from the lips of a woman (*Didascalia* 15). Epiphanius, the fourth-century heresy hunter ridicules the catechetical instruction of Marcionite Christians by reporting that they even give women the authority to baptize (*Panarion* 42.4). It is interesting to note that women's leadership in evangelizing and baptizing is not contested until the third and fourth centuries.

PROPHECY

In Christian communities women prophets performed functions similar to those performed by women in Greek and Roman religions. Prophecy permeated every aspect of Greco-Roman social life. Professional prophets, or diviners, provided guidance for governments in matters of military expeditions, the founding of colonies, and the timing of festivals. They also consulted with private citizens and provided counsel to individuals in matters of marriage, travel, and the bearing of children. In all these arenas prophets were interpreters of a divine will because they spoke under the influence, inspiration, or possession of a divine spirit.

In the first Christian community at Corinth prophets and especially women prophets provided inspired leadership in personal and communal matters. Through a meticulous analysis of Paul's rhetoric in his letter to the Corinthians, Antoinette Clark Wire is able to reconstruct a profile of the women prophets.[21] Although they entered the community possessing little social status, their new identity as Christian prophets gave them wisdom, power, and rank, and their self-understanding as new creations made in God's image clothed them with honor and authority. They demonstrated their authority and their freedom by rejecting the Jewish prohibition against eating meat offered to idols; setting aside their veils and their sexual abstinence (associated with prayer and prophecy) served to enhance their authority.[22] Together they possessed a collective wisdom, signifying that they had the mind of Christ and were able to interpret spiritual things. This they communicated during Christian worship through "prayer and prophecy," which included songs, praise, psalms, and ecstatic prayer in tongues intermingled with teaching, exhortation, and instruction. Although Paul attempts to regulate the attire of women prophets, he does not object to their leadership roles.[23]

A manual on church organization shows that by the second century the functions of women prophets were institutionalized as a church office. The *Statutes of the Apostles* instructs churches to ordain two widows for the ministry of mediating revelations. "Let them ordain three Widows, two to continue together in prayer for all who are in trials, and to ask for revelations concerning that which they require."[24] Some revelations answered to individual needs for healing or advice; other revelations would be messages for the community as a whole. Paul in his letter to the Corinthians had also characterized prophetic words as those that edify, comfort, and encourage (1 Cor 14:1).

The activities of a woman prophet, Maximilla, and her associate Priscilla, initiated a resurgence of prophetic manifestations in the second century that was called by its supporters the New Prophecy. Its opponents called the group Montanists after the first significant male among the leadership.[25] The movement had followers as far away as Lyon and Africa. When an outbreak of persecution in Lyon brought a group of Christians to the brink of their martyrdom, they used their authority as confessors to support the prophecy movement by sending letters of endorsement to Phrygia. Irenaeus of Lyon, a major second-century theologian, saw in this outpouring of prophetic gifts the fulfillment of Joel's prophecy about the coming of the Spirit and a sign of the end-time (*Adversus Haereses* 3.11.9).

From Tertullian, an African theologian and supporter of the movement we have a description of the activities of a local prophetess:

> We have now amongst us a sister whose lot it has been to be favoured with gifts of revelation, which she experiences in the Spirit by ecstatic visions amidst the rites of the Lord's day in the church; she converses with angels, and sometimes even with the Lord; she both sees and hears mysterious communications; some hearts she discerns, and obtains directions for healing such as need them. Whether in the reading of the Scriptures, or in the chanting of psalms, or in the preaching of sermons, or in the offering up of prayers, in all these religious services matter and opportunity are afforded her of seeing visions. (*On the Soul* 9)[26]

During prophetic ecstasy women prophets received revelations about individuals, discerned their internal states, and provided counsel and guidance for them.

So highly did their communities value their oracles that they wrote them down, collected them into books, and circulated them widely. Tertullian appealed to one of these oracles to support his understanding of the nature of the soul. However, a second-century opponent, Hippolytus, protested that the oracles of the Montanist prophetesses were revered more than Christ, "They magnify these wretched women above the Apostles and every gift of Grace, so that some of them presume to assert that there is in them a something superior to Christ" (*Refutation of Heresies* 8.12).[27] The fourth-century church historian Eusebius accused them of creating a new scripture.

In another fourth-century controversy over the authority of Prisca and Maximilla, a detractor denounces them for daring to compose books under their own names. It was as bad as praying without a head covering, writing without the covering of a male author.[28] Nonetheless, the written authority of the women prophets remained a source of identity and strength for the Montanist church for three centuries. The fourth-century Christian emperor Constantine was unsuccessful in suppressing the Phrygian adherents of the New Prophecy, although he confiscated their churches and forbade them to assemble in private homes. At the end of that century the emperor Theodosius unleashed a severer persecution, demanding that their books be burned before judges and decreeing the death penalty for those who hid the books. In spite of the fact that followers of the movement were declared heretical and persecuted by the imperial church, a few of their oracles have survived.[29]

Nor did Maximilla's leadership go unchallenged in her own day. When a local bishop opposed her, he was blocked by her supporters and in the end was unsuccessful in challenging her authority. According to another account a bishop Sotas tried to "drive the demon out of Priscilla." He also was unsuccessful (Eusebius, *Ecclesiastical History* 5.18.13).[30] Interestingly, a similar story is told about an outstanding prophetess in Cappadocia. During a time of severe persecution in Caesarea, a woman with a prophetic gift assumed leadership of the beleaguered community. She set an example for courage through her asceticism (she went barefoot in the snow) and impressed many by predicting a major earthquake. She presided over the Eucharist and baptized new converts in her congregation—in effect, assuming the role of the bishop (Cyprian, *Letter* 75.10ff.).[31] Her opponent Firmilian claimed she was possessed and described an encounter in which she was subjected to an exorcism. Again the attempt to "exorcise" her failed and she continued as the leader of her congregation. When the religious authority of women could not be suppressed, it was subverted by attributing it to demonic powers.

TEACHERS

Although the role of teacher was never institutionalized as a church office, teachers within the Christian community enjoyed an authority that sometimes put them in competition with their bishops. The highly regarded head of the school in Alexandria, Origen, was censured because of rivalries with his bishop, Demetrius. A century later in the same city, a popular teacher, Arius, was expelled by Bishop Alexander for refusing to submit to episcopal authority. Christian teachers often came to their vocation because their families possessed the resources to secure an education for them, either by sending them to school or by hiring a tutor. Reading, writing, and declamation were taught through studying and reciting the classical texts (Homer in Greek and Virgil in Latin). Advanced study required a mastery of rhetoric—at this stage one could become a teacher. Only the dedicated would go on to study philosophy. Basic literacy and a thorough grounding in the scriptures (the Christian classics) qualified an individual as a teacher within the churches.

For the Christian community the work of teachers fell into two categories: catechizing the converts and instructing the faithful. The role of teacher itself was not gendered. Priscilla clearly acted out of her authority as a teacher when she sought out Apollos and instructed him on the interpretation of the Prophets. She had been trained in the Jewish scriptures and had a profound understanding of Christian teachings. Three centuries later she was honored by Chrysostom, the court preacher of Constantinople, who devoted a sermon to her gifts as a teacher (*First Homily on Greetings to Priscilla and Aquila*). A fourth-century papyrus refers to a Kyria, a woman teacher (*didaskalos*).[32] In a Syriac church order, *Testament of Our Lord,* the order of widows is specifically assigned the task of teaching and catechizing. Again reflecting the importance of gender segregation in this society, the widows were to teach the women.

The influence of another woman, Philoumene, a second-century Christian teacher and founder of a Gnostic school, is attested by the list of theologians who challenged her views: Tertullian, Origen, Hippolytus, Rhodon (a student of Tatian), Pseudo-Tertullian and Epiphanius.[33] She converted Apelles, a disciple of Marcion, to her own theological system. In becoming Philoumene's disciple, Apelles rejected the Marcionite doctrine of two gods (a good and distant Father and a jealous, vengeful Creator) and espoused Philoumene's teaching that there is only one God, a good God who created the lesser gods or angels, who in turn created the world, souls, and bodies. Although not perfect, they too were good creators. Even Philoumene's theological opponents praised her for teaching that Jesus had a real physical body. But she taught that Jesus did not receive his physical body from a virgin birth; rather, he created a body for himself out of the four elements. After undergoing a real crucifixion, real death, and real resurrection, he dissolved his body back into its original elements and ascended. Thus, for Christians the resurrection will not be a bodily resurrection but a return of the preexistent soul to heaven.

Perhaps the most striking element of Philoumene's system is that she believed that the soul was gendered. In their original form of existence, souls were male and female, and it is the gendering of the soul that produces the male and female bodies. Salvation is the return of male and female souls to their original state, freed of their bodies. Anne Jensen suggests that if maleness and femaleness were part of the original identity of souls then it is probable that Philoumene would have rejected a gender hierarchy in the church.[34] (In fact, in several of the Gnostic churches women held the offices of bishop, presbyter, and deacon.[35]) Philoumene's teachings were published and widely circulated; Rhodon read them in a work called *Apophthegmata* (Wise Sayings); Tertullian refers to them under the title of *Phanerosis* (Revelations). However, Rhodon called her "possessed," and Tertullian in a rhetorical move typical of him calls her an "empty-headed whore." He had also called the leader of the Cainites a wanton woman (*De praescriptione Haereticorum* 41.5).

INTERPRETING GENDER CONFLICTS

While women's leadership in early Christian churches had much in common with women's religious leadership in Greek and Roman societies, there is one striking difference—women's leadership in some Christian circles was bitterly contested. After a sweeping study of women's religious leadership in Greek and Roman societies and in Jewish and Christian communities, Ross Kraemer concludes, "Only among Christians is women's religious leadership an issue. Only Christians both attempt, sometimes successfully, to exclude women from religious office and community authority and argue about it."[36] Why is women's religious leadership controversial only among Christians? What is it about leadership in the Christian context that made its interaction with the gender system of the ancient Mediterranean different from that of Greek and Roman religions?

MALE HONOR AND FEMALE SHAME

The rhetoric of those who opposed women's leadership reveals both cultural convictions about gender and changing beliefs about Christian leadership. As we saw above, when Tertullian wanted to discredit the leader of the Cainites he insinuated that she was unchaste, "And the women of these heretics, how wanton (*pocaces*) they are! For they are bold enough to teach, to dispute" (*De praescriptione Haereticorum* 41.5). The Latin term *pocaces* means "bold," "shameless," and "impudent." Paul accuses a woman prophet who prophesies without a veil of being shameless. In 1 Corinthians 11:6, he argues, "If a woman prophesies without her head covered it is a shame to her; she dishonors her head." Her indiscretion is as shameful as having her head shorn. Why were boldness and shamelessness associated with women's ministries? Clearly Tertullian and Paul are writing as rhetoricians, trained to strike the right emotional chords of outraged propriety.

Ancient writers were able to conjure up an image of the shameless woman by invoking a set of ethical standards that defined male honor and female shame.[37] In this sexual division of moral labor, honor was considered an aspect of male nature expressed in competitiveness and a natural desire for precedence that resulted in a reputation based on achievement. A woman's reputation rested on her sexuality, on a public demonstration that she was sexually exclusive. Shame, the defining quality of womanhood, meant that a woman understood her sexual vulnerability and was careful to avoid all appearances of sexual indiscretion.[38]

Because maleness symbolized authority and prestige, and femaleness, submission to authority, deference, and passivity, there were tensions surrounding women's exercise of leadership roles. Although a woman, practically speaking, could undertake leadership roles based on her social status, wealth, and power, in so doing she failed to manifest those culturally defined characteristics of personality that signified a woman's concern for shame and risked being regarded as morally corrupt.

For a man to seek honor through the skillful deployment of his resources of social status and wealth was perceived as appropriate to the cultural meaning of maleness—since maleness connoted honor. However, for a woman, the process of achieving honor—challenge, competition, public identity—contradicted what a woman as an embodiment of femaleness should signify, namely, submission, passivity, timidity, and sexual restraint.

This tension underlies Paul's dispute with the women prophets of Corinth. Their prophetic roles were leadership roles, involving authority, precedence, prestige, and honor. These attributes (associated with maleness) conflicted with the cultural role of women, that is, to symbolize shame, submission to authority, sexual exclusiveness, deference, and passivity. Paul's solution to this tension was his injunction that women prophets should wear head coverings. Paul contends that women prophets will be perceived as refusing their female role of passivity, deference, and submission to authority if they do not wear veils. However, if they wear veils, the veil as a symbol will show that they recognize the precedence of man over woman and the authority of male over female (1 Cor 11:7–10). Paul could be comfortable with women's leadership in the Corinthian congregation if the women prophets were willing to signal publicly that they were not breaking with woman's cultural role of functioning as a symbol for shame. By wearing veils they would be publicly manifesting the values of submission to authority, thereby reaffirming the symbolic function of femaleness to signify shame, although at the same time they would be exercising leadership roles of authority and precedence.[39]

Like Paul, Tertullian, an African leader of the third century, sees in the practice of veiling a way for women to manifest their concern for shame while being in positions of authority. Tertullian is concerned with the authority, precedence, leadership, and honor of the virgins within the African congregations. The virgins were part of the clergy and sat in special seats reserved for them along with the presbyters, widows, and bishop. Their number and their commitment to a life of chastity were for the rest of the church one of its proudest emblems. By not wearing veils, these virgins signified their unmarried state. For the church these young women, unveiled and dedicated to God, were like a public and visible offering.

Tertullian objected to this practice. The honors bestowed on the virgins offended Tertullian's sense that femaleness should be associated with submission, passivity, and sexual exclusivity. For Tertullian, the vow of chastity itself was not enough to demonstrate a woman's concern for sexual exclusivity. There must be a public, visible demonstration of the concern for modesty and chastity, which could best be shown by the wearing of the veil. In fact, Tertullian warns that women who have taken the vow of virginity, "after being brought forward and elated by the public announcement of their good deed, laden by the brethren with every bounty and charitable gift"—will no doubt become sexually active, since they are on public display. If they do not use the veil to signify their concern for shame (sexual exclusiveness) they will in the end become pregnant and add to their guilt by attempting abortions and by contriving to conceal their motherhood. For Tertullian also, a veiled virgin can continue in her position of prestige, authority, precedence, and honor, because she is publicly demonstrating her concern for shame, for sexual exclusiveness (*On the Veiling of Virgins* 5).

Public Man and Private Woman

Another Greco-Roman belief about gender—that public roles were masculine and that women should confine themselves to the domestic sphere—appears in the rhetoric of detractors of women's leadership in the third century. Cross-cultural studies by anthropologists indicate that the distinction between public and private and the relegation of women to the private sphere is a near-universal phenomenon.[40] In most cultures women are involved primarily in domestic activities, because of their childbearing function. Their lives are focused on the "particularistic" concerns of children and home. Men occupy themselves with the formation of the "universalistic" superstructures such as politics and warfare, which link particular domestic groups. Women are associated with the private sphere and men with the public sphere.

In the ancient Greco-Roman version of the public–private gender ideology, definitions of social space played an important role. The social and economic functions of the *oikos* (household) were carried out in the covered places, in contrast to the functions of the *polis* (city), which occurred in the open or in public spaces. In the words of a second-century B.C.E. writer, "Men should be generals and city officials and politicians, and women should guard the house and stay inside and receive and take care of their husbands."[41] Women were assigned the task of child-rearing. As the manager of the *oikos,* a wife was responsible for the production of textiles; the distribution of food and clothing; and the education, training, and disciplining of slaves. Her activities defined women's space, the physical space of the household. In terms of this ancient public–private ideology, public space was male space because it was defined by the masculine activities of citizenship: voting, debating, public speaking, and holding public offices. Wherever men engaged in the pursuit of the public welfare, politics, law, or warfare became public spaces.

Because Christianity developed within the matrix of Greco-Roman society, cultural beliefs about a public male sphere and a private female sphere were assimilated into the Christian social order. However, in the first two centuries this assimilation had a positive effect on women's leadership. In terms of the division of Greco-Roman society into public and private domains, the early Christian house-churches were located in the private domain. The public sphere was that of the state, concerned with the common good—politics, warfare, and public justice. The concerns of the private domain were economic and familial.[42]

The earliest Christians conceived of themselves explicitly as an "alternative" family or household. In the preaching of Jesus the bonds between the followers of Jesus were like familial bonds, and indeed superseded them. The Christian communities of the apostolic period designated themselves a "household church" (*hē kat' oikon ekklēsia,* literally, "coming together at home") (1 Cor 16:19; Phlm 2; Col 4:15). The position of head of a household also qualified an individual for leadership roles. Because household management involved administrative, financial, and disciplinary responsibilities, it prepared an individual to assume corresponding responsibilities in the community.[43]

Up until the third century, early Christian worship took place in the homes of prosperous householders. Women and men as heads of households possessed important resources for the early Christian communities. First, they owned homes that were large enough for the communal gatherings, which probably took place in the dining room, or *triclinium.* Prayers, preaching, and exhortation were carried out in the context of a communal meal, and the meal itself was provided out of the resources of the household's store of food — grain, olive oil, cheese, and fruit. Such gifts of food and hospitality counted as a form of benefaction and established the householder in the role of patron. While male and female householders who served as patrons of house-churches may not have always been the titled leaders of those churches, there are many similarities between the duties of householders and those of early "bishops" and "presbyters." Architectural evidence suggests that after the middle of the third century Christian communities were able to buy private houses and adapt them for worship through minor remodeling.[44] However, not until the erection of basilicas (modeled on the Roman public reception hall) in the fourth century did architectural space clearly define Christian worship as public.[45]

As long as Christian worship was conducted in private space, the public–private gender ideology did not constitute a cultural barrier to women's leadership. First- and second-century Christians, familiar with the authority and leadership role of the female head of household, would have perceived women's leadership within the church as not only acceptable but natural.[46] Nor would the specific leadership functions exercised in the first- and second-century church have constituted a barrier to women whose skills and experiences as managers amply prepared them to assume roles of teaching, disciplining, nurturing, and administering economic resources.

Because women's leadership in the churches was perceived as being exercised in a quasi-private sphere, it did not threaten ingrained social prejudice. But by the third century, Christian churches were beginning to perceive themselves as more similar to institutions of the public sphere than institutions of the private sphere. As this transition from the private to the public sphere took place, women's leadership in the churches became controversial and problematic. Not until the third century do we find Christian writers invoking the public–private gender ideology to oppose women's leadership.

Origen of Alexandria appeals in his commentary on 1 Corinthians 14:34–35 to this gender ideology in his polemic against the women prophets associated with the New Prophecy:

> In short let a woman learn from the man who is her own, taking "man" in its generic sense, as the counterpart of woman. For it is improper for a woman to speak in an assembly, no matter what she says, even if she says admirable things or even saintly things; that is of little consequence since they come from the mouth of a woman. A woman speaking in an assembly— clearly this abuse is denounced as improper, an abuse for which the entire assembly is responsible. (*Fragments on 1 Corinthians* 74)[47]

Although a woman's leadership and teaching may be above reproach, the fact that she performs her ministry in the public space of the assembly makes her speaking disgraceful. Tertullian in his controversy with the consecrated virgins insists: "It is not permitted for a woman to speak in church. Neither may she teach, baptize, offer, or claim for herself any function proper to a man, least of all a public office" (*On the Veiling of Virgins* 9.1). For Tertullian, the space of Christian worship has become public space and Christian ministries have become public offices and therefore are open to men only. Chrysostom gives this public–private gender ideology a Christian baptism:

> Our life is customarily organized into two spheres: public affairs and private matters, both of which were determined by God. To woman is assigned the presidency of the household; to man all the business of the state, the marketplace, the administration of justice, government, the military and all other such enterprises. (*The Kind of Women Who Ought to Be Taken as Wives* 4)[48]

From the third century on, Christian writers increasingly see the church as constituting a space analogous to that of the state, concerned with government, justice, and war. The parallels are no longer drawn between the church and household. While Greek and Roman women who served as priestesses could officiate at public temples, lead public processions, hold public offices, and receive public honors, there was still a public space from which women were excluded, that of the Forum — the assembly of citizens and the city councils where political issues were proposed, contested, and debated, and where votes were cast. When church governance was conceived of as analogous to the processes for the governance of the state, the space of Christian worship became public space and the offices of the church became masculine. However, women's leadership, although sharply contested in certain contexts, did not disappear. Documentary and literary sources provide evidence of women's leadership throughout this period and into the succeeding centuries. The obstacles posed by the changing models of leadership and the Greco-Roman conventions about public and private space were serious, but in the end they were only obstacles; women could find ways of circumventing them.

NOTES

1. See Elisabeth Schüssler Fiorenza, *In Memory of Her: A Feminist Theological Reconstruction of Christian Origins* (New York: Crossroad, 1983), 41–67.

2. Ibid., 109.

3. Ibid., 140–50.

4. Bernadette Brooten, "Early Christian Women and Their Cultural Context," in *Feminist Perspectives on Biblical Scholarship,* ed. Adela Yarbro Collins (Biblical Scholarship in North America 10; Chico, CA: Scholars Press, 1985), 65–92.

5. Bernadette Brooten, *Women Leaders in the Ancient Synagogue: Inscriptional Evidence and Background Issues* (Brown Judaic Studies 36; Chico, CA: Scholars Press, 1982).

6. Ibid., 41–56; see also *Maenads, Martyrs, Matrons, and Monastics: A Sourcebook on Women's Religions in the Greco-Roman World,* ed. Ross Kraemer (Philadelphia: Fortress, 1988), 218–20.

7. *Maenads,* ed. Kraemer, 220.

8. Egypt: *Cahiers de Recherches de l'Institut de Papyrologie et d'Egyptologie de Lille* 5 (1974): 264 No. 1115; Phrygia: *Greek, Roman and Byzantine Studies* 16 (1975): 437–38; Greece: *Bulletin de Correspondence Hellenique* 101 (1977): 210, 212; Sicily: *L'Annee Epigraphique* (1975): 454. A letter from an African bishop mentions a woman elder in Cappadocia (Cyprian, *Epistle* 75.10.5).

9. Asia Minor: (Phoebe of Cenchreae) Romans 16:1; Greece: *Supplementum Epigraphicum* 29 (1978): 425; Melos: M. Guarducci, *Epigrafica greca* IV (Rome, 1978), 368–70; Macedonia: G. H. R. Horsley, ed., *New Documents Illustrating Early Christianity* (Sydney, 1977), 109; Delphi: M. Guarducci, *Epigraphia greca* IV (Rome, 1978), 345–47; Bithynia: *Zeitschrift für Papyrologie und Epigraphik* 18 (1975): 46; Cappadocia: *Supplementum Epigraphicum Graecum* 27 (1978): 9478a; Jerusalem: M. Guarducci, *Epigrafia greca* IV (Rome, 1978), 445.

10. Dorothy Irvin, "The Ministry of Women in the Early Church: The Archaeological Evidence," *Duke Theological Review* 2 (1980): 77–78.

11. Ibid. See also Joan Morris, *The Lady Was a Bishop: The Hidden History of Women with Clerical Ordination and the Jurisdiction of Bishops* (New York: Macmillan, 1973).

12. Ross Kraemer has collected documentary evidence for women holding priestly office: Chrysis of Delphi, Tata of Aphrodisias, Berenice of Syros, and Flavia Vibia Sabina of Thasos (*Maenads,* 211, 216–17).

13. Ross Kraemer, *Her Share of the Blessings* (Oxford: Oxford University Press, 1992), 80–92.

14. Ibid., 50–70.

15. Valerie Abrahamsen, "Women at Philippi: The Pagan and Christian Evidence," *Journal of Feminist Studies in Religion* 3 (1987): 17–30.

16. Schüssler Fiorenza, *In Memory of Her,* 169–84.

17. Bernadette Brooten, "Junia . . . Outstanding among the Apostles (Romans 16:7)," in *Women Priests: A Catholic Commentary on the Vatican Declaration,* ed. Leonard Swidler and Arlene Swidler (New York: Paulist, 1977).

18. Schüssler Fiorenza, *In Memory of Her,* 180.

19. It is likely Clement is referring to Philippians 4:3, where he greets a woman, calling her *syzyge* (companion or yokefellow).

20. Edward Hennecke and Wilhelm Schneemelcher, *The New Testament Apocrypha* (2 vols.; Philadelphia: Westminster, 1964), 2:322–89.

21. Antoinette Clark Wire, *The Corinthian Women Prophets: A Reconstruction Through Paul's Rhetoric* (Minneapolis: Fortress, 1990).

22. The famous prophetess at Thyatira also celebrated this freedom, which grievously offended the writer of the Apocalypse (Rev 2:20–23). See also Adela Yarbro Collins, "Women's History and the Book of Revelation," in *Society of Biblical Literature 1987 Seminar Papers,* ed. Kent Richards (Atlanta: Scholars Press, 1987), 83.

23. Other first-century prophetesses were the four daughters of Philipp and Amnia of Philadelphia. In later controversies about women's prophetic office, Mary the mother of Jesus, was claimed as a prophetess and also Anna in the temple.

24. *The Statutes of the Apostles,* trans. G. Horner (London, 1904), 304. Anne Jensen finds evidence in a second-century Gnostic group for ordination to a prophetic office. See *Gottes selbstbewusste Töchter: Frauenemanzipation im frühen Christentum* (Freiburg: Herder, 1992), 263–64.

25. Maximilla was supported by another woman prophet, Prisca, and Montanus, who was an advocate for them. Anne Jensen argues that Maximilla was the earliest leader of the movement. She makes an important distinction between second-century sources that are either sympathetic or cautiously critical and hostile fourth-century sources. The fourth-century accounts of the New Prophecy are distorted by the imperial church's repudiation of prophetic authority and its antipathy toward women leaders. The use of a traditional rhetoric of slander against female leaders, the equation of Montanus with the paraclete, and oracles attributed to Montanus appear only in the fourth-century sources. Although Montanus was not founder of the movement that bears his name (Montanism), later heresiologists were more comfortable attributing leadership to a man. Eusebius calls Maximilla and Priscilla followers of Montanus.

26. Trans. Kraemer (*Maenads,* 224).

27. Trans. Kraemer (*Maenads,* 225).

28. See Jensen, *Gottes selbstbewusste Töchter,* 334. Mary's Magnificat was written under the covering of the Gospel writer!

29. Ronald Heine, *Montanist Oracles and Testimonia* (Macon, GA: Mercer University Press, 1989).

30. See Jensen, *Gottes selbstbewusste Töchter,* 275–86. Later sources describe this confrontation as taking place between Montanus and the bishop.

31. See Jensen, *Gottes selbstbewusste Töchter,* 352–58.

32. *Zeitschrift für Papyrologie und Epigraphik* 18 (1975): 317–23.

33. Jensen has carefully extracted the essence of Philoumene's teachings from the polemics of her theological opponents. By keeping clearly in the foreground the issues of the second

century—a good God and an imperfect world, the proper use of Jewish scriptures, the incarnation and the resurrection of the body—she is able to show Philoumene's position on these questions. See *Gottes selbstbewusste Töchter,* 365–426.

34. Most of the writers who insist on a gender hierarchy believe that it is limited only to this world; heaven will be what Kari Børresen aptly calls a salvational democracy. See *Subordination and Equivalence: The Nature and Role of Women in Augustine and Aquinas* (Washington, DC: University Press of America, 1981).

35. Elaine Pagels, *The Gnostic Gospels* (New York: Random House, 1979), 61–63.

36. Kraemer, *Maenads,* 175.

37. Bruce Malina, *The New Testament World: Insights from Cultural Anthropology* (Atlanta: John Knox, 1981), 44; see also David Gilmore, *Honor and Shame and the Unity of the Mediterranean* (Special Publication of the American Anthropological Association 22; Washington, DC: American Anthropological Association, 1987).

38. Malina, *New Testament World,* 28; see also Karen Torjesen, *When Women Were Priests* (San Francisco: Harper, 1993) chaps. 5, 6.

39. The gender issues in 1 Cor 14:34–35 are those of preserving female shame. Paul says it is a shame (*aischron*) for a woman to speak in the assembly. When the writer of 1 Timothy says that a woman may not teach, he is also concerned with female shame. Only men are to recite liturgical prayers; women are to be chaste in dress and adornment (the positive signs of female shame) and are not to teach.

40. See Michelle Zimbalist Rosaldo, "Woman, Culture, and Society: A Theoretical Overview," in *Woman, Culture and Society,* ed. M. Z. Rosaldo and Louise Lamphere (Stanford, CA: Stanford University Press, 1974), 17–42; and Rosaldo, "The Use and Abuse of Anthropology: Reflections on Feminism and Cross-Cultural Understanding," *Signs* 5 (Spring 1980): 389–417. Rosaldo has suggested that the public–private distinction is a universal—though "nonnecessary"—aspect culture and society. Rayna Rapp offers a review of some responses to Rosaldo's initial statement of her theory and questions the value of a universal model to explain historically distinct phenomena ("Review Essay: Anthropology," *Signs* 4 [Spring 1979]: 497–513, esp. 508–11).

41. Mary Lefkowitz and Maureen Fant, *Women's Life in Greece and Rome* (Baltimore: Johns Hopkins University Press, 1982), 104.

42. Although the references to Christianity in Roman literature of the period do not explicitly connect Christianity with the private sphere of the household, they do indicate that non-Christians viewed Christianity as distinctly "nonpublic." Christianity is associated with the private "clubs" or voluntary associations and with mystery cults (often organized as voluntary associations), which were likewise viewed as both separate from and (at least potentially) threatening to the public order.

43. Karen Torjesen, *When Women Were Priests,* chap. 2; Schüssler Fiorenza, *In Memory of Her,* 84–95, 160–204.

44. See Carl H. Kraeling, *The Christian Building at Dura-Europos* (Locust Valley, NY: J. J. Augustin, 1967); and Gorbo Virgilio, *The House of St. Peter at Capharnum* (Publications of the Studium Franciscanum, Collectio minor 5; Jerusalem: Franciscan Printing Press, 1969).

45. See Sir Thomas Graham Jackson, *Byzantine and Romanesque Architecture* (Cambridge: Cambridge University Press, 1920; reprint, New York: Hacker Art Books, 1975), 1:17ff.; and H. Kahler, *Die Frühkirche: Kult und Kultraum* (Berlin, 1972), 54ff.

46. While both men and women, in practice, functioned as heads of households and household managers, men of the propertied classes achieved their identity through

participation in public life and distanced themselves from the domain of the household. It was these social arrangements among elite families that generated the public–private gender ideology in which men are associated with the public sphere and women with the domestic sphere.

47. *Journal of Theological Studies* 10 (1909): 41–42.

48. Trans. Elizabeth Clark, in *Women in the Early Church* (Lewiston/Queenston: The Edwin Mellen Press, 1987), 360.

RECOMMENDED READINGS

Brooten, Bernadette. *Women Leaders in the Ancient Synagogue: Inscriptional Evidence and Background Issues.* Chico, CA: Scholars Press, 1982.

Burrus, Virginia. *Chastity as Autonomy: Women in the Stories of Apocryphal Acts.* Lewiston/Queenston, Edwin Mellen Press, 1987.

Clark, Elizabeth. *Women in the Early Church.* Wilmington, DE: Michael Glazier, 1983.

Jensen, Anne. *Gottes selbstbewusste Töchter: Frauenemanzipation im frühen Christentum.* Freiburg: Herder, 1992.

Kraemer, Ross. *Her Share of the Blessings.* Oxford: Oxford University Press, 1992.

——, ed. *Maenads, Martyrs, Matrons, and Monastics.* Philadelphia: Fortress, 1988.

Morris, Joan. *The Lady Was a Bishop: The Hidden History of Women with Clerical Ordination and the Jurisdiction of Bishops.* New York: Macmillan, 1973.

Schüssler Fiorenza, Elisabeth. *In Memory of Her: A Feminist Theological Reconstruction of Christian Origins.* New York: Crossroad, 1983.

Topping, Eva Catafygiotu. *Holy Mothers of Orthodoxy.* Minneapolis: Light and Life Publishing, 1987.

Torjesen, Karen Jo. *When Women Were Priests: Women's Leadership in the Early Church and the Scandal of Their Subordination in the Rise of Christianity.* San Francisco: Harper, 1993.

Wire, Antoinette Clark. *The Corinthian Women Prophets: A Reconstruction through Paul's Rhetoric.* Minneapolis: Fortress, 1990.

PART FOUR

Transforming the Master's House: Building a "Room of Our Own"

❖ Feminist Interpretation
and Liturgical Proclamation

MARJORIE PROCTER-SMITH ♦

> To proclaim emancipatory transformation, women are empowered to take
> back the Scriptures: to speak of them and to hear them, painfully, angrily,
> prophetically, hopefully, lovingly, and gracefully.[1]

THE LITURGICAL CONTEXT provides its own radical reinterpretation of biblical texts. The biblical text is removed from its literary context and placed
in a radically different context which interprets the text by altering the mode
(from written to spoken), combining the text with other texts, creating
beginnings and endings for the text, providing nonbiblical commentary
in the form of antiphons, hymns, prayers, and sermon, and placing the
text in a larger liturgical context which itself may be governed by a
theological theme or occasion of the church or secular year.

This radical recontextualizing of scripture by the liturgical context holds
both possibilities and perils for feminist proclamation. After offering a
definition of feminist emancipatory proclamation, this essay will consider
first the problems that face those who would engage in such proclamation
in a liturgical context, and then the possibilities that the context offers.

FEMINIST EMANCIPATORY PROCLAMATION

Feminist emancipatory proclamation asserts the need for women to speak
freely and with power in the context of the worshiping assembly, that is,
to claim our authority to interpret the Bible for ourselves and to proclaim
the word for women's lives in our times. In order to claim such authority,
a feminist theology of proclamation must be developed which takes account
of the androcentric and patriarchal character of the Bible and of the tradition

of patriarchal proclamation and at the same time is committed to empowered speaking by women on behalf of women.

Feminist proclamation grows naturally out of women's claiming their power to speak. It is accountable to women and to women's struggles against their own and other women's oppression; thus feminist proclamation is committed to change. This commitment to women takes precedence over commitment to scriptural texts, recognizing that many scriptural texts have been and continue to be used to inhibit women's emancipation. At the same time, feminist proclamation claims the authority of scripture on behalf of women, finding in the texts not only the story of the silencing and oppression of women but also the story of biblical women's struggle for emancipation, their resistance against forms of oppression, their courage and hope.

Feminist proclamation is contextual and embodied. It is grounded in working to bring about change in women's lives in church and society, since to proclaim women's emancipation without working to bring it about is to contribute to women's oppression.

Feminist proclamation is dialogical, communal, and participatory. It may take the form of public proclamation by a single individual, but the content and purpose of the proclamation are born out of ongoing honest dialogue among women. It is particularly critical that this dialogue include women of different races, classes, cultures, and so on, including as much diversity as is embodied among women, lest the proclamation give the illusion of universality. Therefore feminist proclamation is also fluid. Emerging out of ongoing dialogue among women, suppressed questions, denied experiences, silenced voices begin to surface, to reshape the meaning of feminist proclamation.

Finally, feminist emancipatory proclamation is empowering. It seeks not to speak for women but to empower women to speak up and speak out on their own behalf. Thus not only is feminist proclamation grounded in work to improve women's lives in church and society; it is itself part of that work. As emancipatory proclamation, it does not give women the power to speak, but calls forth that power which is already present in the struggles, the courage and the hope of women's lives.

PROBLEMS OF LITURGICAL PROCLAMATION

Basic problems facing feminist proclamation are the Bible as word of God, the choice of texts for liturgy, contemporary models of preaching, and liturgy as interpreter of the text.

AUTHORITY OF THE BIBLE

According to common understanding, the purpose of reading scripture in Christian worship is to proclaim the word of God to the assembly, whether the reading is understood as proclamation itself or as a basis for the preacher's proclamation. Thus the first problem that must be faced in developing feminist proclamation is the authority of the Bible.

Feminist biblical interpretation that is critical rather than apologetic directs attention to the dangers of uncritical acceptance of biblical authority for women and other oppressed people. Feminist interpretation recognizes not only the male bias of biblical texts but also the use of the Bible to support patriarchal interests. South African biblical scholar Itumeleng Mosala notes that "the Bible is the product, the record, the site, and the weapon of class, cultural, gender, and racial struggles."[2] This is confirmed by others who point to the use of biblical injunctions of obedience to authority and affirmations of male dominance to justify violence and oppression of women, children, and other subjugated persons.[3] This criticism locates authority not in an ancient text or even in the interpretation of an ancient text, but in the struggle of oppressed people for freedom and dignity.

By contrast, the use of the Bible in Christian liturgy has functioned as an authoritative statement, as "word of God" to be accepted and obeyed. It serves, as Elisabeth Schüssler Fiorenza has said, as "not simply a record of revelation but revelation itself."[4]

In many liturgical traditions the reading of the Bible is accompanied by verbal and nonverbal affirmations of its authority, such as prayers, acclamations, processions, elevations of the Bible, restrictions on who may handle or read from the Bible, and so on. Such actions serve to reinforce the religious authority of the book and of the book's interpreter (the preacher or homilist). Location of authority away from the community in general and from women in particular is intensified in traditions that restrict or forbid women's access to the pulpit or emphasize the role of the ordained preacher as authoritative interpreter of the text.

At the same time, many women and other oppressed people have found important resources in the Bible for their own struggles for freedom and dignity. Texts that proclaim emancipation and justice can sometimes work to subvert patriarchal authority, which would use the Bible to curtail the freedom of some. However, the authority of the Bible in these cases still rests in the choice and interpretation of texts by those who are or have been suffering and struggling against oppression, and not in the texts themselves; nor do all oppressed groups find courage in the same texts.

Claiming the authority of scripture for the emancipation of women and other oppressed people is a necessary, albeit difficult, move for women of biblical religions. Such a claim, however, must be made without resorting to apologetic interpretations of difficult texts. This presents a problem when the liturgical context announces in word and gesture that this text is the "word of God." Such a context undermines critical reading and hearing of a text.

CHOICE OF TEXTS

The reality that some texts are useful as resources for emancipation while others contribute to oppression raises the question of the choice of texts for worship. By whom and by what criteria are such texts chosen?

All systems of scripture readings involve some form of *lectio electa,* or selected readings, whether in the form of a lectionary system constructed by a team of scholars or in the week-to-week decisions of a pastor. Lectionary systems in use in North American churches—including the lectionary of the Episcopal *Book of Common Prayer* (1979), the lectionary of the Lutheran *Book of Worship* (1978), and the *Common Lectionary,* produced by the Consultation on Common Texts in 1983 (and its 1992 revision) and now in use officially in the United Methodist Church in the United States and on a trial basis in the Presbyterian Church both in the United States and in Canada, in the United Church of Canada, and in the Anglican Church in Canada—are more or less derived from the Roman Catholic three-year eucharistic lectionary of 1969.[5]

Contemporary lectionary reform has been motivated at least in part by critiques of older lectionaries which point to the paucity of scripture included in them and the absence of readings from the Hebrew Scriptures in particular. Thus the newer lectionary systems have as a primary goal increasing the amount of scripture read in Sunday worship. An examination of the texts on women that are included in these new lectionaries, however, reveals that biblical texts that recount stories of women tend to be omitted or made optional texts, and that when women are included in the lectionary texts it is because they are adjunct to a central male character.[6]

The hermeneutical principle on which contemporary lectionary systems are based is androcentric. Because lectionaries are necessarily selective, they must choose certain individuals and events or themes in the biblical text to lift out. Since the Bible itself is androcentric, the central actors are usually men, and the pivotal events are told from men's experience. Thus the lectionary intensifies the androcentrism of the Bible by omitting less central characters and events: typically events involving women. If one hears only the biblical texts read in church Sunday after Sunday, one will perceive the Bible as being even more androcentric than if one simply sits down and reads the entire Bible through.

On the other hand, the lectionary system as a means of selecting texts for public worship opens the way for a feminist reconstruction. A lectionary is constructed on the principle that the purpose of the reading is the building up of the community, and that not every biblical text is always appropriate for that purpose. The process of selection can be used to the benefit of women, by asking what texts are emancipatory and what texts are oppressive.

Another problem raised by the issue of selection of texts is the question of canon. Contemporary Sunday lectionaries confine themselves to the official biblical canon (as defined by the tradition constructing the lectionary). But feminist critique has pointed out the extent to which the biblical canon silences and mutes women's voices and the ideological significance of that silencing. The present canon, then, is distorted and incomplete and needs to be supplemented with noncanonical texts and feminist amplifications of canonical texts.

A particularly knotty problem of selection of texts is whether and in what way to use negative texts. Even granting that the entire Bible is androcentric and patriarchal, certain texts proclaim the subordination of women to men, of slaves to masters, of children to parents so explicitly that it is difficult to see any reason to include them in a lectionary.

Some argue that such texts should never be proclaimed as God's word to the assembly.[7] Others, arguing that such texts are already known to most worshipers, prefer to include them in order to confront them and locate them historically and culturally. There are four uses to which such texts might be put in the context of worship.

They might function as educational texts, which would then be explained or interpreted to the congregation. The weakness in such an approach is twofold. First, the liturgical function of lections normally presupposes the authority of the text being read. Thus, such interpretation, by default, often resolves itself into apologetics for the text or the author. Further, such an approach assumes that worshipers are willing and able to hear instruction on the historical and cultural background of an ancient text and that such instruction is an adequate form of proclamation.

Second, they might function as objects of critique. The use of negative texts for the purpose of critique would demand the construction of new liturgical forms of presenting the readings, in such a way that the authority of the text is not proclaimed but is subverted. This would mean, among other things, locating authority in the community rather than the text. Juxtaposing conflicting texts in a liturgical context would also help to decenter the power of the negative text by offering internal critique, as it were.

Third, negative texts might serve as subjects of a rite of exorcism, which is how in fact they are often used in feminist worship gatherings. Such rites do not merely subvert the authority of the text but reject it outright, naming the text as evil, repudiating its power over us, and casting it out.

A fourth possibility is to make such texts the content of a ritual of lament, recognizing the power such texts have exerted over us as women, giving men the opportunity to confess their use of such texts to oppress women and to repent of that use, and lamenting the harm done by the use of the texts.

MODELS OF PREACHING

This essay will consider two of the numerous preaching models in existence as being most closely related to the topic of liturgical proclamation and feminist biblical interpretation: liturgical preaching and biblical preaching.

Liturgical preaching insists on the importance of the liturgical context of the sermon, emphasizing the connection between the sermon and the season of the church year, and between the sermon and the other elements of the liturgical event. Thus liturgical preaching, while understood to be biblical in the general sense of taking one or more scripture texts for its starting point (normatively, such preaching centers on the Gospel text), focuses more on the liturgical context, such as baptism or the Eucharist, Lent or Epiphany.[8]

Biblical preaching insists on the priority of the biblical text, whether assigned by a lectionary or chosen by the preacher. The authority of the text is assumed, and the purpose of the preaching task is, in part, to discover the "word of God" in a given text for the community. Such submission to the text, it is often assumed, will reveal an essential unity in the biblical message.[9] Although the use of historical-critical methods for studying the text are recommended, the purpose of such methods is to ensure that the preacher does not "violate" the meaning of the text.

All contemporary models of preaching associate the preaching with the "word of God," suggesting that the words of the preacher are somehow comparable to the words of the Bible and are thus above criticism. The nonverbal elements of preaching suggest the same thing, when the preacher speaks from an elevated place in the church to which lay people do not normally have access or when the preacher wears clothing that indicates special status and education. The verbal model as well, in which the preacher does all the talking, communicates a message of domination, regardless of the content of the message.[10]

These models of preaching fail to take account of feminist biblical interpretation and its challenge to the authority of the Bible, nor do they recognize the ambivalence (if not alienation) many women bring to the proclamation of the biblical word. They stress the preacher's necessary submission to the authority of the word of scripture as if there were no problematic or even contradictory texts in the Bible, and they assume that every preacher can find the "word of God" in any biblical text that might be assigned by a lectionary.

Feminist models of preaching would be more concerned with the violation of people than the violation of texts, would integrate feminist biblical translation and interpretation into sermon preparation, and would call forth the authority of the community rather than defend the authority of the biblical text. Feminist models would also develop reciprocal gestures to replace the present gestures of dominance and submission common to the preaching task and would create new worship spaces which affirm the participation of the whole community in the proclamation of the word.

LITURGY AS INTERPRETER OF THE TEXTS

By means of the juxtaposition of scripture texts, the use of interpretive nonbiblical texts (hymns, antiphons, introductory comments, etc.), and location in the church calendar, the liturgical context interprets the chosen biblical texts. In traditions that follow a form of the church year the texts are chosen to express an aspect of the season or feast. The present pattern is to select three readings and a psalm: one from the Hebrew Scriptures (except during the seven-week Easter season, when the first reading is taken from the book of Acts), one from an epistle, and one from a Gospel. Although the texts do not necessarily correspond to one another Sunday by Sunday (the *Common Lectionary* uses a broader system of correspondence), they are intended to reflect some aspect of the season or feast, according to the interpretation of those who choose the texts. Taken out of their literary context, then, three texts (or four, including the psalm) are placed in a new context in which they are presented as if they were related to one another.

For example, the *Common Lectionary* (but not *The Revised Common Lectionary*), the Lutheran lectionary, the *Book of Common Prayer* lectionary, and the Roman lectionary all pair Genesis 2:18–24, the creation of the woman from the rib of the man, with Mark 10:2–16, the saying about divorce and the blessing of children (Proper 22, year B). Since the rest of the creation story is found elsewhere in the lectionary, the interpretation suggested by this pairing of texts is that the woman was created for the purpose of marrying and having children. This is confirmed by the psalm chosen for the day: "Your wife will be like a fruitful vine within your house" (Psalm 128). Such an interpretation already provided by the liturgy undermines any possibility that the sermon will be able to offer critique of either text or of their usual interpretation.

In a similar way, hymns, antiphons, ritual actions and gestures also provide an interpretation of the texts. The use of verbal and nonverbal proclamations that the reading is the "word of God," the restriction of access to the book, the reading of the book from an elevated or otherwise restricted space by certain people only—all offer an interpretation of the texts which virtually precludes critical interpretation in the sermon.

Some traditions include prayers before the readings which emphasize the contemporary applicability of the ancient texts and typically include requests for knowledge and obedience to the word of God.[11] Emphasis on the contemporaneity of the texts undermines any effort in the sermon to relativize the power of a patriarchal text by placing it in its original historical context. Even apart from such explicit prayers, all liturgies assume that the texts chosen and read have been chosen and read precisely for their contemporary significance. The function of the sermon, then, is to make clear to the assembly the significance of the texts for them. This liturgical function of the reading of scripture, which is quite distinct from the reading of scripture for the purposes of Bible study, makes the responsible selection of texts even more critical.

Traditions that follow the church year are provided with yet a further level of interpretation of the texts, according to which the texts are interpreted as reflecting some aspect of the season or feast. The basic elements of the church year are christological feasts: the incarnation (Advent–Christmas–Epiphany) and the death and resurrection (Lent–Easter–Pentecost). Studies of the lectionaries built around these cycles demonstrate the extent to which these christological events are interpreted androcentrically, focusing on male actors, such as the male disciples and apostles in the Lent–Easter–Pentecost cycle. The exception is the presence of

Mary and Elizabeth during the Advent–Christmas–Epiphany cycle, where, however, their childbearing role is prominent.

Sanctoral cycles are even more androcentric, with the normative saint being male, celibate, and clerical or monastic. Women, when included in the sanctoral cycle, are identified as virgins and/or martyrs, and typically are celibate.[12] The Lutheran sanctoral departs from this pattern by including biblical women (Lydia, Dorcas, and Phoebe, January 27), hymnists (Catherine Winkworth, July 1), and social reformers (Florence Nightingale and Clara Maass, August 13), but men still outnumber women on the calendar.[13]

Absent from either the christological cycle or the sanctoral cycle are events that commemorate women's experiences either by celebration or lament. Only Mother's Day, a secular holiday, influences the Christian calendar — and then only to glorify women's childbearing experiences without regard to the struggle that those experiences normally entail for women, and often to reiterate women's submission to men as well.

POSSIBILITIES FOR FEMINIST LITURGICAL PROCLAMATION

The liturgical context into which scripture texts are placed is an androcentric and patriarchal one. The hermeneutical principles that guide lectionary development, the nonverbal language that accompanies the readings, the models of proclamation of the message, all reflect patriarchal interests and serve patriarchal needs.

However, the radical reinterpretation of scripture which the liturgical context provides is open also to feminist construction. The basic premise that the purpose of reading scripture in worship is to build up the community suggests that this goal is not realized until the needs and interests of women are considered in the choice and proclamation of texts — indeed, not until women representing the rich variety of women's lives participate in the choosing and proclamation.

As discussed earlier, selectivity is *already* a basic principle of liturgical use of the Bible. Feminist principles of lectionary selectivity, recognizing the basic androcentric and patriarchal character of the Bible, must amplify the silenced voices of women in the text, draw attention to evidence of women's resistance against their oppression, and supply missing pieces of the story of biblical women. This may be done by the use of feminist typology, feminist translation of biblical texts, and feminist amplification of texts.

Feminist Biblical Typology

The use of biblical typology is an ancient liturgical practice, intended to draw parallels between different events in order to emphasize the continuation of the patterns into the present. It is a process first of identifying a recurring pattern, and then drawing analogies with other events. Historically, the Christian use of typology has functioned often to the detriment of women and Jews by creating stereotypes which then serve the interests of Christian patriarchy and Christian anti-Judaism.

Feminist biblical typology is already functioning in the identification of some biblical texts as reflecting repeated historical patterns recognized by women. The woman's search for the lost coin (Luke 15:8-10) has become a type of women's search for their lost tradition, or for value in Christian tradition. The woman bent double (Luke 13:10-17) is often used as a type of women's struggle for recognition and authority in the church. The woman who anointed Jesus' head with oil (Matthew 26:6-13; Mark 14:3-9) serves as a type of women's liturgical and prophetic leadership as well as the tradition's resistance to that leadership.

Still other feminist typologies will continue to emerge as women continue to articulate their experience in the church and in the world, and to recognize patterns of oppression and of women's strategies of resistance both in their own lives and in the scriptures.

Feminist Translation

Feminist translation of scriptures is necessary for the development of feminist emancipatory proclamation. Although inclusive translation, which corrects androcentric language to include women, is useful, it alone is insufficient for liturgical proclamation. The pastoral and ethical demands of liturgical proclamation require an effort to subvert and supplant the patriarchal and misogynist elements of any text that is to be proclaimed to the worshiping community as the "word of God." Such translation must assist the community in reading between the lines, in the silences and gaps, and behind the lies and evasions of the androcentric text.

At the same time, feminist translation would draw attention to, rather than gloss over, the hostility of some texts for women and other oppressed people, in order that recognition and repentance of the human cost of proclaiming such texts as word of God may be carried out in the worship assembly.

FEMINIST AMPLIFICATION

The liturgical context is at least potentially multisensory. Minimally, a text that is often approached primarily as written literature is re-presented as spoken. The biblical text ceases, at least to some extent, to be written text and becomes once again oral. It also has at least the possibility of being presented through image and action as well as spoken word in the liturgical setting.

This offers possibilities for amplification of the text which may go beyond the written or even the read text. Jane Schaberg's suggestion that written texts of Gospel stories of the call of the male disciples be amplified with the inclusion of a blank page marked "The Call of the Women Disciples"[14] lends itself well to liturgical proclamation, which may include drama, ritual act and gesture, dance, art, and music, as well as sermon. In such a broadened context, both the marginalized voices and the hostile patriarchal voice in the biblical witness can be presented.

The model of feminist amplification also reminds us that a distinction must be drawn between texts that proclaim emancipatory transformation (and these may be emancipatory only in feminist translation or amplified proclamation) and texts that are hostile to emancipation and thus cannot be proclaimed as "word of God." Such hostile texts can, and should, however, be used in liturgies of lament, exorcism, and repentance.

Clearly, multiple models of the use of the Bible in feminist liturgical proclamation are necessary in order to deal with the complex and painful relationship that exists between women and other oppressed people and the Bible. Texts must not be limited to the prevailing narrow role of "word of God." They must also be allowed to function as objects of critique, lament, exorcism, and witness to the oppression as well as the emancipation of the people of God. Only in this way can women begin to proclaim the scriptures "painfully, angrily, prophetically, hopefully, lovingly, and gracefully."

NOTES

1. Rebecca Chopp, *The Power To Speak: Feminism, Language, God* (New York: Crossroad, 1989), 47.

2. Itumeleng J. Mosala, *Biblical Hermeneutics and Black Theology in South Africa* (Grand Rapids: Eerdmans, 1989), 193.

3. See Leland T. White, "The Bible, Theology and Cultural Pluralism," *Biblical Theology Bulletin* 16 (1986): 111–15; Susan Thistlethwaite, "Every Two Minutes: Battered Women

and Feminist Interpretation," in *Feminist Interpretation of the Bible,* ed. Letty M. Russell (Philadelphia: Westminster, 1985), 96–110; Sheila Redmond, "Christian 'Virtues' and Recovery from Child Sexual Abuse," in *Christianity, Patriarchy, and Abuse,* ed. Joanne Carlson Brown and Carole Bohn (New York: Pilgrim, 1989), 70–88.

4. E. Schüssler Fiorenza, *Bread Not Stone: The Challenge of Feminist Biblical Interpretation* (Boston: Beacon Press, 1984), 25.

5. Horace T. Allen, Jr., "Common Lectionary: Origins, Assumptions, and Issues," *Studia Liturgica* 21 (1991): 14–30; Consultation on Common Texts, *The Revised Common Lectionary* (Nashville: Abingdon Press, 1992).

6. See Marjorie Procter-Smith, "Images of Women in the Lectionary," in *Women—Invisible in Theology and Church,* ed. Elisabeth Schüssler Fiorenza and Mary Collins, *Concilium* 182 (Edinburgh: T. & T. Clark, 1985), 51–62; Jean Campbell, "The Feminine as Omitted, Optional, or Alternative Story: A Feminist Review of the Episcopal Eucharistic Lectionary," in *Proceedings of the North American Academy of Liturgy* (Valparaiso, IN: NAAL, 1990), 59–67.

7. Schüssler Fiorenza, *Bread Not Stone,* 18.

8. See O. C. Edwards, Jr., *Elements of Homiletic: A Method for Preparing to Preach* (New York: Pueblo Publishing, 1982).

9. See William D. Thompson, *Preaching Biblically: Exegesis and Interpretation* (Nashville: Abingdon, 1981).

10. See Christine Smith, *Weaving the Sermon: Preaching in a Feminist Perspective* (Louisville, KY: Westminster/John Knox, 1989); Marjorie Procter-Smith, *In Her Own Rite* (Nashville: Abingdon, 1990), 131–35.

11. See *The Service for the Lord's Day: The Worship of God,* Presbyterian Church (U.S.A.) and Cumberland Presbyterian Church (Philadelphia: Westminster, 1984), 101–11; *The United Methodist Hymnal: Book of United Methodist Worship* (Nashville: United Methodist Publishing House, 1989), 6.

12. See Shawn Madigan, "Called to be Holy, Made to be Saints," *Liturgy* 1 (1980): 32–36.

13. *Lutheran Book of Worship* (Minister's Desk Edition; Minneapolis: Augsburg; Philadelphia: Board of Publication, Lutheran Church in America, 1978), 41–45.

14. Jane Schaberg, "Response: Special Section on Feminist Translation of the New Testament," *Journal of Feminist Studies in Religion* 6 (1990): 74–85.

RECOMMENDED READINGS

Campbell, Jean. "The Feminine as Omitted, Optional, or Alternative Story: A Feminist Review of the Episcopal Eucharistic Lectionary." In *Proceedings of the North American Academy of Liturgy,* 59–67. Valparaiso, IN: NAAL, 1990.

Chopp, Rebecca. *The Power To Speak: Feminism, Language, God.* New York: Crossroad, 1989.

Duck, Ruth C. *Gender and the Name of God: The Trinitarian Baptismal Formula.* New York: Pilgrim Press, 1991.

Procter-Smith, Marjorie. "Images of Women in the Lectionary." In *Women—Invisible in Theology and Church,* edited by Elisabeth Schüssler Fiorenza and Mary Collins, 51–62. *Concilium* 182. Edinburgh: T. & T. Clark, 1985.

———. *In Her Own Rite.* Nashville: Abingdon, 1990.

Redmond, Sheila. "Christian 'Virtues' and Recovery from Child Sexual Abuse." In *Christianity, Patriarchy, and Abuse,* edited by Joanne Carlson Brown and Carole Bohn, 70–88. New York: Pilgrim Press.

Schaberg, Jane. "Response: Special Section on Feminist Translation of the New Testament." *Journal of Feminist Studies in Religion* 6 (1990): 74–85.

Schüssler Fiorenza, Elisabeth. *Bread Not Stone: The Challenge of Feminist Biblical Interpretation.* Boston: Beacon Press, 1984.

Smith, Christine. *Weaving the Sermon: Preaching in a Feminist Perspective.* Louisville, KY: Westminster/John Knox, 1989.

Thistlethwaite, Susan. "Every Two Minutes: Battered Women and Feminist Interpretation." In *Feminist Interpretation of the Bible,* edited by Letty M. Russell, 96–110. Philadelphia: Westminster, 1985.

Thompson, William D. *Preaching Biblically: Exegesis and Interpretation.* Nashville: Abingdon, 1981.

Winter, Miriam Therese. *WomanWord. A Feminist Lectionary and Psalter. Women of the New Testament.* New York: Crossroad, 1990.

Wren, Brian. *What Language Shall I Borrow? God-Talk in Worship: A Male Response.* New York: Crossroad, 1989.

◆ Womanist Interpretation
and Preaching in the Black Church

KATIE G. CANNON ◆

THERE IS AN INTIMATE CONNECTION between the new modes of critical inquiry created by African-American women in the theological academy[1] and the central role that preaching plays as a cultural phenomenon in the black church community.[2] It is new because, until most recently, black preaching has not asked questions about womanist interpretation and womanist theological studies have not included homiletics. It is significant because the majority of the faithful who have heard and continue to hear black preaching are women.

While the majority of these churchgoers have little trouble testifying that a good sermon is a many-splendored art form, the articulation of an analysis by which we elucidate and delegitimize patriarchal teachings is not as easily arrived at. When sermons are written and presented in the interest of men, the categorical definitions of theo-ethical concepts lend an evidently weighty authority to androcentric conclusions about male preachers and masculine-centered culture.[3] It is therefore important to analyze sermonic texts in terms of their socioecclesial locations and theological interests, with special attention to their gender dimension. Such methodological analysis of sermonic texts needs to be the task of womanist interpretation.

My own proposal for the form this womanist interpretation should take is based on the convergence of a feminist liberationist theoretical interpretation inspired by Elisabeth Schüssler Fiorenza's groundbreaking scholarship and Isaac R. Clark's seminal work on black homiletics.[4] These two dynamic areas of interpretative discourse offer a challenging nexus for womanist scholars concerned with radically rethinking and revisioning "how duties and roles are advocated, how arguments are constructed and how power is inscribed"[5] in the black church community.

A womanist critique of homiletics challenges conventional biblical interpretations that characterize African-American women as "sin-bringing

Eve," "wilderness-whimpering Hagar," "henpecking Jezebel," "whoring Gomer," "prostituting Mary Magdalene," and "conspiring Sapphira." A womanist hermeneutic identifies the frame of sexist-racist social contradictions housed in sacred rhetoric that gives women a low image of ourselves. This analysis deconstructs biblically based sermons that portray female subjects as bleeding, crippled, disempowered, objectified, purified madwomen. It enables us to ask hard questions about the responsibility of black preachers to satisfy the *whole* congregation's spiritual hunger, with their intellectual grasp, mastery of scripture, social analysis, and constructive homiletical skill. Both areas of research, feminist liberation interpretation and preaching in the black church, reinforce each other, by raising questions, clarifying problems, and amplifying issues that shape our collective consciousness about "the survival and wholeness of an entire people."[6]

FEMINIST LIBERATIONIST INTERPRETATION

Following Schüssler Fiorenza's methodology, I would argue that the essential task of a womanist hermeneutic consists in analyzing how black sermonic texts "participate in creating or sustaining oppressive or liberating theo-ethical values and sociopolitical practices."[7] Womanist analysis provides an interpretative framework that holds together the spiritual matrix of black religious culture while exposing the complex, baffling contradictions inherent in androcentric language. I am arguing for a critical evaluation of sermonic texts, including an analysis of when and how women are mentioned, and whether these sermons adequately reflect African-American reality.[8]

Schüssler Fiorenza's methodology can be likened to detective work, which does not rely solely on historical "facts" nor invent the evidence. Instead, it engages in an imaginative reconstruction that rests on observation and inference and employs a critical analysis of whether scriptural texts in sermons mention women only as problems or as exceptions. The task of womanist homiletics is to unearth what black preachers are saying about women and what we are saying about men.

A critical study of black sermons shows that African-American church traditions and redactional processes follow certain androcentric interests and perspectives that do not reflect the historical contributions of African-American women's leadership and participation in the life of the church. By showing the detailed and numerous androcentric injunctions about women's nature, place, and behavior in black preaching, we are able to identify and critique sermonic texts that express and maintain patriarchal historical conditioning. We are also able to highlight those sermons which reproduce and shape the liberative reality for all members of the worshiping community.

A womanist adaptation of Schüssler Fiorenza's integrative heuristic model seeks to provide means of ethical assessment that help the black church community look at the practices and habits, assumptions and problems, values and hopes embedded in its Christian cultural mind-set. It does so with the hope of renewing and reforming the faith-justice praxis in the black preaching tradition. It is essential that womanist interpretative practices be employed not only in the critique of androcentric preaching with its references to patriarchal relationships of inequality. We must also use womanist methodology at the constructive stage of sermon preparation and delivery.

PREACHING IN THE BLACK CHURCH

The history of black preaching begins with the emergence of the black church as an invisible institution in the slave community during the seventeenth century.[9] Utilizing West African religious concepts in a new and totally different context and blending them syncretistically with orthodox, colonial Christianity, black women and men developed an extensive religious life of their own.[10] The black church community was the only social institution in which African Americans could exercise leadership and power, and the preacher and preaching were held in the highest esteem. Preaching was one of the principal instruments used by enslaved black leaders. They preached what they knew about the progression from patriarch to priest to prophet to Jesus to Paul and testified to what they had seen, exalting the word of God above all other authorities. The preacher sought for close, empathetic, communal identification with the congregation. Holding forth in the pulpit on Sundays and throughout the week as one of God's earthly representatives, the preacher was the dominant, influential spokesperson for the community at large. The black preacher served as the arbiter of intellectual/moral life and the principal interpreter of canonized sacred writings.[11]

The continued self-inventiveness of black preaching is the result of gifted orators who gathered Bible stories, deeds, and sayings from their given theological contexts and transposed these words of faith into patterned episodes in clear language amenable to their listeners. Black preaching is a running commentary on scripture passages, showing how the Bible is an infinite resource that provides hearers with ways in word and deed for overcoming oppressive situations.

Because of the oral proclivities of African-American Christian culture, a written sermon cannot be understood apart from its delivery. The sermon is a combination of serious exegesis and imaginative elaboration of the stories in the Pentateuch, the sayings in wisdom literature, the prophetic writings, and the New Testament. It is an unhampered play of theological fantasy and at the same time an acknowledgment of the cultural maturity and religious sophistication of traditional themes.

The homiletical explorations of Isaac R. Clark penetrate to the soul of black preaching, providing us with insight into the way in which oral religious thought is organized and conceptualized. To be sure, Clark speaks of black preaching in the broadest sense, as a fundamentally creative, artistic cultural form of African-American Christian speech that exhibits a distinct, expressive style and flavor for communicating existent religious beliefs and theo-ethical considerations in an articulate oral pattern. According to Clark, preaching as the spoken representation of the dimensions of the holy is "divine activity wherein the Word of God is proclaimed or announced concerning contemporary issues with a view toward ultimate response to God."

Black preaching is a narrative that exhibits all of the formal structures of rhetorical prose, such as a text, title, introduction, proposition, body, and conclusion. It is the major medium for making scriptural proclamation relevant to our times. By figuratively dramatizing biblical conflicts of dominance and submission, assertion and deference, the righted and the outlawed, the propertied and the dispossessed, the black preacher calls into question "the social network of power/knowledge relations."[12] In each preaching event, the religious practices and deep-seated theo-ethical beliefs of the black church are reinvented in and through a specific scriptural interpretation. Investigation of the integral connection between the preacher who creates the sermon, the sermon's internal design, the world that the sermon reveals, and the religious sensibilities of the congregation that are affected by the sermon invites us to a higher degree of critical consciousness about the invisible milieu in which we worship.

Divine activity refers to the customary three-tiered configuration that places the black preacher in the mediating position between God and the congregation. With one ear to the ground hearing the cries and longings of the people and the other ear at the mouth of God the preacher has a special obligation to instruct the hearers in defining, interpreting, and solving problems related to the life we live, the life we dread, and the life we aspire to live. The preacher has power and privilege to determine precisely what biblical text will be used and whose experiences are central and endowed with force and continuity in the encoding of norms and values for the black church community. Throughout the sermonic delivery the preacher must communicate that the authority for the sermon emanates from a guiding force beyond the preacher, in God.[13]

Word of God focuses on the Word that becomes flesh and dwells with us as the living God, and does not simply apply to the "words" of canonized scripture that we read and hear. The God-self is present as the content of the preached word. The Holy Spirit must work through the critically conscious preacher so as to present the person and work of Jesus Christ as recorded in the Bible to the body of believers.[14] Jesus, the kerygmatic Christ, pulsates with a quality of "isness," a particular contemporaneity which identifies the sacredness spoken of during the sermon with recognizable aspects of the congregation's everyday raw material of existence.[15] Preaching in the black church is a dynamic process that matches the scriptural texts with temporal sequences, provides etiological explanation for evil and suffering inflicted by human agency, and emphasizes the close union of heaven and earth, God and people.

Black preaching concentrates a lot of attention on Jesus, who acts decisively and speaks pointedly.[16] The Gospel stories about Jesus are linked back to quite definite events of the Greco-Roman world and to the life of the present-day community. However, in the final analysis it is not the historical Jesus who occupies the central place but the divine power that holds sway over him as the Word Incarnate.

Proclaimed or *announced* is the preacher's indicative mode for declaring the biblical ideas, beliefs, and systems of thought in the vernacular of the hearers. To be most effective and efficient, the preacher artfully amplifies sacred referencing in a language that includes the idiomatic and colloquial forms most recognizable to black churchgoers. The exposition of the scriptural text must be delivered with vigor and vitality in order to bear witness to the preacher's enthusiasm for being called to this sacred task. The language of black preaching is a mode of action and not simply a countersign of thought. Parishioners participate in a call-and-response dialogue with the preacher that subjects biblical preaching to dynamic, in-the-moment expressions of resurrection.

The narrative strategies of black religious lore recapitulate the lives and decisive actions of biblical ancestors, who are not thought to belong merely to the past but are also considered to be living on, in, with, and beyond their faith descendants. Black preaching takes great liberty in tapping into the inexhaustible treasures of wisdom and spiritual power lodged in the biblical canon.[17] Black preaching encourages proclamations of the "good news" Bible stories in ways that are interactive, memorable, and commonly public.[18] Anthropomorphism within the black preaching tradition transforms biblical characters, adventures, and behavior supposedly peculiar to everyday folks into a larger context of experience so that the finite mind can grapple with the eternal creative act.

Contemporary issues are determined by gifted communicators transforming and reinterpreting their divine call as it interfaces with scripture and the existential circumstances of the hearers. Clark's study of sacred rhetoric suggests a number of intriguing approaches that open up windows to the biblical concepts structured into the imaginative core of the black worship experience. By communicating with gestures, facial expressions, and chanted deliveries, the black preacher builds a compelling sermon by preserving and "making plain" the stories of the Bible that have been handed down through the years.[19] Equilibrium is maintained by sloughing off memories that no longer have present relevance while proclaiming the religious inheritance of ancestral mothers and fathers that enhances narrative variation for audience responses in similar but new situations.

The black sermon is more than a mere tangent to social history.[20] It has a special affinity with contextual reality, insofar as it connects the experience of finitude with the transcendent dimensions expressed within the biblical culture of bygone days. It encompasses vivid descriptions, colloquial diction and concrete imagery drawn from both the Bible and daily life, symbolizing liberating possibilities between actuality and hope, real and ideal, earth and heaven. In other words, Bible stories are relived, not merely heard; the preacher gives enough details and embellishes the actions with metaphors to keep the story moving so that the hearers stay abreast of their present-day identification with the biblically based narratives.

Given the complexity of and ambiguity in the black church community, preachers verbalize their homilies with more or less close reference to the African-American life world, assimilating the abstract world of theology to the more immediate, familiar world of everyday life and struggle. Homiletical proclamation is enmeshed with historical and social events in the African-American community, engaging knowledge in the arena where human beings struggle with one another, binding the knower and the known.

The overall objective and purpose of preaching are to call the worshiping congregation to an *ultimate response to God.* According to Clark, the black preacher's primary activity is to inform, engage, and create contradictions within situations of complacent security in order to invite the congregation to make a decision for or against emancipatory praxis. Preaching not only helps us to know what we believe and why, but it is the medium through which events of transformative understanding shake up creeds, question social power, and transform traditions. The preacher thinks through complex problems and articulates solutions by verbalizing a "why crisis" that motivates the listeners to contemplate the complicated series of theo-ethical assertions. The constant exposure to the abounding iniquity in the world opens the congregation to a gracious message of deliverance.

Clark's rhetorical methodology shows why black preaching has acquired a particular and unique physiognomy, why certain theo-ethical themes and motifs are present and others absent, why certain stylistic treatments are accepted and others rejected. In other words, this signifying process enables us to see how theo-ethical canons, standards, and conventions are produced and maintained in African-American homiletical texts. Hence, black sermons are characterized by the combination of biblical retrospect with exhortation in which the worshiping community is called forth to be among the chosen, fully grasping and proclaiming the character of Yahweh as the liberating God of history. Black sermons have a great deal to teach us concerning the congregation's call to possible redemption through the fullest imaginative response.

Clark solves effectively the problem of intellectually organizing the data of text and context by developing a rhetorical methodology of heavy patterning in terms of definition, elaboration, exemplification, and justification, in order to establish a line of continuity inside the mind. The syntax, rhythm, and balanced pattern of repeating these four formulary essentials help implement rhythmic discourse. They act as retention and ready recall aids in their own right. Moreover, they form the substance of thought itself. Clark's coordinated homiletical structure, through which the syntactic and theological ideas are generated, expands the aesthetic dimensions of black preaching, realizing the most effective, consistent, innovative "telling of the old, old story."

WOMANIST QUERIES

My particular concern is with the way in which a womanist critical evaluative process, when understood in its contextual framework, can suggest the possibilities and limitations for liberating the negative and derogatory female portraiture in black preaching. An intensive examination of sermonic texts shows how preachers follow certain androcentric interests in objectifying and commodifying black women. Even in "text-led" biblical preaching where the representation of woman may occupy a central place in the expository structure, women are often occluded. By unmasking the detailed and numerous androcentric injunctions, womanist hermeneutics attempts to expose the impact of "phallocentric" concepts which are present within black sacred rhetoric.

For instance, when we turn to the experience of black churchwomen, in order to establish criteria for interpreting and determining the value of sermonic texts, we need to ask, what difference does it make that African-American Christians hear sermons full of linguistic sexism, in which images of and reference to women are seldom positive? As womanist theologians, what can we do to counter the negative, real-world consequences of sexist wording that brothers and sisters propagate in the guise of Christian piety and virtue? How disruptive are such gender-biased androcentric sermons for social relations within the temporal circumstances of the African-American family? What is the correlation between what is preached in church on Sunday and what Abbey Lincoln describes as the African-American woman's social predicament?

> Her head is more regularly beaten than any other woman's, and by her own man; she's the scapegoat for Mr. Charlie, she is forced to stark realism and chided if caught dreaming; her aspirations for her and hers are, for sanity sake, stunted; her physical image has been criminally maligned, assaulted, and negated; she is the first to be called ugly, and never yet beautiful. . . .[21]

As clergywomen committed to the well-being of the African-American community how are we refuting gender stereotypes that are dehumanizing, debilitating, and prejudicial to African-American women?[22] Can we change male supremicist attitudes by prescribing alternatives to discriminatory word usage? What happens to African-American female children when black preachers use the Bible to attribute marvelous happenings and unusual circumstances to an all-male scenario? The privilege, power, and prerogative in developing such sermons are in themselves significant. The marginalization of women within the cast of characters constitutes a significant choice within these larger patterns of decisions.

What are the essential liberating strategies that African-American clergywomen use in our own sacred rhetoric that will continue to encourage an ethic of resistance? What are we doing that will allow a womanist interpretation to emerge, an analysis that shows how black women who are subjected to patriarchal teachings and relations of domination are complex, life-affirming moral agents? I maintain that a womanist analysis provides the internal analytical categories of the valuation system for this genre of sacred rhetoric.

The sensibilities of womanist interpretation of preaching in the black church require sacred orators to be responsive to the emotional, political, psychic, and intellectual implications of our message. We anticipate and embrace both power and subsequent actions in the creation and in the delivery of our sermons. Therefore, we must identify the qualities and considerations that result in the identification of an "ideal" black church-woman and the production of the "realized" Christian woman. In appreciating the complexity of the genius of black preaching, we must be able to analyze how this genre is both sacred and profane, active and passive, life-giving and death-dealing. Womanist interpretation calls for the balanced tension between the accuracy of the spoken word—organization, language, fluidity, and style—and the expressed political aim of our sermonic content. In order to present coequal discipleship the preacher must reflect on the sacred words that underrepresent, truncate, and distort African-American women's image, voice, and agency.

A womanist hermeneutics seeks to place sermonic texts in the real-life context of the culture that has produced them. The basic premises of sermonic development aim to operate inside boundaries both of canonized scripture and of the circumstances in which the sermon is written and delivered. Images used throughout the sermon invite the congregation to share in dismantling patriarchy, by artfully and deftly guiding the congregation through the rigors of resisting the abjection and marginalization of women. A womanist interpretation requires each component of black homiletics to adhere to the emancipatory practice of a faith community. The preacher is obliged and expected to show the listeners how to "trace out the logic of liberation that can transform patriarchal oppression."[23]

Womanist hermeneutics regards sociocultural context as an important component of the sermon. The preacher's testimonial function is necessarily looked at within a personal-existential framework. These utterances of the preacher must be examined in the situation in which they are produced and delivered to the hearers, that is, in terms of the preacher's and congregation's own experiences. Nothing prohibits us from asking questions about the role of social factors in shaping sermonic texts and what part the preacher's gender plays in selecting the kinds of biblical stories and sayings which she or he uses in preaching.

Womanist analysis of sermons inquires into the depictions of women's experiences, of missionary circles, of mothers and female saints of the church, and of the women officers and leaders in the ecclesiastical community. This practice removes men from the "normative" center and women from the margins. It leads to the alteration of prevailing masculine models of influence. To avoid perpetuating traditional, binary assumptions, womanist theory offers a helpful strategy for focusing on the oppression of women while simultaneously providing conventions of liberation.

Using Clark's tools and methods on preaching in the black church and interfacing them with Schüssler Fiorenza's most recent writings on feminist liberationist criticism, we can provide precise answers to these questions: (1) How is meaning constructed? (2) Whose interests are served? (3) What kind of worlds are envisioned in black sacred rhetoric? Every choice that a preacher makes in constructing a sermon will have certain connotations, inherited from the sermons that preceded it. Preaching in the black church is as much affected by issues of misogyny, androcentricity, and patriarchy as by homiletical form. Within this complex discursive construction of sacred rhetoric, women and men who cast their lot with us must make an intervention, no matter how slight, in the dominant religious discourse of our time.

NOTES

1. The canon of womanist discourse is growing. Among many, see Toinette Eugene, "Moral Values and Black Womanists," *Journal of Religious Thought* 44 (Winter/Spring 1988): 23–34; "Roundtable Discussion: Christian Ethics and Theology in Womanist Perspective," *Journal of Feminist Studies in Religion* 5/2 (Fall 1989): 82–112 (lead essay by Cheryl J. Sanders; responses to the essay by Katie G. Cannon, Emilie M. Townes, M. Shawn Copeland, Cheryl Townsend Gilkes and bell hooks); Delores S. Williams, "Women's Oppression and Lifeline Politics in Black Women's Religious Narratives," *Journal of Feminist Studies in Religion* 2 (Fall 1985): 59–71; eadem, "The Color of Feminism: Or Speaking the Black Woman's Tongue," *Journal of Religious Thought* 43 (Spring/Summer 1986): 45–58; and Emilie M. Townes, ed., *A Troubling in My Soul: Womanist Perspectives on Evil and Suffering* (New York: Orbis, 1993).

2. See Joseph A. Johnson, Jr., *The Soul of the Black Preacher* (Memphis: C.M.E. Publishing House, 1970); Charles V. Hamilton, *The Black Preacher in America* (New York: William Morrow, 1972); Henry H. Mitchell, *Black Preaching* (Philadelphia: Lippincott, 1970); idem, *Celebration and Experience in Preaching* (Nashville: Abingdon, 1991).

3. See Robyn R. Warhol and Diane Price Herndl, eds., *Feminisms: An Anthology of Literary Theory and Criticism* (New Brunswick: Rutgers University Press, 1991).

4. Elisabeth Schüssler Fiorenza, *In Memory of Her: A Feminist Theological Reconstruction of Christian Origins* (New York: Crossroad, 1983); Isaac Rufus Clark was an extraordinary homiletician and master teacher for twenty-seven years at the Interdenominational Theological Center in Atlanta, Georgia. Throughout this discussion I refer to my learning from his lectures and class notes.

5. Elisabeth Schüssler Fiorenza, *Revelation: Vision of a Just World* (Minneapolis: Fortress Press, 1991), 3.

6. This is an essential component in Alice Walker's definition of "womanist" in her collection of essays *In Search of Our Mothers' Gardens: Womanist Prose* (New York: Harcourt Brace Jovanovich, 1983), xi.

7. Schüssler Fiorenza, *Revelation*, 3.

8. One could critique the sermons in the following anthologies: Walter B. Hoard, ed.,

Outstanding Black Sermons, Vol. 2 (Valley Forge, PA: Judson Press, 1979); Robert T. Newbold, ed., *Black Preaching: Selected Sermons in the Presbyterian Tradition* (Philadelphia: Geneva Press, 1977); Milton E. Owens, Jr., ed., *Outstanding Black Sermons,* Vol. 3 (Valley Forge, PA: Judson Press, 1982); William M. Philpot, ed., *Best Black Sermons* (Valley Forge, PA: Judson Press, 1972); James Henry Young, ed., *Preaching the Gospel* (Philadelphia: Fortress Press, 1976).

9. See Albert J. Raboteau, *Slave Religion: The "Invisible Institution" in the Antebellum South* (New York: Oxford University Press, 1978); and David Charles Dennard, "Religion in the Quarters: A Study of Slave Preachers in the Antebellum South, 1800–1860" (Ph.D. diss., Northwestern University, 1983).

10. See Benjamin E. Mays, *The Negro's Church* (New York: Institute of Social and Religious Research, 1933); Harry V. Richardson, *Dark Glory: A Picture of the Church Among Negroes in the Rural South* (New York: Friendship Press, 1974); Carter G. Woodson, *The History of the Negro Church* (Washington, DC: Associated Press, 1921).

11. See Gayraud S. Wilmore, *Black Religion and Black Radicalism: An Examination of the Black Experience in Religion* (Garden City, NY: Doubleday, 1972); and Jualynne Dodson, "Nineteenth-Century A.M.E. Preaching Women," in *Woman in New Worlds,* ed. Hilah F. Thomas and Rosemary S. Keller (Nashville: Abingdon, 1981), 276–89.

12. Elisabeth Schüssler Fiorenza, *But She Said: Feminist Practice of Biblical Interpretation* (Boston: Beacon Press, 1992), 3.

13. See Gerald L. Davis, *I Got the Word in Me and I Can Sing It, You Know: A Study of the Performed African American Sermon* (Philadelphia: University of Pennsylvania Press, 1985); James H. Robinson, *Adventurous Preaching* (Great Neck, NY: Channel Press, 1956); and Bruce Rosenberg, *Can These Bones Live?* (Urbana: University of Illinois Press, 1988).

14. James Forbes, *The Holy Spirit and Preaching* (Nashville: Abingdon, 1989).

15. See Jacquelyn Grant, "Womanist Theology: Black Women's Experience as a Source for Doing Theology, with Special Reference to Christology," *Journal of the Interdenominational Theological Center* 13/2 (Spring 1986): 195–212; and Kelly D. Brown, "God Is as Christ Does: Toward a Womanist Theology," in *Journal of Religious Thought* 46/1 (Summer/Fall 1989): 7–16.

16. E. L. McCall et al., *Seven Black Preachers Tell: What Jesus Means to Me* (Nashville: Broadman, 1971).

17. Cain Hope Felder, ed., *Stony the Road We Trod: African American Biblical Interpretation* (Minneapolis: Fortress Press, 1991).

18. C. L. Franklin, *Give Me This Mountain: Life History and Selected Sermon,* ed. Jeff Todd Titon, foreword by Jesse Jackson (Urbana: University of Illinois Press, 1989); Samuel Gandy, ed., *Human Possibilities: A Vernon John Reader* (Washington, DC: Hoffman Press, 1977); William Lloyd Imes, *The Black Pastures* (Nashville: Hemphill Press, 1957); Sandy Ray, *Journeying Through the Jungle* (Nashville: Broadman, 1979); Gardner Taylor, *The Scarlet Thread: Nineteen Sermons* (Elgin, IL: Progressive Baptist Publishing House, 1981).

19. See Williams E. Hatcher, *John Jasper* (New York: F. H. Revell, 1908); and Ralph H. Jones, *Albert Tindley: Prince of Black Preachers* (Nashville: Abingdon, 1982).

20. See Samuel D. Proctor, *Preaching About Crisis in the Community* (Philadelphia: Westminster, 1988); and Kelly Miller Smith, *Social Crisis Preaching* (Macon, GA: Mercer University Press, 1984).

21. Abbey Lincoln, "Who Will Revere the Black Woman?" *Negro Digest* (September 1966): 18.

22. One could critique sermons written and published by African-American women in

the following anthologies: Ella Pearson Mitchell, ed., *Those Preaching Women: Sermons by Black Women Preachers,* 2 vols. (Valley Forge, PA: Judson Press, 1985, 1988); Helen Gray Crotwell, ed., *Women and the Word: Sermons* (Philadelphia: Fortress Press, 1977); Justo L. Gonzalez, ed., *Proclaiming the Acceptable Year: Sermons from the Perspective of Liberation Theology* (Valley Forge, PA: Judson Press, 1982); David A. Farmer and Edwina Hunter, eds., *And Blessed Is She: Sermons By Women* (San Francisco: Harper & Row, 1990); Annie L. Milhaven, ed., *Sermons Seldom Heard: Women Proclaim Their Lives* (New York: Crossroad, 1991).

23. Schüssler Fiorenza, *But She Said,* 9.

RECOMMENDED READINGS

Cone, James H., and Gayraud S. Wilmore, eds. *Black Theology: A Documentary History,* Vol. 2: *1980–1992.* Maryknoll, NY: Orbis, 1993.

Gandy, Samuel, ed. *Human Possibilities: A Vernon John Reader.* Washington, DC: Hoffman Press, 1977.

Kelly, Leontine T. C. "Preaching in the Black Tradition." In *Women Ministers,* edited by Judith L. Weidman, 67–76. San Francisco: Harper & Row, 1985.

Mitchell, Ella P., ed. *Those Preaching Women: Sermons by Black Women Preachers.* 2 vols. Valley Forge, PA: Judson Press, 1985, 1988.

Pipes, William H. *Say Amen, Brother! Old Time Negro Preaching: A Study in American Frustration.* With an Introduction by Cornel West. Detroit: Wayne State University Press, 1992.

Sanders, Cheryl J. "The Woman as Preacher." In *African American Religious Studies: An Interdisciplinary Anthology,* edited by Gayraud S. Wilmore. Durham, NC: Duke University Press, 1989.

Schüssler Fiorenza, Elisabeth. *Discipleship of Equals: A Critical Feminist Ekklesia-logy of Liberation.* New York: Crossroad, 1993.

——. *But She Said: Feminist Practices of Biblical Interpretation.* Boston: Beacon Press, 1992.

Smith, Kelly Miller. *Social Crisis Preaching: The Lyman Beecher Lectures, 1983.* Macon, GA: Mercer University Press, 1984.

Taylor, Gardner C. *Chariots Aflame.* Nashville: Broadman Press, 1988.

Townes, Emilie M., ed. *A Troubling in My Soul: Womanist Reflections on Evil and Suffering.* Maryknoll, NY: Orbis, 1993.

Warren, Mervyn A. *Black Preaching: Truth and Soul.* Washington, DC: University Press of America, 1977.

◆ Shifting the Paradigm:
Feminist Bible Study

ALISON M. CHEEK ◆

CONSCIOUSNESS RAISING THROUGH feminist Bible study involves the attainment of some freedom with the text. It is most effective in groups composed entirely of women. When women come together without men present we learn to trust our communal insights and our own experiences of oppression and liberation in a patriarchal church and world.

For women to meet separately in a congregational setting there may have to be some preliminary education. It is necessary to find ways to interpret to those upset by exclusion the different dynamic that occurs in mixed groups and in gender-specific groups. If you are the pastor of a church you will be able to accomplish this more easily than if you have to convince a pastor, but the group will have fewer hurdles to jump if the pastor is sympathetic to the issue.

Public announcement and advance notice of a Bible study group are helpful. If the parish has a bulletin or newsletter, an announcement worded with care will help attract a wide spectrum of participants. Women in Bible study groups usually have differing levels of consciousness about social oppression, depending on their culture and context. Some may be resistant to addressing gender oppression; heterosexism may be totally unconscious; participants are likely to have varying levels of understanding of race and class issues. Not many women will come with the confidence to be their own interpreters of the text.

Is there a way in Bible study groups to loosen the weave of the biblical text and its familiar interpretation so that women may come to see ourselves as theological agents, with a part to play in forming and transforming our religious tradition? Both tools and strategies are needed to shift from an androcentric model of biblical interpretation to a critical feminist one.

SHIFTING THE PARADIGM

An overall framework that provides tools for a critical feminist interpretation of biblical texts is Elisabeth Schüssler Fiorenza's fourfold hermeneutical model: *a hermeneutics of suspicion,* which does not take androcentric texts at face value, and which analyzes the patriarchal interests of the authors of the texts; *a hermeneutics of remembrance,* which moves beyond specific texts on women to reconstruct women's history obscured by androcentric historical consciousness; *a hermeneutics of proclamation,* which assesses all scriptural texts and evaluates them theologically for their oppressive impact or liberating tendency; and *a hermeneutics of creative actualization,* which stimulates our creative powers to recall, embody, and celebrate the achievements, sufferings, and struggles of the biblical women who are our forebears in the faith.[1] The potential for consciousness raising is implicit in this model.

An invaluable visual aid in consciousness raising is the drawing of patriarchal pyramids, which Elisabeth Schüssler Fiorenza has introduced in her teaching.[2] Such pyramids immediately make visually apparent women's subordinate position in the power structures of society. In addition, the pyramid shows with visual clarity that patriarchy is not simply the domination of all women by all men. Social location determines where particular categories of men and women fall on the domination and subordination scale and where power relations lie. Patriarchy used in this sense refers to a political and social system in which a hierarchy of subordinations and dominations in regard to economic status, race, and gender are integrally related to one another. Feminism is then seen as the political oppositional term to patriarchy.

The presentation in diagram form of the classical Aristotelian model of a patriarchal society is helpful for its clarity (see appendix 1). Although throughout history modifications have taken place in the layers, it is still basically the political-social structure in Western culture today. When it is apparent that we are structurally linked with our foresisters in the first and second centuries we are able to identify with their struggles. Seeing the model in the form of a diagram has the effect of cutting through the rhetoric that obscures power structures when the relationship between men and women is addressed simply in terms of complementarity. When women grasp this conceptual tool, consciousness is raised. Moreover, we can no longer talk about women's reality without differentiating between women who are privileged and who have access to some power, and women who are doubly and triply oppressed by the patriarchal system.

When white, middle- and upper-class women are not conscious of these interrelated structures, we tend to shift from an androcentric paradigm to a gynocentric one. Once women are able to analyze the structures of oppression for men of color and women of color, for women trapped in poverty and men trapped in poverty, for gay men and lesbian women, for women and men crippled by colonial exploitation and militarism, and for those dominated by cultural imperialism, the impulse is not to move to a gynocentric paradigm but to a feminist one.

It is with these tools in hand that I have approached feminist Bible study. Strategy, however, is dictated by context. My own work has been primarily with middle- and upper-class white women, and I have tried to use Bible study as a way to raise consciousness about gender, class, and race issues in order to encourage solidarity in the struggle for liberation (salvation) for all oppressed people. I have been particularly interested in the use of imagination in Bible study groups as a means of undercutting resistance to new ideas, of enabling us to break out of dominant interpretations that are oppressive, and of helping form community where experience of struggle may be shared and become the touchstone for interpreting biblical passages.

In the following section I offer some practical observations and two experimental designs from my experience with feminist Bible study groups in Episcopal parish churches, a women's conference, and a seminary class. These suggestions may or may not be useful for Bible study groups in other contexts. They may, however, provide a basis for experimentation and modification, or for contrast. The groups for which the studies were designed were women's groups, the parish and conference groups consisting mainly of white, middle- and upper-class women and the seminary class consisting of twelve white women, a Korean-American woman, a Japanese woman, and a woman from northern India.

STUDY ONE
MARY AND MARTHA (LUKE 10:38–42):
A FOCUS ON GENDER

SESSION ONE

1. As each woman arrives, welcome her and hand her a blank name card. Ask her to write her name on it and one word that describes herself.

2. When everyone has arrived, go around the room inviting each one to introduce herself and talk about the self-descriptive word on her tag.

This initial exercise quickly breaks the "passive response to leader" syndrome. From the outset the participant becomes an agent in the process and centers on her own immediate experience as she searches for a descriptive word. To encourage participants to become their own interpreters of the Bible, I invite them to engage with a Bible passage with a minimum of introduction to it.

3. *Introduction:*

When it comes to doing Bible study, where we end up with a passage very much depends on where we begin, and how we begin. In this series of meetings I'm inviting you to interact with some biblical texts and we are going to begin with ourselves as church. And that, of course, is where the New Testament began. It arose out of the shared life of Christian communities

When we want to understand and evaluate biblical texts, our touchstone will be the *totality* of our experiences as women and as persons called by God — as church. As women-church. We have already begun with ourselves — by naming ourselves, and introducing ourselves, and naming some aspects of ourselves and sharing that. Now I want to invite you to use your imagination to envisage what the New Testament calls "the new creation." To embrace a new creation we have to break out of old structures, old ways of thinking, So, for a Christian, conversion involves consciousness raising.

4. Divide the large group into small groups of four to six. Have the room looking as attractive as possible. Give thought to the arrangement and use of space. Set the tone. To enhance creativity, an atmosphere of lightness and freedom and respect for one another makes a difference. Have some extra Bibles handy.

5. *Directions:*

When you look at the Bible passage, let your imagination flow. The wilder the better. We're not looking for any "right" interpretation or "wrong" interpretation. It's not possible to make a mistake in this exercise. We're just taking our experience and using our imagination to explore possibilities.

6. *The text at face value.* Hand out cards saying: "Luke 10:38–42: Read the story. Share your responses to it. Flesh out the characters in your imagination. How does it feel to be in their shoes?"

7. *A hermeneutics of suspicion.* When the groups are well under way, go to each one and ask if they would be willing to shift gears. Designate each group as either a Martha group or a Mary group and give out a second card saying: "If I were Martha (Mary) this is what I would have to say about the story Luke wrote about me. . . ."

8. After sufficient discussion time has passed, hand around a third card, saying: "Choose a spokesperson to play your character when we all come back together. Begin by saying: I am Mary (Martha) and Luke wrote a story about me. . . ."

9. When the groups are ready, have the Marthas and Marys do their role-plays.

10. Take plenty of time to debrief the players and to allow everybody to talk about their experience of the total process.

This gives an opportunity to affirm insights and excitements and to deal with anxieties and uneasiness. Timing will differ according to the composition of groups. It is important for the leader to have an easy and open style, and not to be worried about getting through everything planned. It is more valuable to project comfort with the moment. This allows each person to value what she is in the midst of and to value her own thoughts, experiences, and input into the discussion. It is helpful to let the process flow. Since the story of Mary and Martha is a very loaded one for women, it is good to be able to spend more than one session on it, so that there may be opportunity to move a little from its very powerful internalization to a new perception of it.

11. Suggest that there may be good reason why we are uncomfortable with one woman being set up against the other (as most groups are), and that there could be more to this story than meets the eye. Invite participants to spend some more time on it next session in order to dig deeper.

12. Suggest that they read John 11:1–44 and 12:1–11 before the next session for a different portrayal of Mary and Martha.

Session Two

1. Ask if there are any thoughts, feelings, or questions left over from the last session.

2. After responding to them, turn back to the text with the whole group. Look at it again, asking some questions of the text. For example: What does it say that Mary does? What does it say about Martha? Does it say anything about a meal?

This is a time for group pooling of knowledge and for sharing information about feminist scholarship. It can be done in a conversational way, even if most of the information comes from the leader. Discuss translations, texts, and alternative meanings of the Greek word "to serve" in New Testament writings;[3] garner knowledge about women's history in the Mediterranean world in the first and second centuries; discuss Luke's interests and context; look at Acts 6:1–6 for a correlation in structure; gather up all the evidence for women's leadership roles as founders and leaders of house-churches, as missionaries and apostles, as prophets and teachers. This becomes a time for engaging in a *hermeneutics of remembrance.*

Turn back to the text to see whether it is a *descriptive* text or a *prescriptive* text. Why are women's leadership roles being challenged? The diagram of the patriarchal pyramid can be introduced, and participants can be encouraged to reflect on the tension between a discipleship of equals lived out in Christian households and house-churches and the structure of the state, of which the patriarchal household was the basic unit. Apologetic interests on the part of the New Testament authors become apparent. Look at the differences between Luke's portrayal of Martha and Mary and that of John's Gospel. What *hermeneutics of proclamation* is called for with this passage? Is it liberating or oppressive?

3. Invite the participants to play again with their imaginations.
Introduction:

If this should be a story that Luke devised with Martha and Mary as representative figures symbolizing two kinds of discipleship, what about the real Marys and Marthas of Luke's time? What was actually going on with women? What were women in leadership roles doing? How were women participating in the decision making of the house-churches? Could we imagine Mary and Martha as important leaders in the early church?

Talk in small groups for a while and see if you can imagine how you would tell stories about Martha and Mary if *you* were writing them, not Luke.

4. After some discussion time, hand out a card to each group that says: "Mary and Martha are very old now. They spend most of their day sitting under the fig tree with children playing about them. Sometimes the children pester them to tell stories about their lives." Choose somebody from your group to be Martha and/or Mary and tell a story.

5. Debrief the players and groups after the role-plays. Ask the participants to think during the week how *they* would like to be remembered by future generations.

STUDY TWO
HAGAR AND SARAH (GENESIS 16:1-15; 21:1-7; 21:8-20):
A FOCUS ON CLASS AND RACE

Whereas the story of Mary and Martha lends itself to an exploration of issues of gender and of androcentric consciousness and patriarchal interests, the Genesis narratives that include stories of Hagar and Sarah provide in addition the potential for raising consciousness about race and class issues. The following design has been used successfully to raise consciousness among white women concerning oppression among women. The litany referred to in the opening exercise is found in appendix 2.

1. Hand out copies of the litany "Rich Woman, Poor Woman."[4] Have the group read it through to themselves. Then divide into two groups and read it as a litany.

I comment that what we have before us is the report of one historical event told from the perspectives of two different social realities.

2. Hand out typed copies of the rich woman's story (extrapolated from the litany) and the poor woman's story. Have the two groups sit quietly and read their particular stories, trying to enter imaginatively the reality of their woman.

3. Invite the "poor women" to listen to the "rich women" as they read aloud their story and to try to make a leap of imagination to enter their reality. Then reverse the procedure with the "rich women" listening to the "poor women" and trying to enter imaginatively into their experiences.

4. Once again read the whole piece as a litany.

This is a powerful exercise, upsetting to everybody, and takes quite a while to talk out when finished.

5. Next have somebody read aloud Genesis 16:1-15, and another Genesis 21:1-7.

6. Divide into two groups at random. Designate one a Hagar group and one a Sarah group and give out cards that say:

You have heard read Genesis 16:1-15 and 21:1-7.
Now read together as a group Genesis 21:8-20.
Imagine yourself as Hagar (Sarah).
Discuss it together.
Choose one person to tell the story from Sarah's (Hagar's) perspective.

7. Have the groups role-play their characters for the whole gathering; then debrief and discuss the experience.

I then ask: "What would have to happen for Hagar and Sarah to meet and speak freely with one another about their realities?"

(This portion of the study may best be done in a second session.)

8. Divide back into two groups to discuss this question. Then have each group choose a "Sarah" and a "Hagar" to have a face-to-face conversation.

I suggest that the other "Hagars" and "Sarahs" could sit around them as coaches and supporters. This interchange can be a very intense experience for everyone and time needs to be left to talk about it afterward. I only do this session when the group has jelled and some trust has grown up among participants.

In this particular design the women readily moved from the modern-day litany to the biblical text and made the connections. In addition, the element of race is a part of the story. Participants simply took the texts at face value, and I made no attempt to do any biblical critical analysis of the passages, since, for use in one or two sessions, they are a very powerful consciousness-raising medium as they stand.

AN OVERALL FRAMEWORK

In feminist Bible study that functions as consciousness raising, only a little can be expected to be accomplished in each session. You may try such designs and perceive no real movement in the participants between the role-playing at the beginning of the study and the role-playing at the end of each session. What is being asked here of many women is a huge paradigm shift. Consciousness raising can be a slow process and people cannot go faster than they can manage. Nevertheless, a dent is made by such a method of Bible study and often very exciting and liberating movement takes place with women who are able to risk entertaining a new perspective. These women then need a continuing community of support for exploration and action. The ending of a Bible study series is as critical as its beginning.

For women who are locked into a doctrinal approach to Bible study, the use of imagination and the sharing of life experiences can sometimes open new doors. For those who feel anxious about "tampering with the words of scripture," a book such as Barbara Hall's *Joining the Conversation* can sometimes be reassuring and enlightening.[5] In it Hall demonstrates the freedom with which the authors of Matthew and Mark exercised their imaginations as they retold the parable of the Great Feast.

Although consciousness raising may be a slow and patient process, nevertheless even with a short series—and certainly with a continuing parish group—it is possible to work with the overall framework provided by Schüssler Fiorenza's fourfold hermeneutical model in ways that are radically transforming. When, over time, all of its elements are included, the Bible becomes an invaluable spiritual source and resource for change and salvation.

Ways to go about such Bible study are as limitless as our imagination and creativity. After women have learned to turn a critical eye on the Bible and have tasted a first rush of liberation, a time comes when all the old verities seem to be slipping away. Then there is a readiness to dig for what rings true for us in the biblical record. The kind of reconstruction Schüssler Fiorenza does at the beginning of the second section of *In Memory of Her* yields a gold mine of material around which a series could be structured.[6] The Sophia section alone, introducing the whole issue of language, symbols, and identification, could be worked into a series in imaginative and creative ways.

At the end of a Bible study series a satisfying recapitulation can be made with each woman participating in the creation of a closing ritual. Participants are invited to bring poems, symbols, stories, artifacts, songs, food, reflections, etc. which gather up the significance of the study for them, and so to contribute to a shared closing event.

In all of these ways it is possible to reclaim our heritage, creatively transform it for our health and salvation, feed and nourish, challenge and strengthen each other, analyze and strategize out of our communal wisdom for political action in living out our calling to create a just and good world. With pain and laughter, with relinquishment of privilege and solidarity of purpose, with true listening and honest sharing, with growing trust and sensitivity toward one another, and with commitment to structural change, we move toward actualizing the fundamentals of our faith.

Appendix 1

Participants may be encouraged to draw pyramids of their own social context

I. Aristotelian Patriarchal Model of Society

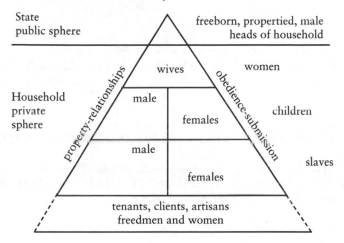

State
public sphere

freeborn, propertied, male
heads of household

property-relationships

wives

women

obedience-submission

Household
private
sphere

male

females

children

male

females

slaves

tenants, clients, artisans
freedmen and women

II. "Constantinian" Patriarchal Model of Church

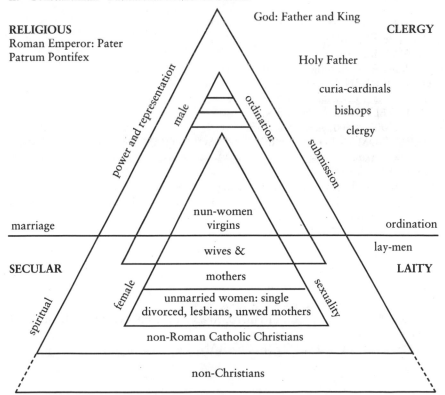

RELIGIOUS
Roman Emperor: Pater
Patrum Pontifex

God: Father and King

CLERGY

Holy Father

curia-cardinals

bishops

clergy

power and representation

male

ordination

submission

marriage

ordination

nun-women
virgins

wives &

lay-men

SECULAR

mothers

LAITY

female

unmarried women: single
divorced, lesbians, unwed mothers

sexuality

spiritual

non-Roman Catholic Christians

non-Christians

Reprinted by permission of Elisabeth Schüssler Fiorenza

Appendix 2

This reflection was written by a working-class Chilean woman in 1973, shortly after Chile's socialist president Salvador Allende was overthrown. A U.S. missionary translated the work and brought it with her when she was forced to leave Chile.

I am a woman.
 I AM A WOMAN.
I am a woman born of a woman, whose man owned a factory.
 I AM A WOMAN BORN OF A WOMAN, WHOSE MAN LABORED IN A FACTORY.
I am a woman whose man wore silk suits, who constantly watched his weight.
 I AM A WOMAN WHOSE MAN WORE TATTERED CLOTHING, WHOSE HEART
   WAS CONSTANTLY STRANGLED BY HUNGER.
I am a woman who watched two babies grow into beautiful children.
 I AM A WOMAN WHO WATCHED TWO BABIES DIE BECAUSE THERE WAS NO
   MILK.
I am a woman who watched twins grow into popular college students with summers abroad.
 I AM A WOMAN WHO WATCHED THREE CHILDREN GROW, BUT WITH
   BELLIES STRETCHED FROM NO FOOD.
But then there was a man;
 BUT THEN THERE WAS A MAN;
And he talked about the peasants getting richer by my family getting poorer.
 AND HE TOLD ME OF DAYS THAT WOULD BE BETTER AND HE MADE THE
   DAYS BETTER.
We had to eat rice.
 WE HAD RICE.
We had to eat beans!
 WE HAD BEANS.
My children were no longer given summer visas to Europe.
 MY CHILDREN NO LONGER CRIED THEMSELVES TO SLEEP.
And I felt like a peasant.
 AND I FELT LIKE A WOMAN.
A peasant with a dull, hard, unexciting life.
 LIKE A WOMAN WITH A LIFE THAT SOMETIMES ALLOWED A SONG.
And I saw a man.
 AND I SAW A MAN.
And together we began to plot with the hope of the return to freedom.
 I SAW HIS HEART BEGIN TO BEAT WITH HOPE OF FREEDOM, AT LAST . . .
Someday, the return to freedom.
 SOMEDAY FREEDOM.
And then.
 BUT THEN.
One day.
 ONE DAY.
There were planes overhead and guns firing close by.
 THERE WERE PLANES OVERHEAD, AND GUNS FIRING IN THE DISTANCE.
I gathered my children and went home.
 I GATHERED MY CHILDREN AND RAN.

And the guns moved farther and farther away.
    BUT THE GUNS MOVED CLOSER AND CLOSER.
And then they announced that freedom had been restored!
    AND THEN, THEY CAME, YOUNG BOYS REALLY . . .
They came into my home along with my man.
    THEY CAME AND FOUND MY MAN.
Those men whose money was almost gone.
    THEY FOUND ALL OF THE MEN WHOSE LIVES WERE ALMOST THEIR OWN.
And we all had drinks to celebrate.
    AND THEY SHOT THEM ALL.
The most wonderful martinis.
    THEY SHOT MY MAN.
And then they asked us to dance.
    AND THEN THEY CAME FOR US.
Me.
    FOR ME, THE WOMAN.
And my sisters.
    FOR MY SISTERS.
And then they took us.
    THEN THEY TOOK US.
They took us to dinner at a small, private club.
    THEY STRIPPED FROM US THE DIGNITY WE HAD GAINED.
And they treated us to beef.
    AND THEN THEY RAPED US.
It was one course after another.
    ONE AFTER THE OTHER THEY CAME AT US.
We nearly burst we were so full.
    LUNGING, PLUNGING . . . SISTERS BLEEDING, SISTERS DYING . . .
It was magnificent to be free again!
    IT WAS HARDLY A RELIEF TO HAVE SURVIVED.
And then we gathered the children together.
    AND THEN, THEY TOOK OUR CHILDREN.
And he gave them some good wine.
    AND THEN THEY TOOK THEIR SCISSORS.
And we gave them a party.
    AND THEY TOOK THE HANDS OF OUR CHILDREN . . .
The beans have almost disappeared now.
    THE BEANS HAVE DISAPPEARED.
The rice: I've replaced it with chicken or steak.
    THE RICE: I CANNOT FIND IT.
And the parties continue, night after night, to make up for all the time wasted.
    AND MY SILENT TEARS ARE JOINED ONCE MORE BY THE MIDNIGHT CRIES
       OF MY CHILDREN.
And I feel like a woman again.
    THEY SAY, I AM A WOMAN.

NOTES

1. See Elisabeth Schüssler Fiorenza, *Bread Not Stone: The Challenge of Feminist Biblical Interpretation* (Boston: Beacon Press, 1984), 15ff.

2. Ibid., 116–17; see also Elisabeth Schüssler Fiorenza, *Discipleship of Equals: A Critical Ekklesia-logy of Liberation* (New York: Crossroad, 1993), 226.

3. See Elisabeth Schüssler Fiorenza, *But She Said: Feminist Practices of Biblical Interpretation* (Boston: Beacon Press, 1992), chap. 2.

4. Printed in *Ecumenical Decade, 1988–1998: Prayers and Poems, Songs and Stories*, WCC Publications (Geneva: World Council of Churches, 1988), 67.

5. Barbara Hall, *Joining the Conversation: Jesus, Matthew, Luke & Us* (Cambridge, MA: Cowley Publications, 1985).

6. Elisabeth Schüssler Fiorenza, *In Memory of Her: A Feminist Theological Reconstruction of Christian Origins* (New York: Crossroad, 1983).

RECOMMENDED READINGS

Cannon, Katie Geneva, and Elisabeth Schüssler Fiorenza, eds. *Interpretation for Liberation*. Semeia 47. Atlanta: Scholars Press, 1989.

Collins, Adela Yarbro, ed. *Feminist Perspectives on Biblical Scholarship*. Chico, CA: Scholars Press, 1985.

Hall, Barbara. *Joining the Conversation: Jesus, Matthew, Luke & Us*. Cambridge, MA: Cowley Publications, 1985.

Pobee, John S., and Barbel Von Wartenberg-Potter, eds. *New Eyes For Reading*. WCC Publications. Geneva: World Council of Churches, 1986.

Schüssler Fiorenza, Elisabeth. *Bread Not Stone: The Challenge of Feminist Biblical Interpretation*. Boston: Beacon Press, 1985.

———. *But She Said: Feminist Practices of Biblical Interpretation*. Boston: Beacon Press, 1992.

———. *In Memory of Her: A Feminist Theological Reconstruction of Christian Origins*. New York: Crossroad, 1983.

Weems, Renita J. *Just A Sister Away: A Womanist Vision of Women's Relationships in the Bible*. San Diego: Lura Media, 1988.

Williams, Delores. *Sisters in the Wilderness: The Challenge of Womanist God Talk*. Maryknoll, NY: Orbis, 1992.

23

❖ A Method of Conscientization: Feminist Bible Study in the Netherlands

LIEVE TROCH ♦

IN THE LAST FEW YEARS many changes and shifts have occurred in the academy in feminist hermeneutics and feminist Bible study. The analysis of familiar presuppositions in Bible study has deepened our understanding of the texts; their contexts and our own have challenged us to embrace new understandings of the authority of the Bible.

In the Netherlands, feminist Bible study is becoming a familiar activity even in the inner circles of Roman Catholic parishes and Protestant church communities, although the perspectives covered by such study range from feminine interpretations whose primary aim is rescuing the Bible to an interpretation or point of departure that rejects the Christian tradition as a whole.

In this article I will reflect on my experiences of feminist Bible study with groups of women who are not theologically trained. After focusing on some of the specifics of the Dutch situation, I will discuss a methodology of feminist Bible study that I have used through the years. Finally, I will describe some of the ways women are transformed as a result of this feminist Bible study.

I will limit my reflections to experiences with groups of women. Having worked with mixed-gender groups and men-only groups, I have observed that different dynamics are involved for men and different methods need to be used with them to help them deal with the texts, notions of authority, guilt feelings, and use of power. As Carol Christ has pointed out, women's awakening to their grounding in the powers of being is different from men's.[1] Each has different behaviors and assumptions to learn and unlearn.

CONSCIOUSNESS RAISING

The term "consciousness raising" has found its way into articles and discussions since Paulo Freire introduced the word "conscientization" as part of a pedagogical system for liberating those who are victims of an oppressive system. This concept embraces more than an intellectual moment. It refers to a process in which oppressed people learn to perceive social, political, and economic contradictions and to take action against the oppressive elements of reality. This process is dialogical in that in naming the world and its contradictions the world reappears and requires new naming. Learning is therefore not based on the banking model of education; rather, the model of education as problem posing is the instrument for liberation and revolutionary praxis.[2]

In the 1960s and 1970s, women's discussion groups—in which consciousness raising was central—arose in the Netherlands, as in other parts of the world. In these groups women "heard each other into speech" and acquired a new understanding of and control over their own lives.[3] However outdated this concept sounds, I believe that these groups and this coming together still function to bring women out of their isolation.

> The fact that today the expression consciousness raising has become dated and more than slightly unpleasant, as any word will that has been appropriated, diluted, digested and spewed out by the media, does not diminish the social and subjective impact of a practice—the collective articulation of one's experience of sexuality and gender—which has produced and continues to elaborate, a radically new mode of understanding the subject's relation to social-historical reality. Consciousnessraising is the original critical instrument that women have developed toward such understanding, the analysis of social reality and its critical revision.[4]

Among feminists, earlier analyses of society as structured according to a principle of sex/gender dualism have given way to a broader definition of patriarchy understood as a system of power based on hierarchical constructs of class, sex, race, sexual behavior, etc. From an initial *Sitz im Leben* among white, middle-class women, these groups now function as connecting groups for women from different races and classes. When women work systematically on feminist Bible study, new stories emerge; the reality of women's lives changes and becomes new. Through this process women also create a new reality of spiritual life in the deepest meaning of revolutionary praxis.

I would like specifically to emphasize in this article the powerful possibilities of feminist Bible study to encourage attitudes other than the hierarchical position: in exorcising the victimization of women, and in making women visible as conscious agents of history and religion, women learn to exorcise the dualism of the oppressor/oppressed from their own body and mind. This is a most difficult task, as it requires perceiving new forms of relationship that rarely exist. Besides developing self, voice, and mind, women also learn in groups of feminist Bible study to understand their bodies as places of change.[5] This learning brings them to new relationships in society and with each other, and to new dimensions of ethical, political, and spiritual praxis.

THE DUTCH SITUATION

The Women and Faith Movement began in the Netherlands in the late 1970s. Women of different church denominations found each other in dynamic groups of consciousness raising in and on the edge of the churches. Feminist Bible study was one of the first activities taken up by those groups of women which developed a feminist awareness of their position in church and society. I will highlight some developments that occurred in the way different groups worked in the field of feminist Bible study.

CONTEXT OF THE EMERGING GROUPS

Women who participate in feminist Bible study groups all have some history with the Bible. For most of them it is a history of both help and abuse. Formulating this history is an important moment in the beginning of the feminist Bible study process. In the Netherlands during the last twenty years much educational work has been initiated by the churches. Both Catholics and Protestants have given extensive attention to Bible study in the process of empowering people to take part in church activities. During these educational processes many active churchwomen and men are confronted with different models of exegesis and interpretation. For many people, the hermeneutical tools and methods function as new ideologies. The androcentric character of the texts and their interpretations remain largely intact. The models of exegesis that have been used can be divided for the most part into two categories: (1) Those employing historical-critical reflection. This method often leads to pardoning the authors of texts that can be defined as abusive to women. Because the author was writing in a historical milieu that cannot be compared to our own, the text is reduced

to merely an interesting phenomenon. The relevance of the text to everyday experience is hardly raised. (2) Those which invite psychologizing or
a psychoanalytic approach to the text. The experiences of the believers
become the departure point for free association with the texts. Minimal
reflection on or analysis of these experiences often leads to a mode of conduct with the Bible that ends in private piety or private imagination. This
approach often involves reading the texts from an exclusively Christocentric
perspective with emphasis on the exemplary function of Jesus and the
invitation to imitation. The early Jesus movement and communities
disappear from sight, as does the political analysis of the current context.

We must take into account these two approaches to Bible study when
beginning a feminist Bible study process, because they both limit *and* open
possibilities for a new perspective.

COPING WITH DIVERSITY IN CHURCH DENOMINATION, CLASS, AND RACE

In the growing Women and Faith Movement, differences in denominational
affiliation — that is, Catholic or Protestant — were immaterial to women when
they worked together on programs focusing on the role and position of
women in church and society. Their differences became more obvious when
they began feminist Bible study. Many Catholic women have little experience
in reading biblical texts. Their experience of the Bible is more with those
who interpret the Bible, and less with the text itself. They know the texts
primarily through listening to sermons. Women are accustomed to listening to stories. Because they are expected to remain passive while they listen,
they are not encouraged to break out of a culture of silence.[6] Learning
to unravel interpretation and to work independently with texts are complementary moments in coming to consciousness. Protestant women are
more accustomed to the texts, and they are more conditioned to believing
in the authority of the Bible.

Nevertheless, many feminist theologians prefer to work with groups of
women in a mixed constellation: both Protestants and Catholics, women
active in their churches and women on the margin of the church, and women
from different economic and social positions and levels of education. It
is my experience that a group consisting of women with such a variety
of backgrounds will have the opportunity to engage in various levels of
consciousness raising. They will also find that their oppression as women,
regardless of their place in the patriarchal constellation of multiplicative

oppressions is a unifying factor for them. The different relationship of the women to the biblical texts and their authority relativizes their different positions from the outset. In the presence of diversity, women are able to break through the culture of silence and to articulate their suspicion concerning the biblical text and its androcentric interpreters.

With regard to differences of class, women on welfare who are part of the Women and Faith Movement began to challenge the churches and other women in the movement. They expressed concern about the growing economic division between rich and poor in both the so-called First and Third worlds and pointed out that those people most affected by poverty are women. Out of their personal experiences and perspective, these same women rewrite biblical texts. These creative actualizations have appeared in journals and workshops and have had a shocking impact on other women in the movement.

A similar situation has taken place as a result of the work of a group of black women. Only a small percentage of the women of color in the Netherlands belong to the Christian tradition; most are Muslim. Nevertheless, at seminars and national conferences of critical Christian movements and the women's movement, Christian black women have challenged white women through dramatizations of the story of Hagar and Sarah in Genesis. By these performances, they have challenged the white interpretation of the text, which usually puts Sarah at the center of the story. At the same time they have highlighted the ongoing racism and neocolonialism that are part of our society.

As a result of Judith Plaskow's essay "Blaming Jews for Inventing Patriarchy,"[7] a group of Christian and Jewish feminists have met on a regular basis since 1984. They call themselves the Tamar group, and through reading and studying women's stories in the Hebrew Bible, they share their traditions. In similar groups, Christian women become conscious of the Christian assumptions and theological constructions they bring to the text. Scholars are more involved than grassroots women in this Jewish– Christian dialogue, whereas more grassroots women are involved in discussions of race and class.

THE EKKLĒSIA OF WOMEN
AS A HERMENEUTICAL PRINCIPLE OF REVELATION

Considerably different approaches toward feminist Bible study are evident among scholars. These concern the authority and the value of the text and the history of the interpretation of the text.[8] It is obvious that church denomination, theological schools of education, personal history, and engagement with feminist grassroots movements and their particular methodologies account for this variety of perspectives.

For the last fifteen years feminist consciousness has shaped my critical reading of the Bible. At the same time, Elisabeth Schüssler Fiorenza's critical theology of liberation based on feminist Bible study has sharpened my feminist consciousness.[9]

Because feminist hermeneutics grounds its analysis and reflection in the experience of women's oppression, suffering, and resistance, as well as in the experience of women with the Bible, and because I work with women, it has become very clear to me that we can never again try to rescue the Bible or some of the texts for their own sake. Confrontation with the shifts in feminist Bible study has helped me to recognize an ever-deepening spiral of the shifting meaning of authority and to discover the roots of communities of resistance and solidarity.[10] The concept of womenchurch as elaborated by Schüssler Fiorenza helps me in the struggle of the living communities of the present to claim the discipleship of equals through the texts.[11] Taking seriously the concept of *ekklēsia* of women has consequences for the method of working with texts and with groups and for the position of the theologian engaged in the process.

MAKING CHOICES

It is essential in groups that consciousness of abusive experiences, abusive interpretations, and abusive texts be allowed to surface. This means that in a process of feminist Bible study there are built-in moments of (1) analysis of the dynamics of the personal, economic, and social reality of women; (2) dealing with the history of interpretation of certain texts; and (3) reading the texts, especially including the so-called texts of terror.[12] I would argue that it is very important to hold these elements together in one process. Through this the authority both of the interpretation and of the text itself is questioned. Although women find this process confusing, I find it a necessary means of drawing attention in a radical way to the androcentric limitations of the Bible, as well as its claims to be the sole locus of revelation. Those who lead feminist Bible study with women must therefore be prepared to engage in a lengthy process with a group. Short meetings or one-time lectures reflect the traditional banking model of education and reduce feminist Bible study to an "interesting topic" to be studied. In the process of creative articulation and imagining of their own reality and its interpretation, women learn to trust their own reading of the texts. Through this way of working both the women and the educator gain new theological understandings and newly lived and shaped spirituality.

Often I have experienced that a feminist Bible study group appears capable of creating commitment on a level beyond patriarchal divisions such as church denomination, culture, and race. Diversity within the group makes possible an analysis of the social and economic situation needed for real consciousness raising. Patriarchal divisions which can also set women against each other can be analyzed within such a process and utilized toward the transformation of power relations.

POSITION OF THE THEOLOGIAN: MIDWIFE IN CONNECTED TEACHING

The theologian in the process of feminist Bible study who focuses on consciousness raising clearly cannot limit herself to teaching differing principles of feminist Bible study in a teacher–pupil model. Even less can she withhold her own theoretical perspective in this field.

The authors of *Women's Ways of Knowing: The Development of Self, Voice and Mind* present the model of the teacher as midwife.[13] A teacher who adopts such a model is able to help women articulate their latent knowledge and to stimulate and encourage further reflection. I find this model an appropriate one for the leader of a consciousness raising group. In group process, new and often unexpected issues may arise. Women should be challenged to explore these new lines of thinking, to relate them to their own latent knowledge, and to articulate their discoveries. The leader as midwife creates space for women to make their suspicions explicit and helps women become aware of the culture of silence which stifles their suspicion.

On the other hand, the women in the groups should not be manipulated to make particular decisions or certain choices; it must be possible for them at any given moment to stop the process of further consciousness raising. This requires a respectful attitude and an ethical awareness on the part of the theologian. Many times women prove that a model of discipleship of equals as a source or criterion for revelation is latently present among them. Women who work with one another in study groups have less difficulty with the implications of this model for biblical authority and the new possibilities for revelatory moments than do some theologians.

I have seen theologians act in an authoritative manner many times, thereby hindering the process of conscientization of a group because of their anxiety that the group will follow a direction different from the one the theologians themselves would have chosen. Even so, it is of great importance that a theologian does not hide the process of her own thinking. Hiding the tools and abilities one possesses can activate unnecessary complicating mechanisms of power.

In facilitating group process in a discipleship of equals, a leader must acknowledge the differences in women's knowledge and insight without organizing these insights in a hierarchical fashion. One woman's contribution should not be upheld as "authoritative" at the expense of another's. Such a group process is unconventional and requires an understanding of authority in dialogue. The results of such a search are not predictable. The process is risky and requires enormous exertion from both the group and its leader. Participants must persistently resist the temptation to revert to traditional hierarchical patterns. A continuous analysis of the economic, social, and global context in which women participate should vigilantly guard the discipleship of equals as something to work on beyond liberal concepts.

FOUR STORIES, FOUR SPIRALS

In this section, I would like to give some examples of a process and method of working that lead to feminist consciousness and to knowledge and ability to use the hermeneutical tools for women. The implications of this feminist consciousness for theologians and women involved in the process will be addressed in a few concluding remarks.

Katharine Doob Sakenfeld argues that the choice to read certain texts is primarily motivated by particular interests and by the need to attack or explicate a certain interpretation.[14] I would like to demonstrate through the examples from four texts how women in a Bible study group can work toward a full understanding of the discipleship of equals as a hermeneutical principle for revelation. The choice of texts, the abusive interpretation, the tracing of androcentric interpretation and the androcentrism in the text itself, the invisibility of women, the reconstruction of hidden struggle, and the resistance of women are all issues that can be addressed in group process.

The biblical texts can also be used to evoke the creativity of women, to aid them in analyzing their current situation, to help create new relationships among them, and to build communities of resistance supported by the heritage of a powerful her-story of struggle and resistance. Women familiar with the hermeneutics of the creative actualization of the text provide new insights that further the work of systematic and practical theologians.

Each of these four texts has had a different function in the consciousness of women. The first text, the story of Mary and Martha in Luke 10:38-42, is well known primarily because of interpretations that discuss "the proper role" for women as assigned by the text. The second is the largely unknown text of the midwives Sifra and Pua in Exodus 1, a text that calls for the glorification of strong women. The third is the story of the woman who suffered from severe bleeding, a story often used to portray Jesus as the first feminist (Mark 5:21-43). Finally I will look at the story of the daughter of Jephthah, known as a "text of terror" (Judges 11:29–40).

Reading these texts anew and uncovering several layers of meaning make feminist Bible study with its entire range of issues and choices accessible to women. After going through these processes, women grow in ability to apply the tools they have acquired to other texts in which women are *not* mentioned.

MARTHA AND MARY (LUKE 10:38–42)

> Redeeming women's experience from the interpretation, redeeming the text from the interpretation, redeeming the women and "the church in her house" from the text.[15]

Research has proved abundantly that stories shape both our identity and the imagination needed for building new reality. But women do not possess many stories or tales that enable them to create a new identity. Women, however, *do* live with certain Bible stories and their interpretations. The silence that surrounds stories women know to be false should be broken.

The story of Martha and Mary is a story that, through its traditional interpretation, has prevented the honest search for identity among women. The women it portrays are caricatured as rivals. Women, reading this story, often feel confused because they are required to make a choice between Mary and Martha. In this way they are robbed of their power. They usually invent a personal solution to cope with the disturbing message, thereby challenging already the authority of interpretation and text. By making women aware of this intuitive exegesis and hermeneutics of suspicion, the road is cleared for a number of following steps. Women have some awareness of the abuse in the Bible, but this awareness is embedded in a culture of silence. After sharing their suspicion, women can make the step from identifying the abuse toward a feminist historical reconstruction of women and men being church "in her house" and acting as true disciples. This reconstructed memory is an essential source of identity and can destroy the false historical memory of the self.

It becomes clear in the process how deeply the interpretive sexist framework is rooted in the minds and bodies of women themselves. Interpretive frameworks provide total frameworks, and it is difficult to disengage from them in order to construct new ones.[16] Giving time to the analysis of the interpretation and the history of abuse of women by this text and its interpretation opens toward the creation of new frameworks. I would argue that analyzing the patriarchal interpretations and texts not only provides new ways of dealing with the Bible, authority, and the divine but also new options for women in terms of how they might reconceive their identity. This process needs to be repeated over and over again using different texts.

SIFRA AND PUA (EXODUS 1): FROM AN ANDROCENTRIC TO A FEMINIST VIEW

The midwives Sifra and Pua said to Pharaoh: "Because the Hebrew women are not like the Egyptian women; for they are vigorous; before the midwife comes to them, they are delivered." (Exodus 1:19)

On reading the rather unfamiliar text of Exodus 1 in women's groups, women feel less hindered or determined by previous interpretations, for almost automatically while reading, women focus on the courageous actions of the two midwives initiating the struggle for liberation of Israel and on the acts of civil disobedience against Pharaoh.[17] These women are seen as examples of women opposing patriarchy.

But other steps also need to be taken in the process of consciousness raising: (1) An analysis of the fact that the text is little known by women will show that even their obvious heritage has been kept from them in the storytelling. (2) Awareness must grow that focusing on these women as prominent figures separates them from the broader movement of resistance of women and thereby makes this movement invisible. The midwives may become too easily the "exceptional" figures.

It is interesting to view the text through the eyes of the midwives. We then no longer focus only on their relationship to the patriarchal world and their struggle not to be incorporated in the patriarchal game. We might see that the midwives view themselves in relation to other women. The midwives define themselves not as disobedient to Pharaoh but according to their own crafts-woman-ship: What is Pharaoh talking about? In a normal situation women can take care of themselves; during labor they do not even need midwives!

This line of thinking moves women beyond the patriarchal setting of the text and toward an understanding of "crafts-woman-ship," an exploration of relationships among women, the possibilities of an insider-outsider position in the patriarchal power game, and a political analysis of their own position in the struggle against patriarchal strategies.

She Told the Whole Truth (Mark 5:33–34): On Reconstruction and Creative Actualization

The story of the woman who suffered from severe bleeding in combination with the raising of the daughter of Jairus from death is well known. The classical way of working with this text focuses on the appraisal of Jesus, who ignores the laws of the outcast to which this woman belongs because of her loss of blood. In touching Jesus she comes to life and is no longer limited by her illness, which was related to her being a woman.

This interpretation, which I have earlier defined as Christocentric, is liberating, at first glance. But it draws the attention away from this woman and her possible position in the theological design of the first Jesus communities.

In a closer reading of the text, women focus on the action, courage, and endurance of the woman herself: she initiates; it is she who touches him, believing that her touch will be adequate. She breaks through the stigmatization of being an outcast, which leads to her full presence in the community. Again the pitfall of isolating a strong and exceptional woman, with guts, looms. Analysis herein clears the way to contemplate the sentence "and she told him the whole truth." In a process of creative actualization and historical imagination, this woman, and with her many more, can be recognized as the messenger and designer of an alternative theological thinking at the center of the first Jesus communities. Her "truth" is different from the truth designed by the Jairuses and according to which she had to live. Her vision of life, society, the political, social, and religious position of women surely must have been different from what was allowed to her in the context of a patriarchal design. She proclaims this her truth and she proclaims it as "the whole truth." This creative reconstruction raises the challenge for women today to create their own theology, while reflecting on new relationships.

By reading in this way, women themselves come to see that revelation begins with their own process of reading and with the challenge to design a new reality. Authority then is the result of a dialogical happening, and the Bible is experienced as a source of help in the struggle for autonomy, not as the only possible source for revelation or as the final legitimization for their struggle.[18]

She Became a Tradition in Israel (Judges 11:39–40)

This history of struggle and resistance creates space for new spiritual and political community building. Phyllis Trible, in her book *Texts of Terror,* has sought in an intriguing manner for the means to handle texts imbued with male violence. Yet in her attempt to read these texts *"in memoriam,"* she does not escape the danger of rescuing the biblical texts for their own sake, for she does not critically evaluate the revelation of the androcentric texts. The God of Jephthah in Judges 11 escapes unscathed, although the reading helps women to name the violence done to them. Acknowledging sexual, military, and patriarchal violence enables women to develop an understanding of the connection between personal and political violence.

Many Protestant women are familiar with this text and its most horrifying interpretations taught in Sunday schools. Catholic women, because they are less likely to have been exposed to the Hebrew Bible, can more easily discover the hidden history of theological and liturgical resistance in the text once they are encouraged to think critically within a feminist framework. In this way, room is made for an understanding and definition of God different from Jephthah's understanding and definition. The revelation of another God takes place in the recognition of the resistance of the daughter of Jephthah and her girlfriends: they leave for the mountains, as did Moses and Jesus. They cast their relation with the divine in a subversive liturgy: they no longer believe in the God of Jephthah; other visions and experiences must have determined their new theological thinking and their "reality." Women in the process of rereading this text experience the subversive liturgical tradition as a challenge to express a spirituality of struggle by developing their own rituals and celebrations. The countertradition within the tradition of Judges is almost hidden in the texts. With an intentional effort, we are able to see, if only for a moment, the margin as the center.

Such discoveries, made by women when interpreting the texts from their own perspective, have far-reaching consequences for women's new definition of God, Christology, community building, and liturgy.

SOME CONSEQUENCES OF
THE HERMENEUTICAL PRINCIPLE
OF THE DISCIPLESHIP OF EQUALS

What are the consequences of the process of feminist Bible study for both theologians and grassroots women. For me as a theologian, working with women's groups in an intensive process of feminist Bible study is an important stimulus for the development of my systematic reflection and academic work. New interpretations of the texts emerge and force me to a more radical rethinking of Christology and soteriology. In my work as an academic theologian I am obliged to take care that these new interpretations emerging from the reality of women's lives will not be lost again but are introduced into theological interpretive structures.

In the dialogical cooperation of the group, the participation of everyone is constitutive for the *ekklēsia* we are becoming, and often it is difficult to go about it in an honest way. The group teaches me that, as a theologian, I have to beware of manipulation. When the women come to their own speech, the questions with regard to authority which I share with them can return like a boomerang. In this process of dialogical cooperation, the women can assist the theologian in ridding theology of its oppressive character and help her to make the right choices and priorities in the selection of themes for theological reflection.

For many women, having a better grasp of the stories means having a better understanding of their own existence and self. Recovery of the lost self goes hand in hand with the discovery of resistant women in the past. The painful sharing of the anger we have for what was and still is done to women comes together with the joy of the new power that surfaces. The shift from text to her-story, from the margin to the center, from victim to the struggle, makes the transformation of reality possible.

Most striking to me in this consciousness-raising process is how women begin to search for new horizons and other contexts. Women become curious to know more about the experiences of women of different race and ethnicity, class and culture, because they acknowledge the limitations of their own context. Beyond their curiosity grows the need for ongoing economic and political analysis and strategizing. Building communities across economic and racial differences is an often difficult and painful process with such pitfalls as guilt feelings, victim behavior, romanticism, universalizations, liberal tolerance, etc. And finding an entry into the past—that is, reclaiming the discipleship of equals—opens possibilities for a new political analysis of the present situation.

During an intensive process of feminist Bible study in the Netherlands, one woman brought two wooden spoons with her from her kitchen cupboard: one with a hole in it and another without a hole. They were helpful tools to find the words for her changing reality: "Until now," she said, "I have been stirring with a wooden spoon with a hole in it. Now, because I feel there is more power within me, I bought a spoon without a hole. I want to use it to scrape the bottom, investigate everything, and make a new mixture."

I will close by referring to birds and plows as metaphors for the story of women. Birds undertake enormous flights, out into the blue; they go to survive, so as not to die of cold and hunger. Many women plow hard on both virgin territory and reclaimed land. Where the land is plowed, birds land in the furrows. The birds behind the plows and the birds in the sky are the same. In swarms they walk the fields, picking and searching, and then with enormous power they take to the skies. Birds live on the land, close to the plowers, and in the air.

NOTES

1. Carol P. Christ, "Nothingness, Awakening, Insight, New Naming," in her *Diving Deep and Surfacing: Women Writers on Spiritual Quest* (Boston: Beacon Press, 1980), 13–26.

2. Paulo Freire, *Pedagogy of the Oppressed* (New York: Seabury, 1972).

3. Nelle Morton, "1971: The Rising Woman Consciousness in a Male Language Structure," in *The Journey Is Home* (Boston: Beacon Press, 1985), 11–30.

4. Teresa de Lauretis, *Alice doesn't: Feminism, Semiotics, Cinema* (Bloomington, IN: Indiana University Press, 1984), 186.

5. Paula M. Cooey, "The Word Become Flesh: Woman's Body, Language, and Value," in *Embodied Love: Sensuality and Relationship as Feminist Values*, ed. P. M. Cooey (New York: Harper & Row, 1987), 17–33.

6. Mary Field Belenky et al., *Women's Ways of Knowing: The Development of Self, Voice, and Mind* (New York: Basic Books, 1986), 25–26.

7. *Lilith* 7 (1980): 11–12.

8. See *The Bible and Feminist Hermeneutics, Semeia* 28 (Atlanta: Scholars Press, 1983); Letty M. Russell, ed., *Feminist Interpretation of the Bible* (Philadelphia: Westminster, 1985);

Adela Yarbro Collins, ed., *Feminist Perspectives on Biblical Scholarship* (Chico, CA: Scholars Press, 1985); *Interpretation for Liberation, Semeia* 47 (Atlanta: Scholars Press, 1989).

9. See esp. Elisabeth Schüssler Fiorenza, *In Memory of Her: A Feminist Theological Reconstruction of Christian Origins* (New York: Crossroad, 1983); eadem, *Bread Not Stone: The Challenge of Feminist Biblical Interpretation* (Boston: Beacon Press, 1984).

10. Sharon Welch, *Communities of Resistance and Solidarity: A Feminist Theology of Liberation* (Maryknoll, NY: Orbis, 1985).

11. Elisabeth Schüssler Fiorenza, "Womenchurch: The Hermeneutical Center of Feminist Biblical Interpretation," in her *Bread Not Stone*, 1–22; see also her *Discipleship of Equals: A Critical Feminist Ekklesia-logy of Liberation* (New York: Crossroad, 1993).

12. This is the title of a book by Phyllis Trible in which she elaborates four Bible texts obviously abusive to women (*Texts of Terror: Literary-Feminist Readings of Biblical Narratives* [Philadelphia: Fortress, 1984).

13. Belenky et al., *Women's Ways of Knowing*, 217–19.

14. K. D. Sakenfeld, "Feminist Uses of Biblical Materials," in *Feminist Interpretation of the Bible*, ed. Russell, 55–64.

15. Elisabeth Schüssler Fiorenza shows the androcentric layers in this text, which serve to make women invisible in the early communities, and also the abuse done to women by Luke's use of them in his description of early conflicts in the communities. The text veils and unveils at the same time ("Theological Criteria and Historical Reconstruction: Martha and Mary, Luke 10:38–42" [Berkeley, CA: Center for Hermeneutical Studies in Hellenistic and Modern Culture, 1986], 1–25; see also her *But She Said*, pp. 51–76.)

16. Sallie McFague, *Metaphorical Theology: Models of God in Religious Language* (Philadelphia: Fortress, 1982), 79–83.

17. This interpretation is also elaborated by J. Cheryl Exum, "You Shall Let Every Daughter Live: A Study of Exodus 1, 8–2, 10," *Semeia* 28 (1988): 63–82. She underlines the refusal of cooperation.

18. Kwok Pui Lan, "Discovering the Bible in the Non-Biblical World," *Semeia* 47 (1989): 30.

RECOMMENDED READINGS

Belenky, Mary F., et al. *Women's Ways of Knowing: The Development of Self, Voice, and Mind.* New York: Basic Books, 1986.

Cannon, Katie G., and E. Schüssler Fiorenza, eds. *Interpretation for Liberation. Semeia* 47. Atlanta: Scholars Press, 1989.

Christ, Carol P. *Diving Deep and Surfacing: Women Writers on Spiritual Quest.* Boston: Beacon Press, 1980.

Collins, Adela Yarbro, ed. *Feminist Perspectives on Biblical Scholarship.* Biblical Scholarship in North America 10. Chico, CA: Scholars Press, 1985.

Cooey, Paula M., S. A. Farmer, and M. E. Ross, eds. *Embodied Love: Sensuality and Relationship as Feminist Values.* San Francisco: Harper & Row, 1987.

Freire, Paulo. *Pedagogy of the Oppressed.* New York: Seabury, 1973.

Morton, Nelle. *The Journey is Home.* Boston: Beacon Press, 1985.

Russell, Letty M., ed. *Feminist Interpretation of the Bible.* Philadelphia: Westminster, 1985.

Schüssler Fiorenza, Elisabeth. *In Memory of Her: A Feminist Theological Reconstruction of Christian Origins.* New York: Crossroad, 1983.

Trible, Phyllis. *Texts of Terror: Literary-Feminist Readings of Biblical Narratives*. Philadelphia: Fortress, 1984.

Troch, Lieve. "The Feminist Movement in and on the Edge of the Churches in the Netherlands." *Journal of Feminist Studies in Religion* 5/2 (1989): 113–28.

Welch, Sharon. *Communities of Resistance and Solidarity*. Maryknoll, NY: Orbis, 1985.

◆ Teaching Feminist Biblical Studies in a Postcolonial Context

KATHLEEN O'BRIEN WICKER ◆

FOR THE PAST twenty years, I have taught feminist biblical studies to religion majors and other undergraduates and to graduate-level students in Women's Studies in Religion and New Testament. My primary institutional affiliation has been with a private women's college that is part of a cluster of five undergraduate colleges, a graduate school, and a more loosely related school of theology.

My pedagogical strategies over the years have reflected the American scholarly discourse among feminists about women's and feminist studies. As I reviewed my course syllabi in light of this project, I recognized a progressive emphasis on "women in," "women as," "women's," and "gendered" readings of the biblical texts in my courses. More recently, I have come to understand how women/gender issues are necessarily related to considerations of race/ethnicity and of class. A sabbatical at the University of Zimbabwe in 1989 made me aware of the importance of including international perspectives in my courses. "African Religions and Their Literary Representations," a course that I taught with an African-American woman colleague, Sue E. Houchins, after my return from Zimbabwe, has been important in further expanding my traditionally Euro-American, North Atlantic perspective and in sensitizing me to the phenomenon of colonization.

My discovery that the writings of John William Colenso, the Anglican bishop of Natal in South Africa, influenced some of Elizabeth Cady Stanton's biblical interpretations has also shaped my approach to this essay. While evangelizing the Zulu people, Colenso recognized the problematic nature of the Anglican doctrinal claim that the Bible was inspired. In 1863, Colenso published *The Pentateuch and the Book of Joshua Initially Examined,* using the then new critical methods of biblical scholarship to demonstrate that not all biblical texts are factually true.[1] During the course of the heresy trial that followed the publication of his work, Colenso also came to recognize the collaboration of Christianity in the colonial system. This insight undoubtedly appealed to Stanton as much as did his challenges to the veracity of the text, since she regarded many nineteenth-century American Christian churches as collaborating in the colonization of women.[2] Stanton's metaphorical use of the term colonization is more accurately referred to today as discursive colonization, which must be distinguished from the historical colonization that Colenso witnessed in southern Africa.[3]

In this essay I address historical and discursive forms of colonization, colonial paradigms of education and of biblical studies, and feminist models of education and of teaching biblical studies. I raise the following questions: What are colonization and colonialism? What is the political agenda of education? Who carries out this agenda? How does feminist education contrast with colonial education? What is biblical studies? How do colonial and feminist biblical studies differ? What distinguishes the pedagogy of colonial and feminist biblical studies? I then describe my course on the Gospels as an example of teaching feminist biblical studies.

COLONIZATION AND COLONIALISM

Colonization is both a historical fact of political and geographic conquest and a metaphor, a discursive formulation. Historical colonization involves a set of power relationships: appropriation of land, control of resources, organization and socialization of people, definition of values. Discursive colonization also deals with power relationships in which metaphors are actualized in experience. Thus, Ngugi Wa Thiong'o can say that to be colonized is to be an exile, separated metaphorically and/or geographically from one's "history and a past style of living, from race, from class, and ultimately from self."[4] Historical colonization is the focus of certain parts of this discussion. Discursive colonization dominates the whole argument.

Feminisms distinguish themselves from the historical and discursive colonial power systems in ways that I will describe below. But because the discursive practice of colonization includes the universalizing of particular experiences, Euro-American feminism, as a culturally specific movement that has attempted to speak in the name of all women, is also in need of decolonization.[5] Though I contrast colonial and feminist educational systems and approaches to pedagogy and to biblical studies, I also recognize that feminism is implicated with colonialism. I suggest educational strategies to aid in its decolonization.

WHAT IS THE POLITICAL AGENDA
OF EDUCATION?

Ghanaian philosopher Anthony Appiah has observed, "When the colonialists attempted to tame the threatening cultural alterity of the African . . . the instrument of pedagogy was their most formidable weapon."[6] One colonial strategy was to educate Africans for a subordinate role. Another was to totally integrate them into the culture of the colonial power.[7] A number of African novelists make these varied educational strategies and their consequences the subject of their fictive narratives.

To illustrate, in Senegalese writer Cheikh Hamidou Kane's novel *Ambiguous Adventure*, the Diallobe chief must decide whether to allow children of his community to attend a colonial school.

> "If I told them to go to the new school," he said at last, "they would go *en masse*. They would learn all the ways of joining wood to wood which we do not know. But, learning, they would also forget. Would what they would learn be worth as much as what they would forget? I should like to ask you: can one learn this without forgetting that, and is what one learns worth what one forgets?"[8]

The chief's sister, the Most Royal Lady, nonetheless influences him to allow the children to attend, even though she recognizes even more clearly than the chief the implications of the decision. She says:

> The school in which I would place our children will kill in them what today we love and rightly conserve with care. Perhaps the very memory of us will die in them. When they return from the school, there may be those who will not recognize us. What I am proposing is that we should agree to die in our children's hearts and that the foreigners who have defeated us should fill the place, wholly, which we shall have left free.[9]

Novelist Kane recognizes education as a process that inculcates sets of values and codes of behavior, a particular historical perspective, modes of knowing, and technological sophistication in ways that reflect and tend to reproduce the culture of the dominant group. Children educated in colonial schools become alienated from their parents and from their traditional culture. If colonial education "succeeds," they will become more French than Diallobe in their self-identification. They will, in Ngugi's terms, become exiles.

The rhetoric of colonial education suggests inclusion, belonging, integration of conquered peoples into the culture of the colonizers. But can colonial education contribute to the strengthening of the traditional community,

even as it imparts new knowledge and technology and access to new systems
of power? Ngugi explores this issue in his novel *The River Between*. The
prophet Mugo commissions his son, Waiyaki, to attend a mission school
to learn "all the secrets of the white man," but not his vices, and still to
"be true to [his] people and the ancient rites."[10] When Waiyaki was excluded
from the mission school for refusing to disavow traditional practices, he
founded schools among his people. Later, when the community rejected
both him and his schools as colonizing agents, he realized that education
must strengthen the community. In his downfall, Waiyaki had a new vision:
"education for unity. Unity for political freedom."[11]

Ngugi's novel raises important questions. Can colonized minds ever truly
act in the best interests of a community that wishes to preserve, or to recover,
its own values and traditions? Or are they bound to perspectives that distort
traditional cultures according to a colonial or patriarchal vision? Despite
Mugo and Waiyaki's desire to use colonial education for the good of the
community, the latter's exclusion at the end of the novel suggests that the
community and perhaps also Ngugi do not share his optimism.

When black feminist Audre Lorde asserts that "the master's tools will
never dismantle the master's house,"[12] she is claiming that it is impossible
to achieve the inner transformation of an oppressive system. Feminists like
Mary Daly share her pessimism.[13] Other feminists, such as Judith Butler,
recognize that women, like other colonized peoples, have been implicated
in the discursive system that they critique. Butler argues that feminists may
not be able to destroy the system but they can weaken or displace it through
parody and other strategies of subversion.[14] Anthony Appiah sees a similar
phenomenon occurring in postcolonial Africa where "European languages
and European disciplines have been 'turned,' like double agents, from the
projects of the metropole to the intellectual work of postcolonial cultural
life."[15]

Many feminist teachers within the academy recognize the validity of the
questions raised by Ngugi and Lorde. But they resist the impulse toward
withdrawal and instead pursue the strategy of subversion in the hope of
preserving and developing liberating visions for a redefined and reconstructed future which includes all people, while respecting the differences
among them.

WHO CARRIES OUT THE EDUCATIONAL AGENDA?

Teachers play a critical role in the process of acculturation called education. The most effective teachers in all educational systems are those who

have internalized the educational agenda and who work to inculcate its values and skills in their students. In colonial systems, upper-class males are often privileged as learners. Whether the teachers are male or female, the Western tradition which is disseminated in colonial systems has privileged European and Euro-American men's thoughts and deeds.

Novelist Mariama Bâ describes a colonial teacher at a Senegalese girls' school in her novel *So Long a Letter*.

> . . . the white woman . . . was the first to desire for us an "uncommon" destiny . . . to lift us out of the bog of tradition, superstition and custom, to make us appreciate a multitude of civilizations without renouncing our own, to raise our vision of the world, to make up for our inadequacies, to develop universal moral values in us. . . .[16]

In this description, Bâ has highlighted the dilemmas that confront this colonial teacher. Unlike many of her colleagues, she values women's education. She recognizes women's potential to play an important role in their society. She views traditional culture as a "bog of . . . superstition and custom," which has a negative impact, especially upon women. Yet she wants her students to appreciate their own as well as other cultures. While she strives to inculcate "universal moral values" in her students, she appears unaware that they are as culturally and contextually conditioned and determined as those she wishes them to reject. Nor does she recognize that the moral values of Western culture are also oppressive of women.

The dilemmas the teacher confronts are dramatized in the life of the novel's heroine, Ramatoulaye. Bâ makes clear the difficulty Ramatoulaye's education and new values create for her in traditional culture. Her lofty career as a teacher demands that she exercise great care never "to warp a soul."[17] She pursues this career along with raising twelve children. It taxes her energies and makes her suspect in the eyes of her husband's family. When her husband chooses to take a second wife, she finds it impossible to renounce cultural constraints and to lead an independent life in the international culture which was to be her "uncommon destiny."

Ramatoulaye regards teachers as responsible for the care of souls. This formulation, reflecting a dualistic Western philosophical paradigm, is problematic for feminists.[18] But, granting the validity of the concern underlying the formulation, how does a teacher ensure that no mistake is made in the care of the students who are entrusted to her? How can she be sure that her vision will liberate them? How self-reflective is she about the bases for her own convictions? Does she have clear insights about how souls are warped, and sensitive strategies to prevent her from warping them? These concerns are more characteristic of a feminist than of a colonial educational agenda.

THE CHALLENGE OF BIBLICAL STUDIES

Some critics claim that the Bible warps all women's souls, because it is irredeemably patriarchal, and all non-Western people's souls, because it is irreversibly Western. The Bible indeed reflects its origins in a patriarchal culture. It describes a social organization in which women are clearly secondary. In addition, the Bible's canonization has narrowed the range of texts the Christian community regards as revelatory. Its canonical status severely inhibits the process of discarding texts no longer considered inspired by feminist and non–North Atlantic communities, though Zimbabwean theologian Canaan S. Banana has recently called for just such a move.[19] The Bible's patriarchal worldview has become normative in many Christian communities, and biblical exegesis by Euro-American, North Atlantic male scholars has in the past rarely challenged this orientation. Thus the Bible is a problematic text to study and to teach for feminists, and others who feel marginalized in the text and the tradition.

COLONIAL AND FEMINIST
BIBLICAL INTERPRETATION

Biblical interpretations that I regard as discursively colonial make one or more of the following assumptions. They regard the patriarchal perspective as divinely validated, and they reject nonpatriarchal readings of the Bible. They affirm an inherent superiority of men over women, and of the public, male-dominated sphere over the private, to which women are relegated. These interpretations also assume that Christianity is the only true religion, or is superior to all other religious traditions. They accept political assertions made in the text, such as the legitimacy of dominating the sons of Ham, because the text justifies them in theological terms.[20] They use the categories orthodoxy and heresy to invalidate certain interpretations of the tradition. They decontextualize the biblical texts in ways that absolutize injunctions addressed to particular situations.

Feminist biblical interpretations question these major hermeneutical principles of colonial biblical interpretation. They reject the validity of the patriarchal worldview, the claims of men's inherent superiority over women, and the hegemony of the public sphere over the private. Many regard these views as rooted in certain Greek philosophical traditions and in social practices of antiquity. Feminists understand Christian anti-Judaism as an expression of the historical tension that existed between early Christian communities and Jews, and they condemn Christian anti-Semitism as unwarranted and unjustified.[21] They also resist legitimating other historical expressions of Christian imperialism, including those forms which were evident during the European colonization of Africa.

FEMINIST PERSPECTIVES ON THE BIBLE AS REVELATION

Adjudicating the truth claims made about scripture has a long and complex history. Bishop Colenso of Natal is representative of nineteenth-century challenges to the doctrine that "the Bible is in all its parts the Word of God" and "every part of the Bible is infallibly inspired."[22] Charged with heresy, Colenso argued that "the Bible is not itself the Word of God, but it contains it, and assuredly God's Word will be heard in the Bible by all who devoutly listen for it."[23] Colenso's perspective struck a responsive chord in Elizabeth Cady Stanton, who took an even more radical stance toward the truth claims of scripture.[24]

Feminist biblical scholars, including Stanton, question theories of biblical inspiration that exclude human participation in the process of biblical writing. They recognize that biblical texts reflect the patriarchal cultures that produced them. Consequently, they reject the notion that this patriarchal perspective is inherently valid or divinely legitimated. They regard the extrabiblical texts of Judaism and Christianity as important sources for understanding the historical contexts of biblical texts. They also believe biblical traditions may be understood in a variety of ways and that no one interpretation should be privileged. Some question the legitimacy of a canon of scripture itself, since the agenda of canonization, saving the text, excludes subsequent generations from sharing in the process of tradition formation.

Contemporary feminist interpreters have moved beyond the nineteenth-century challenge to the historical accuracy of the Bible. They ask how a text like the Bible, which is historically conditioned and interpreted, can promote the full humanity of women and men of all races, ethnic backgrounds, and classes. A number of paradigms have been suggested by feminists for resisting the patriarchal claims of and about the Bible. Several are summarized below.

Elisabeth Schüssler Fiorenza recommends that the Bible be regarded not "as archetype but as historical prototype or as a formative root-model of biblical faith and life."[25] This allows the Christian vision of liberation and salvation to be informed by the Bible but not derived from or dictated by its specificities. For Rosemary Radford Ruether, the "prophetic-liberating" or "prophetic-messianic" traditions in the Bible have provided the norm for judging scripture and tradition and for the critique of colonial cultures which do not promote the full humanity of oppressed peoples.[26]

A number of feminist scholars, including Nelle Morton, Sandra Schneiders, and Lynda Sexson, recognize the metaphoric nature of biblical language and of the claim that the Bible is the "word of God."[27] All metaphoric language is tensive, suspended between the "is" and "is not" of the metaphor. This perspective allows the text to have a revelatory function, while protecting it from literalization or banalization.[28] Nelly Ritchie, in describing how Latin American women move from their particular experience to the Bible, from the Bible to action, and then back again to the Bible, suggests the necessity of a process of mutual validation between experience and text.[29]

FEMINIST APPROACHES
TO TEACHING THE GOSPELS

Both the method and the content of the undergraduate course I teach on feminist approaches to the Gospels are affected by the considerations I have discussed above.

Colonial pedagogy assumes an expert teacher, who "knows the truth," and students, who must assimilate the "truth" the teacher conveys, without regard for their experience. But feminist psychologists tell us that critical thinking or "separate knowing," knowing separated from experience, must be complemented by "connected knowing." In the latter approach, students reflect on experiences that relate to the ideas or issues they are studying.[30] If students in a class represent a diversity of racial, ethnic, and class groups, they must be encouraged to see how their experiences are relevant to their education. If they are not a representative group, it is even more important that different voices be heard in the readings for the class. Diverse perspectives are important for preparing our students to live in a multicultural world. They help them to avoid universalizing their relatively homogeneous experiences. They also contribute to the decolonizing of our feminisms.

Although the students read biblical interpretations of the Gospels by women from many countries and cultures, the use of "feminist" in the course title indicates that the perspectives that inform the issues, and my orientation as teacher, are primarily those of Euro-American and middle-class women. The use of the plural "approaches" affirms my view that there is no single feminist approach to the biblical texts, so alternative feminist readings are considered. Presenting multiple interpretations of texts is also a way to resist colonial claims to an absolute truth, to respect differences, and to reject the Western impulse to create artificial unities.[31]

The claim that the Gospels are revelatory texts is addressed at the beginning of this course, since all subsequent interpretations depend on the response to this claim. Students need to recognize their presuppositions about the text and to identify the implications of these presuppositions. They must also evaluate the claim many feminists make about the priority of experience in interpreting the text. They often interpret the criterion of experience to mean that truth is relative. However, an examination of the interpretative experience in all areas of human perception suggests that the biblical texts are themselves hermeneutical. They often contain interpretations that are in tension, an insight reflected in the decentering hermeneutical strategy used by some womanists.[32] Equally, all appropriations of them are necessarily interpretative.

Historical and literary critical studies of the Gospels that discuss how the historical Jesus both is and is not mediated to us through these texts are examined. These studies also analyze the literary relationships among the Gospels, and their historical and theological differences. A comparison of the canonical and the noncanonical gospels highlights the distinctiveness of the former, while the study of the latter texts recognizes the diversity of traditions within the early Christian communities.

Reading the Gospels from feminist perspectives allows students to explore the liberating potential of these texts for women. Elisabeth Schüssler Fiorenza's comprehensive and imaginative feminist theological reconstruction of Christian origins provides an important perspective on women's place in the ministry of Jesus and in the life of the early church. Jesus was and is significant for women, she claims, because he was the leader of a religious renewal movement within Judaism that advocated a liberating inclusivity and equality for all.[33]

Women who understand Jesus' work as "the liberation of the poor and oppressed and the reestablishing of a just order"[34] often move Jesus from his historical context into metaphor. In this way they can relate him to the realities of their lives. Lynda Sexson has described metaphor as the process by which we make our ordinary lives sacred.[35] Many writings of women of color reveal the powerful metaphoric images that result from this process.

Jacquelyn Grant has developed a womanist Christology rooted in African-

American women's triple oppression under racism, classism, and sexism. Connecting herself with a tradition that goes back to nineteenth-century African-American women such as Jarena Lee and Sojourner Truth, Grant asserts that the theology of black women emerges both from their personal experiences of divine revelation and the biblical witness. Jesus, recognized as both divine and human, is "the divine co-sufferer, who empowers them in situations of oppression."[36] Indeed, because black women endure a triple oppression, "this Christ, found in the experiences of Black women, is a Black woman."[37]

Cameroonian theologians Thérèse Souga and Louise Tappa suggest that African women experience a "threefold captivity—cultural, spiritual, socio-economic": in traditional culture; in the church, through the negative attitudes toward women which the missionaries transmitted; and in international imperialism.[38] Because of this, "Christ is in solidarity with women, for they incarnate the sufferings of the African people."[39]

Elizabeth Amoah and Mercy Amba Oduyoye of Ghana reject the image of a royal Christ ruling over an eschatological kingdom as a colonial metaphor which justified their oppression. They claim that a savior "who breaks the power of evil and empowers us in our life's journey"[40] is a more powerful image for Africans. Because they equate Jesus with women who are "the least" in African culture, the contemporary Christ figure for them is a woman. "Jesus is Christ—truly woman (human) yet truly divine, for only God is the truly compassionate One."[41]

Korean theologian Chung Hyun Kyung says that Asian women accept the traditional image of Jesus as suffering servant but distinguish between suffering imposed from without and suffering that is the result of a struggle for justice. Jesus' suffering, as well as their own, reflects the latter.[42] When Asian women use the image of Jesus as lord, it is as lord of the poor and oppressed, not the problematic lord image that Western colonialism used to justify political and economic exploitation.[43]

Asian-American theologian Rita Brock suggests that people find liberation from brokenheartedness and achieve wholeness as human beings not through the historical Jesus but in the Christa-community.[44] A similar image was suggested by a Korean factory worker: "Jesus Christ emerges from the broken-body experiences of workers when they affirm life and dare to love other human beings in spite of their brokenness."[45]

TEACHING FEMINIST BIBLICAL STUDIES

The title of Jo Anne Pagano's "meditations on teaching," *Exiles and Communities: Teaching in the Patriarchal Wilderness,*[46] resonates with those of us who teach feminist biblical studies. As feminists, we no longer tolerate the exile of women's experiences from the dominant patriarchal discourse about what it is to be human. As Christian feminists, we claim ourselves as integral and equal partners in the community of our heritage. We are committed to eliminating barriers that perpetuate women's exile within the Christian community. As academic feminists, we belong to a dominantly patriarchal academy whose traditions we have assimilated, but we also work to create another community within the academy, one that provides the voices of women's experiences, understandings, and interpretations. As feminist teachers, we are concerned with diversifying our teaching styles to respond more effectively to our students' ways of knowing. We also seek to decolonize our feminisms by diversifying the content of our courses. We incorporate the varied racial, class, and cultural experiences of our students or those they will encounter in this pluralistic world. As teachers of feminist biblical studies, we assist students in locating themselves in or in relation to the Jewish and Christian traditions. We also urge them to examine critically their received ideas of race/ethnicity and of class. We utilize research that helps us contextualize biblical texts so their meaning can be more fully understood. At the same time, we recognize the importance of knowing how biblical texts have been interpreted historically and of exploring their significance for us today. We share Ramatoulaye's concern for the well-being of our students, and we express that concern by resisting and subverting colonization and using our varied individual experiences and cultural heritages to create a new world order.[47]

GLOSSARY OF TERMS

Decentering—a hermeneutical strategy that avoids privileging a single interpretative framework by affirming multiple oppressions.

Decolonization—the process of identifying the ideological assumptions and assertions of historical and discursive colonization in order to reevaluate or to reject them.

Discursive Colonization—the psychological domination of people through appeals to authority, based on the asserted superiority of one race, gender, class, or culture over another.

Historical Colonization—the political, economic and social domination of people of less developed countries by those from more developed countries.

NOTES

1. I have had access only to the People's Edition of John William Colenso, *The Pentateuch and the Book of Joshua Critically Examined* (London: Longmans, Green, 1870).

2. Stanton cites Colenso three times. See Elizabeth Cady Stanton and the Revising

Committee, *The Original Feminist Attack on the Bible (The Women's Bible)* (New York: Arno Press, 1974), Part I: 96, 120–21, 135–36.

3. For the distinction between historical and discursive colonialism, see Laura E. Donaldson, *Decolonizing Feminisms: Race, Gender, and Empire-building* (Chapel Hill and London: University of North Carolina Press, 1992).

4. Ngugi Wa Thiong'o, "George Lamming and the Colonial Situation," in *Homecoming: Essays on African and Caribbean Literature, Culture and Politics* (New York: Lawrence Hill, 1972), 128. However, it would be a mistake to view colonized peoples simply as passive victims of colonial powers. Jean and John Comaroff discuss the ways in which the Southern Tswana attempted to use the English missionaries strategically for their own goals (*Of Revelation and Revolution: Christianity, Colonialism, and Consciousness in South Africa* 1 [Chicago: University of Chicago Press, 1991]).

5. See Donaldson, *Decolonizing,* passim.

6. Kwame Anthony Appiah, *In My Father's House: Africa in the Philosophy of Culture* (New York: Oxford, 1992), 55.

7. Gerdien Verstraelen-Gilhuis discusses an instance of the former strategy ("African Education as seen from Le Zoute, 1926: An International Conference on Christian Missions in Africa," in *A New Look at Christianity in Africa* [Gweru: Mambo Press, 1992]). For the latter approach, see V. Y. Mudimbe, *The Invention of Africa: Gnosis, Philosophy, and the Order of Knowledge* (Bloomington: Indiana University Press, 1988); and Christopher L. Miller, *Theories of Africans: Francophone Literature and Anthropology in Africa* (Chicago: University of Chicago Press, 1990), 119.

8. Cheikh Hamidou Kane, *Ambiguous Adventure,* trans. Katherine Woods (London: Heinemann, 1986), 34.

9. Ibid., 46.

10. Ngugi Wa Thiong'o, *The River Between* (Oxford: Heinemann, 1988), 20.

11. Ibid., 143.

12. Audre Lorde, "The Master's Tools Will Never Dismantle the Master's House," in *Sister Outsider: Essays and Speeches* (Trumansburg, NY: Crossing Press, 1984), 110–23.

13. Mary Daly, *Beyond God the Father: Toward a Philosophy of Women's Liberation* (Boston: Beacon Press, 1973).

14. Judith Butler, *Gender Trouble: Feminism and the Subversion of Identity* (London: Routledge, 1990), esp. chap. 1 and conclusion.

15. Appiah, *Father's House,* 55. Benedict Anderson observes that any print languages can be used to articulate postcolonial imagined communities (*Imagined Communities* [rev. ed.; New York: Verso, 1991], 133–34).

16. Mariama Bâ, *So Long a Letter,* trans. Modupé Bodé-Thomas (Oxford: Heinemann, 1989), 15.

17. Ibid., 23.

18. Lynda M. Glennon, *Women and Dualism: A Sociology of Knowledge Analysis* (New York and London: Longman, 1979).

19. Canaan S. Banana, "The Case for a New Bible" (seminar paper presented at the University of Zimbabwe, June 14, 1991).

20. Sue E. Houchins and Kathleen O'Brien Wicker have illustrated the retention of the Ham myth in an African novel in "The Blessing of Ham: Resacralizing and Recontextualizing the Narrative of Nation" (paper presented at the Society of Biblical Literature meeting, 1991).

21. Rosemary Radford Ruether, *Faith and Fratricide: The Theological Roots of Anti-Semitism* (New York: Seabury, 1979).

22. John William Colenso, *A Letter to the Laity of the Diocese of Natal* (London: Longman, Green, Longman, Roberts, & Green, 1864), 10.

23. Ibid.

24. Stanton, *Feminist Attack,* 61.

25. Elisabeth Schüssler Fiorenza, *Bread Not Stone: The Challenge of Feminist Biblical Interpretation* (Boston: Beacon Press, 1984), 14.

26. Rosemary Radford Ruether, *Sexism and God-Talk: Toward a Feminist Theology* (Boston: Beacon Press, 1983), 22–23.

27. Nelle Morton, *The Journey Is Home* (Boston: Beacon Press, 1985); Sandra M. Schneiders, *The Revelatory Text: Interpreting the New Testament as Sacred Scripture* (San Francisco: Harper, 1991); Lynda Sexson, *Ordinarily Sacred* (New York: Crossroad, 1982).

28. Schneiders, *Revelatory Text,* 29–33.

29. Nelly Ritchie, "Women and Christology," in *Through Her Eyes: Women's Theology from Latin America,* ed. Elsa Tamez (Maryknoll, NY: Orbis, 1989), 84.

30. Mary Field Belenky et al., *Women's Ways of Knowing. The Development of Self, Voice, and Mind* (New York: Basic Books, 1986), esp. 100–130, 214–29.

31. Susan Thistlethwaite, *Sex, Race, and God: Christian Feminism in Black and White* (New York: Crossroad, 1991).

32. Laura E. Donaldson, "From the Woman's Bible to the Womanist Bible: Sexual Difference and the Crisis of Feminist Hermeneutics" (paper presented at the Society of Biblical Literature meeting, 1990). For other examples of womanist interpretations of the Bible, see Clarice J. Martin, "Womanist Interpretations of the New Testament: The Quest for Holistic and Inclusive Biblical Translation and Interpretation," *Journal of Feminist Studies in Religion* 6/2 (1990): 41–61; Renita J. Weems, "Reading *Her Way* Through the Struggle: African American Women and the Bible," in *Stony the Road We Trod: African American Biblical Interpretation,* ed. Cain Hope Felder (Minneapolis: Fortress Press, 1991), 57–77.

33. Elisabeth Schüssler Fiorenza, *In Memory of Her: A Feminist Theological Reconstruction of Christian Origins* (New York: Crossroad, 1983).

34. Jacquelyn Grant, *White Women's Christ and Black Women's Jesus: Feminist Christology and Womanist Response* (Atlanta: Scholars Press, 1989), 138.

35. Sexson, *Ordinarily,* 1–4.

36. Grant, *Black Women's Jesus,* 212.

37. Ibid., 220.

38. Thérèse Souga and Louise Tappa, "The Christ-Event from the Viewpoint of African Women," in *With Passion and Compassion: Third World Women Doing Theology,* ed. Virginia Fabella and Mercy Amba Oduyoye (Maryknoll, NY: Orbis, 1989), 26.

39. Ibid., 29.

40. Elizabeth Amoah and Mercy Amba Oduyoye, "The Christ for African Women," in *Passion and Compassion,* ed. Fabella and Oduyoye, 38.

41. Ibid., 44.

42. Chung Hyun Kyung, *Struggle to be the Sun Again: Introducing Asian Women's Theology* (Maryknoll, NY: Orbis, 1991), 53–57.

43. Ibid., 57–59.

44. Rita Nakashima Brock, *Journeys by Heart: A Christology of Erotic Power* (New York: Crossroad, 1988).

45. Kyung, *Struggle,* 72.

46. Jo Anne Pagano, *Exiles and Communities: Teaching in the Patriarchal Wilderness* (Albany: State University of New York Press, 1990).

47. Research grants from the Athwin Fund, Scripps College and the American Academy of Religion supported the development of a number of ideas expressed in this article.

RECOMMENDED READINGS

Chung Hyun Kyung. *Struggle to be the Sun Again: Introducing Asian Women's Theology.* Maryknoll, NY: Orbis. 1991.

Colenso, John William. *The Pentateuch and the Book of Joshua Critically Examined.* London: Longmans, Green, 1870.

Donaldson, Laura E. *Decolonizing Feminisms: Race, Gender, and Empire-building.* Chapel Hill and London: University of North Carolina Press. 1992.

Fabella, Virginia, and Mercy Amba Oduyoye, eds. *With Passion and Compassion: Third World Women Doing Theology.* Maryknoll, NY: Orbis. 1989.

Grant, Jacquelyn. *White Woman's Christ and Black Women's Jesus: Feminist Christology and Womanist Response.* Atlanta: Scholars Press. 1989.

Pagano, Jo Anne. *Exiles and Communities: Teaching in the Patriarchal Wilderness.* Albany: State University of New York Press. 1990.

Schneiders, Sandra M. *The Revelatory Text: Interpreting the New Testament as Sacred Scripture.* San Francisco: Harper, 1991.

Sexson, Linda. *Ordinarily Sacred.* New York: Crossroad. 1982.

Tamez, Elsa, ed. *Through Her Eyes: Women's Theology from Latin America.* Maryknoll, NY: Orbis. 1989.

Thistlethwaite, Susan. *Sex, Race, and God: Christian Feminism in Black and White.* New York: Crossroad. 1991.

Contributors

Janice Capel Anderson is Assistant Professor of Philosophy at the University of Idaho. Her publications include "Matthew: Gender and Reading," *Semeia* 28 (1983); "Mapping Feminist Biblical Criticism," *Critical Review of Books in Religion* (1991); and *Mark and Method,* co-edited with Stephen D. Moore.

Karen Baker-Fletcher is Assistant Professor of Theology and Culture at the School of Theology at Claremont in Claremont, California. She has published articles in the *Journal of Feminist Studies in Religion,* the *Journal of Religious Thought,* the *New York Times,* and *Theology Today.* Her sermon, "Whose Responsibility?" was published in *Prophetic Voices: Black Preachers Speak on Behalf of Children,* edited by Allegra Hoots for the Children's Defense Fund.

Rita Nakashima Brock holds the Endowed Chair in the Humanities at Hamline University, St. Paul, Minnesota, and is the author of *Journeys by Heart: A Christology of Erotic Power,* as well as other essays on feminist theology and Asian American women.

Claudia V. Camp is Associate Professor of Religion at Texas Christian University, Fort Worth, where she has taught since 1980. Her research interests lie in the areas of wisdom literature, methodology in biblical interpretation, and feminist interpretation. Her publications have focused on female sages and female imagery in the wisdom literature, including a book, *Wisdom and the Feminine in the Book of Proverbs.*

Katie G. Cannon is Associate Professor of African American Studies in the Religion Department at Temple University in Philadelphia, Pennsylvania. She is the author of several articles and books on womanist ethics, including *Black Womanist Ethics;* she is the co-author, with Carter Heyward, of *Alienation and Anger: A Black and a White Woman's Struggle for Mutuality in an Unjust World.*

381

Elizabeth A. Castelli is Assistant Professor of Religious Studies and Women's Studies at the College of Wooster in Wooster, Ohio. She is the author of *Imitating Paul: A Discourse of Power*.

Alison M. Cheek is Director of Feminist Liberation Theology Studies at the Episcopal Divinity School in Cambridge, Massachusetts.

Carol Devens-Green is Associate Professor of History at Central Michigan University, editor of the *Michigan Historical Review*, and the author of *Countering Colonization: Native American Women and the Great Lakes Missions, 1630–1900*. She was a 1990–91 Rockefeller Fellow in the Women's Studies in Religion Program at the Harvard Divinity School, where she did research on gender and racial issues in the interaction between nineteenth-century Native American women and women missionaries.

Monika Fander was a theological consultant to the Catholic Bible Society of Germany for its Year of the Bible. From 1983 to 1988 she was an assistant in New Testament at the University of Münster. Her doctoral dissertation was on the topic of women in the Gospel of Mark, with special consideration of cultural and historical aspects.

Ivone Gebara is a Brazilian feminist ecumenical theologian working with various groups in Brazil and other countries. She is the author of several books and articles.

Carolyn De Swarte Gifford is the editor of the selected edition of the journals of Frances E. Willard, forthcoming from the University of Illinois Press in 1994. She is also on the editorial board of the Historical Encyclopedia of Chicago Women, forthcoming from Indiana University Press in 1996.

Elisabeth Gössmann, a medievalist, is an honorary professor of Seishin Women's University in Tokyo and is also affiliated with the Ludwig-Maximilian University in Munich. She has written books and essays on mariology, medieval philosophy and theological anthropology, and Hildegard von Bingen. She is the editor of *Archiv für philosophie- und theologiegeschichtliche Frauenforschung* and co-editor of *Wörterbuch der Feministischen Theologie*.

Ada María Isasi-Díaz was born and raised in La Habana, Cuba. She is an activist theologian and frequent lecturer and writer on *mujerista* theology, Hispanics, and women and church issues in the United States and Latin America. At present she is Assistant Professor of Ethics and Theology at Drew University in Madison, New Jersey.

Brigitte Kahl teaches at the Theological Faculty of Humboldt University in Berlin. She is an ordained minister of the Evangelical Church.

KWOK Pui Lan is Associate Professor of Theology at the Episcopal Divinity School in Cambridge, Massachusetts. She is the author of *Chinese Women and Christianity, 1860–1927* and co-editor of *Inheriting Our Mother's Gardens: Feminist Theology in Third World Perspective.*)

Elizabeth Struthers Malbon is Professor of Religion at Virginia Polytechnic Institute and State University. She is the author of *Narrative Space and Mythic Meaning in Mark* and *The Iconography of the Sarcophagus of Junius Bassus*. Currently she is at work on a narrative commentary on Mark's Gospel.

Melanie A. May is Associate Professor of Theology and Dean of the Program in the Study of Women and Gender in Church and Society at Colgate Rochester Divinity School in Rochester, New York.

Lauree Hersch Meyer teaches courses on biblical hermeneutics and feminism at Bethany Theological Seminary in Oak Brook, Illinois.

Barbara H. Geller Nathanson is Associate Professor and Chair of the Department of Religion at Wellesley College in Wellesley, Massachusetts. Her research focuses on aspects of the history and archaeology of the Jewish communities of Roman and Early Byzantine Palestine and the relationships of those communities to the larger environments of which they were a part.

Teresa Okure, SHCJ, a native of Nigeria, is the Academic Dean of the Catholic Higher Theological Institute of West Africa in Nigeria and a professor in Sacred Scripture. She is the author of *The Johannine Approach to Mission: A Contextual Study of John 4:1–42,* the co-author of *32 Articles Evaluating the Inculturation of Christianity in Africa,* and has also written several articles on mission and scripture interpretation.

Judith Plaskow is Professor of Religious Studies at Manhattan College. She is the author of many articles and books on feminist theology, including *Standing Again at Sinai: Judaism from a Feminist Perspective.*

Marjorie Procter-Smith is Associate Professor of Worship at Perkins School of Theology at Southern Methodist University in Dallas, Texas. She is the author of *In Her Own Rite: Constructing Feminist Liturgical Tradition,* co-editor with Janet Walton of *Women at Worship: Interpretations of North American Diversity,* and is presently working on a book on feminist prayer as an act of resistance.

Elisabeth Schüssler Fiorenza is the Krister Stendahl Professor of Divinity at the Harvard Divinity School. She was the first woman president of the Society of Biblical Literature (1987), is co-editor with Judith Plaskow of the *Journal of Feminist Studies in Religion* and is also an active editor of the international journal *Concilium*. Her book *In Memory of Her: A Feminist Reconstruction of Christian Origins* (1983) has been translated into eight languages. Among her other recent books are *Bread Not Stone: The Challenge of Feminist Biblical Interpretation, Revelation: Vision of a Just World, But She Said: The Rhetoric of Feminist Interpretation for Liberation,* and *Discipleship of Equals: A Critical Feminist Ekklesia-logy of Liberation.*

Mary Ann Tolbert is Professor of New Testament and Early Christianity at Vanderbilt University in Nashville, Tennessee. She has written several articles on feminist biblical interpretation. Her most recent book is *Sowing the Gospel: Mark's World in Literary-Historical Perspective.*

Karen Jo Torjesen holds the Margo L. Goldsmith Chair of Women Studies in Religion at the Claremont Graduate School in Claremont, California. Her most recent book is *When Women Were Priests: Women's Leadership in the Early Church and the Scandal of Their Subordination in the Rise of Christianity.* She is currently working on a book on the social construction of the doctrine of woman's nature.

Lieve Troch studied theology at the universities of Leuven, Belgium, and Tilburg, the Netherlands. Following twelve years of pastoral work, she has taught systematic and feminist theology at the University of Nijmegen/Heerlen, the Netherlands, since 1988.

Kathleen O'Brien Wicker is Professor of Religious Studies at Scripps College and the Claremont Graduate School in Claremont, California. Her special interests are women in antiquity and African religions and literature.

Index

Index of Subjects